Reading
Improvement
for Adults

7790 1

PAUL D. LEEDY

The Reading Institute,
New York University

McGraw-Hill Book Company

NEW YORK   ST. LOUIS   SAN FRANCISCO   LONDON
TORONTO   SYDNEY   MEXICO   PANAMA

A Note on the Design of This Book

This book was set on the Linotype in Electra, a type face designed in 1935 by W. A. Dwiggins. Electra is a simple and very readable type which avoids any eccentricities that might catch the eye and interfere with the reading of the text. It is not based on any historical model and, as a result, does not echo any particular time or fashion. One of its very desirable characteristics, particularly for a book of this kind, is the lack of undue contrast between thick and thin strokes.

The size of the text type used in this book is 10-point with 3-point leading.

Preface

This book has been written for the adult who wants to learn how to read faster and with greater understanding. *Reading Improvement for Adults* brings modern reading techniques to the businessman, the engineer, the professional man, the college student, and the busy housewife who know how to read already and who want to read more quickly and with increased comprehension. It is not intended for those with physical or psychological defects—there are many good books devoted entirely to remedial reading.

Today millions of adults are faced with a formidable number of letters, memos, and reports to read in their daily work. In addition, there are professional and trade journals and books that should be read, and must be read with understanding, if one is going to keep up with advances in his field.

And how about the daily paper, the monthly and weekly magazines, and the books to be read for pleasure? Is twenty-four hours a day enough?

You can, by conscientiously following the rules and doing the exercises in this book, bring about a remarkable increase in your reading speed, and you will discover that you are actually understanding more of what you have read.

Whether you study alone or in an evening adult education class, an executive training program, or college, you will benefit by the application of the principles laid down here.

Basically, reading improvement requires a twofold emphasis: on reading speed and on comprehension. Increased reading speed alone is valueless. "With all thy getting, get understanding." The principal emphasis of this book is on *understanding*. The most efficient reader is he who comprehends most rapidly what the author is trying to convey.

The approach is a practical one. A glance through the table of contents will convince the reader that an attempt has been made to meet most of the general needs as well as the specialized demands that confront the average adult reader. The reading of graphs and other visual aids, business correspondence, and technical material and reading for the purpose of sheer enjoyment have all been discussed.

Each chapter begins with a practical analysis of a particular problem that faces the reader. Specific steps are spelled out to suggest a solution for the problem. An immediate application is indicated for the suggestions which have been given. There are sections in each chapter designed to help the reader improve his visual and perceptual skills—a type of training that is very important to good reading. Each chapter also contains two selections which give practice in reading informative material for speed and level of comprehension. Finally, for each chapter there is an inventory check list of the reading habits of the individual reader. For those who need them, vocabulary and general background helps have been included in Chapter 20 and in the Appendix.

My aim has been to present a program of reading improvement which is comprehensive in scope, mature in approach, and relevant to the world of today—and tomorrow—a program which has produced results with both college students and adults. Out of my years of experience, both as supervisor of adult reading at The Reading Institute of New York University and from teaching college students and adults how to read better and more effectively, this book has been largely written.

To mention all those to whom I am indebted is impossible. Their inspiration, their help, and their suggestions stretch back across the years, and for everything that they have contributed, I am sincerely thankful. Especially do I wish to acknowledge my indebtedness to Dr. Nila B. Smith, Director of The Reading Institute of New York University, who read most of the manuscript and offered many helpful suggestions. I am deeply appreciative of the assistance of Dr. Leonard Carmichael, Secretary of the Smithsonian Institution, and formerly director of the Tufts College Research Laboratory of Sensory Psychology and Physiology, who very kindly reviewed the visual aspects of reading as presented in this volume. To Dr. Paul B. Diederich, of the Educational Testing Service, the author is indebted for many helpful suggestions for improving the comprehension questions. Finally, for the invaluable help in typing much of the manuscript, in proofreading it, and in preparing the Table of Reading Rates, I am greatly indebted to my wife.

PAUL D. LEEDY

Contents

List of Reading Selections

Chapter One

You *can*
improve your reading!

So you want to read better?

You want to read faster, with greater comprehension.

In short, you need the know-how that will help you master the printed page quickly and conclusively.

In this you are not alone. Millions of men and women also yearn for the same skill, the same ability. Their problem is the same as yours.

And it is to meet this problem head on, and to help you solve it, that this book was written. The chapters that follow are planned as lessons in reading improvement. Each chapter has been carefully designed to help you advance with the least amount of lost motion, in a progressive, orderly fashion, along the entire front of better reading at the adult level.

Improvement in reading is the result of improvement in a number of areas, all of them more or less directly related to the specific act of reading itself. For the person who reads well calls upon far more resources than are at first apparent. The possession of an adequate vocabulary, for example, is of inestimable value in comprehending the exact meaning quickly and accurately. Quite as important, although dealing with another phase of the reading process, is proficiency in perception and the acquisition of a wide and disciplined visual span. The person who reads well also has a vast fund of incidental general knowledge: all sorts of miscellaneous facts and bits of information that find a familiar and responsive echo in the material that he reads. This "general-knowledge quotient" is, in fact, so important that it might almost be said that as a person's general factual knowledge background expands, the satisfaction which he derives from reading proportionately increases. Clear, analytical thinking is another factor which affects in no small way the ability to read well.

In short, effective reading is the result of the acquisition of a set of skills and habits—reaction patterns to the printed page—which makes "reading" the page more rewarding and less laborious. Good reading habits are those immediate responses to a page of print as a result of which the thought comes off the page faster, easier, and more clearly. They save the reader time and effort. Yet, the establishing of good habits of reading is no different from forming any other habit patterns. Repetition and practice largely turn the trick.

A great deal depends on you and your desire to learn. Seek out every opportunity to apply in your everyday reading what you will learn in the pages that follow. Every time your eyes fall upon a line of print you have an opportunity to improve your reading skills.

Topflight readers are not born; they're made. And into the making of a good reader goes a lot of dogged persistence, some simple sincerity of purpose, a willingness to try some new approaches and to change the old ways of doing things, to break faulty but tenacious habits of incorrect reading, and to look at the printed page in a new and different light.

Those who read really well are few in number. If you are a mediocre or slow reader, you are one of the multitude. Perhaps the more efficient reader *is* more efficient because he knows a few facts about the mystery of the printed page; perhaps he has worked a little harder to apply what he does know to *all* his reading. In this may lie the secret of his power.

But you, too, can read better than you do. There may be some secrets that you do not know. Or knowing, you may not be applying what you know in terms of practice to the page which you are now reading.

Some of our troubles stem from the past. About this we shall talk at greater length in the next chapter. After grade school we were caught up in the jet stream of life and carried ever farther and farther away from anything which looked like reading instruction. Not that we haven't done a lot of reading in those long intervening years! We're like shipwrecked sailors in a sea of print. Somehow we've managed to survive. Luckily, most of the time, we've managed to keep our heads above the waves. But it's been a rough haul. Many of us are tired of battling the sea. We are in desperate need of learning how to swim as the experts swim, instead of struggling as drowning men who want only to save their lives.

And we *can* learn to read better than we do. For reading is knowing what to do with a page of print. Reading is knowing where to look to discover main ideas and supporting details. Reading is knowing how to appreciate the organization of thought and how to interpret and evaluate that thought as it lies open upon the page before us.

All this will take some effort. It may even take some doughtiness of spirit to read in somewhat new and unconventional ways from those in which we have always read, for we feel confident that the way in which we have always done things, the method by which we have always read is the *only* way to read. And for most of us it *is*, for it is the only way we have ever known. Never have we read, consciously looking for paragraphs and the main divisions of the author's thought or for directional words or for punctuation signals down the lanes and highways of the printed word. How did *we* read? Why, we just picked up a book and *read*. Starting at the first word of the first paragraph, we read each word unto the very end. What more could we do? Reading is reading, isn't it? One might just as well say, farming is farming and, in the middle of the twentieth century, yoke his oxen to a wooden plow and go out to plow his field!

The reading of this book will not, by virtue of that fact alone, make you a better reader. No more can you learn to swim by merely reading about swimming. It takes the book plus the pool to make the swimmer; and, in addition, it takes a lot of splashing before you're really tops.

This book will give you the information and suggest some techniques that will make you a better reader. It will attempt to give you, in one simple package, a road map to the highway of print. What is suggested here is practical. It has been seen to work successfully with thousands of men and women, college students, professional and nonprofessional people, the great rank and file of readers who, like most of us, are floundering when, with a little help and a lot of practice, we could swim like the experts.

In this text you will progress steadily from one reading technique to another, and you will be constantly evaluating your achievement. Success

in one respect begets success in another. It is very important as you progress that you are aware of your progress. Do not expect the line of
progress, however, to climb steadily ever upward. The line of reading
improvement, like life itself, is a matter of ups and downs. But in the
end the line should be up. The trend should generally be toward more
skillfulness and less struggle with the printed page. You *can* read better
than you do!

How this book is planned to help you

In general, the chapters in this book will follow a uniform plan in organization and arrangement. The material in each chapter, except the
introductory and concluding chapters will be presented as follows:

1. *General Discussion.* It is important that you understand the ways
in which you get ideas from the printed page, that you see clearly how
ideas are handled, developed, organized, and presented, so that you will
know how to approach whatever you intend to read. You should know
how paragraphs are put together, how written material is structured, and
how to crack the shell of words so that the thought may fall out, clear
and meaty, before your very eyes.

There is also much that no one has ever specifically told many of us
about reading in its more mature aspects. To be sure, there is a great
deal that we already know that we have picked up from courses in grammar and English composition, from teachers who have taught us the
anatomy of the paragraph and the structure of the theme. But strangely
enough, many of us have not related these bits of information to the
problem of reading. Reading is but writing in reverse.

Each chapter will begin, therefore, with a practical discussion of some
of the aspects of better reading; some of the ways in which you can get
at the thought behind the print faster, easier, and more accurately.

2. *Practice Material.* Immediately following the discussion in each
chapter, you will have an opportunity to apply what you have just
learned. Exercises, usually in the form of short paragraphs, will give you
a chance to try your skill. This is mere practice area. With the exception
of a very few instances, you will not read this material against time.
There will be no need to hurry or to give these exercises surface treatment. They should be considered as practice opportunities. Here you
may learn to do by doing. In each succeeding chapter you will want to
apply all the skills and techniques suggested in preceding chapters. Al-

ways you have but one aim in view: to improve your reading skills all along the front. A solid grounding in fundamentals is very important in establishing better and more mature reading habits.

3. *Perception and Visual-span Developments.* It is amazing how little most of us see at a single glance. And of that little that we do see, it is even more amazing how inaccurately most of the time we see it. And yet, in reading, glance absorption of visual data is a very valuable aid. Our eyes race across a line of print. Combinations of letters, each with its distinctive profile and characteristic shape, become for us in a split second of time a word, a thought, a concept.

If each of us were clutching for pennies from a barrel of pennies, he would be the richer who had the larger hand, for a big hand can hold more pennies in a single grasp. Transfer this comparison to the reading field. We talk about an eyeful. But how much is an eyeful? Some eyes pick up no more than tidbits: a word at a time, a single item, a simple detail. Others take in half a line at a sweep! The more words in a line you can grasp at a single fleeting glance, the faster, the easier your reading will be.

In each chapter, therefore, you will find an important section containing exercises whose purpose is to develop your visual span and perceptual acuity. They are of different types and kinds, each one designed for a particular purpose. Work at them faithfully. They are exercises only, but by doing each one a few minutes each day, you will soon realize that you are seeing more faster.

4. *Reading for Speed of Comprehension.* Thinking of improvement in reading as merely "speeded reading" is a grave mistake. Greater speed alone is valueless, unless it is coupled with other factors of reading improvement. Instead of increasing only your speed, you will want to improve your total reading proficiency.

A fourth section of each chapter will be devoted to two articles, general in nature, timely, and interesting, to be read for speed and level of comprehension. The reading of these articles will test how well you are able to synthesize everything that has been presented into a workable whole. This means your ability to put into practice on the production line of reading efficiency a correct approach to the material you are about to read, correct eye movements and visual perception, an adequate vocabulary and general knowledge background, and, in short, an application of all the skills and techniques of better reading.

You will notice the terms "speed of comprehension" and "level of comprehension" which we have used. These are terms which are used professionally to describe what happens, or indeed what should happen, in the improvement of reading. They are significant terms because they emphasize the one goal of all reading, better *comprehension*. Those who speak of "speed and comprehension," do so as if these two were separate and unrelated factors. This, however, is not the case. Basically, we read to comprehend. For some of us this process of comprehension takes a long time. We have to read, and ponder, and re-read the same words before the meaning finally shines through. Our "speed of comprehension" is slow. But speed of comprehension by itself means very little, for most of us read slowly when the material involved is of a very difficult or technical nature. We say that "it takes a lot of thought to read this." What we mean, of course, is that the rate at which we comprehend, the time that elapses from the time our eyes behold the words until our minds understand the thought, is relatively much longer than it would be for "normal," "easy" reading. We have not "read" in the best sense of the word until we have grasped the meaning—in other words, comprehended.

Our aim, therefore, in this book is to learn how to get the meaning off the page, from behind the words, in a shorter space of time. That is "speed of comprehension."

But give two men a piece to read. One will be able to tell you much more about what the author has said than the other. He will "remember" more. This may not be memory at all; it is, perhaps, that he understands more fully during the process of his reading the thought which the author is trying to convey through his choice of words. In other words, one may well comprehend at a higher level than the other. Thus, our two terms, which we shall use at the end of each major reading assignment as a measure of your efficiency in reading—"speed of comprehension" and "level of comprehension"—are chosen advisedly. The first refers to the *quantity* of written material that a given mind can handle in a given space of time; the other refers to the *quality* of the operation of that same mind in grasping the meanings, nuances, associations, and relationship of meanings which the author is trying to convey through the words which he has chosen. Sometimes the author's thoughts are clear and his writing is lucid; at other times his thought is abstruse or his writing is involved. The good reader handles each situation on its own merits and as conditions dictate.

This does not mean, however, that difficult reading will be read as rapidly as easy reading. Your pace will vary depending upon the difficulty of the text. But it should be clearly pointed out that a slower pace in climbing a steeper intellectual hill is not inferior reading. It may not, of course, equal the speed that one might employ on the straightaway of unobstructed thought, but that makes no difference. It is one of the principles of reading, as it is one of the laws of dynamics, that speed must be sacrificed to power. This book does not suggest that speed is the ultimate criterion of all reading. You not only want to get there; you want to get there with all the facts on board!

Coming into vogue is the "reading index." This is an attempt to see as a single factor the two criteria of comprehension. The reading index is the product of the speed of comprehension and the level of comprehension divided by 100. This gives a net reading efficiency score, which in some instances is preferred over two fluctuating scores. We shall use the reading index in conjunction with the rate and level evaluations.

In the back of the book you will find tables and charts designed for keeping a record of your progress chapter by chapter. The serious student keeps this data accurately and studies it carefully. Here is the fever chart of your reading health. It will indicate your progress of recovery from the ills you may now have.

5. *Reading Habit Index.* In the area of reading improvement, as in the area of human behavior, the truth remains that what one *knows* to do and what one does in fact are sometimes vastly different things. And what one *does* is of the two by far the more important.

You will read better only when you practice those skills and heed that knowledge in which you have been instructed. Up to this time, old ineffectual habits have bound you down and have hindered your progress. You will be liberated from your slow, laborious reading when new, free habits take the place of old ones. For that reason it is extremely important that you evaluate your reading behavior at the close of each chapter.

This is the reason why each chapter closes with a "reading habit index." It is meant to be a valuable instrument in aiding you to read better. It will indicate your good points and your poor points and will serve as a guide to future action. The reading habit index may reveal the reasons for your improvement or the causes for your failure. Its purpose is to act as a reading barometer to tell you whether your sailing is fair or foul. The reading habit index is a means of helping you to recognize those areas where you will need to practice more assiduously those habits which you already know to be right and good.

6. *Vocabulary and General-knowledge Background.* Vocabularies differ greatly as we take a cross section of the population. Some of us have quite adequate vocabularies for the reading of this book and its selections. Others may recognize a need for help in this respect. Because of this disparate situation, vocabulary improvement exercises have not been included in the chapters themselves. But at the end of the book a section is devoted to this purpose. Each person will need to evaluate his own needs. If the vocabulary in this book gives you trouble, turn to the vocabulary section in Chapter Twenty, and before you begin a new chapter, familiarize yourself with the meanings of the words in that chapter which are likely to be unfamiliar.

What is true of vocabulary is true of your knowledge in general. The more you know the better you read. Constantly in your reading, references are made to items of general, or common, knowledge. The good reader always has a broad background of miscellaneous facts, of broad knowledge, which help him to understand more fully the meaning of what the author has to say. There are times when in reading we come across a phrase or reference whose implications are unknown to us, and when this happens, the lights go off and the power fails momentarily in the comprehension mechanism and, gliding over the phrase, we come to more familiar words, when the power flashes on again. The more the lights go off, the less adequately we are likely to comprehend. (In that last sentence there was need for some general-knowledge background. One who has never ridden by electrical transportation—subway trains, in particular—could not comprehend the meaning as fully as those who have.) A high general-knowledge quotient is reflected in improved comprehension. The more you know, the better you read.

In all, improving your reading efficiency should be a lot of fun, yet at the same time it should prove to be a challenging line of combat: a campaign against the domain of print. The personal qualifications for a successful fight are determination to succeed and unremitting pressure on the front. The succeeding chapters will outline the tactical strategy for the campaign. Meanwhile, a few practical hints may help you open your offensive with increased advantage to yourself.

Practical hints for better reading

1. *Set aside a certain time* each day for reading improvement practice, preferably when you are not too tired.

2. *When you read,* READ! Don't permit your mind to wander or your attention to lag. When you read, your mind should be working like a nest of termites: it should be riddling, reducing, digesting, consuming the ideas that underlie the printed word. Don't be distracted: turn off the radio or television and get off by yourself where you can read—and concentrate.

3. *Before beginning an exercise in this book, have all the materials ready that you will need:* pencil, a note pad, some paper clips, an eraser, a stop watch or a watch with a second hand, and a dictionary.

4. *When you come upon an unfamiliar word, make mental note of it.* See if you can determine its meaning from the context; if not, jot it on your scratch pad and look it up after you have finished reading. Then—and this is *most* important—use it in the live currency of conversation as soon and as often as possible until that word becomes a part of your normal, usable vocabulary.

5. *Put the new skills that you have learned into practice.* Use the reading improvement techniques suggested in this book every time you pick up a page of print. You cannot expect to break your old habits and substitute new and more efficient ones by attacking your reading problem in a half-hearted, occasional way. You are fighting the impregnable bastion of established habit—behavior patterns entrenched across the years! It means an all-out assault if you are to succeed.

The book as a whole is designed on a well-integrated pattern for reading improvement. You will begin in the early chapters of the book by getting thoroughly acquainted with the broad, basic principles of efficient reading. Later on you will be introduced to the most effective ways of reading such specialized forms of writing as newspapers, technical reports, correspondence, and miscellaneous material.

But, first of all, what is it that makes a good reader? Let us look for a little while at what it really means to read well.

Chapter Two

What does it mean to read well?

G OOD READERS are rare.
Dip into the adult population almost anywhere and you'll come up with Mr. Average Reader. As a specimen for study he is an interesting fellow. Most of the time he is candidly honest and utterly realistic. He recognizes that his skills with print are definitely inadequate for the job he has to do and for the demands that are made on his time. That he *is* a slow reader he seems to accept with outward equanimity; inwardly he is disturbed by his inefficiency in the face of the pressures that are constantly upon him.

Yet when he looks around he is comforted, for he recognizes his counterpart in practically everyone with whom he associates. Their reading skills are no better than his. And so he consoles himself with the thought that misery finds its image everywhere!

He doesn't know *why* this is so, but it is, for as he looks around him— at the office, on the bus, in the train—wherever people are reading, there he sees himself. He sees that they do just about what he does when he picks up a page of print. Most of them are slow, word-by-word readers, even as he is, sluggishly pushing their eyes along the lines of print. Some of Mr. Average Reader's associates even move their lips as they read.

There are a few who do so noticeably, others do it almost imperceptibly, while still others wag their heads as their eyes travel across the page. Nearly all of them go back to re-read the section that they have just been perusing because they have "missed the point" or because they're not sure "what it's all about."

But there is another aspect to Mr. Average Reader, and that is his anchor to windward: he believes that, if he only knew how, he could read faster than he now does and with a great deal more comprehension of the meaning. And his belief is well founded.

Generally speaking, Mr. Average Reader and all his friends can improve their reading skills considerably. In fact, we can all read better than we do. And it is the purpose of this book to help you do just that. We shall attempt to explain in this chapter some of the reasons why we are such poor readers, and in future chapters we shall aim to point out how we can become better ones. There is no magical formula. Good reading is a developmental process. The acquisition of effective reading skills is like the development of any habit pattern: in general, it is a gradual, progressive matter in which conscientious practice and hard work play a large role.

But why as a college and an adult population are we such poor readers? And in using that term we are thinking of the qualitative as well as the quantitative aspect of our reading. Good reading, of course, is far more than speeded reading. To read well means to engage in a complex activity, partly visual, partly psychological. It is basically a process of translation. The reader must translate the printed symbols which lie before his eyes so that the writer may communicate to him ideas—ideas which the writer had in his own thinking originally but which, in order to communicate to others, he was forced to cast into words and sentences.

Why we read as we do

Let us go back and look at some of the reasons why most mature readers read slowly and comprehend inadequately. Research indicates that the average adult reads about 200 to 250 words per minute and comprehends about 70 per cent of what he has read. These figures are, of course, open to wide questioning, but are presumably for materials of average readability and difficulty with standard comprehension questions. Also, these are figures derived from observation of mature readers en masse, and at the adult level there are wide divergencies to this supposed norm. But in any event, this is just about the speed and comprehension level of an average sixth-grade child.

This is a rather appalling situation. Why is this so? Some of the reasons may become much more obvious if we reflect for a moment upon our own experience in being taught to read. We began to read when we were in the first or second grade, and our formal instruction in reading *as a subject in the school curriculum* continued through fifth or sixth grade. After that, the instructional aspect of reading tapered off sharply. You could read orally, probably quite well; and it was, therefore, assumed that you could read silently just as well. By the usual tests you were a proficient reader: you could look at the words and pronounce them correctly, you could understand what they meant, and even the standardized tests did not rate you too low in reading ability.

Termination of instruction in any other subject at the sixth grade would have been unthinkable. Mathematics as a subject began for you as "number facts" in the first grade and progressed with you through high school and into college, perhaps even unto vector analysis or the calculus. With English, history, and science the story is very much the same: these subjects began in the lower grades and advanced as you advanced. But not so, reading. For most of us, reading *as a subject of instruction* ceased to be a part of our educational program when we were about eleven years old.

After sixth grade the program for reading improvement was a simple one: simply provide more and more reading; give the student a heavier reading load, for by this time—so it was generally assumed—you were able to go forward on your own resources, which in all too many cases were merely those of a word-by-word reader. But in the accepted viewpoint of the day, you were fully equipped, with sixth-grade reading skills, to tackle the reading demands of high school, of college, and of life.

It is very enlightening to go back twenty-five years and to discover that very few indeed were the voices that suggested that adults needed to learn to read; not, of course, in the sense of learning phonics and word attack, but in the sense of learning ways in which to master the printed page.

Well, what happened after sixth grade? The ideas became more and more complex as they were presented to us in print. Assignments in reading became longer and longer. And we grew to adulthood with a level of reading development that was grossly inadequate for our everyday needs. Each day, from a reading efficiency standpoint, we were getting further and further behind the proverbial eight ball!

As adults on the production lines of the workaday world few of us have ever gotten out from behind that ball. Voluminous piles of business and professional material demand that the adult of today be a skillful and rapid reader if he is to cope successfully with the demands of the present. But most of us are trying to do a man's job with a boy's strength, from a reading standpoint, and it's a rough deal.

Fortunately, reading education has come a long way in recent years— for our children nowadays it is not what it was for us. Educators are recognizing the need for reading skills at the developmental level which will prepare our boys and girls for the reading load which will be placed upon them. We are planning more carefully now so that they may be better prepared than we were for the vast reading demands which will be expected of them. But the demands have skyrocketed so rapidly that it is difficult for any of us to keep pace with them. A fast-moving world has enormously increased the need for communication through the printed word. That means more reading for everyone—now, and in the years to come.

Reading is thinking—plus!

Essentially reading is a mental process. As E. L. Thorndike phrased it, "Reading is thinking." And since it is thinking, if you would read well you must think well: you must be intellectually awake and mentally alert. When you read—*think!* Keep your mind on what the author is saying. But at the same time your mind, like a dancing will-o'-the-wisp, should play over and around the words of the author with a swarm of questions. The good reader is in an interrogatory mood as he reads: What is the main idea that the author is presenting? How is he organizing his thoughts? Is there a pattern of presenting the facts? If so, what is it? What sort of person wrote this? What is his purpose? What is my purpose in reading this? All these, and many other thoughts of similar nature, should be romping through the reader's mind as he reads. He should be thinking *with* the author—then comes a place where he should *sense* what the author *must* say next—and be far ahead of him— out there, waiting for the author to catch up to him, the reader. This is what Thorndike meant when he declared, "Reading is thinking."

But reading is not only thinking. It is also evaluating the material read and defining the author's purpose in writing and your purpose in reading it. This threefold approach to reading—thinking, evaluating, defining—must proceed simultaneously as the reader advances along the lines of print. The words themselves are of relatively minor importance to the first-class reader. He is absorbed in the thought that the author is presenting and how that thought fits with other thoughts. This, to him, is of much greater consequence than the words themselves. We are speaking now of the usual factual, nonfictional type of material that comprises much of our business and professional reading. With literature and poetry the situation is somewhat different. But most of our reading is utilitarian, factual, functional. To the topflight reader of such material, the words are but the garb in which the thought is wrapped. The thought is the all-important desideratum.

If you are *really* reading, therefore, when you pick up a page of print, something happens. You react to that page immediately. A chain reaction begins. Certain questions pop inevitably into your head. You look for certain specific things. But do you? Wouldn't it be interesting to know? All right; keep your eyes moving straight ahead. Don't roam back over any of the lines that you have just read. Answer the following questions (jot down your answers in the blanks; this will make interesting reading later on):

1. What is the general subdivision topic of the chapter that is now being discussed?

    _____

2. How many such general subdivision thought areas have been discussed in this chapter thus far? _____ What were they entitled?

    _____

3. Don't look back now, but what was the last principal thought (main idea) presented in the paragraph immediately preceding these questions? What were you reading about?

    _____

4. Have you been conscious of reading any of the preceding paragraphs in this chapter in a basically questioning, or interrogatory, mood?

    _____

5. What is the title of this chapter that you are now reading?

_____

If you are an efficient reader, a wide-awake, mentally alert reader, you should have done very well on that little quiz. It was basically a test of you *as a reader*—a mature reader. Turn now to the Appendix, to the Answer Key, and let's see how well you really did do. After you have checked your answers, allow yourself 20 per cent for each question answered correctly. What is your Reading Efficiency Index?

Let's enter it here for future reference: _____%

Every page should present to you the challenge of a puzzle. "Here," you should think to yourself, "is a page of print. Thought is locked up in these words: facts, ideas, opinions are here. What is the best way that I can 'crack' this wordy shell so that I may grasp the kernel of thought within?"

The page should break down for you into main ideas or principal thoughts, supported or supplemented by subsidiary ideas, details, and ancillary facts and data. You should also make certain evaluations, certain critical appraisals as you read the page, that require clear thinking and careful analysis of what the writer has said. You should, as an expert reader, have not only perfect command of the facts, but be able to relate them logically to each other, beginning with the principal fact or main idea, and show how all the other data is grouped around this central point. You should be able to "read between the lines," without injecting your own ideas, prejudices, or biased opinions; you should read and clearly understand the author's implications, attitudes, and feelings even when these differ sharply with your own views. And you should be able to do all this quickly and skillfully. This, in part, is what it means to read well.

All these phases of reading will be explained and amplified in later chapters. Now, however, we should look specifically at what happens when we read a line of print.

Fixations and eye span

Have you ever watched carefully the movements of a person's eyes while he is reading? If not, take a mirror and hold it at such an angle that you will be able to see reflected in it the eyes of the person reading.

For this experiment it is better if the subject read a book or printed material with book-length lines. Watch intently. You will notice his eyes travel in little skips and jumps: a dart, a pause; a dart, a pause; a dart, a pause. These brief pauses are known as *fixations*. The movements of the eyes are controlled by six small but powerful muscles attached to the outside of the eyeball. These muscles act coordinately to pull the eyes in a series of small jerks as they sweep the axis of vision across the line of print. When these muscles become fatigued, we say that our "eyes are tired," or that we "feel eyestrain."

But let us get back to the fixations—the brief pauses between the jumps. It is during these fixations that the eyes do the reading. During the darts, or interfixation movements, the eyes see nothing.

How many fixations did the person whom you were watching make in reading a single line of print? The number of fixations per line depends upon two things: (1) the length of the line of print and (2) the amount of printed material the eyes can take in at one pause—an "eyeful," so to speak. As a general rule, the average book should be read with two or three fixations per line. Usually there are from ten to twelve words in such a line of print. This means that the eyes should be able to take in a span of three or four words at a glance. At that rate—three hops—and you are ready for the next line. Like this:

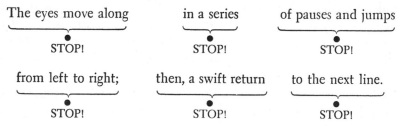

Try reading those two lines again. Focus the center of your vision at the point of the arrow. Look intently at the arrow point, yet try to see as "wide" as possible. The first line is grouped; you will need to do your own grouping in the second line. Let's try it now:

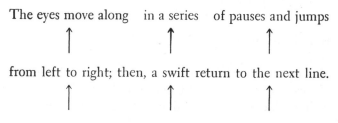

Were you conscious of seeing the outer edges with your marginal field of vision. This is your seeing potential. Actually, fixations are not as severely limited as you might have concluded from the diagram above. Rather there is a peripheral area which is probably very important from a reading standpoint. Some researchers seem to feel that "peripheral vision may aid in the determination of where the next fixation pause is to be located." [1]

Perhaps a more realistic representation of fixation and perceptual span might be the following, where the area in braces represents the image at the foveal, or optical center, and the area between bars comprises the peripheral area of visual awareness:

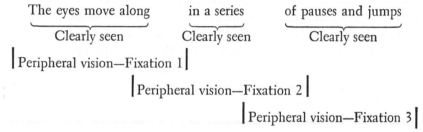

The eyes move along   in a series   of pauses and jumps

Clearly seen   Clearly seen   Clearly seen

|Peripheral vision—Fixation 1|

|Peripheral vision—Fixation 2|

|Peripheral vision—Fixation 3|

Sometimes with a narrower column, like the columns of so many pocket digest magazines, where there are two narrow columns to the page, the eyes of a good reader tick down the column with the swinging action of a pendulum: left, right; left, right; left, right. Like this:

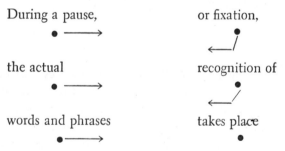

During a pause,   or fixation,

the actual   recognition of

words and phrases   takes place

Sometimes, however, with poor readers the eyes take in only verbal tidbits. The reader goes inching along the line, stopping, looking at every word, before he goes on to the next one. Where he encounters unfamiliar words—words that look strange to him—he may pause, "sound

[1] Leonard Carmichael and Walter F. Dearborn, *Reading and Visual Fatigue*, p. 61, Houghton Mifflin Company, Boston, 1947.

out" the word that is causing trouble, before he proceeds. This is word-by-word reading, but it is practiced by millions of adult readers who engage in it unwittingly. They read a line of print like this:

Word-   by-   word   reading   is   a   habit

that   has   had   its   begin-   ning   in   child-

hood   when   you   learned   to   read   orally.

As children many of us learned to word-read from the habit of reading orally from the basic reader. We *learned* to read that way; we have never read any *other* way.

It must be obvious by now how extremely important eye-span development is to efficient reading. If the eyes can scoop up a whole group of words at a time and then leap to the next group, reading time is cut to a fraction, fatigue is lessened—every time those six tiny muscles must jerk to a stop, and then streak to another stop, *they* feel the strain, whether you do or not—and reading is being done phrase by phrase rather than word by word.

This book will provide certain exercises and suggest certain methods whereby the eye span can be widened. You will want to scoop up larger eyefuls of print when you race across the page. Each chapter will, therefore, contain material for widening your perception span or for improving your perception generally. And with that we come to a brief discussion of another phase of reading efficiency.

Regressions

Legend and mythology tell of the dire consequences that befell those who looked back. One woman was turned into a pillar of salt; another vanished into Hades. Let that be a lesson to you. Do not look back; keep your eyes forward. In reading as in motoring, look ahead.

But despite the fact that we know better, how many of us are not guilty of the backward glance? While reading, we convince ourselves that we have missed something. In a split second, before we realize what we have done, back we look, re-reading the words our eyes have just passed over. Such backward glances and re-readings are called, technically, "regressions."

But *why* do we regress? The answer is simple, stark, and uncomfortable. We regress for two reasons, principally: (1) we are dreaming instead of reading or (2) we are in the grip of a vicious habit, looking back when there is no need to do so.

Most of the time, regressions indicate that the reader, instead of tending to business and concentrating upon his reading has been mentally doing something else. You wouldn't drive your car when you're in a trance. You shouldn't read, either, when you are in the same condition.

Next time you find yourself impelled to regress, stop! Force yourself to give account of the reason why you are regressing.

"I missed something," you sheepishly confess.

"But *why* did you miss something? What were you doing that you didn't see what you missed back there?"

"I guess I was thinking of something else."

"I guess you were," you reprimand yourself. Give yourself a "going over" such as a traffic cop might if you had run through a stop light because you didn't have your mind on your motoring.

Now, what happens at this point? Do you go back to see what you think you missed? You do not! You face dead ahead—down the avenue of print. Give yourself one final "lacing out." (This, incidentally, will do a great deal toward breaking that habit of "trance reading" that you've acquired across the years.)

Say to yourself, "Now, get on the ball; tend to business from now on; if you're going to read, let's read, and what you missed, you missed! Go on, now, keep your mind on the book—and read!"

Here is probably what will happen: ahead of you, somewhere down the highway of print, you will meet again and recognize that fact, that thought, that idea, which you were positive that you had failed to see and to comprehend back there where you stopped and wrestled with yourself. The eye sees more than we are aware that it does, and the brain records more than we are aware that it does. So that, in the instant that you have the urge to regress, drive yourself on. In doing so, in all probability, you will be doing two very wonderful things from a reading viewpoint: (1) you will be replacing a bad reading habit—the habit of regressing—with a better one, and (2) you will be convincing yourself that practically all of your impulses to regress are without foundation.

Only when the thought goes completely to pieces should you go back to locate the difficulty, but not until you have forced yourself to read to the end of the paragraph in which the regression impulse occurred. Then, when you do go back, you should always analyze *why* you did not get the thought when you passed over it the first time. Too much inconvenience, you complain? A little inconvenience may be your best tutor in teaching you to think while you read.

In any event, remember that regressions are one of the greatest hindrances to rapid, efficient reading. They must be dealt with severely. If the correcting of regressive tendencies causes you some delay for the time being, it may be time well spent. Perhaps you will learn the sooner to take heed of your evil ways and to remember that when you read, you *read!*

Perception

Perception is a broad term. It has a tendency to mean all things to all men. Here, however, we shall use the term to mean a grasping of certain specific data through the medium of the visual sense. There is some danger, however, in trying to present in a simplified form and in layman's language so complex a psychological factor. Professor Allport has devoted a sizable volume [2] to the description and definition of perception.

Perhaps the etymology of the word itself gives as well as any source the broad, basic idea of perception. The word comes from two Latin elements, a prefix, *per*, meaning *through*, and *capere*, to *take*. Perception, then, in the visual sense is that data which is taken through the eye. In its simplest and most unsophisticated sense, we might say that perception is merely seeing visual data. We may see either accurately or inaccurately, but the aim of the perceptual exercises in this book will be to encourage rapid, accurate seeing of greater and greater amounts of visual data.

Let us take a practical example which shows the perceptive faculty at work—the mere act of looking at an item of information discriminatingly and with enough attention to remember its salient features. For example, you consult an index in a book to locate information upon some specific subject. And this is one of the skills of the study type of reading—the ability to use an index efficiently. Upon perusing the index you find that the page on which the desired information is to be found is, let us say, page 256. And then, before you can consult the page, you see other page numbers in passing. You are not certain exactly what the number was. Was it 265 or 255? Maybe it was 295; no, you think it *was* 265. But,

[2] Floyd H. Allport, *Theories of Perception and the Concept of Structure*, John Wiley & Sons, New York, 1955.

then, it may have been 296 or 269. By this time you are completely confused. By the way, don't look back, but what was the number?

Our eyes travel at lightning speed. They grasp data in a split second
and then dash on. Some adults have trouble at times with very common
words whose configurations are similar. This is especially a hindrance to
rapid reading, and may be one of the causes of regression. To read well
we must see words with unerring accuracy. *If* and *of, in* and *on, where*
and *when, then* and *them,* and dozens of similar words that look alike
may be very readily misread and confused unless we possess a high
degree of perceptual accuracy. Why not test yourself for perceptual
accuracy?

Read this sentence: [3]

FINISHED FILES ARE THE RESULT

OF YEARS OF SCIENTIFIC STUDY

COMBINED WITH THE EXPERIENCE OF YEARS

Now count the *F*s in that sentence. Count them *only once;* don't go
back and count them again. How many *F*s did you find? Enter the number here: _____. Now turn to the Answer Key to find the correct answer.

You will find perception exercises of many kinds in the course of the
following chapters. Each one is designed to help you improve your perceptual accuracy, speed your recognition, widen your eye span. Each
exercise has been planned with a particular end in view. By improving
your perceptual skill you are laying the foundation for improvement in
one phase of your reading.

But first, we must find out what your skill in *reading* is at this time.
The next chapter is designed to help you to do precisely that.

[3] Reprinted through the courtesy of The Shaw Walker Co.

Chapter Three

How well
do you read–now?

THIS IS the very beginning of your effort to improve your reading habits and skills. Let's take account of stock. How well do you read now?

In the next few pages you will have an opportunity to find the answer to that question. You will evaluate your own status as a mature reader. The rest of this chapter is devoted to three simple tests, each one just a little more difficult than the one before it. Each test will evaluate, among other things, your speed of comprehension and level of comprehension at each of the three stages of difficulty.

Each test will follow the same general pattern: you will have a selection to read which you will read as rapidly as possible, always making sure, however, that at the same time you are understanding the full meaning of the author's thought. These are not "speed of reading" tests —they are rather tests of your reading ability, as nearly as that can be determined in this small compass. You will time yourself on the reading selection. Then you will answer certain questions on the passage which you have just read.

You will want to do all three tests at one time, proceeding from one to the other, without interruption. You will want to have a quiet place in which to work: some place where you will not be disturbed. You will need a watch with a second hand, a pencil, an eraser, and a scratch pad. In taking the tests please observe the following directions carefully:

1. Read each selection only once. Do not go back to re-read; do not refer to the reading selection for any purpose after you have finished reading.
2. Read as rapidly as you can, but never sacrifice the understanding of what you are reading merely to read rapidly. This is a test of your speed of comprehension—not speed alone.
3. In each test the timing procedure is the same: When you begin to read, jot down in the blank at the beginning of the selection the exact time in minutes and seconds. As soon as you have finished reading the selection and before you begin to answer the questions, again jot down the time, minutes and seconds, in the blank at the end of the selection.
4. Answer the questions after you have completely finished reading the selection, without referring back to it again. You do not time yourself in the question-answer part of the test, but do not spend any more time on any one question than is necessary. Work rapidly, but make accuracy your aim.
5. When you have finished Test I, go on immediately to Test II. Note the time, jot it down, then proceed as in Test I. After finishing Test II, then do Test III. Do your best.

And now, are you ready? Here is the first test. It might be better to wait until the second hand of your watch reaches 60 before you start.

Jot down the time *just before* you begin to read: MINUTES _____

SECONDS _____

Begin, now, to read the following selection.

Test I

Today events happen with lightning speed. An earthquake levels a town in lands beyond the horizon, and our newspapers carry the story within minutes of the disaster. We board a plane and keep pace with the sun across the broad expanse of a continent. We hear the voices from our radio loudspeakers before those in the rear of the great broadcasting studio have heard those same voices. We have built machines that hurtle through space faster than the speed of sound, and we have bounced our signals off the face of the moon. Whereas our forefathers thought of "lands beyond the mountains," we think of extragalactic universes, space travel, and the outer fringes of the realms of light.

We live in a world where not only the pace has been quickened, but where the horizons have been pushed back. Ours is indeed a big, round, wonderful world. And because it is such a wonderful world, we should try to absorb as much of its wonder and to enjoy as much of its beauty as possible. But no one can savor the wonders of the modern world unless he learns what these wonders are, and to do this he must read and read well. For the modern world staggers the imagination with the daily wonders which it holds.

In terms of total productive effort the world has never beheld the likes of modern man. In each succeeding decade man builds upon the establishment of the work of his hands until he is, at the present moment, being deluged under the very flood of his own activity. Think, for example, what is going on around the world in terms of human productive effort. Man tills the soil and burrows in the depths of the earth so that the crude product of his labor can be transformed by other men into a miracle fit for the market place. He goes down, down into the very roots of the mountains for his precious ores, he refines the sea for its metal, and he taps the energy of the sun.

In countless laboratories men perform their weird rituals of search and synthesis. Look at a map of the earth. Try to visualize what is happening in terms of human endeavor at every dot that represents a town or city on that map. See that dot correctly, and you will see men—busy men—in factory and in laboratory, in office, and in mill. Everywhere they are tackling new problems, trying new procedures, and experimenting with newer and better ways of handling old and familiar things.

All this activity makes news. Sooner or later word of what is going on trickles down to the level of every man, and to learn of it he is compelled to read. The schoolboy with his textbook and the engineer with his journal are companions in quest of knowledge of what man has done and what he is planning to do. Countless millions read the daily paper to learn of man's activity with his fellow man. And man has found that the sharing of this news is good and that the world is a safer and a better place in which to live when he shares his knowledge and pools his facts. To do this, each man writes down what he would share with others, and it is then circulated for all to read.

This is different from anything known before in the history of the world. In ancient times the written word was encountered only occasionally. What writings there were, were like springs in the wasteland of man's ignorance and illiteracy. A clay tablet, a stray parchment, an occasional scroll—these were the reading materials of the ancient world. In all the populace but few men were able to read, and there was relatively little reading matter for these very few. Then Gutenberg gave to the world the press and movable type, and the spring became a trickling stream. And that stream has grown and widened, and man has had to learn to read. No longer is reading reserved for kings and wise men, nor even for the educated and the elect; it is now a skill at which every man must be adept.

We are surrounded by the kingdom of print. From whirling presses pour forth a flood of words, ever widening and deepening and more voluminous. This has been a sudden deluge. The trickle has swollen into a torrent within a very short time. Until the end of the first quarter of the twentieth century the world progressed fairly well without too much "paper work." Then the flood descended, and man was unprepared for its impact because his skills were inadequate and his pace was slow.

But though words have suddenly engulfed us on every side, the end result is good. Everywhere life is better because of the printed word. As the days pass, one truth stands out with ever-increasing clarity: whatever a man is, or whatever he hopes to be, will be conditioned by the skill with which he reads the printed page. This ability to read, more than any other single skill, will mark him as one who is equipped to live competently in the highly literate world of today and the even more communicative world of tomorrow.

Among other things he should know accurately and unerringly what he has read; and, if he has become skilled in the art of reading, he will have no trouble in keeping clearly in his own mind the main thought and the supporting details. He will find little difficulty in divorcing the author's thoughts from the author's words and in clothing those thoughts anew in words of his own choosing, to the end that by so doing he can make the thought clearer and more concise in his own mind. He needs to know also not only how to read the lines, but how to read *between* the lines. Quickness at comprehending not only the stated fact but the implied thought is a mark of the skillful reader.

But accuracy of comprehension is but one side of the shield. Today's reader also reads with speed. He touches the page deftly and gets its message in a flash. This is a necessary skill for those who live in the age of lightning speed. The old half-formed habits and half-learned skills are incapable of serving the man or the woman who, in turn, must serve today's world.

Skills that help the reader to grasp above all else the thought of what he reads, to organize and summarize, to think actively while following the author's presentation carefully—these are the skills that the reader of today must have.

Compare with these requirements your own reading skill. How well are you prepared to face the reading demands of the age of speed and to feel comfortable? How competent are you to confront the new era when the printed word shall become increasingly more important? These are questions which he who must do battle with the printed word, ofttimes as a part of his livelihood, should soberly consider in this increasingly literate and communicative world.

What time is it now? MINUTES _____

SECONDS _____

What is your reading time for this selection? MINUTES _____

SECONDS _____

Comprehension quiz

Now, answer the following questions. Do not refer back to the article.

How Clearly Do You Recognize the Main Ideas?

In the article which you have just read, the author has presented certain main ideas. These main ideas were amplified, or supported, by certain details. Below are ten statements. Five of these are statements of main ideas. Instead of being exact quotations from the article, these statements are paraphrased. See if you can select those statements which are main ideas. Indicate the statements you have chosen by encircling the item numbers.

1. Nowadays events happen with lightning speed.
2. Some men plow their fields; others look for ore.
3. We have built machines that hurtle through space faster than the speed of sound.
4. In terms of productive effort the world has never beheld the likes of man.
5. In ancient times the written word was encountered only occasionally.

6. Man builds upon the efforts of preceding generations.
7. The expert reader finds no trouble in being able to rephrase **quickly and** accurately the thought of the author.
8. We are surrounded by a river of print.
9. Every dot on a map represents unimaginable human effort and **endeavor.**
10. Man's labor makes news.

How Well Did You Comprehend the Details?

There was a certain amount of factual data in the article which you have just read. Test your comprehension of the facts by completing the following statements. Only one word goes in each blank.

1. In the modern world, in addition to an accelerated pace, we have also

   pushed back the _____.

2. The author suggests the use of a _____ in visualizing modern man's activity.

3. The author suggests that the modern problem associated with reading

   began with the advent of _____.

4. Quickness in comprehending not only the stated facts but also ___ ____

   _____ ._____ is a mark of the skilled reader.

5. To know what is going on in the world, man must ___ _____.

Now, go on to the next test. You will follow the same general procedure as you did with this test. After you have finished all the tests, we shall score them and discuss the meaning of the scores in terms of your own reading skills and needs.

Are you ready for the next test? You will want to time yourself on the reading portion of this test as you did in the one you just completed.

Here is the second test.

Test II [1]

Time now? MINUTES _____

SECONDS _____

Begin to read.

Long before the age of electronic communication, the Lamaistic

[1] E. Wayne Marjarum, *How to Use a Book,* Chap. 2, pp. 22–26, Rutgers University Press, New Brunswick, N. J., 1947.

priests of Tibet devised a wondrous means of hailing their deities. They write out their prayers on a long strip of paper and then wind the paper about a cylinder which revolves on an axle. To pray, they need only to spin the prayer wheel. One cannot but wonder at the ingenuity of the device. *There* is broadcasting. But still more wonderful must be the rapidity with which the gods can read when the worshiper is feeling unusually sorry for himself, for, presumably, the more he needs the gods, the faster he whirls the mill.

The flood of books, circulars, and pamphlets which the world presents for our daily inspection makes one wish he could read as fast as a Tibetan god. Lacking such supernal endowments, we are forced to do the next best thing, which is to read as fast as we can. Most of us could read faster than we do. Laboratory methods have revealed much in recent years about our reading habits and capacities, and the results of experiments are somewhat amazing. It has proved possible for subjects willing to undertake the training to increase their reading speeds two-fold, in some cases to a rate three or four times as fast as the ordinary rate of vocal speech.

A preliminary to all such training is the eradication of habits which impede reading, and the worst of these is the tendency to pronounce the words. In old-fashioned schools the youngsters were frequently encouraged to read their lessons aloud. The masters in the "blab schools," as they were called, having accommodated their nerves to the infernal cacophony, could easily spot the idlers—they didn't make enough noise. And you yourself have seen persons form the words on their lips, with or without actual sound. Many others who appear to read silently are actually readying their organs of speech for each sound, shifting the position of the tongue and the other organs toward, if not to, the positions they would take in articulating the word. Examine yourself carefully and honestly to see if this is true of you. If it is, do not hesitate to apply mechanical aids. Some specialists recommend that one should, if necessary, practice regularly reading with some object in his mouth to inhibit and finally stop the habit of "vocalization." Since the speed with which we talk is only a fraction of that with which we read silently, it can easily be seen that even an incipient use of the vocal organs acts as a brake. It may seem to the reader that such advice is impertinent, but he would be surprised to find how frequently this habit is to be observed by persons whose work gives them much opportunity to notice.

Closely related to this immaturity is the effect which some kinds of work produce upon reading habits. Proofreaders, copyists, and particularly teachers, the very nature of whose occupation is to scrutinize every written symbol on the page, get so in the habit of close inspection that even when reading for general purposes they see every misplaced comma, every slip in typesetting, and even check at the end of a sentence to make sure that the period is there. Only a deliberate effort to ignore such matters is likely to help them, and the resolution to be less careful must be renewed many times.

Laboratory studies of reading habits, with the aid of a motion-picture camera focused upon the eyeball of cooperating subjects, illustrate the most important difference between slow readers and fast. As you know, you have a direct line of vision which you use in sighting a rifle or aligning a row of fence posts. It corresponds to a point in the back of the eye called the yellow spot, where the rod- and cone-shaped tissues are very highly concentrated. But when aiming a rifle or putting the cross hairs of a telescope upon a target, you are aware of other objects on which your eye is not directly fixed, particularly if they are in motion. This kind of seeing is peripheral vision. To see how useful peripheral vision is for reading, slip a dime between the pages of a closed book, keeping your forefinger on it to guide your eye so that when you open the book your glance will fall immediately on the dime and nothing else. Next, open the book, and keep your eye on the center of the coin. Try to see how much you can read of the surrounding material while focusing on the dime. Then let your eye wander to the edges of the dime, but not beyond, and try again to see if you cannot read a few words without actually looking at them. You will find that your peripheral vision can be used for reading—not very efficiently, of course, but it can definitely be used.

Now when you read a line of a book, your eye does not travel in a continuous sweep from left to right. If it did, your line of vision would traverse each letter and each word at about the same speed. Actually, your eyeball, instead of rotating slowly, moves in a series of little jerking movements. Your center of vision is applied successively to a series of points in the line, resting upon each for a fraction of a second, and then jumping to another point to the right. In short, you don't look at all the letters with your yellow spot; you look at a few of them, and peripheral vision does the rest. You are so familiar with the general configuration of the letters in a word like *apple* that it is quite sufficient for you to look at one letter, for example the second *p*. When short words occur together, you read several of them at once. Instead of reading individual symbols, you read clusters, and the more words you apprehend in any one cluster, the faster you can read.

What time is it now? MINUTES _____

SECONDS _____

How long did it take you to read this selection? MINUTES _____

SECONDS _____

Comprehension quiz

In the selection which you have just read, the author stated or implied certain facts and ideas. From the four choices for each question, select the one which best completes the statement.

1. With training you can increase your reading speed to
   a twice what it was before you began training.
   b three to four times as much as the average adult reading rate.
   c no more than the normal rate of vocal speech.
   d twice as much as the normal rate of vocal speech.

2. The practice of vocalization in adults is
   a usually found in those who, as children, attended old-fashioned schools.
   b seldom found in those who move their lips while they read.
   c a frequent cause of slow reading.
   d the habit of pronouncing every word aloud.

3. The author implies that the most important difference between slow readers and fast ones is
   a the difference between jerking along a line of print and sweeping your eyes across it.
   b the difference between a low retinal concentration of rods and cones and a high concentration.
   c that slow readers are usually in the habit of checking to see that each sentence has a period.
   d the difference between the use that each makes of peripheral vision in the act of reading.

4. You are more likely to see objects peripherally especially if they are
   a in action.
   b of considerable size.

c brightly colored.

d arranged in a straight line.

5. Which of the following choices is the best title for the selection which you have just read?
   a The Reading Skills of Gods and Men
   b Habits and Reading
   c Peripheral Vision and Reading
   d Recent Research Investigates Reasons for Slow Reading

What Is Your Word Power?

The following ten words have been taken from the selection which you have just read. Following each word are four choices. Check the choice which you feel is nearest in meaning to the key word. Do *not* refer to the article while doing this part of the test.

1. apprehend: *a* distrust   *b* recognize   *c* estimate
   d grasp

2. articulate: *a* speak   *b* mumble   *c* separate   *d* sparkle

3. cacophony: *a* harmony   *b* rhythm   *c* discord   *d* chorus

4. configuration: *a* calculation   *b* form   *c* seizure
   d drawing

5. incipient: *a* beginning   *b* sickening   *c* late
   d surrounding

6. inhibit: *a* reside   *b* restrain   *c* inherit   *d* depress

7. impede: *a* mediate   *b* accuse   *c* hinder   *d* remove

8. impertinent: *a* impenetrable   *b* impulsive   *c* calm
   d inappropriate

9. peripheral: *a* spherical   *b* external   *c* elliptical
   d indistinct

10. supernal: *a* celestial   *b* sumptuous   *c* miraculous
    d additional

Now, go on to the final test. You will follow the same general procedure that you did with this test. After you have finished Test III, we shall score all of the tests and discuss the meaning of the scores in terms of your reading skills and needs.

Are you ready? You will want to time yourself on the reading of this test. It will be more difficult than the test you have just taken. Do not sacrifice meaning for speed. You will need to comprehend the author's thought particularly in Test III.

Here is the third test.

Test III [2]

> Time now? MINUTES _____
>
> SECONDS _____
>
> Begin to read.

The growth of conscious purpose and self-direction—all that is implied in the historic concepts of the soul and the person—was made possible by man's special skill in interpreting his own nature and working his experiences into a meaningful and valuable whole, upon which he could draw for future actions and operations. That skill rests upon a special aptitude, embedded in man's very physiology: the ability to form and transmit symbols. Man's most characteristic social trait, his possession of an extra-organic environment and super-organic self, which he transmits from generation to generation without using the biological mechanism of heredity, is dependent upon his earlier conquest of the word.

During the last century this essential fact about man's nature has been obscured by the false assumption that man is primarily a "tool-using animal." Carlyle called him that long before Bergson suggested that the term Homo Faber, Man the Maker, should replace Homo Sapiens. But man is not essentially distinguished from his animal relatives either by the fact that he lives in groups or performs physical work with tools. Man is first and foremost the self-fabricating animal: the only creature who has not rested content with his biological form or with the dumb repetitions of his animal role. The chief source of this particular form of creativity was not fire, tools, weapons, machines, but two subjective instruments far older than any of these: the dream and the word.

Without dwelling on the function of symbolization, one cannot begin to describe the nature of man or plumb the deepest spring of his creativeness. That is why I pass over many other attributes, fully taken into account today by anthropology and psychology, to dwell on man's role as interpreter. Language, the greatest of all human inventions, is the most essential key to the truly human. When words fail him, as we find

[2] From *The Conduct of Life,* copyright, 1951, by Lewis Mumford. Reprinted by permission of Harcourt, Brace and Company, Inc., Chap. 2, pp. 39–42.

in the few authenticated cases of wild children reared without the benefit of human society, man is an animal without a specific life-plan, compelled to imitate the wolfish habits of the animal in whose brood he has been suckled and reared.

One can, of course, only speculate on the way in which man invented and perfected the various tools of symbolization. But in the primary instance of speech, the word was made possible by changes in the bodily organs including the larynx, the tongue, the teeth, and not least the creation of mobile lips: in the earliest skulls identifiable as man, the anatomists find the speech centers already relatively well developed. The enlargement of man's powers, through his quicker ability to learn by trial and correction, demanded a special instrument for dealing with the multiude of sensations and meanings, suggestions and demands, that impinged upon him. Every sensation, as Adelbert Ames has experimentally demonstrated, is a prognostic directive to action: hence even the simplest stimulus must be interpreted, for whether we accept it or reject it depends not only upon its own nature but upon our purposes and predispositions and proposals. Even the purest sensation must be translated and re-ordered, before the organism will in fact see it, hear it, or answer it. In that response, the entire organism co-operates; and what is actually seen or heard or felt is only what makes sense in terms of the organism's immediate purpose or its historic plan of development.

At every moment of his waking existence, man senses, interprets, proposes, acts in a single unified response: but between the starting point and the end, the intermediate steps of interpretation and planful reorganization are critical, for it is here that error, miscalculation, and frustration may intervene. With the development of language, man created an instrument of interpretation that gave him a way of traversing the largest possible field of life. What he took in of the world expressed his own nature: what he expressed of himself partook of the nature of the world; for it is only in thought that organism and environment can be separated.

Now other creatures than man respond to immediate signals: the snarl of a dog has meaning for another dog, and the upraised white tail of a doe tells the fawns, as plainly as words, "Follow me!" But man, at a critical moment in his development, began to invent signs, in the form of audible words, which represent an event or a situation even when they are not present. By this act of detachment and abstraction, man gained the power of dealing with the non-present, the unseen, the remote, and the internal: not merely his visible lair and his daily companions, but his ancestors and his descendants and the sun and the moon and the stars: eventually the concepts of eternity and infinity, of electron and universe: he reduced a thousand potential occasions in all their variety and flux to a single symbol that indicated what was common to all of them.

Similarly, by kindred means, man was able to give form to and project his inner world, otherwise hidden and private: by words, images, related sounds, it became part of the public world, and thus an "object." This extraordinary labor-saving device, for extracting, condensing, and preserving the most complicated kinds of events, was perhaps another manifestation of the creative uses of his exuberance and vital proliferation. Man's possession of a "useless instrument," his special voice-producing organs, with their wide range of tones, plus a love of repetition, which one observes in the fullest degree in infants, opened up playful possibilities. If man is an inventor or an artist, the first object of his interest is his own body: he falls in love with his own organs long before he seeks to master the outside world.

"We must never forget," the distinguished philologist Jespersen once observed, "that the organs of speech . . . are one of mankind's most treasured toys, and that not only children but also grown people in civilized as well as savage communities, find amusement in letting their vocal cords and tongue and lips play all sorts of games." Out of this original organic overflow, man found too a way to shape a meaningful, orderly world: the world realized in language, music, poesy, and directed thought. The gift of tongues is the greatest of all gifts: in the beginning was the Word.

Speech, human speech, affected a miraculous transformation in human society: by such magic Prospero tamed Caliban and released Ariel. Speech, at first probably inseparable from gesture, exclamatory, disjointed, structureless, purely emotive, laid the foundation for a more complex mechanism of abstractions, the independent structure of language itself; and with language, human culture as an extra-organic activity, no longer wholly dependent upon the stability and continuity of the physical body and its daily environment, became possible. This broke through the boundaries of time and place that limit animal associations.

What time is it now? MINUTES _____

SECONDS _____

What is your reading time for this selection? MINUTES _____

SECONDS _____

Comprehension quiz

Now, answer the following questions. Do not refer back to the article.

In the selection that you have just read, certain facts and ideas were either stated or implied. From the four choices in each question, choose the one which best completes the statement.

1. The author says that man's "ability to form and transmit" symbols is
   a the result of man's "extra-organic environment."
   b "a special aptitude, embedded in man's physiology."
   c embedded in the world around him.
   d the result of "the biological mechanism of heredity."

2. Man is unique in that he
   a is able to communicate by means of "immediate signals."
   b acts from a set of single, unified responses.
   c "is first and foremost the self-fabricating animal."
   d can communicate with others of his race.

3. We may infer from what the author says that man gained the ability to think in terms germane to the concepts of a nuclear age when he
   a "gained the power of dealing with the nonpresent."
   b learned to think.
   c learned to employ fire and make weapons.
   d "broke through the boundaries of time and place."

4. Language began as a result of
   a the need to express the thought of the human race.
   b man's need to communicate with his fellow men.
   c man's need to interpret the "concepts of eternity and infinity."
   d man's interest in his vocal organs.

5. Human speech was probably at first
   a learned from animals.
   b inseparable from gesture.
   c imitative of natural sounds.
   d used as magic, in the way Prospero employed it.

How Clearly Do You Recognize the Main Ideas?

The ability to recognize and recall the main ideas of the author is one of the very first steps toward improving your comprehension. In

Test I you were asked to identify the main ideas in a selection which was easy to read and hence in which the ideas were easy to identify. Now, try again, on the selection you have just read. As before, you will have a list of ten statements: five of these are statements of main ideas; five are details that merely support the main ideas. Instead of being exact quotations, some of the ideas, as before, are paraphrased. See if you can select the main ideas; indicate your choice by circling the number of the statement.

1. We have beclouded our vision with reference to the real nature of man by a false assumption concerning his tool-using ability.
2. Human speech affected a miraculous transformation in human society.
3. The gift of tongues is the greatest of all gifts.
4. When words fail him, as we find in the few authenticated cases of wild children reared without the benefit of human society, man is an animal without a specific life-plan, compelled to imitate the wolfish habits of the animal in whose brood he has been suckled and reared.
5. Man is the only creature who has not rested content with his biological form or with the dumb repetitions of his animal role.
6. Without dwelling on the function of symbolization, one cannot begin to describe the nature of man or plumb the deepest spring of his creativeness.
7. Language is the essential key to the truly human.
8. "We must never forget," the distinguished philologist Jespersen once observed, "that the organs of speech . . . are one of mankind's most treasured toys, and that not only children but also grown people in civilized as well as savage communities, find amusement in letting their vocal cords and tongue and lips play all sorts of games."
9. The enlargement of man's powers, through his quicker ability to learn by trial and correction, demanded a special instrument for dealing with the multitude of sensations and meanings, suggestions and demands, that impinged upon him.
10. One can, of course, only speculate on the way in which man invented and perfected the various tools of symbolization.

What Is Your GKQ (General-Knowledge Quotient)?

The highest level of reading demands that the reader not only understand and retain the information resident upon the printed page and that he acquire this quickly and efficiently, but that he contribute something on his part, from his fund of general knowledge, to the words and thought of the author, so that what the author has written may take on added meaning in the mind of the reader. Allusions, figures of speech, references of one sort or another, all demand that the reader meet the author halfway, so that the full implication of the author's words may be appreciated. In Test III there were several instances where the reader needed to call upon his general knowledge of the facts of literature, anthropology, history, and biology to understand fully the text. In this way general background information and knowledge become definitely a factor in comprehension. Let's find out what your GKQ is. Do not refer to the text. Answer the following questions with a simple, straightforward, informative statement.

1. What is the meaning of "Homo sapiens"?

_____

2. ". . . The creation of mobile lips in the earliest skulls identifiable as man . . ." Who were some of these earliest "men"?

_____

3. The author closes one of his paragraphs with these words: "In the beginning was the word." This is a famous quotation. What is its source?

_____

4. To what literary situation does the author refer in the words "by some such magic Prospero tamed Caliban and released Ariel"? Who was the author and in what work does this situation take place?

_____

5. What is an electron?

_____

What Is Your Word Power?

One of the reasons why so-called "difficult" reading is difficult is the fact that the author frequently employs a vocabulary in which many of the words have specific meanings derived from their association with the other words within the context. The question in this test is not whether you know *any* meaning of the word, but whether you can sense the meaning which the author had in mind when he chose a particular word to express his thought. Here it is necessary for you to understand the idea which the author is expressing and to fit the meaning of a particular word to that idea.

In the sentences given below you are to give a synonym for the key word. Select a synonym which will express the specific meaning in view of the thought expressed in the entire sentence.

Although the sentences following are taken from the article which you read in Test III, they have been edited for the purposes of this test.

1. Man's ability to form and transmit symbols rests upon a special aptitude, embedded in his very physiology.

   aptitude: *a* sense   *b* organ   *c* talent   *d* quality
   e need

2. Man's most characteristic social trait is his possession of an extra-organic environment.

   extraorganic: *a* natural   *b* extraordinary   *c* expanded
   d external   *e* large

3. Man is first and foremost the self-fabricating animal: the only creature who has not rested content with his biological form or animal role.

   self-fabricating: *a* creative   *b* cooperative   *c* self-satisfied
   d tool-using   *e* selfish

4. The chief source of man's particular form of superiority was not fire, tools, weapons, machines, but two subjective instruments far older than any of these: the dream and the word.

   subjective: *a* primitive   *b* ancient   *c* inner   *d* powerful
   e superior

5. The enlargement of man's powers demanded a special instrument for dealing with the multitude of sensations and meanings that impinged upon him.

   impinge: *a* impend   *b* encroach   *c* enclose   *d* rest
   e weigh

6. Every sensation is a prognostic directive to action.

   prognostic: *a* obvious   *b* unmistakable   *c* probable
   d proximate   *e* predictive

7. At every moment of his waking existence, man senses, interprets, proposes, acts in a single unified response: but between the starting point and the end, the intermediate steps of interpretation and planful reorganization are critical, for it is here that error, miscalculation, and frustration may intervene.

   critical:　　*a* understood　　*b* hazy　　*c* climactic　　*d* crucial
   　　　　　　e useless

8. Whether we accept a stimulus or reject it depends upon our purposes and predispositions and proposals.

   predisposition:　*a* prejudice　　*b* thought　　*c* susceptibility
   　　　　　　　　d predetermination　　*e* feeling

9. By the invention of signs, in the form of audible words, man reduced a thousand potential occasions to a single symbol.

   potential:　　*a* different　　*b* drinkable　　*c* unforeseen
   　　　　　　d righteous　　*e* latent

10. The developing of language was perhaps another manifestation of the creative uses of man's exuberation and vital proliferation.

   proliferation:　*a* rapid growth　　*b* warmth　　*c* interests
   　　　　　　　d well-being　　*e* energy

Evaluate your reading habits

Reading improvement is a matter, in part at least, of the establishing of correct reading habits. There are certain things that an efficient reader does, certain approaches that he has, certain techniques that he uses. There is a certain way in which he attacks a reading situation so that he may comprehend quickly and effectively the thought behind the words on the page.

All sound reading improvement programs recognize the fact that a person cannot significantly improve his reading skills until he forms habits that are consistent with effective reading. This book endorses that viewpoint. It is of utmost importance, therefore, to determine at the outset whether your habits are those of a good reader or not. To determine this fact the following Reading Habit Inventory may be helpful. It may also help you to focus your attention on your individual needs and your particular assets.

The purpose of this inventory is to help you evaluate your own read-

ing habits. Answer it honestly. Put wishful thinking aside. Do not con-
trive to outwit the inventory. Simply read each statement, and then
try to evaluate it as objectively as possible. Say to yourself, "Now, what
do I *really* do most of the time when I read?" Such an approach may
help you to make a realistic decision with reference to your actual
reading habits.

At the close of each chapter you will also have an opportunity to
evaluate briefly some of the more important habits which you should
possess, if you are a really effective reader. As you progress from chapter
to chapter you should find that after a while you really are doing more
things in your reading as they should be done. When this realization
comes, it will spell progress in an important area of reading improvement.

Reading Habit Inventory

For each of the following statements, check under Never, Rarely,
Sometimes, Usually, or Always. Do not omit any of the items. Be truthful and utterly realistic. Represent your reading habits as they actually
are.

Never Rarely Sometimes Usually Always

1. When I pick up a page of
print, I notice the paragraphs
specifically.

2. I read as I drive, with varying
rates of speed, depending upon
varying reading conditions.

3. While reading, I find it easy to
keep my mind on the material
before me.

4. After I have been reading for
a while, I stop reading for a
few moments and rest my eyes
by looking at some distant
object.

5. I am alert to the role which
punctuation plays in aiding me
to get the meaning.

6. When I pick up a piece of

Never   Rarely   Sometimes   Usually   Always

reading matter for the first time, I look for certain specific items which will aid me in reading the piece more efficiently.

7. I read groups of words at one glance.

8. I notice a distinctive style, or flavor, of the author.

9. I enjoy reading.

10. I can read for long periods of time without a feeling of eye fatigue or tiredness.

11. After I read a paragraph, if required to do so, I could sum up the main idea clearly and briefly in my own words.

12. I make a practice of skimming articles frequently.

13. In reading a paragraph I usually try to see the organization of its thought content: I look for the main idea, and the details which support it.

14. I do not lose my place, or skip words or lines, while reading.

15. I am mildly conscious of grammatical structure while reading.

16. I feel comfortable and perfectly at ease while reading.

17. In reading larger units of writing (articles, chapters, etc.) I try to see the outline and total structure of the author's thought.

18. I have little difficulty in remembering what I read.

19. When I read, especially for

	Never	Rarely	Sometimes	Usually	Always
any length of time, I make sure that the page before me is adequately illuminated.					
20. When I read, I am reading for some definite purpose, and I try to keep that purpose clearly in mind as I read.					
21. I read the preface of a book.					
22. In reading more difficult material, after reading a paragraph or a section, I pause to summarize in a momentary flashback the material I have just covered.					
23. While reading, I am aware of questions which arise in my own thinking about the material being read.					
24. While reading, I hold the page 15 to 20 inches from my eyes.					
25. I am aware that with practice a person can improve his reading skills, and I make a conscious effort generally toward that end.					

Count the checks in each column to obtain:	(A)					
Multiply by:	(B)	0	1	2	3	4
to obtain:	(C)		%	%	%	%

Now add the figures in row C for your final score: _____%

Analysis of Your Reading Habits

Now, analyze your reading habits. What does the above Inventory mean? If you have marked it carefully and conscientiously, it should prove a helpful guide in aiding you to develop more effective reading habits than those you now have. This means that ultimately you will be a more efficient reader.

To analyze your reading habits, carefully check on the chart below, under the number of the item of the Inventory statement, the category (Always, Usually, Sometimes, Rarely, Never) as you marked it in the Inventory above. Out of the 25 items that you marked, certain of them attempted to appraise your habits associated with certain specific reading techniques. Other items attempted to evaluate the more important matters associated with ocular hygiene and visual efficiency. Finally, a few items sought to probe some of the emotional factors which may aid or hinder your total reading efficiency.

Note the line in the forms below marked, "Danger Line." As you transcribe your check marks from the Inventory above, you will find that you have checked either above or below this danger line. The check marks *below* the danger line indicate that in these matters you need to give attention to your reading habits and practices. Try to put into practice each time you read, the procedures suggested by the Inventory statements of those items which you have checked below the danger line.

1. What does the Inventory indicate as to my reading techniques? To find out, transcribe a check mark from the Inventory to the proper box in the chart following:

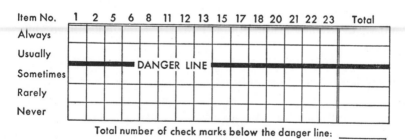

Item No.	1	2	5	6	8	11	12	13	15	17	18	20	21	22	23	Total
Always																
Usually																
DANGER LINE																
Sometimes																
Rarely																
Never																

Total number of check marks below the danger line: _____

2. What does the Inventory indicate about my visual factors in reading? Check the following chart to find out:

Item No.	4	7	10	14	19	24	Total
Always							
Usually							
DANGER LINE							
Sometimes							
Rarely							
Never							

Total number of check marks below the danger line: _____

3. What does the Inventory indicate about my emotional factors in reading? Check the following chart to find out:

Item No.	3	9	16	25	Total
Always					
Usually					
■ DANGER LINE ■					
Sometimes					
Rarely					
Never					

Total number of check marks below the danger line: _____

Total number of check marks in all three charts *above* the danger line:_____

Divide 25 into the *total* number of check marks you have *above* the danger line. This will give you your percentage score of *desirable* reading habits: _____%

How Well Did You Read?

You have now completed taking the tests designed to give you some indication of your present reading ability. Each of the tests was of a different level of difficulty: Test I was fairly easy reading; Test II, standard or average reading; and Test III, fairly difficult to difficult reading.

Now turn to the Appendix to the Table of Reading Rates. Consult that section of the table entitled, "Preliminary and Final Evaluation Tests—Reading Rates." Under the heading, Chapter Three, you will notice columns of figures for Tests I, II, and III. In the extreme left-hand column find the number of minutes and seconds, representing your reading time for the first test. In the next column to the right you will find the words per minute which you were reading. Find your rate for each of the three tests.

Then turn to the Answer Key. Check each of your answers with those suggested in the Key. In the completion questions, if you have an answer equivalent in *meaning,* but different in wording from the answer that is suggested in the Key, give yourself full credit. If, however, your answer differs substantially from the one suggested in the Key, deny yourself credit. In every case, where there is any question in your mind, check back into the text to try to see the reason for the answer suggested in the Key.

Fill in the "Summary of Your Reading Skills." You will note that following each of the rate-comprehension entries there is a blank for the reading index. You get the reading index by multiplying the rate by the comprehension and dividing the product by 100 (pointing off two decimal places). For example, if you are reading at 250 words per minute at 80 per cent comprehension level, the reading index would be 250×80 = 20,000. Divide 20,000 by 100. The reading index is 200. The importance of this figure will be discussed later in the text, but you should work out the reading indexes now for future reference.

For those desiring to work out *exactly* the number of words per minute which they have read, it is necessary to time your reading to the exact second, with a stop watch or other accurate timing device. Convert your reading time to seconds, find the number of words in the article, divide the reading time into the total word count, and multiply the result by 60. Your answer will be your rate of reading in words per minute. For the reading selections in this book, the exact total word count is given in the Table of Reading Rates, pages 435–441, opposite the 1:00-minute designation in the time column (the first figure in each column, under the title of the article).

If your scores on certain sections of the tests are below 80 per cent, you should give special attention to the building of more proficient skills in these areas. If your word power score is below 80 per cent, you should give extra attention to the building of a more powerful vocabulary. Chapter Twenty will help you. Consult it before you read each chapter.

Also, if your general-knowledge quotient is below 80 per cent, you need to acquire a broader factual background for reading.

The vocabulary-building material is designed to help you *before*, rather than after you have made your mistake. If your scores indicate at this point that you need help with respect to your vocabulary, turn to Chapter Twenty *before* you begin Chapter Four. There you will find a list of words which will occur in the chapter. Use your dictionary; get the meanings of these words well in mind *before* you begin to read.

Summary of Your Reading Skills

Date: _____

Your speed and level of comprehension:

Test I: Fairly Easy Reading

Rate	_____wpm
Comprehension	_____%
Reading Index	_____

Test II: Standard, or Average Reading

Rate	_____wpm
Comprehension	_____%
Reading Index	_____

Test III: Fairly Difficult to Difficult Reading

Rate	_____wpm
Comprehension	_____%
Reading Index	_____

Your ability to comprehend main ideas:

Test I	_____%
Test III	_____%

Your word power:

Test II	_____%
Test III	_____%

Your general-knowledge quotient:

Test III	_____%

Your habits of reading:

Inventory of Reading Habits	_____%

Individual diagnostic chart

The Reading Skills Summary is a composite picture of your initial reading achievement. The chart which you are about to fill in will be your guide to further reading improvement. It will indicate the specific areas in which you have not achieved a satisfactory score. It is in these areas that you will need to give special attention to the development of those specific skills and techniques which will help to make you a more efficient reader.

In the column entitled Minimal Satisfactory Score you will find a level of achievement indicated. Any score which you made on the tests which falls below this minimal score indicates unsatisfactory reading skill performance. Compare your scores with the minimal achievement scores in each category. Then mark an X in the appropriate column.

If your score is *above* the minimal satisfactory score, put an X in the left-hand column. If it is *below* the indicated minimal satisfactory score, put an X in the right-hand column.

Reading Skills Area	*Level of Material*	*Minimal Satisfactory Score*	*Your Score*	*Satisfactory: (Minimal Score or Above)*	*Unsatisfactory: (Below Minimal Score)*
Rate:					
Test I ....Fairly easy		600 wpm	_____	_____	_____
Test II ....Average		500 wpm	_____	_____	_____
Test III....Fairly difficult		400 wpm	_____	_____	_____
Comprehension of details:					
Test I ....Fairly easy		80%	_____	_____	_____
Test II ....Average		80%	_____	_____	_____
Test III....Fairly difficult		80%	_____	_____	_____
Comprehension of main ideas:					
Test I ....Fairly easy		80%	_____	_____	_____
Test III ..Fairly difficult		80%	_____	_____	_____

Reading Skills Area	Level of Material	Minimal Satisfactory Score	Your Score	Satisfactory: (Minimal Score or Above)	Unsatisfactory: (Below Minimal Score)
Word power:					
Test II ....Average		90%	____	____	____
Test III....Fairly difficult		80%	____	____	____
General-knowledge quotient...		80%	____	____	____
General reading habits		90%	____	____	____
Total satisfactory scores				____	
Total unsatisfactory scores *					____

* You should have a total of *not more* than three check marks in this column.

Chapter Four

Why paragraphs?

HAVE YOU ever glanced down a column of print and, seeing those little indentations, wondered why they were there? The real reason that they are placed there is to make reading easier for you. Those paragraph indentations are set there so that the thought will come off the page faster and so that you will be able to read with greater comprehension. Yet most people never notice paragraphs while they are reading. Having an eye for paragraphs is one of the first signs that you really know what to do with a page of print.

Paragraphs are units of writing which every reader should master. As a general rule, they have structure, organization, and purpose. They have been constructed around one idea according to specific rules of writing. They provide a means by which an author may, in an expanded form, show the reader his thought.

But do not expect that every paragraph will be a perfect example of writing or follow a given form. Not every writer is equally skillful in his ability to express his thought. And so you must expect to find paragraphs of all kinds. In reading you must take paragraphs as you find them.

Each paragraph should revolve around one thought, and by far the great majority of them do. Within the paragraph, however, you usually find one sentence which states clearly the main thought of the paragraph. This sentence is commonly called the "topic" sentence. This sentence is different from the others within the paragraph. It is more inclusive. It glows with the concentrated white heat of the *whole* idea. The other sentences will break down the thought within this topic sentence as a prism breaks down the rays of light. They will help you to see the central thought in all of its meanings. The entire thought-spectrum, as it were, is presented sentence after sentence, as each sentence explains, illustrates, contrasts, or parallels the topic sentence of the paragraph. As the author elects, the topic sentence may or may not be expressed. But regardless of that fact, the thought of every other sentence tends toward the topic sentence as iron filings are pulled toward the center of a magnetic field. You should always be sensitive to the central pull of the thought within the paragraph. In reading, keep clearly in your own mind the pivotal idea around which the rest of the paragraph revolves.

How to recognize a main idea when you see one

It is not the topic sentence, however, which we will consider first. To ask many readers to find the topic sentence is to send them out blindfolded to catch butterflies. Those who may have some success will probably snatch at the first, or last sentence of a paragraph—and hope! Somebody, somewhere, at some time or other, told them that this procedure was a fairly safe one. But, shift the topic sentence elsewhere within the paragraph, and you leave them bewildered, confused, and lost.

How, then, would you track down the statement of the main idea?

Let us take a paragraph and see, step by step, exactly how to proceed. The way in which you approach a paragraph will indicate whether you know how to read with the skill and maturity characteristic of the truly efficient reader.

Develop a technique of paragraph reading, so that as soon as your eyes alight upon the page, you see the paragraph as a unit of writing and you automatically look for the main idea of that paragraph as expressed in its topic sentence. This is the first habit which the good reader should acquire. Where there is no topic sentence as such expressed within the paragraph, you should sense the main thought clearly, and immediately frame a topic statement in your own thinking.

But one does not find a main idea merely by being told to look for it. There must be a *way* of looking. Along the road somewhere there must be some specific guideposts to help you find the path to the main idea. We shall, therefore, begin by spelling out, as specifically as possible, the way in which you may go about locating the statement of the main thought.

The first thing that you will want to do is to locate the *noun* that dominates the paragraph.

Let your eyes sweep down over the following paragraph: [1]

A flat fragment of rock lying on the surface offers a special attraction to many subterranean animals. When sun shines on the stone, warmth is conducted through it far more rapidly than through an equal depth of earth. The rock becomes a radiant heater—one that is waterproof. These are its virtues. Elsewhere air spaces in the soil act as a blanket of insulation, resisting changes in temperature. And as heat gradually gets through porous ground, these same spaces draw off and squander the moisture that is so essential to the animals there.

This is the way most readers see a paragraph. It is merely a block of words upon a printed page. Skillful readers, on the other hand, look at a paragraph in much the same manner that a physician looks at his patient. There is much to observe that the layman never sees.

Take, for instance, that paragraph that you just read. Did you notice the *one* word around which the meaning of the whole paragraph revolved? Did you notice how the idea pertaining to that word was repeated over and over again throughout the paragraph? There is only *one* thing the author is talking about in that paragraph, only *one* noun that the author emphasizes again and again. This noun is the dominant or topic noun of the paragraph. It is the noun at the dead center of the main idea. Every paragraph has such a noun as its focal point—the pivotal axis, upon which thought the paragraph turns. It is an axiom that a correctly constructed paragraph discusses one thought and one thought only. That axiom is a cue for the reader.

When a gem is turned, a rainbow of color darts from its center. A paragraph is similar to a gem. Inspect a paragraph from various angles. The topic noun will flash from every sentence new meanings that will add to a fuller understanding of the thought contained in the topic sentence. These various meanings the reader must see clearly if he is to appreciate the full impact of the central thought which the author is trying to convey. The reading of each sentence of the paragraph, then, is a slight turning of the gem. Every statement throws just a little additional light upon the meaning of the main idea.

[1] Margery and Lorus Milne, A *Multitude of Living Things*, Chap. 8, pp. 93–94, Dodd, Mead & Company, New York, 1947.

Let us look at the paragraph again. Here it is:

A flat FRAGMENT of rock lying on the surface offers a special *attraction* to many subterranean animals. When sun shines on the *stone*, warmth is conducted through *it* far more rapidly than through an equal depth of earth. The *rock* [*fragment*] becomes a radiant *heater*—one that is waterproof. These are *its* virtues. Elsewhere [*than beneath a fragment of rock*] air spaces in the soil act as a blanket of insulation, resisting changes in temperature. [*In contrast, the fragment acts as a radiant heater.*] And as heat gradually gets through porous ground, these same spaces draw off and squander the moisture that is so essential to the animals there [*which moisture, if it were under the fragment of rock would be conserved; and, thus, the fragment would be a special attraction to many subterranean animals*].

Here it may be well to point out the structure of this paragraph. The observant reader will see that by implication, the thought carried to its logical conclusion forms a perfect circle, with the concluding statement being the same as the opening statement of the paragraph.

Notice how the italicized words all emphasize the *one* thing the author is discussing. Observe in sentence after sentence that the author emphasizes in a variety of ways that the one thing that he is discussing is a "fragment"—"a flat fragment of rock." And he is discussing this as an attraction for the denizens of the world underground, the tenants of the soil.

Now, let's go back to the comparison of the paragraph to a gem, which we suggested earlier. Turn the paragraph now, slowly, in your mind. Note the various rays of light which dart from it, illuminating the main thought. Sometimes, as in the case of the inferences in the last two sentences, the rays may be reflected, but if you observe closely the author's angle of thought, you cannot miss seeing the inference he had in mind.

It will help you in reading *any* paragraph to acquire the skill of turning it over in your own mind. By so doing you will get, in so far as it is possible, the accurate, exact meaning of what the author is trying to convey.

Communication is one of our most vital and, at the same time, one of our most perplexing problems. This is because of the failure of words to convey *exactly* what we have in mind. Let's not hamper communication through the printed word unduly by clumsy and inexact reading.

For example, the inexact reader would say that in the paragraph just quoted that we were reading about a rock. No, we were not reading about a rock! The author is discussing "a flat *fragment* of rock." There is a difference between a rock and a *fragment* of a rock, as you will see if you try to visualize them. Here the reader's sensitiveness to word concepts enters the scene—his sensitiveness to connotative as well as denotative meanings. *Rock* connotes massiveness. But that is not what the author has in mind. He is thinking of a *fragment* of a rock, a "flat fragment"—a slab or sheet of rock, which has been broken off—and he calls it variously a *stone*, a *heater*, an *attraction*. He contrasts conditions under it with the blanket of cold, porous soil of the same depth: "warmth is conducted through it [the *fragment*] far more rapidly than through an equal depth of earth."

This book will emphasize constantly the habit of reading for the meaning behind the words. This paragraph presents a splendid example of this point. The last two sentences, taken by themselves, seem to be divorced from the meaning of the rest of the paragraph. They depend upon the reader's skill in interpreting the *meaning* which lies *beneath* the words—the thoughts that the author had in mind, but did not express. Note that in the last two sentences of the paragraph the author does not mention or refer to the rock fragment at all. But, for these words to mean anything at all in terms of what the author has said, you realize at once that the whole *idea* of the "fragment" of rock is present, in spite of the fact that the word itself does not occur more than once. The idea travels on, propelled by its own momentum, so that the thought within the bracketed parts of the paragraph is as obvious as though it were fully expressed.

The whole paragraph, in fact, revolves with beautiful unity around one word, *fragment*. That word is the *dominant* noun of the paragraph.

The topic sentence of any paragraph is a broad, general statement about the dominant, or topic, noun. In the rest of the paragraph the author usually explains exactly what he had in mind when he wrote that topic statement. The reader must be adept, therefore, at evaluating the *relative* importance of the thought in each sentence of the paragraph in order to find the principal, over-all, or topic sentence. With practice you can become very skillful in locating the topic sentence quickly and unerringly. Constantly ask yourself whether any particular statement could sum up everything else that the paragraph contains, or whether it is just a statement of a fact which, with other statements similar to it, point toward a broad, main idea

Up to this point you have been given two steps toward cracking the paragraph—the basic unit in reading. These steps are:

1. Look for the noun or pronoun that dominates the paragraph.
2. After you find the dominant noun, locate the sentence within the paragraph that makes the most generalized statement about this noun. That sentence will be the topic sentence.

Sentences in paragraphs are somewhat like little cubicles that nest inside each other. All of them are contained within the larger outer box. Just so, the sentences of a paragraph may be conceived as all fitting, *from a thought standpoint,* within the all-inclusive topic sentence.

Now we come to a danger point, that is, the position of the dominant noun of the paragraph in the topic sentence.

1. Usually the dominant noun is the *subject* of the topic sentence.
2. In some instances, however, it is in the direct-object position in the topic sentence.

Let us illustrate each of these situations by an example. The paragraph about the "fragment of rock" which we have just been discussing is illustrative of the topic noun as the *subject* of the topic sentence. As an example of the topic noun in the *direct-object* position, take the following:

Man has always had a *tendency* to make himself comfortable. This *inclination* in man's nature is first seen in the earliest records of the race. Man learned to use fire, and in so doing he found a substitute for the warmth of the sun. This same *proclivity* to be comfortable led him to wrap himself in the skins of animals. *It* also inspired him to light a pine knot, a rush, or a dish of oil that its smoky flickering might dispel the murkiness of his cave, making it a more comfortable place in which to live. This *tendency* is still at work. Television and atomic energy are merely modern expressions of the primitive *bent* toward a fuller, easier, and more comfortable way of life.

Probably the most important question of all is this: How do you know that the sentence that you select really is the topic sentence?

There is a very simple way of checking.

1. Read the topic sentence (or the sentence that you think is the topic sentence).
2. Then, immediately ask the question, "What does that mean?"
3. Read each of the remaining sentences of the paragraph, but preface the

reading of each one with the words, "It means that . . ." and then read the sentence.

4. Follow the reading of each sentence with a re-reading of the topic sentence. By so doing you will discover the relationship that every other sentence in the paragraph has to the topic sentence.

Try this technique on the paragraph we have just been discussing. Note how smoothly the meaning runs; how unified the thought of the whole becomes. For example:

Man has always had a tendency to make himself comfortable. (*What does that mean? It means that* . . .) This inclination in man's nature is first seen in the earliest records of the race. (*Because* . . .) Man has always had a tendency to make himself comfortable. (*What does that mean? It means that* . . .) Man learned to use fire, and in so doing he found a substitute for the warmth of the sun. (*Because* . . .) Man has always had a tendency to make himself comfortable. (*What does that mean? It means that* . . .) This same proclivity to be comfortable led him to wrap himself in the skins of animals. (*Because* . . .) Man has always had a tendency to make himself comfortable. (*What does that mean? It means that* . . .) It also inspired him to light a pine knot, a rush, or a dish of oil that its smoky flickering might dispel the murkiness of his cave, making it a more comfortable place in which to live. (*Because* . . .) Man has always had a tendency to make himself comfortable. (*What does that mean? It means that* . . .) This tendency is still at work. (*Because* . . .) Man has always had a tendency to make himself comfortable. (*What does that mean? It means that* . . .) Television and atomic energy are merely modern expressions of the primitive bent toward a fuller, easier, and more comfortable way of life. (*Because* . . .) Man has always had a tendency to make himself comfortable.

From this exercise it is quite obvious that the well-written paragraph is a closely knit structure. The topic sentence is, in fact, the master sentence.

Sometimes, however, a paragraph will seem to be only a loose collection of facts, a truncated pyramid. Such paragraphs seem to have no focal point, no topic noun. Such paragraphs are distinctive. You will soon learn to recognize them on sight. You feel immediately the looseness of their structure. That is because such paragraphs lack the topic sentence.

One of the best ways to get the feel for the paragraph without the topic sentence is to read a number of paragraphs, purposely omitting in each one the topic sentence. You will sense immediately there is not the basic cohesion that is necessary to hold everything together into a closely knit unit.

When you meet such paragraphs in your reading—and you occasionally will—take *all* the sentences into consideration. Try to determine what the common denominator of the thought is that underlies them all. Say to yourself, "What *one* thing are all these sentences talking about?" Read them over carefully; think of the *one* factor that seems to be common to all of them. Find the topic noun. Then, with the topic noun as the subject, cast the topic sentence so that in it you bring all the threads of thought together into a common bond.

Here, for example, is such a paragraph:

In London the underground is a subway; in the United States it is a subversive organization. British drivers fill their tanks with petrol, but here in the States we fill our tanks with gas. To the Britisher, elevators are lifts and radio tubes are valves. And whereas our politicians run for office, theirs stand for it.

Notice that there is no master statement in that paragraph. Each sentence, rather, is an illustration and an example. But an example of what? What *one thing* is being emphasized by each sentence? The answer to that question reveals the topic noun of the paragraph. This is it: each sentence is an example of the *difference* in the British and American way of saying things.

Now, let's take the topic noun, and make a statement about that topic noun, according to the thought—the total thought—expressed in the paragraph:

The *difference* between our everyday speech and that of the Britisher is at once apparent in the terms each uses for common, everyday things.

That is the topic sentence of the paragraph. That is the main idea, the basic thought, of which the sentences given in the paragraph were merely examples.

There is another type of paragraph which on the surface looks a great deal like the paragraph without a topic sentence. It is the transitional paragraph. This is a special type of paragraph, almost purely functional in nature, with slight thought content. The transitional paragraph is usually found as a bridging device between large blocks of thought, between the divisions of an article, or the larger thought areas of more extensive pieces of writing. The purpose of the transitional paragraph is to get the reader safely and smoothly from one topic which has already been discussed over to a new topic which is about to be discussed. The skillful reader soon learns to recognize this type of paragraph when he sees it. Fortunately, this is not too often.

Up to this point we have proceeded upon the assumption that the normal paragraph structure is the type of writing that you will most frequently meet in general reading; that, on the whole, a paragraph contains one main idea; that in most cases the statement of that main idea is usually incorporated in a topic sentence, expressed within the paragraph; that this sentence is usually in either the initial or final position, but that occasionally it occurs medially or may be entirely lacking; and that the paragraph as a whole is the development or enlargement or working out of the main idea so that the reader may appreciate it from various angles. In other words, we have assumed that the paragraph is a thought unit which is self-contained and whose structure is fairly definite. As a general rule, this is so.

But there are some deviates. There are some paragraphs that do not apparently fit into the normal patterns of paragraph structure. They disappoint us when we attempt to analyze them because they do not behave in the way in which we have been led to expect they would. They are abnormal: either dwarfed or double-headed. Sometimes one paragraph is broken up into two or more; again, one paragraph will contain two main thoughts. But, as the master reader sees these abnormalities, he instantly recognizes a partial thought, or a double one, almost as soon as his eyes alight upon them. The reader who has trained himself to look for the *main* thought of the paragraph will have no trouble in recognizing the irregular paragraphs.

Why do these unconventional forms appear? There are several reasons. Some writers are not sensitive to the paragraph as a thought unit. Others follow their whims. They allow the over-all appearance of the page to guide their paragraphing. When they feel that the type is beginning to look too heavy or too solid, they begin a new paragraph whether they have a new thought or not. Still other writers have been influenced by newspaper style: the paragraphs are short, most of the time scarcely more than a single sentence. But these are unusual forms and we shall discuss them later.

The next chapter will continue the discussion of the paragraph as an aid to better reading, discussing the behavior of the thought within the paragraph. But first of all, you must be able to find the main idea. This is basic to all else. Let's see how skilled you are in this technique.

Practice in the technique of reading paragraphs

In each of the paragraphs indicated:

1. Draw a box around the topic noun.
2. Encircle all repetitions of the topic noun, i.e., synonyms or pronouns which substitute for the topic noun.
3. Insert between brackets above the line any additional words that you must supply to show the full meaning that the author had in mind, but did not express, with relation to the topic noun.
4. Underline the topic sentence.
5. Check the topic sentence as suggested on pages 54–55.

Here is a sample paragraph to show you what to do: [2]

Comment

The [Delaware] is a small river. From (its) source to the mouth of the Delaware Bay, south of Cape May, the flowing (waters) travel a distance of only 326 miles. The importance of the (river,) however, is out of proportion to (its) size because (it) flows right through the heart of one of the country's greatest industrial areas. That is precisely why the waters of the (river) are in such great demand.

This is the topic sentence. We are talking about the Delaware River.

All words in brackets complete the thought but were not in the original paragraph.

All words which refer to the topic noun are encircled.

Part One

Analyze, according to the directions given above, each of the following paragraphs in this text:

[2] "The Delaware River Water Controversy," *Business Review* (The Federal Reserve Bank of Philadelphia), June, 1954, p. 4.

Part Two

The second part of this exercise is to test your ability to grasp the central idea of a paragraph clearly, and to express that idea again, unhesitatingly, in your own words. Here are the directions for this part of the practice exercise:

1. Read each of the following paragraphs *only once*. Do not go back to re-read any part of the paragraph. Make yourself grasp the thought as you read. Read from the beginning of the paragraph to the end; then, close the book.
2. Take a sheet of paper, and *in your own words*, write *a complete sentence* (not a fragment)—a single, declarative statement—in ten words or less, expressing completely the main thought of the paragraph.
3. You should be able to read the paragraph *and* to summarize it in your own words within one minute.

Try your skill on the following paragraphs:

These practice paragraphs are merely to get you started. In addition to these, take paragraphs at random from your reading and apply the same techniques to them until you have formed the habit of summarizing the main thought of the paragraph while you are reading it.

Learn to Develop Your Visual Span

The expert reader, like the well-trained athlete or the accomplished musician, has spent much time in practicing in order to develop certain basic skills and techniques. The athlete spends hours punching the bag or throwing the ball so that he may develop certain muscles and coordinate his movements so that these will aid him in the heat of the game. The musician, likewise, spends hours upon the practice of scales and etudes to perfect his keyboard skill and musical technique.

The reader also needs to practice. He needs to practice widening his eye span, improving his perception, and learning to see more at a single glance.

This training is sometimes done with a tachistoscope, an instrument which casts upon a screen in a split second's duration certain phrases of varying widths. In the instant during which he sees the phrase, the student is asked to read it. The whole idea is to wake up the normally little-used peripheral reading areas of the retina, causing them to be more sensitive to the word images that fall upon them.

In this text we shall help you to develop those visual skills and abilities that are associated with tachistoscopic training.

These exercises may seem tedious at first, and you may be tempted to slight them. They are, however, a very important part of your total program of reading skill development. Work at them conscientiously. It will be easy for you to cheat. You have no one to discipline you but yourself. In like manner, you have no one to cheat but yourself.

You will reach limits. Again, that is the purpose of these exercises. But you will also be able to push back those limits, with practice, so that after a few days you will realize that you are doing better than you did at first. It will encourage you if you keep a careful record of the limit of your achievement for each practice period. After several days you will see clearly that the limits *are* being pushed back.

First, you will want to develop an increased eye span. With these exercises an eyeful a few weeks from now should mean more, in terms of reading, than an eyeful does now. This is how you will do it.

On the following pages you will see certain phrases arranged in pyramidal fashion, getting wider and wider as you progress down the page. Here is what you do:

1. Take a 3- by 5-inch card and put a small arrow about midway across the card, with the point of the arrow pointing to the edge of the card as in this illustration:

2. You will find a black guide line running down the middle of page 62 broken only by phrases of varying lengths. Place the card over the phrases, with the point of the arrow pointing to the black guide line.
3. Draw the card down the page, so that the first phrase is visible. Be very careful to look only at the *point* of the arrow. Fix your attention on the point, but try to *see* on either side of this point, right *and* left, as far as possible. At first you may be able to see easily the *whole* phrase. If so, keep your eyes fixed on the arrow point at the center of the line. Move the card down to the next phrase, and the next, and so on, until you are aware that you are having difficulty seeing the ends of the lines. Try, try to see more. Try to push back the margins of your usable vision. This will widen your eye span. Do not let your eyes shift or steal a sidewise glance. Keep them glued to the center-line point. Work at this for five or ten minutes at a time. In each succeeding practice try to take in the whole phrase more rapidly, until you can see each of them with one quick glance.

At the extreme right of each phrase you will find a figure. This is the width of the line. The numbers refer to the width in units of type of the phrase. Keep trying until you can see all of the phrases in one fixation. There are two sets of phrases for you to practice on. Alternate your practice. Work on the first group, then on the second. Your one aim in this exercise is to widen your eye span.

You will find reading less fatiguing if you learn to take in more words at a single glance. Be sure to carry over these achievements in eye-span development to your everyday reading. Try to see just as much of the line of print at a single glance as you possibly can in a single fixation.

Do you have your card ready? Place the point of the arrow so that it points to the center guide line above the first phrase. You will then be ready to pull it down so that the first phrase is visible.

an old habit   12

habits to form   14

eyes on the line   16

look at the center   18

do a little each day   20

drill makes the reader   22

see with a wide eye span   24

steady practice helps much   26

try to do this when you read   28

look steadily at the mid-point   30

are you still seeing both edges?   32

if so, your eye span is excellent   34

learn to read   13

read everything   15

you are improving   17

practice this daily   19

stretch your vision   21

work only a few minutes   23

don't let your eyes shift   25

s-t-r-e-t-c-h your eye span   27

see more, and yet still more!   29

this is to help you read better   31

can you possibly see all of this?   33

How well did you do? Each time you work at this exercise, record in the blanks below the maximum span you were able to read. You will want to compare your achievement later with this, your initial attempt.

Date	*Duration of Practice* *(Minutes)*	*Maximum Span Read*
_____	_____	_____
_____	_____	_____
_____	_____	_____
_____	_____	_____
_____	_____	_____
_____	_____	_____
_____	_____	_____
_____	_____	_____
Average:	_____	_____

Reading for Speed of Comprehension—1

The following selections are fairly easy to read, but they are placed here to test your speed of comprehension. At the end of each chapter you will find similar selections. They may tend to become slightly more difficult as you progress through the book, but in every case their purpose is to test your growth in the speed with which you are able to comprehend the main thoughts and specific facts in each selection.

Read each article as rapidly as you can, but not too rapidly to grasp the meaning. Always let your first concern be that you are getting the thought of the author—that you understand what he is saying, that you see the facts in their relationship to each other. Use every approach and technique that you possess toward this end. You do not need to read these selections the way you have always read. Quite to the contrary, it is hoped that as you learn, chapter by chapter, new ways of attacking the printed page, that you will *not* read just as you have always read. Put the ideas that you gather from the discussions in these chapters to work in the reading of these selections.

Be paragraph-conscious when you read. Look for the main ideas. Try to relate the details to the main idea of the paragraph. As you read, think to yourself: "There's a new paragraph. This must be the beginning of a new thought. Presumably this paragraph is talking about *one* thing. Yes, it deals with (*here insert the topic noun*). Certainly, there is the topic sentence. Now, let's see, how does the author explain that general statement . . . ?"

Then read on, looking for the way in which the author presents the facts to support the main idea. Your mind should be working all the time you are reading. The above thoughts should streak across your mind while you are reading as meteors streak across a sky full of stars.

You will want to time your reading to each of the selections at the end of the chapters. They are to be read for *speed* of *comprehension*.[3] The best time to read is at the same hour each day, at a time when you will have no interruptions. Avoid trying to read for speed of comprehension when you are very tired. Give yourself a chance to do your best. Time your reading of the selections accurately. This is of greatest importance. A stop watch is best for the purpose but, lacking that, use any watch with an easily seen dial and second hand. Jot down the *exact* time *when you begin to read*. There is a space at the beginning of each selection for this data. Read as rapidly as you can, and still get the meaning. When you have finished reading, note the exact time you read the final word of the selection. Jot down this time in the blanks provided at the end of each selection for this purpose. Then, answer the comprehension questions. You do *not* time yourself on answering the questions.

For every selection, follow this same procedure. Do exactly as you are directed.

Are you now ready to read? If so, what time is it? Jot it down here:

MINUTES _____

SECONDS _____

Now, begin to read:

[3] Perhaps, if you have forgotten the meaning of the phrase, "speed of comprehension," you may wish to turn back to pp. 5–6 at this point and review the discussion there given.

THE HERITAGE OF THE PRINTED WORD [4]

by Storer B. Lunt

There is no denying that in these times that are again trying men's souls the book takes on a heightened significance. There have been other critical times in our history when the printed word has brought the realities of the period into sharp focus and contributed powerfully in shaping the destiny of our nation. Consider the writings of Thomas Paine, think of the writings of Jefferson and the founding fathers, of Lincoln, or more recently those of Wilson and Roosevelt. Consider the impact of such a book as *Uncle Tom's Cabin,* or again on the reverse side of the shield a book like *Mein Kampf,* that powerful creed of wickedness which finally served the enemies of the very evil it proclaimed. Statesmen and politicians disappear. Wars come and go. And when the breath is stilled and the smoke of battle has disappeared over the horizon, there remains the constant and unbroken flow of the printed word and the books that record the history, the philosophy, and the moral values of the world. There is no question—books are the silent and imperishable springs of the eternal truths and of the best in man and his recorded thinking.

I hold that we are blessed and fortunate in our heritage of the printed word through the literature of England. With the exception of the literature of ancient Greece, there is no body of writing comparable to the heritage of English literature shaped over a thousand years; and it is from this that our contemporary writings stem. And with her literature England has also given us humor. What other nations besides England and ourselves have been able to laugh their way through their wars? Where else can we turn for a Shakespeare or a Gilbert and Sullivan or a George Bernard Shaw? Or in our times, for a James Thurber, an E. B. White, or an Ogden Nash? Consider the impact of English literature on the world. Ponder the glory and wonder of the English Bible with a translation that has never been equaled in any other language.

England's history and the history of her literature have been of infinite variety. In recent years her empire may have been whittled down, but

[4] An address given on July 8, 1951, by Storer B. Lunt, President, W. W. Norton & Company, Inc., at the meeting of the American Library Association held in Chicago. Reprinted by permission of the author

the flowering of English literature is still the intellectual and moral empire of the world. Both literature and humor England has given to us, and along with our religion it is the best heritage we have. And we must not let it down.

Let us admit that in recent years the use of books has been intruded upon by other organized holds on the minds of men. I think it perhaps a mistake to define the radio and television precisely as instruments of communication. These instruments of modern commotion are actually more instruments of impact. They require more a passive participation— often none whatsoever. They represent the easier way. They are a substitute—for the lazy mind. There is no time for reflection. One cannot stop to think. One cannot re-read and ponder a paragraph. One grows to take it as it comes. In large part it is split-second entertainment, addressed primarily to the trigger-happy mind. Right now television is the latest American toy, but it will in time outlive its novelty and assume its place among the other gadgets in the American household.

I am all for the solitary reader. It is he who is the vital citizen. It is he who in the long run is the opinion maker. As publishers we fail if we do not encourage the kind of product which reflects a deep personal experience in contemporary life. In this confused and terribly complicated world there is a crying need for companionship and understanding. A voluntary meeting of minds is essential and the most rewarding of all human experiences. I like to think of that Yankee farmer to whom Emerson had loaned his copy of Plato's *Republic*. In returning the book to Mr. Emerson he said, "You know, that man has a great number of my ideas." I need hardly remind you that Mr. Emerson's farmer dwells in every community in the land.

Books supply the nourishment of calm democratic minds. Let books be available and accessible over the land. Let us guard them jealously and fight for their complete freedom and full circulation. If you are subject to the prejudices and pressures of any censorship, tell the world about them. Truth and taste are the only criteria for judging a book and in a democracy truth shall prevail and the press shall be free. We have heard a great deal of nonsense of late on the score of censorship with a recitation of certain case histories and a complete ignoring of countless other case histories which are the common experience of every book publisher. I don't recall Henry Thoreau blaming the Mexicans in the 1840's because most of the first edition of *Walden* gathered dust in his attic. The public at that time simply did not want his book. Today I believe there are nine different editions of *Walden* on the market and *Walden* has moulded men and moved nations.

In conclusion let me say that while we honor and celebrate the heritage of the past, we must at all times bear in mind that the present is here and now and that in a democracy we are ever and always at the point of no return. With a sense of the past we live in the present and we are all pioneers of the future. Remember Pasteur's observation that discoveries occur only to the minds of men that are prepared. Our job is to brighten the tools of the past and to provide new tools for the machinery of the thoughtful and informed citizens of the land. Democracy functions only through an informed and enlightened citizenry. And to that end let me assure you that the typewriter is mightier than the television set.

What time is it now? MINUTES _____

SECONDS _____

What is your reading time for this selection? MINUTES _____

SECONDS _____

Now, test your comprehension of what you have read by answering the following questions.

Comprehension quiz

Part One

Select the statement which best completes the sentence in terms of what you have read. Do not refer back to the article while you are taking the quiz.

1. In "times that try men's souls"
    a we need more writers like Thomas Paine.
    b the printed word flourishes more than at other times.
    c we need more books than at other times.
    d the printed word has helped us to focus our minds on reality and to conspire with destiny.

2. The radio and television are considered as instruments of
    a communication.
    b impact.
    c confusion.
    d information.

3. With reference to radio and television the author's attitude is one of
   a apprehension.
   b regretful but detached concern.
   c indifference and unconcern.
   d patient and philosophic understanding.

4. The story of Emerson lending his book to a farmer is told to illustrate
   a the desirability of farmers reading Plato.
   b that Mr. Emerson was a friendly sort of person.
   c the need for a meeting of minds.
   d the prevalence of Platonic thought in New England in Emerson's day.

5. The author implies that *Walden*
   a was censored unjustly.
   b gathered dust in Thoreau's attic because the Mexicans did not like it.
   c was written before the public was ready for it.
   d was unpopular because it was sympathetic to the Mexican cause while we were at war with Mexico.

Part Two

One of the marks of an efficient reader is his ability to recall the author's thoughts in the order in which the author presented them. Below are five statements; they are paraphrases of the author's thoughts. Their order is disarranged. In the blanks to the left of the item numbers, place 1 before the statement which should be first, 2 before the statement which should come next, and so forth. Assign each statement a number according to the place it occupies in the sequence of the author's thoughts.

_____ 1. I applaud the solitary reader.

_____ 2. We are fortunate in having the heritage of English letters.

_____ 3. Let us venerate the past but remember that we must produce books consonant with the challenge of the future.

_____ 4. The times give a book added significance.

_____ 5. In the modern world other influences have encroached upon the domain of the book.

How well did you comprehend what you have read? Check your answers with those given in the Answer Key. Each correct answer is worth 10 per cent.

What is your level of comprehension? ———%

What is your speed of comprehension? ———wpm

(To find your speed of comprehension refer to the table in the Appendix)

What is your reading index (R × C/100)? ———

The reading index is a convenient figure used to express the composite factors of rate *and* comprehension. It is obtained by multiplying the rate (R) by the comprehension (C), and dividing the product by 100 (pointing off two decimal places):

$$\frac{\text{Rate} \times \text{comprehension}}{100} = \frac{R \times C}{100} = \text{reading index (RI)}$$

Plot your progress after you complete each chapter. A graph form for this purpose is in the Appendix.

Reading for Speed of Comprehension—2

Here is another article to read to test your speed of comprehension. Try to push your speed of reading just a little faster; aim to comprehend and to remember the facts just a little more accurately. Progress comes by inching along steadily.

Apply now some of the suggestions the author of the preceding article gave you for more efficient reading. Put them to work immediately in the reading of the article that follows.

All of us talk about work. Most of us work for a living. "Work, work, work!" You have heard those words said many times. Perhaps you have said them yourself, with that disgusted, monotonous tone that reveals all too clearly your own thoughts and viewpoint.

What is work? Have you ever honestly answered that question satisfactorily? The author of the following article gives some stimulating and thought-provoking ideas on work and working.

Time the reading of this article as you did the preceding one. Are you ready to read? If so, what time is it now? MINUTES ———

SECONDS ———

Now, begin to read.

WHAT IS WORK? [5]

by William J. Reilly

Most Americans have the ridiculous notion that anything they do which produces an income is work—and that anything they do outside "working" hours is play. There is no logic to that.

I have a friend who is a locomotive engineer. I know he loves the feeling of masterfulness and responsibility that comes over him when he gets behind the throttle and blows that whistle.

But when he comes into his house on a typical night his wife is apt to say, "George, the Carlburgs want us to come over and play bridge tonight."

Suddenly George feels all fagged out. He mutters irritably, "Have we got to go? I've had a hard day. You know I don't like bridge and play it miserably. Besides, Willard is such an old windbag."

Now, to George, playing bridge at the Carlburgs' is the purest kind of work, infinitely more exhausting and harassing than his activities at the throttle. And he is right.

As we define work in career counseling, it is doing something you don't enjoy doing. You may not enjoy it simply because it bores you, or because you don't have the knack of doing it, or because you have to be with people you don't like. Whatever the reason, you just don't like it. So it is work, even if it's playing bridge at the Carlburgs'.

How many Americans are there who don't enjoy their jobs? All of my studies indicate that a decided majority are dissatisfied and wish they were doing something else. Imagine how much frustration all this vocational maladjustment is causing! No wonder so many people are irritable nowadays.

What about yourself? Is your job work or fun? If it is work, then you would probably be wise to take immediate steps to get out of it. Your life is too short and too valuable to fritter away in work.

If you don't get out now, you may end up like the frog that is placed in a pot of fresh water on the stove. As the temperature is gradually increased, the frog feels restless and uncomfortable, but not uncomfortable enough to jump out. Without being aware that a change is taking place, he is gradually lulled into unconsciousness—boiled.

[5] William J. Reilly, *How to Avoid Work*, Chap. 1, pp. 1–6, Harper & Brothers, New York, 1949.

Much the same thing happens when you take a person and put him in a job which he does not like. He gets irritable in his groove. His duties soon become a monotonous routine that slowly dulls his senses. As I walk into offices, through factories and stores, I often find myself looking into the expressionless faces of people going through mechanical motions. They are people whose minds are stunned and slowly dying.

I see accountants who wish they were teachers or explorers, and salesmen who wish they were cabinetmakers. I recently talked with the son of a wealthy lawyer who was grimly studying law. He said, "Oh, I'll plow through these courses somehow." Deep in his heart, he wants to be a geologist, but of course, he said, he couldn't disappoint Dad.

When a person is in a job he dislikes, he reacts by being moody and nervous. He becomes tired easily and is a victim of indigestion and insomnia. As he continues to feel frustrated, he becomes rebellious, figuratively kicks at people, grows sour on the world. Yes, forcing yourself to work at a job you dislike is like wearing a lead vest to run a race— it's just plain exhausting.

Most people think that once you get started in a certain field, you can't very well change. This is sheer nonsense. No matter who you are, what you've been doing, or how old you are, you can change to a job environment more agreeable to your nature. There is no such thing as a one-and-only career for anyone. Frequently there are several possible careers open to you that will be equally satisfying. It is only when you get caught in a job that is wholly alien to your nature that you develop ulcers and a nervous breakdown.

Life really begins when you have discovered that you can do anything you want. Amelia Earhart expressed it well when she wrote: [6]

"I flew the Atlantic because I wanted to. If that be what they call 'a woman's reason,' make the most of it. It isn't, I think, a reason to be apologized for by man or woman. . . .

"Whether you are flying the Atlantic or selling sausages or building a skyscraper or driving a truck, your greatest power comes from the fact that you want tremendously to do that very thing, and do it well."

Actually, there is only one way in this world to achieve true happiness, and that is to express yourself with all your skill and enthusiasm in a career that appeals to you more than any other. In such a career, you

[6] Amelia Earhart, "Flying the Atlantic," *The American Magazine*, August, 1932. p. 15.

feel a sense of purpose, a sense of achievement. You feel that you are making a contribution. It is not work.

A doctor who has felt the pulse of life and the still of death does not feel he is working when he must leave a party to deliver a baby.

A farmer who owns his own land is not working when he labors fifteen hours a day to get in a crop.

A carpenter is not working when he builds a cottage he is proud of.

A natural-born politician is not working when he spends sixteen hours a day stumping a county for votes.

A mother is not working when she cleans the house so that she can give her daughter a surprise party. As one mother said, as she stood over a steaming tub washing her baby's diapers, "Whatever we do for those we love is never work. I'm proud of my little family. Not a one of them has ever been any trouble to me. It's been fun."

All of us are much more creative than we suspect. A mechanic is creative when he figures a way to construct a more efficient monkey wrench. A department head is unconsciously acknowledging his creativeness when he points with pride to one of his best salesmen and says, "Why, when I got hold of Eddie he was nothing but a bum!" A mother who goes in for interior decoration and a housewife who paints in oils in her spare time, are creative when they add touches of individuality and of beauty to their homes.

To my mind, the world would be a much pleasanter and more civilized place to live in, if everyone resolved to pursue whatever is closest to his heart's desire. We would be more creative and our productivity would be vastly increased.

Altogether too much emphasis, I think, has been placed on what we *ought* to do, rather than what we *want* to do.

To some people, doing what you want to do seems almost sinful. But, believe me, it is not sinful. It is not selfish. It is not something a person should feel guilty about. If your life is important, why waste it in disagreeable work that has no meaning to you?

The greatest satisfaction you can obtain from life is your pleasure in producing, in your own way, something of value for your fellowmen. That is creative living!

When we consider that each of us has only one life to live, isn't it rather tragic to find men and women, with brains capable of comprehending the stars and the planets, talking about the weather; men and women, with hands capable of creating works of art, using those hands only for routine tasks; men and women, capable of independent thought, using their minds as a bowling-alley for popular ideas; men and women, capable of greatness, wallowing in mediocrity; men and women, capable of self-expression, slowly dying a mental death while they babble the confused monotone of the mob?

For you, life can be a succession of glorious adventures. Or it can be a monotonous bore.

Take your choice!

What time is it now? MINUTES _____

SECONDS _____

What is your reading time for this selection? MINUTES _____

SECONDS _____

Now, answer the following questions. Do not refer back to the article.

Comprehension quiz

Each of the following statements has four choices. Choose the word or phrase which completes the statement most accurately, *according to the thought of the author as expressed in the article.* A word of caution should be given at this point: You will have to be careful *always* to distinguish between what the author has said—*what you have read*—and what you may already know, or think, from your own standpoint about the same matter. This is a test of your *ability to read.*

1. The author implies that work is
   a any activity which produces income.
   b one's occupational pursuit.
   c a state of mind.
   d putting in overtime on the job.

2. Vocational maladjustment is the cause of much
   a irritability.
   b failure.
   c family argument.
   d apologizing for one's failures.

3. The author implies that if a situation is uncongenial to you, and you don't do something to correct it,
   a it will soon cause your death.
   b you'll wake up some day to find that you're in hot water.
   c you'll soon find that it won't worry you any longer.
   d soon you will be incapable of doing anything about it

4. The author advocates
    a avoiding lowly tasks whenever possible.
    b doing those things which are expected of us.
    c doing one's duty without complaint.
    d following the course of one's heart's desire.

5. The best workers are those who
    a have the best training.
    b enthusiastically express themselves in their work.
    c are the pluggers—the steady, reliable ones on whom you can always depend.
    d feel a high sense of responsibility and do not want to disappoint others who believe in them.

6. We are all living below our potential
    a happiness.
    b creativity.
    c individuality.
    d enthusiasm.

7. Amelia Earhart is quoted to illustrate the fact that
    a life's greatest satisfactions come from being able to do what you most desire.
    b flying the Atlantic was a great feat for a woman.
    c once you get started in a certain direction, you cannot very well change your course.
    d every woman has a reason for her actions.

8. Which of the following quotations sums up the author's position?
    a "It takes all kinds of people to make a world."
    b "All work and no play makes Jack a dull boy."
    c "The fault, dear Brutus, is not in our stars,
       But in ourselves, that we are underlings."
    d "Half a loaf is better than none."

How well did you comprehend what you have just read? Check your answers against those given in the Answer Key. Each correct answer is worth 12½ per cent.

What is your level of comprehension?   _____%

What is your speed of comprehension?   _____wpm

What is your reading index (R × C/100)? _____

Reading Habit Index

At the close of every chapter you will want to take an inventory of your resources. You will want to check against your past performance. See how well you did on an exercise in this chapter as compared with your achievement on a comparable exercise in another chapter. You will be striving for improvement, and you have a right to expect it. But there is one underlying area of your development which you are likely to underestimate—your habits of reading. Presumably, you will be building a new set of reading habits to take the place of those which have not served you well. You will be told to do certain things, but even though ministers tell their congregations to practice certain virtues, there is still vice among us. Sometimes we need to have the index finger of accusation—or of commendation—pointed directly at us. That is what the reading habit index will do in each chapter. You will honestly evaluate your reading practices. *Index* means "to point out." That is what the reading habit index will attempt to do, to point out the good habits which you should be forming, to point out the bad reading habits which you need to forsake.

Evaluate your own reading habits by checking the statements below which apply to your reading practices. Be honest and realistic. Do not mark the column that you feel you *should* mark if you are going to be a good reader. Mark the one which represents what you actually do when you read.

Give yourself 4 points for each "Always," 3 points for each "Usually," 2 points for each "Sometimes," 1 point for each "Rarely," and no credit for "Never." The maximum score is 20 points.

	Never	Rarely	Sometimes	Usually	Always
1. When I pick up a page of print I notice paragraphs, and I am aware of them as units of writing as I read along.					
2. I expect every paragraph to have a topic noun, and I *look to find it.*					
3. I consciously try to see more of the line of print as I read.					

	Never	Rarely	Sometimes	Usually	Always
4. I can recognize quickly the fact that a paragraph has a topic sentence.					
5. I look for the meaning behind the words, and I read to get the thought as a thought, which I could express readily in my own words, if need be.					

Reading habit index score: _____

Date: _____.

Chapter Five

How flows
the thought?

Vᴵᴇᴡ ᴀ paragraph as you view a rapids below a falls. As the currents of water behave there, so do the currents of thought behave within the paragraph. From the over-all view the thought-stream flows always in one general direction—that is, the direction set by the topic sentence. But as you read through the paragraph, you will see countercurrents, ideas that run opposite to the main thought of the paragraph. These countercurrents serve only to emphasize the direction of the main stream. There will also be whirlpools and eddies: the turning of the author's thought, playing upon an example or an illustration, so that the reader may see more clearly the fuller meaning of the principal thought which the author is attempting to convey.

As a reader, you should be alert to what is happening. You should recognize the eddies and the currents, the countercurrents and the on-rush of the mainstream of thought as it flows through the paragraph. Look for the movement of thought within a paragraph as you might look for the movement in the flow and swirl of waters in a stream.

Each sentence a part of the stream of thought

In a paragraph each sentence is important. There is usually one sentence, however, which is the *most* important. This sentence, its significance, and how to find it we have discussed in the previous chapter.

One by one, other sentences, like tributaries, add to the onward flood of the author's thought or run counter to it. By every contrivance within his command, an author tries to make the reader see what he means by his main statement. He uses every device to tumble it over, turn it around, and show you all sides of it. He permits some sentences to drift parallel to the main idea; then he reverses the stream of thought and by a contrast movement emphasizes the more the direction in which the thought of the main idea flows.

Here is a paragraph. As you read it, see if you can discern the way in which the author has channeled the main thought of the paragraph and directed it through the sentences that cause it to twist and turn, cause it to be now accelerated, now retarded, and again brought almost to a standstill, so that the reader may see that topic idea in its various manifestations, all the while discerning more and more clearly the fullness of the basic thought.

We have a number of vocabularies, instead of only one vocabulary. This is our "word-hoard," as the Anglo-Saxons put it. The smallest part of our word-hoard is our speaking vocabulary. We use fewer words in expressing our spoken thoughts than anywhere else. Next in size comes that group of words which we call upon when we want to express our thoughts in writing. For many people their writing vocabulary does not much exceed their speaking vocabulary, because most people write, on the whole, very little. Third, we have a reservoir of words, whose meanings we know when we read them. True, we may not know the meanings of all these words in our reading vocabulary; but when we meet them on the page before us, they give us, for the most part, little trouble. Finally, there is our recognition vocabulary. It is the least practical of all our word-hoard in actively expressing our thoughts. But that is no reason for ignoring this important category. In fact, these words may be vital, future vocabulary in the making. Once upon a time we have seen these words somewhere—they have a familiar look—but their meanings are indistinct. They are mere shadowy ghosts that glide in and out of our thinking and elude our grasp when we attempt to use or define them. In spite of their inaccessibility for general use, however, this group of words is a very real asset. It constitutes the most promising of our several vocabularies.

Now, as you read that, were you aware of the direction, and the change of direction of thought in that paragraph? Did you note certain words as being particularly important because upon these words the *direction* of the thought turned? Did every sentence contrast, advance, or clarify in some way the thought expressed in the topic sentence?

You should be able to answer all of these questions in the affirmative.

Now, let us look at that paragraph again—torn down and laid out piece by piece. Below are two columns: in the left-hand column you will have the text of the paragraph; in the right-hand column is a running commentary. This right-hand column might be considered as a kind of slow-motion technique showing how a skillful reader's mind might react as he reads that paragraph. Fleeting thoughts and ideas dart in and out of his mind. The mind of the skillful reader almost seems to be doing two things at once: he is reading the text, while at the same time evanescent shimmerings of thoughts, ideas, observations, and reactions to the text itself or to the thought of the author are dancing through the reader's mind. The right-hand column will attempt a kind of "stream-of-consciousness" technique for the purpose of showing how the better-than-average reader reacts to this paragraph. These comments will indicate two principal facts about better reading:

1. That the skillful reader notes every surface movement of the thought. He keeps track of the thought, and what it is doing every instant.
2. That reading *is* really thinking. The mind of the expert reader is active while he is reading—noting, observing, exploring, reflecting, drawing conclusions, dancing over the words and the thought of the author with the lightness of a will-o'-the-wisp.

Let the arrows indicate the flow of thought. The thought of the topic sentence (the main thought of the paragraph) will flow from left to right. Where the thought is stationary, as when an example is used, or a reason given, dots (. . . .) will be used. The underlined words are those which are the key words in effecting the change of thought flow.

	Comment
We have a number of vocabularies,	*This is the topic idea.*
$\longrightarrow$	
<u>instead</u> of only one vocabulary.	*A contrasting idea: "number of vocabularies" versus "only one vocabulary."*
$\longleftarrow$	
This is our "word-hoard,"	*An equivalent statement to the topic statement, parallel and explanatory.*
$\longrightarrow$	
(as the Anglo-Saxons put it.)	*A parenthetical clause which really does not advance the main thought at all.*

The smallest part of our

⟶

From here on the paragraph breaks down "fractionally": each one of the "number of vocabularies" which we have is in turn explained.

word-hoard is our speaking

⟶

"The smallest": Will we have an ever larger and larger pattern?

vocabulary. We use fewer

⟶

Restatement of idea in the last sentence for purpose of intensification and emphasis.

words in expressing

⟶

our spoken thoughts

⟶

"Our spoken thoughts": This harks back to "our speaking vocabulary." That is what we are talking about.

than anywhere else.

⟶

"Than anywhere else": So there is somewhere else that we use more words than here! Where is it? Will the author explain? Keep your eyes open.

Next in size comes

⟶

"Next": So this is No. 2 of the number of vocabularies coming up. "Next in size": Maybe this is where we will use more words—this is the "somewhere else"! And the fractional breakdown continues. The author really is explaining his topic idea, step by step.

that group of words

⟶

which we call upon

⟶

when we want to express

⟶

our thoughts in writing.

⟶

"In writing": So this is the next vocabulary—the WRITING vocabulary. That makes sense; the first one was the SPEAKING vocabulary.

For many people their

⟶

This sentence has the effect of slowing down the flow of thought.

writing vocabulary does

⟶

not much exceed their

⟶

speaking vocabulary,

⟶

because most people write,

. . . .

on the whole, very little.

. . . .

Here the thought eddies. There is no onward progress, but we merely stop while the author takes time to explain the reason for the first part of the sentence.

Comment

Third, we have a reservoir

$\longrightarrow$

of words, whose meanings

$\longrightarrow$

Now the thought is again flowing in the direction of the topic idea: "a reservoir of words." Note the word "third." The author is further explaining what he means by "number of vocabularies"—the topic idea. We have had two explained to this point. Now this one is No. 3. "Reservoir" would suggest to the reader that this might be a sizable vocabulary.

we know when we read them.

$\longrightarrow$

Here is the beginning of an interesting current and countercurrent of thought. The author says we have a reservoir of words whose meanings WE KNOW.

True, we may not know the

$\longleftarrow$

meanings of all these words

$\longleftarrow$

in our reading vocabulary;

$\longleftarrow$

Now, note the change: "we may not know the meanings of ALL *these words." The author contrasts the whole with the partial: he contrasts, on the basis of knowing the meanings of the words, the speaking and writing vocabularies with the reading vocabulary.*

but when we meet them on

$\longrightarrow$

the page before us, they

$\longrightarrow$

give us, (for the most part,)

$\longrightarrow$ . . . .

little trouble. Finally,

$\longrightarrow$

This eddying and swirling of thought is again righted by the BUT, *and the thought flows smoothly until it is interrupted briefly by "for the most part," a purely parenthetical eddy, which might be lifted out of the context without the slightest loss.*

"Finally": This is the cue word for the continuation of the thought flow: the author is about to present the last of the "number of vocabularies."

there is our recognition

$\longrightarrow$

vocabulary. It is the least

$\longrightarrow$

practical of all our word

$\longrightarrow$

hoard in actively express-

$\longrightarrow$

"Least practical": This smallest degree helps to show the continuity of the main idea. "Actively expressing" harks back to the earlier vocabularies which he was discussing.

ing our thoughts. But that

$\longrightarrow$

is no reason for ignoring

$\longrightarrow$

this important category.

$\longrightarrow$

BUT: Here is a contrast word again. THAT *means [the fact that] "it is the least practical of all our word hoard." "*BUT that,*" he says, "is* NO *reason for ignoring this category." There is a kind of double reversal there. The effect is equivalent to a positive assertion: "We should take this category into account."*

	Comment
In fact, these words may be ⟶	*"In fact": This phrase helps to intensify the sentence above.*
vital, future vocabulary ⟶	
in the making. Once upon ⟶	*In these lines the onward advance of the main idea slows down. The author is taking time here to explain what he means by the phrase "recognition vocabulary": words that we have seen somewhere, words with a "familiar look."*
a time we have seen these ⟶	
words somewhere—they ⟶	
have a familiar look— ⟶	
but their meanings are ⟵	*"But": A contrast is coming up! These words* LOOK *familiar, but they are* NOT *familiar: "their meanings are indistinct."*
indistinct. They are ⟵	*This sentence merely repeats what the author has said in the last sentence.*
mere shadowy ghosts that ⟵	
glide in and out of our ⟵	
thinking and elude our ⟵	
grasp when we attempt to ⟵	
use or define them. ⟵	
In spite of their inaccess- ⟵	*"In spite of": The sensitive reader notes this phrase immediately. It indicates a change in the direction of the thought is imminent.*
ibility for general use, ⟵	
however, this group of ⟶	*What was suggested as a change by the phrase "in spite of" is brought about by the word "however." Elusiveness is contrasted with substantiality: this group of words, far from being mere "shadowy ghosts" are "a very real asset" constituting "the most promising of our several vocabularies."*
words is a very real ⟶	
asset. It constitutes the ⟶	*The author's main idea was: "We have a number of vocabularies, instead of only one vocabulary."*
most promising of our ⟶	
several vocabularies.	

While you are reading a paragraph, your mind should play over it like a dragonfly above a stream. It should be delicately poised; shimmeringly responsive to the directional flow of the thought and ideas and keenly aware of the most critical shade of meaning and degree of contrast. At any moment you should know exactly how the thought is behaving. Think to yourself, while you are reading, "What is the author doing now?" "How is he maneuvering his words to show the thought more clearly?"

Take a photograph, for example. Every photograph has many degrees of contrast, from pure white to jet black. These shades and tones of gray, these contrasts and differences, are what make the photograph meaningful—even seeable.

So it is with a paragraph. As you see the thought flow and eddy, and flow back upon itself, and swirl again, you see also with greater clarity what the author is trying to convey.

Words that emphasize the countercurrents of the thought

In every paragraph you will notice that the movement of the thought pivots upon certain words or phrases. It is these words and phrases that give an indication to the reader that the thought direction is going to change. They are like heralds that proclaim the happening of an event. The event in this case is the reversal of the direction of the flow of thought. Here are the most important of these thought-reversing words:

BUT: Probably the chief of the thought-reversers. The word "but" should stand out as a flashing beacon to warn the reader that here is a barrier damming the stream and forbidding onward progress. The thought must swirl around to become a countercurrent to the direction in which it has been going.

Examples: It has been a beautiful day, *but* now it looks like rain.

$\longrightarrow$ $\longleftarrow$

I thought he was my friend, *but* I discovered that he was my

$\longrightarrow$ $\longleftarrow$

enemy.

Other words belonging to this category and having a similar effect upon the thought are:

ALTHOUGH: *Although* he denies it, I am sure he is guilty.

$\longleftarrow$ $\longrightarrow$

"Although" is frequently paired with "yet," as:

    Although he asserts his innocence, *yet* I believe he is guilty.

$\longleftarrow$ $\longrightarrow$

AS A MATTER OF FACT: The meaning implied in the use of this phrase is that something which has been stated is *not* "a matter of fact" and that the information which follows this phrase will turn the situation right.

Example: The situation was, *as a matter of fact*, different from the way in which the newspapers reported it.

EITHER . . . OR: These words imply plainly an alternative situation.

Example: Will you *either* recommend him for a promotion *or* request his resignation?

EVEN IF, EVEN THOUGH: Defiance of the fact is suggested by these phrases.

Example: I expect him to try to reach his destination *even though* there is every obstacle in his way to prevent him from reaching it.

HOWEVER: This word reverses the flow of meaning and is many times almost synonymous with "but":

Example: He said that he would not oppose the plan; *however,* I am sure he will not approve it.

IN SPITE OF: This phrase is an aphetic rendering of the original expression, "in despite of." The word "despite" is frequently used to substitute for "in spite of." The connotation behind the phrase is that of flying in the face of circumstance, opposition, counterattack. Originally, in Latin, from which the word derives, it meant "looking down upon."

Examples: He would not be convinced, *in spite of* all that we could do to persuade him.
    Despite the fact that Mars is the earth's neighbor, it is not a striking object in the sky.

INSTEAD OF: This phrase suggests a substitution, a change in the place of one thing for something else.

Example: Let us debate the main issue *instead of* wasting our time on irrelevant matters.

NEVERTHELESS: This word is a difficult one to deal with from the viewpoint of a straight definition of what the word means; nevertheless, it is possible to suggest several synonyms which will indicate the general meaning of this word. "Nevertheless" is more or less equivalent to "notwithstanding," "however," and "but."

Example: This is the most effective and economic military method of defending the United States from attack; *nevertheless* the Air Force must also be prepared to conduct a successful air offense.

NOT: This little word changes the meaning decisively from the affirmative to the negative. Every skillful reader should watch out for it.

Example: The Middle Ages contended that the earth was flat; the earth is *not* flat.

NOTWITHSTANDING: This is another of a group of words, like "nevertheless," which is a compound of several smaller words. Synonyms for this word might include "in spite of," "despite," "nevertheless," and "although."

Example: This is the heart of the matter, *notwithstanding* all other facts that may be presented.

ON THE OTHER HAND: A phrase which definitely indicates an alternative position—a change from that which is being considered.

Example: I have known personal disappointments and despair, and who has not; *on the other hand*, I look forward to the morrow with courage and high hopes.

RATHER: This word is not an out-and-out indication of direction change; it has various meanings, but among them are meanings which suggest a preferred or accepted alternative, or a situation which is desired to the contrary of that which is also proposed. "Rather" is frequently coupled with "than."

Example: A good name is *rather* to be chosen than great riches.

REGARDLESS: This word means "without heed for," "unmindful of," and suggests frequently in context the deliberate choosing an alternative in the face of contrary facts.

Example: I will not change my mind, *regardless* of the facts.

THE SITUATION BEING IN TRUTH THAT: The phrase connotes that the situation as being represented is at variance with the facts.

Example: Many people seem to suffer from the persecutions of life, *the situation being in truth that* they are neurotic and get a great pleasure out of self-torture.

TO THE CONTRARY, CONTRARY TO: Obviously, these words would reverse the thought flow of the sentence.

Example: Phobos, one of the satellites of Mars, is a small moon, only ten miles in diameter, and, *contrary to* the east-west route of the other bodies in the solar system, rises in the west and sets in the east.

WHEREAS: The word means "while on the contrary."

Example: The one came freely, *whereas* the others held back.

YET: A word like "rather," which has several meanings, some of which indicate a reversal in the stream of thought.

Example: His term of office was on the whole above reproach, *yet* he had his political foes and there were those who questioned his ability.

Onward—faster and faster

Another group of words, instead of showing a reversal of the flow of thought, rather add to the forward movement of the thought-flow. With these words the stream of thought tumbles the rapids and hurries on. Some of these words are:

AND: This is probably the chief of the words that help the thought onward.

Example: He went farther *and* farther, *and* his men went with him.

BESIDES: This word means "in addition to what has already been stated." *Besides* frequently indicates an afterthought.

Example: I did not like the house; *besides* it was too high-priced.

AGAIN: A word that suggests a repetition: "another time," "once more," "in addition," "moreover," "further."

Example: The waves struck the ship, *again* it shuddered from stem to stern; *again* the waves struck, *again* the shudder came.

ALSO: Synonymous with "likewise," "moreover," "besides."

Example: He reported the facts as he found them; he *also* said that if he had been there earlier, he would have seen more

AS WELL AS: Suggests that something else is to follow that is equal with, or no less than, that which has gone before.

Example: He was known for his kind acts *as well as* for his great learning.

FURTHERMORE: The word is a compound of two other words, "more" and "further" and means exactly that: "besides," "in addition."

Example: The facts have led me to this detailed explanation. It is necessary, *furthermore*, that we point up the real achievements of this man by citing further facts in his behalf.

IN ADDITION TO: This is certainly a phrase that advances the thought stream. What is to be said is *in addition to* what already has been said.

Example: Scientists have investigated the nature of hydrocarbons; *in addition to* adding to the literature of chemical research, they have also performed an invaluable service to industry.

MOREOVER: A word, additive in meaning, which signifies that something follows beyond that which has been said.

Example: Good reading depends upon a number of factors; *moreover*, it depends upon the desire within the individual to improve.

SINCE, SINCE THEN: This word, or these words, prepare you for a logical issuance of the thought into a concluding statement.

Example: You have every opportunity to advance yourself at your fingertips; *since* you have not availed yourself of these opportunities, it would seem that you are uninterested in getting ahead.

Other words that might keep the thought flowing in the same direction are the ordinal numbers: "first," "second," "third," etc., and the words "finally" and "in conclusion."

Pools where the thought dwells

Up to this point in our discussion of the words which indicate the direction of the flow of thought, we have been considering either those that reverse or those that advance that movement. But there are some words that lie like pools, deep and motionless, upon the surface of the prose. These words direct you to dwell upon a particular point while the author gives you more light upon the matter, while he clears up some phase of the thought that may be obscure, while he tries to make everything clearer and more understandable. Some of the words and phrases which indicate the pools where the thought dwells are:

BECAUSE: This word dates from the Middle English period of our linguistic development, deriving from *by* and *cause*. It is a signal for an explanation to follow.

Example: I once saw peas, planted in a flowerpot, lift and thrust aside a heavy sheet of plate glass laid over the top. *Because* growth in plants is a gradual thing, we often overlook the power that is contained in the rising shoot and the expanding seed.

FOR EXAMPLE, FOR INSTANCE: These two phrases are practically synonymous in meaning. Following them you should prepare to meet an illustration, a specific instance, of the matter being discussed.

Example: Not all words possess connotative powers; *for example*, articles, conjunctions, prepositions, and many of the common adverbs lack connotative qualities.

IF: This word suggests a condition. The reader will note that when he encounters the word "if," the thought flow stops while the author proposes a conditional situation under which the main thought will operate.

Example: *If* he has the knack of talking their own language—without their ever feeling that he is talking down to them—he can be a great success.

LIKE, AS: These words suggest that a comparison will be drawn. A general statement will probably be illustrated by a specific instance.

Example: Do not trust your memory; carry a pocket notebook with you, *as* Beethoven did, *as* Coleridge did, *as* most intellectual workers do.

PROVIDED, PROVIDED THAT: This expression is almost equivalent to "if." The words "provided," or "provided that," impose a condition on the main idea.

Excmple: There will be no trouble at all with this proposition, *provided that* you keep your part of the bargain.

SPECIFICALLY, TO BE SPECIFIC: These words are synonymous with the expressions "for example" and "for instance." In each case what will follow will be an example illustrating the main idea, or the generalization.

Example: In 1878 Edison began work on the incandescent light; *specifically* by making an exhaustive review of what others had done.

There are other verbal situations where the thought does not really flow, but where rather it dwells until the author is ready to give it further motion. For example, the question is one of these deep pools where the thought lies. The author asks a question, not to advance the progress of the thought, but instead to cause the reader to think. Exclamations are similarly, but much less frequently, used. There are perhaps other instances which the reader will discover for himself, where the purpose of the words is to divert the stream of thought.

All the foregoing categories of words and expressions are important in helping the reader to grasp quickly and accurately what the author is doing with reference to the flow of thought. Wherever words alter, direct, modify, or change in any way the direction of the main idea, or the progress of the main idea, there those words cause some disturbance in the smoothly flowing stream of thought. The skillful reader takes cognizance of all such instances as he reads.

Expert fishermen, for example, can tell by looking at the surface of a stream where the ledges of rock lie, and where the deep pools and countercurrents are. They fish accordingly. The expert reader looks with as quick an eye upon the stream of thought in the prose before him. He sees at a glance much that the unpracticed eye of the ordinary reader fails to notice. Every sentence is for him a telltale current. Certain words indicate the rocky ledges where the thought hurries on, and certain other words indicate the whirlpools and eddies, the drifts and counterdrifts that make the river of factual prose as fascinating and varied as it is refreshing and alluring.

Now, let us see how sensitive you are to the flow of thought in the practice work that follows.

Determining the thought flow

This is an exercise to help you sense the movement of thought within the paragraph. *Read each paragraph for the meaning.* Do the following:

1. Underline the topic sentence.
2. Indicate the thought direction of the topic sentence by an arrow flying from left to right. ($\longrightarrow$)
3. As soon as the direction of the thought changes, bracket the word that indicates the change and reverse the direction of the arrow accordingly.
4. Place within parentheses any parts of the paragraph where the thought remains motionless because the author gives an explanation or a reason or proposes a condition.

Here is a sample paragraph:

You will read rapidly when the text is easy. Short stories, novels, newspaper articles you will take at a brisk pace. You will change your pace, [however,] with different kinds of subject matter. When you read for facts your purpose, and consequently your rate, will be different. Then you will shift into a lower gear. (For example, when you read science, philosophy, or any of the "thought-content" subjects, you will proceed more carefully.) [But] (if the science or philosophy is of the "popular" type), you may cruise through it at a higher speed.

NOTE: In every instance where the *thought* is synonymous with the *thought* of the topic sentence the arrows will fly in the same direction as those of the topic sentence. This is important to remember, because occasionally the "reversing" word is omitted. It is characteristic of the English language for ellipsis of this sort to occur. In the event that it does occur in any of the paragraphs which are to be used for practice purposes, you should supply the missing word by inserting a caret and placing the supplied word in brackets. For example:

Men, to be sure, commonly care about the welfare of their children. [But] Animals accept no such responsibility.

Obviously, the *thought* of these two sentences is not the same; in the second sentence it is, in fact, *opposite* to that of the first sentence. Hence the "but" is inserted and the arrow is reversed. The fundamental rule is: Read always for the meaning *behind* the words. When the *meaning* changes, that is the important fact, even though the author has omitted the word that indicates this change.

Practice in discerning thought-flow in the paragraph

Analyze each of the following paragraphs according to the directions and the sample paragraph given above. In reading each paragraph, proceed phrase by phrase, testing, in each instance, the thought-flow of that particular sentence, or part of the sentence. Be alert for changes in the thought itself, even though the directional words have been omitted. If such omissions occur, supply the directional word which the author should have inserted.

Such a situation emphasizes the importance of reading first and foremost for the meaning—for the thought behind the words. The important question always is, "How flows the thought?" The careful person reads with a mind alert to only one thing: the thought, the meaning *behind* the words. When the meaning changes, that is the important fact, even though the author may have omitted the directional word which indicates this change.

It should also be pointed out that much of the effectiveness of thought contrast occurs in the small subideas that eddy about within the sentence, or in a clause within the sentence. The principal clause of a sentence may be pointed generally in the direction of the main thought of the paragraph, but a portion of that sentence may run counter to the principal clause for one purpose only: to emphasize the main idea the more in the mind of the alert reader.

Analyze each of the paragraphs found in this book on the pages designated in the following list. In reading the paragraph for the purpose of detecting the flow of the thought, proceed phrase by phrase. Keep constantly in mind the thought expressed in the topic sentence. Be alert for changes where directional words have been omitted.

In addition to these paragraphs, take other paragraphs at random from your reading. Analyze them for thought-flow. Develop a sensitiveness to change in the direction of the thought within a paragraph. Only practice will give this sensitiveness to you. Practice until you are *sure* you have it.

Read Rhythmically, Rapidly, and with Increased Eye Span

The following exercise is designed to help you read rhythmically, and to grasp an eyeful at a fixation.

Read this exercise several times each day, with a time lapse between each reading. But each time you read it try to shorten your reading time. You will need a stop watch, or a watch with a second hand—preferably a sweep hand—for timing yourself. Jot down the exact second when you begin, and the exact second when you finish. You may be able to shave only seconds off of your reading time with each practice. For this reason accurate timing is especially important with this exercise. Try to take each group of words in the line with one glance. Look at the mid-point of each group.

Try to feel your eyes "dancing" down the page. You may feel that you pause slightly on the first phrase in the line, and that you take the other two more quickly, then sweep back to the first phrase again.

One further word—and this is very important. Read always for meaning. Push yourself, to be sure, but also be sure that you get the thought, clearly and unmistakably, from each fixation.

The average book page is read with three fixations per line. Practice the exercise. Then pick up another book and practice further, trying to get three rapid, rhythmical fixations per line. Each day, for the next several days, practice the exercise; then practice on a page of a book. Then—read as rapidly as you can, without thinking of fixations. Read only for meaning. The fixations will take care of themselves.

On eye movements

Eye movements	in reading,	like steps
in walking,	are necessary	and important.
But they	should not receive	the prime attention
of the reader	while he is reading.	As in walking,
one does not	pick up each foot	and put it
down again	purposefully and deliberately.	So in reading,

one does not   *try* to place   one's eyes deliberately
along the line   of print.   For to do so
would hinder the reader   as well as   the walker.
   As a general rule   if the mind reads,   the eyes
take care of themselves.   An eyeful is   just so much print.
Beyond this limit,   taking in more   becomes an effort.
That fact, however,   should not deter us.   We should try
to see more and more   and to move   steadily forward.
   Some people's eyes   take tiny steps,   and faltering ones
at that,   along the lines   of the printed page.
As one who has   a faulty gait   needs practice,
so those   with erratic eyes   need training
in forward,   disciplined seeing.   To this end,
these exercises   have been   especially designed.
Look at each group   of words   between the spaces.
Some are larger,   some smaller groupings.   Just so
in reading,   the eyes snatch   varying lengths
of word groups.   Meaning largely   dictates the length
of the phrase   which the eyes grasp.
   The purpose   of reading   an exercise
of this kind,   over and over again   for a few minutes
each day,   is to accustom   the eyes to see
natural groupings   of words   and to force them
to accept   phrase after phrase,   line after line,
down the page   without faltering,   or hesitating,
or turning back,   but to march   dauntlessly forward
across each successive   line of type.
   Some fixation troubles   may have mental   rather than
physical causes.   The trouble is not   with the muscles
of the eye.   It is rather   with the inability
of the mind   to grasp quickly   and unerringly
the successive bits   of information   fed into it
at each fixation   of the eyes.   True, this information
does come piecemeal,   and perhaps   because of this
phrase-by-phrase   injection of ideas   we are likely
not to catch   the full meaning   of each one
as it arrives.   One or two get by   in a momentary lapse
of attention.   The meaning is lost,   and we regress
—go back to find—   the missing link   of thought.

Drive your eyes,	therefore,	down the lines,
as quickly as possible,	but always be sure	to get
the thought	at each fixation	along the line.
These exercises	will help you	to do this consciously.
In normal reading	you will do it	involuntarily.
Drive yourself	—ever more quickly—	down the lines.
But not too fast	to sacrifice meaning	for speed.

Each time that you repeat this exercise, record your time in seconds. Try to show a definite record of improvement by shortening the time that it takes you to read this.

Seconds

1. _____
2. _____
3. _____
4. _____
5. _____
6. _____
7. _____
8. _____
9. _____
10. _____

Average time: _____

Reading for Speed of Comprehension—1

The following selection is slightly more difficult than the articles in the last chapter. The author's purpose is to show you that man is a unique creature upon the face of the earth. He gives you many reasons to support his contention. Read to find these reasons. They may not always be laid out in full view so that you will see them without a little thought on your part. Think along with the author.

Read the article as rapidly as you can without missing the meaning. After you have read the article, answer the questions. Do not go back to reread any part of the article; make yourself get the meaning as you go along.

Time yourself accurately. Are you ready to read? If so, jot down the exact time in these blanks: MINUTES _____.

SECONDS _____

Now, begin to read.

HOMO SAPIENS [1]

by Gilbert Highet

Thinking. Learning, remembering, knowing; imagining and creating new ideas; preserving and communicating knowledge over distances in time and space. Not only is it wonderful in its compass and variety: it is unique. It makes us human.

Animals or Men

Consider our lives. All other activities we share with the other inhabitants of the planet. Animals, birds, reptiles, fish, and insects also struggle for power, as we do. They organize themselves into social groups. Many build. Some control their environment by ingenious inventions. Some of them, like some of us, collect wealth. They fight. They make love. They play games. Some have powers we shall never possess and can scarcely comprehend. Cunning and skillful, that they are. Yet collectively they learn little that is new, and individually almost nothing. Their skills are intricate, but limited. Their art, though charming, is purely decorative. Their languages consist of a few dozen signs and sounds. Their memory is vivid but restricted. Their curiosity is shallow and temporary, merely the rudiment of that wonder which fills the mind of a human scientist or poet or historian or philosopher. They cannot conceive of learning and knowledge as a limitless activity administered by the power of will. Only human beings really learn, and know, and remember, and think creatively as individuals far beyond the limitations of any single group or the dominance of any single need. Knowledge acquired and extended for its own sake is the specific quality that makes us human. Our species has the hair and lungs of animals, reptilian bones, and fishlike blood. We are close indeed to the beasts; often we are more cruel. But we are fundamentally different from them in that we can learn almost infinitely, and know, and recollect. We are *Homo sapiens*: Man the Thinker.

The life of every individual man and woman is made up of many acts and passions. But it is most clearly and consistently seen as a pattern of learning. We think all the time. Our thoughts and our experiences continually form a mass of material which we accept and try to organize.

[1] Gilbert Highet, *Man's Unconquerable Mind*, Chap. 2, pp. 7–13, Columbia University Press, New York, 1954.

It is chiefly in the depth and completeness of its organization that we differ from one another.

We all recognize this: it is a familiar notion. But it is a less familiar concept that all human history—with all its multitudinous glories and disgraces and crimes and heroisms—might be best understood as a process of learning. The process is troubled, delayed, interrupted, reversed sometimes, and sometimes arrested for long periods. Yet it is always traceable, and when in forward movement always admirable.

History as the record of struggles for power is exciting but unrewarding. Dinosaurs tore at one another for ages; some survived; some died: it is all meaningless. Tribes of humn beings have been hunting and rending and enslaving one another for many centuries. This one had the longer claws, that had the stouter muscles, another hid in ambush. It is factual, but is it important? Does it even explain the spread of mankind over the face of the planet, or is it merely a side activity? No: surely our real, our essential history is the story of our learning and thinking.

It was by learning that we ceased to be animals and made ourselves into men. That was the first stage. It was then, far back in the warm jungles, that somehow, cell by cell and reflex by reflex, the wonderful human brain was formed, and with it our two other human powers—the devices by which, even if the world fell into ruins, we could still rebuild it—our fantastically intricate speech, and our ingenious adaptable hands.

Tools

And then, still far back in the darkness of forest and cave, we learned how to use tools. Even better, we learned how to make tools. Prehistoric archaeology is a discipline in which there is much guesswork. But one thing in it is certain, and contains much pathos and much charm: the slow and impressive advance of our distant selves from animalism to humanity, learning, learning, always learning. In any good museum there will be a case full of prehistoric stone tools—hammers, axes, or scrapers—arranged in series. The earliest are scarcely more than lumps of stone, with a few corners chipped off to fit the rough hand roughly. But to gaze at them, those tools of the brutish dawn-men, and then to examine the rest of the series, to see how, very gradually, slow century by century, better stones are selected, and their heft and balance are studied, and instead of being crudely pounded into edged lumps, they are sliced and chipped and flaked and smoothed and rounded and sharpened and polished until they are not only efficient but almost handsome; and then to imagine those remote ancestors working away at them, thinking or learning to think, talking or learning to talk, while they worked, so that the urgent simple need of having a flint fit to kill a wolf developed into the pleasure of possessing an instrument well made for its own sake and even decorative, and the habit of improvisation grew into a craft and a tradition, and the growth of refinement created new powers, needs, hopes, and rituals—ah, it is impossible to look at those stone tools and to imagine their makers without feeling pity, admiration, and affection for our clever industrious ancestors, without seeing them as part of the same series of makers and inventors to which we ourselves belong, and without renewing our reverence for the growth of the human mind.

This is real history, the record of such a growth. After the stone tools came other inventions: the control of fire; the skillful, almost magical, transformation of lumps of earth into hard pottery and durable metal; the creation of the wheels which have ever since been rolling across the face of the earth. And at some long-distant time clever men also invented animal helpers. That is, they took wild creatures—the horses and buffaloes and pigs which they had once hunted and eaten, the wolves they had once fought, the jungle and swamp fowl they had once shot and trapped—and trained them slowly, generation by generation, to live patiently and even willingly in the company of men. It is strange to watch a puppy in a kennel, whining and scratching at the door, eager for the companionship of any human being, and to reflect on the long centuries it took to tame his ancestors, the captured whelps reared with the tough cave-children (reversing the tale of Mowgli and the wolf cubs), playing and feeding and wrestling and sleeping beside the common fire, and then running down the same prey, tearing at the same warm meat and cracking the white bones together, until they became, as they now are, fast friends of man rather than servants. (When the American continent was discovered in 1492, it had millions of inhabitants at many different stages of civilization. They had tame dogs, but no horses; stone tools and soft-metal products, but no iron; no ploughs; and no wheels. Therefore their ancestors had discovered America and moved into it after dogs and stone tools and pottery were invented, but before the invention of horses, wheels, ploughs, and ironworking.)

Plants

Equally wonderful, perhaps more wonderful, was the invention of plants. Almost everything we consume, except animal food, is part of a plant, carefully bred from selected stock: our wheat and sugar, our fruit and roots, the tobacco we smoke, the hemp and cotton we weave—all these and many more were once wild plants growing in the jungle. Some intelligent man or woman found each one of them, tasted or tested it, by patient experiment discovered how to rear it, improved it, fertilized and crossbred it, and thus invented it as surely as Diesel invented his air-fuel-compression-ignition engine. Their names are lost, those inventors, unless they are hidden under Dionysus and Demeter and Hiawatha, for long revered as the gods who taught mankind how to use plants. Yet the studies of modern botanists and archaeologists have told us where they worked. Most of the cultivated plants on earth were developed in a very few regions. Most, by far the most, came from the uplands of western China; next most from India; the next most copious groups came from East Indies; then from the high plains of central Asia, where our wheat was born; then from Asia Minor, home of orchards (and what else was Eden?); next from the Mediterranean area; lastly from Central America, the Andean highlands, and the Amazon basin, that mysterious and fertile region where, within our own generation, an inventor found a poison, curare, and transformed it into a powerful agent of healing.

That was one of the real beginnings of civilization. In that slow patient process, the men improved the plants, and the plants improved the men. They ceased to live at random. They settled down, and grew together. The First Families were founded, with the well-known names: Mr. Farmer, Mr. Miller, Mr. Gardener, and not far away Mr. Weaver, Mr. Potter, Mr. Carpenter, and the mysterious Mr. Smith. (Mr. Hunter lived some way off in the woods; and the hut on the river-bank was the residence of the Fisher family.) Ploughing came in. The land was improved by clearing and draining. The complex craft of irrigation was discovered, a skill which we are still working to develop. Farms and fisheries and crafts, they soon make a market; a market makes a village, and villages grow into towns, towns into cities. Cultivated fields and systematic irrigation make men invent rules and observe seasons: therefore laws were devised, the calendar was established, and astronomy became both a religion and a science.

So it was through learning, through expanding our knowledge, that we moved from primitive animalism to primitive human savagery, and from savagery to civilization. People sometimes say nowadays that the next war will mean "the end of civilization." It might well mean the end of an era in civilization. We, or our surviving remnants, and our descendants, might go savage again for a time. But as long as the planet is livable and as long as we possess, unimpaired, this fifty-ounce organ of exploration and invention and adaptation, the brain, we shall not only be able to reconstruct civilization. We shall be compelled to reconstruct civilization.

What time is it now? MINUTES _____

SECONDS _____

What is your reading time for this selection? MINUTES _____

SECONDS _____

Now, answer the following questions. Do not refer back to the article.

Comprehension quiz

Each of the following statements has four choices. Select the choice which best completes the statement in accordance with what you have read in the article.

1. That which distinguishes man from all other creatures is his ability to
   a use materials skillfully.
   b learn, know, and remember.
   c communicate with others of his species.
   d control his environment.

2. Man fundamentally
   a is akin to the animals.
   b has nothing in common with the animals.
   c is inferior to the animals.
   d is different from the animals.

3. We differ from one another as humans chiefly because of differences in
   a our environmental influences.
   b heredity and social factors.
   c the varying depth and completeness with which we organize our thoughts and experiences.
   d the number of vicissitudes which we have had.

4. Human history might best be understood as a
    a struggle for existence.
    b record of struggle for power.
    c process of learning.
    d process of evolution from cave man to modern man.

5. The author fancies that some mythological characters may have been
    a inventors.
    b gods.
    c heroes.
    d botanists.

6. The author implies that Stone Age man
    a took pride in achievement for its own sake.
    b derived language from imitating the animals.
    c had not yet learned to think creatively.
    d was the first to cultivate plants.

7. Dogs are man's best friend because the dog was
    a the first animal tamed by man.
    b not used as food by the cave man.
    c domesticated before the horse.
    d adopted by the cave man as a member of his family.

8. The theme of the essay is
    a modern man is superior to his cave man ancestors.
    b man is irresistibly constructive.
    c civilization began when man learned to cultivate plants.
    d the next war will mean the end of civilization.

9. This essay principally discusses man's
    a feats and accomplishments.
    b rise from his primitive to his modern state.
    c dreams and ideals.
    d intellect and ingenuity.

10. The author's attitude with regard to man is
    a noncommittal.
    b pessimistic.
    c optimistic.
    d skeptical.

How well did you comprehend what you have read? Check your answers against those given in the Answer Key. Each correct answer is worth 10 per cent.

What is your level of comprehension?   _____%

What is your speed of comprehension?   _____wpm

What is your reading index (R × C/100)? _____

Reading for Speed of Comprehension—2

To most of us a lock is a mystery. It is one of our commonest pieces of everyday mechanism. Almost all of us carry keys, an assortment of them, and we slip them in and out of locks without thinking very much about the lock itself. But let us become locked out, and we try every key in sight in the vain hope that "this, too, might tumble the lock."

We know very little, in fact, about the common lock. In the following article the author tells you a great deal in a small space about locks: their history, their construction, and the keys that fit them.

Read this article to remember the facts. Concentrate while you read. Pay strict attention to what the author says. See how rapidly you can comprehend the thought as you read the article.

Time your reading. Are you ready to begin? Time: MINUTES _____

SECONDS _____

Now, read.

WHAT DO YOU KNOW ABOUT THAT LOCK? [2]

by Rufus Jarman

There have probably been burglars ever since there were people on earth. Locks intended to foil them were among the earliest of the somewhat complicated machines. The oldest known lock in existence was found in a 4000-year-old palace at Khorsabad, near Nineveh. It is an Egyptian type, best of the ancient locks, consisting of a set of wooden pins inside a heavy wooden staple. When a wooden bar was thrust into the staple, the pins dropped into a set of matching holes in the bar, locking it. This principle inspired Linus Yale to invent his lock centuries later.

Ancient Greeks secured their doors by tying intricate knots with cord across the latch. The Romans made the first of the large iron locks, with

[2] An excerpt from Rufus Jarman, "How Burglars Outwit Locks," *The Saturday Evening Post*, July 31, 1954, pp. 20–21, 40, 44, 48.

heavy, delicately shaped keys that can be seen today in movies about dungeons. This type of lock, ornate and ponderous, but not very secure, remained in vogue until the British developed some excellent locks during the latter eighteenth and early nineteenth centuries. Most of these locks were based on a set of lever tumblers, or parallel metal pivots, that had to be aligned before the bolt could be moved.

During the Civil War years Yale perfected his pin-tumbler lock—his most important invention, although he did not realize it at the time. He regarded it at first as suitable mainly for desks, cupboards and such.

One of Linus Yale's last mechanical achievements was the designing of a lockbox for the Boston post office. It was the first of the familiar key-operated boxes, now seen in all first-class post offices.

All pin-tumbler locks, whether for post-office boxes or front doors, work alike. A door lock, probably the most familiar, consists of a brass cylinder which is called the "case." Its diameter is that of a half dollar, and it is anchored into the door. Set into the case is a smaller cylinder the size of a dime, called a "plug." The plug contains the key way, and turns with the key, shooting the bolt. Inside the lock is a line of holes drilled vertically from the top of the key way up entirely through the top half of the plug. These holes match a line of holes drilled vertically into the stationary case. The holes are called pin chambers. The more chambers, the more secure the lock, but five is the most common number. There is a coil spring in the top of each chamber, pushing down on two metal pins of varying lengths, placed end to end.

The mechanism locks when each chamber spring pushes its pins downward so that one pin in each chamber is half into the revolving plug and half into the stationary case. Like small nails, the pins keep the plug from turning until the saw-blade key is inserted. The key lifts the pins the proper distance to put one entirely within the stationary case, the other entirely within the revolving plug. This leaves nothing to pin the revolving plug to the inside of the case, which allows the key to turn and the bolt to move.

In such a lock, every additional pin tumbler multiplies by ten the number of different key combinations that can be made. Thus, a lock with two pin tumblers could be made to fit only 100 different keys. If all locks had only two pin tumblers, a person with 100 keys properly made could open any pin-tumbler lock on earth. A three-tumbler lock has 1000 different key-change combinations; a four-tumbler lock 10,000; and a five-tumbler lock has 100,000. A six-tumbler lock has 1,000,000 different key combinations, and a seven-tumbler lock 10,000,000. However, because so many of these changes are so nearly alike, most manufacturers use only 27,000 key combinations on five-tumbler locks, and cut down proportionately on the other size locks. After making 27,000 five-tumbler locks to fit that many different keys, Yale starts all over again with another batch of the same. The company thinks the chances of two people learning that they have identical keys is very remote. However, to guard against such a possibility identical keys are never sent to distributors in the same locality.

Before Yale, ordinary keys within the public's price range usually had, at most, thirty-six possible key changes. The Yale lock, with its many key combinations and reasonable price, made master-keying practical. A good example of master-keying is in large hotels. The simplest key is the one given the guest; it can open only one room. It is known technically as a single-change key. Next is the maid's key, which unlocks the sixteen rooms in her block (a sub-master key). Then comes the floor clerk's key, which opens all the rooms on a floor (a master key). Over that is the manager's key, which opens all the doors in the house (a grand master key). Above them all is a special-emergency key. By working a final tumbler that the others do not touch, it will open all doors, even those locked from the inside with the key left in the lock (it is a great grand master key).

What time is it now? MINUTES _____

SECONDS _____

What is your reading time for this selection? MINUTES _____

SECONDS _____

Now, without referring back to the text, answer the following questions:

Comprehension quiz

The following paragraphs are a résumé of the article which you have just read. Test your comprehension of the facts by filling in the blanks.

The oldest known lock in existence was found in a _____ [1] -

year-old _____ [2] near _____ [3]. It was made of

_____ [4]. The Greeks secured their doors by _____ [5].

The Romans made their locks of _____ [6]. The _____ [7] were also excellent lockmakers, turning out some of their best work during the _____ [8] and _____ [9] centuries.

Lockmaking reached its acme of development, however, in America. Linus Yale is the man whose name is invariably associated with the perfecting of the _____ [10] type of lock. His ingenuity and inventiveness has made an indelible impression on the lock industry. One of his _____ [11] inventions was the designing of a lockbox for the post office in _____ [12].

Few people know the locksmith's terms for the various parts of a lock. For example, in a lock there is a large, brass cylinder whose diameter is about that of a half-dollar. This cylinder is known as the _____ [13] of the lock. Set into this is a smaller cylindrical component about as big as a dime. This is called the _____ [14]. In this is the slot for the _____ [15]. The cylindrical bores in which the pins are fitted are called pin chambers. In the top of each pin chamber is a _____ [16].

The complexity of a lock depends upon the number of its pin tumblers. Every pin tumbler multiplies the number of possible key combinations by _____ [17]. For example, a lock with two pin tumblers could be made to fit _____ [18] keys.

The problem of making each lock different from the others, so that no one key is likely to open two locks, presents somewhat of a problem to a large lock manufacturer. The Yale company meets this problem by starting all over again with duplications of lock combinations after they have made 27,000 key combinations on five-tumbler locks. Before Yale, the average lock had at most _____ [19] key changes. The Yale lock made _____ [20] practical.

How well did you comprehend what you have read? Check your answers against those given in the Answer Key. Each correct answer is worth 5 per cent.

What is your level of comprehension? _____%

What is your speed of comprehension? _____wpm

What is your reading index $(R \times C/100)$? _____

Reading Habit Index

	Never	Rarely	Sometimes	Usually	Always
1. I see immediately the "directional words" when I glance at a paragraph.					
2. I try to improve my speed of comprehension by pushing myself while reading.					
3. When reading, I am mildly aware of thought flow, and I notice when it runs in an opposite direction to the thought before it.					
4. I have tried to use the words which I did not know in this chapter, or the last chapter, in thinking, writing, or speaking.					
5. I concentrate upon getting the thought—the meaning—and let eye-movements take care of themselves.					

(See directions for scoring, p. 75)

Reading habit index score: _____

Date: _____

Chapter Six

Punctuation: the traffic lights of reading

THE PURPOSE of punctuation is to speed the reader on his way: to get him quickly and directly through the maze of thoughts upon the page. Punctuation aims to keep him out of traffic jams that occur when words follow too closely upon one another and when one thought swerves into the path of another thought without due warning or sufficient pause.

Words and thoughts are like city traffic: they need to be controlled if everything is to proceed smoothly and without interruption. Otherwise, ideas jam up, the reader becomes confused, and the whole verbal tangle results in one unintelligible and meaningless snarl.

Punctuation regulates the speed of reading. On a clear straightaway the reader is at liberty to breeze down the printways until a period brings him momentarily to a halt. Then with a new sentence, and a new spurt of power, he is off to the next thought's end.

Where there is much for the mind of the reader to handle, however, where verbal "pedestrians" are likely to dart out into the stream of verbal traffic (as that word, "however," did a moment ago in this sentence!), where detours must be made around other thoughts, there the punctuation marks—the traffic lights of reading—must be thickly clustered so that without delay the reader may deftly find his way through the maze of words, thus keeping the traffic of thought flowing smoothly.

Note that the last paragraph, 85 words in length, was all one sentence! You were helped immeasurably in threading your way through that labyrinth of words by the fifteen punctuation marks within that sentence. Take all the punctuation out of that sentence, and you will have a rough time with it! No less than six of the eleven points of punctuation in the English language helped to guide you through that passage.

Periods and Exclamation Points

Like the red, amber, and green lights of the traffic lanes, each point of punctuation is a signal of special significance for the reader.

Periods (.) and exclamation points(!) are red lights. They flash a stop signal as he approaches them, and the thought that he has been following comes momentarily to a halt. Beyond these marks of punctuation looms the capital letter of the next sentence. It is the "green light" of a new thought. These items are too familiar to every reader to require an example to illustrate them.

Semicolons

The semicolon (;) is a kind of caution signal—a red light that flashes green just as you are about to stop. It warns the reader that he is approaching the end of one aspect of a thought, but that continuing he will encounter a different phase of that same thought. He will encounter a change in the general direction of the idea; the idea itself will not be changed. For example, look at the following sentence, describing the various hues and colors of early morning in the city: [1]

The light was brown, dark lavish brown hued with rich lights of gold; the light was rich brown shot with gold like the sultry and exultant fragrance of brown coffee; the light was lavish brown like old stone houses gulched in morning on a city street, brown like exultant breakfast smells that come from basement areas in the brown stone houses where the rich men lived; the light was blue, steep frontal blue, like

Brown, dark lavish brown hued . . . with gold;

rich brown shot with gold like the fragrance of ground coffee;

lavish brown;

blue, steep frontal blue;

[1] Thomas Wolfe, *Of Time and the River*, p. 507, Charles Scribner's Sons, New York, 1935, as quoted in *The Face of a Nation*, pp. 126–127, The Literary Guild, New York, 1939.

morning underneath the frontal cliff of build-
ings; the light was vertical cool blue, hazed with   *vertical cool blue;*
thin morning mist; the light was blue, cold flow-   *cold flowing harbor blue*
ing harbor blue of clean cool waters rimed   *rimed with a dancing gold.*
brightly with a dancing morning gold, fresh,
half-rotten with the musty river stench, blue
with the blue-black of the morning gulch and
canyon of the city, blue-black with cool morning shadow as the ferry, packed with its thousand small white staring faces turned one way,
drove bluntly toward the rusty weathered slips.

That sentence is from Thomas Wolfe's *Of Time and the River*. It
deals with one thought: the morning light was composed of many hues.
What happens each time you come to a semicolon? The hue changes.
The semicolons announce that a new phase of the thought is being
presented.

We begin with the browns: "dark lavish brown hued . . . with gold;
rich brown shot with gold like the fragrance of ground coffee; lavish
brown." Then the blues: "steep frontal blue; vertical cool blue;" and
finally the "cold flowing harbor blue."

Another sentence, briefer in scope, may show the use of the semicolon
in another setting:

The power of the atom has been unleased; for better or for worse we have
begun a new era.

In that sentence the part following the semicolon interprets or comments upon the first part.

Commas

The comma (,) is a little fellow who runs through the sentence frequently without being noticed by any but the best readers. Of all the
marks of punctuation the comma is the most profusely scattered over
the page. As an aid to the reader, by helping him to lay hold on the
meaning of the print, the comma is of very great help. In looking for
the nugget of thought in each sentence, the reader runs down the paragraphs until he comes to a sentence which begins like this:

Whether it be the wispy mare's-tail or the towering cumulus with its rumbling thunder and forked lightnings, *every cloud is composed of the same
filmy and diaphanous material*—water vapor.

What is the first thing that the expert reader does, if he is merely looking for the principal thought of that sentence? First of all he relies upon his knowledge of grammatical construction as he learned it (—or if he didn't, he'd better get busy and learn it now, if he ever expects to be a master reader) during his school days. As he races down the printed page, *whether* looms up in front of him. This he recognizes as a subordinate conjunction—a flagman signaling to him that he is entering upon the *subordinate* part of the sentence. Obviously the words that immediately follow cannot express the main idea of the sentence. Such words must lie elsewhere.

Sensing the situation, as an expert driver senses what to do when an unexpected road hazard confronts him, the practiced reader, since he is looking for those words only which express the main thought, skids his eyes along the sentence until he comes to the comma that inevitably announces the end of this preliminary, modifying, dependent part of the sentence. This does not mean that the expert reader ceases to read during this time. It does mean, however, that he throws his power-reading out of gear, takes his foot off the accelerator, and glides through this dependent part of the sentence, noting in passing the general situation, even as a good driver might do.

The comma at the end of the clause is a signal. It flashes to the mind of the reader the fact that he is probably now approaching the main thought. Sure enough, there it is. For the main thing that the author is saying in this sentence is: *every cloud is composed of the same filmy and diaphanous material.*

Let us suppose, however, that the sentence did not end where it does, but that the period was another comma. If, for instance, the sentence read as follows:

Whether it be the wispy mare's-tail or the towering cumulus with its rumbling thunder and forked lightnings, every cloud is composed of the same filmy and diaphanous material—water vapor, which is everywhere present in the atmosphere.

The expert reader would recognize instantly on coming upon the second comma that there were more "road conditions" ahead. Immediately following the second comma he sees the word "which." This tells him at once that another subordinate modifying element is just ahead of him and that he must treat it, in terms of emphasis, similar to the first one, which he has already negotiated.

If, as a boy, he learned his lessons well, he recognizes at once that this sort of construction usually means that the clause which is to follow is a thought that is being tossed in incidentally—and knowing this, he gives it due weight in his reading.

Sometimes you see a row of commas, each tagging along with a word. What does this sight mean? To the reader, as to the writer, it means the same thing: a series, a list, an enumeration.

On this spring day the earth was prodigal with the blossoms of the apple, the peach, the magnolia, and the quince.

Any reader who knows his way around will recognize those commas all in a row. It is a distinctive piece of typographical scenery; one which cannot easily be mistaken. The reader usually takes in at a glance the items, and he quickly summarizes them into a category as his eyes pass over them.

There is one further principal use of the comma that is important for the reader. This is the comma which *precedes* the words "and," "but," "or," "nor," "for." Such a situation is a signal for the reader to press down upon the accelerator of his attention and to go ahead straight down the printways into a new, related idea which is an all but independent thought. In fact, in these cases the reader may very appropriately in his own thinking of the situation, remove the comma and the conjunction entirely, and begin the next word immediately following these with a capital letter, thus making this part of the sentence entirely independent. For example:

He swung the great telescope toward a heaven full of stars, and there he beheld the handiwork of God.

The reader might well consider this sentence as two separate thoughts. The comma, in company with the *and*, indicates where one thought ends and the other one begins:

(1) He swung the great telescope toward a heaven full of stars. (2) There he beheld the handiwork of God.

The expert reader should form the habit of looking for the combination of a comma coupled with a conjunction as a part of his surveying of the typographical landscape. You can learn to see something that looks like this:

, and   , but   , for   , or   , nor

To the eye of the practiced reader these combinations should constitute one symbol, a symbol which means, "Here (for all practical purposes *in reading*) begins a new thought."

Colons

So much for the common little comma. What about the colon? Ask most people what its specific purpose is, and they will hesitate. Many people are not sure. Yet the colon (:) is a common and very important mark.

Here is the herald of the punctuation clan. The colon announces to the reader that what follows it is basically explanatory material. At the end of a statement the colon stands like the pillars of a gateway through which the reader may get a broader, fuller, more expansive view of the meaning. Here is the pattern to look for: statement, colon, further explanation of what the statement means. For example:

One fact, indeed, is certain.

There, that is a statement; but what does it mean? You need an explanation. Now let's take the complete sentence. Notice how the part following the colon explains the statement which precedes it:

One fact, indeed, is certain: you can read better than you do.

There are other uses of the colon: enumeration, direct quotation, usually of an extended nature, salutation—as in a letter—and reference figures. For example, volume 4, page 236, frequently becomes merely 4:236. In one way or another, however, the colon nearly always has an explanatory function.

With regard to the direct quotation, the quotation following the colon is usually an extended one. One might find, for example,

It was a great day, on that nineteenth of November, 1863, when at Gettysburg, on a little knoll south of town, Lincoln spoke the following words:
[Here would follow the Gettysburg Address.]

An enumeration following a colon is a much more common situation and every reader should be on the lookout for it. Here is a typical sentence:

The river was filled with all kinds of craft: tugs, lighters, ferries, motorboats, and flatboats, while among them rode the liners, those mighty leviathans of the sea.

The words that follow the colon obviously explain just exactly what the author had in mind when he said, "The river was filled with all kinds of craft." That sentence, permitted to stand alone, would not give the reader a very accurate picture of just what the author meant by "all kinds" of craft. And to have imagined—well, the reader may have imagined a scene with sailboats, canoes, and yachts—perhaps even battleships, aircraft carriers, and submarines. But apparently here are six categories of craft which were *not* there.

Quotation Marks

Quotation marks (" ") upon the page are an unmistakable sign that someone is saying something—or has said something which we are currently repeating. There is but one exception to this: where a word is enclosed in quotes. There it may mean that we have twisted the meaning of that word, so that we are employing it in a different sense from the meaning usually attached to it. Consider the following use of the word *expert:*

He represented himself as a baseball "expert"—speaking as with the omniscience of God.

When one is reading conversation, especially in fiction, there is a technique that is practiced by expert readers which cuts reading time and wordage considerably. A character in a novel makes some remark, enclosed in quotation marks, and then the author follows the remark with the observation, "he said," "she answered," "the woman observed," "the man snapped," and similar remarks. Now, if the reader is reading with keen attention to the thought that is being expressed, many of these comments are unnecessary. The good reader does not need them because, from the very nature of the situation, from the words *between* the quotation marks, in keeping with the situation as it has already shaped up, and from what the man said under these particular circumstances, he would have *had* to have "snapped" his reply.

Try reading your next novel by cutting down on as much description as you can—read just enough to give you the setting—as you would read the stage directions for a play. Then, read just the words within the quotation marks. See if you can't hear the character speaking. What tone would he use? What would his manner be? To start with, it is better to choose a novel that is heavy on the conversational side. Just leap from character to character. Imagine you are in a room with them all and that they are talking. You are simply listening, looking from one to the other as he speaks. Try it. You may find that your novel will for the first time come strangely alive and the characters will step forth from the page as real persons.

A quotation within a quotation—what somebody said that somebody said—is indicated by single quotation marks. For example:

He said, "She called to me, 'John, I can't go on!' "

Dashes

A set of dashes looming up within the sentence warns the reader that a parenthetical expression—an afterthought or an explanatory statement —usually falls between them. When the expert reader comes upon the first dash, he is on the alert for the second dash, which he expects will follow. And he knows that between the two of them the parenthetical or explanatory material lies.

When a dash occurs terminally, it means that the reader has been following a trail of thought which drops off, sheer, into nowhere. The thought breaks off suddenly, without—

In fiction the use of dashes, usually in conversation and where a cluster of them occur, indicates broken, hesitating speech, or mental confusion:

"Oh, of course, the suit is very well-made, but it doesn't—that is—well— er, the stripes—the stripes going *around*, instead of up and down, make one —well, tend to make one look heavier than he really is."

The dash is also used for emphasis and for the insertion of material within the sentence which is of explanatory nature:

You must take yourself—your whole self—completely in hand.

Parentheses and Brackets

The final four marks that we shall mention stand out boldly and obviously upon the page. They are in the truest sense "eye-catchers."

Little needs to be said about the first two of these marks, the parentheses ( ) and the brackets [ ], except to differentiate their use. When the author wants to include in his text a remark, or an aside, or an item of data which is easily detached (usually added only for explanatory purposes) he inserts parentheses, and places the "parenthetical" remark between them. Parentheses are of the author's own doing. Brackets, on the other hand, indicate to the reader that an item of information has been inserted into the text by someone other than the author, usually an editor of the author's text. For instance,

We hold these truths to be self-evident, that all men are created [politically] equal.

Question Marks

There is another mark, however, which the eye of every good reader should recognize down the printways, far ahead of him. Its characteristic shape and size makes it conspicuous upon the page. Why is this so? Well, for one reason, it is as tall as a capital letter, three times the size of a period or a comma. This is the question mark (?) or the interrogation point. What does it do? It sets the reader to wondering. This mark arouses curiosity. It bestirs the mind of the reader to think of its own accord or to be vigilant for the answer which the author will give in response to the question he asks. All in all, the question mark has a very real value as a traffic device for the speeding reader. It attracts his attention, it wakes him up, it sets him to looking around for an answer to the query which has been proposed. And there is nothing so tantalizing as an unanswered question in which your curiosity has been aroused. A question is the author's device to keep the reader awake and on his toes. And it usually does just that.

Ellipsis

Only occasionally does the reader encounter three periods, one after another, in the line. They are conspicuous because of their tenuous character. They leave a vacant space within the line. They are met with rarely, but when they are, the reader should be prepared to interpret their meaning. They announce to the reader that something has been omitted from the text which was originally a part of it. Usually these marks are used when a part of the material has been deliberately left out because of the exigencies of space, or for some other reason. For example:

We, the people of the United States, in order to form a more perfect Union . . . do ordain and establish this Constitution for the United States of America.

In the above quotation twenty-five words have disappeared from the Preamble. Occasionally asterisks (* * *) instead of periods are used.

Reading in floating gear

Probably an important observation should be made here; namely, that punctuation is largely postulated upon grammatical structure. Basically a sentence is composed of two kinds of material: principal and subordinate. For the reader there are two kinds of emphasis which he will give to the page that he is reading: a primary emphasis when the main thought is being stated and a secondary emphasis when the subordinate elements are qualifying, amending or conditioning (modifying, we call it in grammar) the main thought. The reader's mind slips into power gear while he is driving ahead with the main thought of the author and into floating gear when the conditioning and modifying elements are claiming his attention. In this way he keeps a sense of proportion in his reading and has a keen awareness every moment of what is *most* important and what is next in importance.

In the paragraph following, the parts of it during which the reader's mind is in full gear and driving ahead are italicized. Where there are no italics, the reader's mind is gliding under the power already generated; he is in these parts open to receive conditions, accept limitations, or observe certain modifying circumstances which may limit the main thought.[2]

The United States is now at the very center of the power struggle, whereas in times past we have been on the fringes. Like a spectator, *we have formerly felt free from the immediate consequences of the contest we watched, calm in the belief that there would always be time to deliberate and that our intervention,* if we chose that course, *could decide the issue. We now live,* as we often say, *in a world of bipolarized power.*

Notice the effect of the commas in that selection. They help to set off, for the convenience of the reader, what is more and what is relatively less important. So all punctuation helps the reader to keep track of what is happening to the thought as he speeds along the print lanes.

A reader, therefore, who has a thorough knowledge of grammar and sentence structure will be better equipped to grasp the meaning quickly. He will strike at the heart of the sentence; he will recognize main ideas and subsidiary ideas when he sees them.

The better one reads, the more he is aware of the little marks of

[2] Adapted from Townsend Hoopes, "Civilian-Military Balance," *The Yale Review,* vol. 43, Winter, 1954, pp. 220–221.

punctuation upon the page. They are the signals by which he is able to negotiate the thoughtways of print safely, easily, and quickly. These are the traffic lights that speed every efficient reader on his way.

Application of the use of punctuation as an aid to reading

In each of the paragraphs indicated in the list below, show how each mark of punctuation aids the reader in getting the meaning.

Page	Paragraph beginning
12	After sixth grade . . .
13	Essentially reading is . . .
15	Have you ever watched . . .
21	Our eyes travel . . .
24	We live in a world . . .
28	A preliminary to all such training . . .
32	The growth of conscious purpose . . .
33	One can, of course . . .
34	Similarly, by kindred means . . .
57	Up to this point . . .
71	"I flew the Atlantic . . .
72	When we consider . . .
78	One by one . . .
95	Thinking.
97	This is real history . . .

How Fast and How Accurately Can You See?

The expert reader has disciplined eyes. When the eyes of a skillful reader dart at a page of print, they see more, faster, than the eyes of the ordinary reader. For that reason in formal reading courses an instrument which is known as a "tachistoscope" is employed. With the tachistoscope the instructor can flash upon a screen words or phrases of varying widths at split-second intervals and the reader is supposed to see them.

What is done with an elaborate instrument at the reading center, we can simulate very simply. Follow these directions carefully:

1. Take a 3- by 5-inch filing card, and on the plain, unruled side, about ½ inch from the edge and centered about midway from each side, draw a

line, parallel with the edge 1½ inches long. At the end of the line you have just drawn and at right angles to it, draw two other lines, each about an inch long, surmounting each with an arrowhead at the edge of the card. Now your card should look something like this:

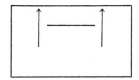

2. Place the card on any page of print—an open book, a magazine, a newspaper—and grasping the lower edge, look steadily at the horizontal line between the two arrows. Gaze at it. Try to look *through* the card. Then, while gazing intently at the line, pull the card toward you with a quick movement, and slide it back again to its original position. In the split second that you saw the lines of print under the card, some few words were momentarily on the page at the same place where the line on the card had been. What were they?

Try this procedure a few times until you become used to handling the card. Always look intently at the line. Do not shift your eyes. As you slide the card down, a line of print will be seen. Slide the card back immediately, but note what words you see.

This practice will help you to tone up your perception. Jot down the words that you see, then count the number of letters in the phrase that you saw with one fixation. This will give you your rapid-perception span. Count each letter and each space. You will measure your perception span in the number of type units you can see with one fixation. For example, the two words "one fixation" is a span of 12 type units (not counting the quotation marks).

Measure Your Rapid-perception Span

Use this book. Prepare a card as described. Pick any page in the book at random. Place the card on the page. Try several rapid perception readings. Then turn over the page and try another location. Do not practice too long on any one page. On the blanks below record what you see, and count the type units. Always confirm your perception. Do this each day. Try to see more letters with increased accuracy.

	Phrase seen	*Type units*		*Phrase seen*	*Type units*
1.	_____	____	1.	_____	____
2.	_____	____	2.	_____	____
3.	_____	____	3.	_____	____
4.	_____	____	4.	_____	____
5.	_____	____	5.	_____	____
6.	_____	____	6.	_____	____
7.	_____	____	7.	_____	____
8.	_____	____	8.	_____	____
9.	_____	____	9.	_____	____
10.	_____	____	10.	_____	____

No. correct ____

Av. type units ____

No. correct ____

Av. type units ____

	Phrase seen	*Type units*		*Phrase seen*	*Type units*
1.	_____	____	1.	_____	____
2.	_____	____	2.	_____	____
3.	_____	____	3.	_____	____
4.	_____	____	4.	_____	____
5.	_____	____	5.	_____	____
6.	_____	____	6.	_____	____
7.	_____	____	7.	_____	____
8.	_____	____	8.	_____	____
9.	_____	____	9.	_____	____
10.	_____	____	10.	_____	____

No. correct ____

Av. type units ____

No. correct ____

Av. type units ____

Reading for Speed of Comprehension—1

The following selection may be considered fairly difficult reading. The prose is fairly compact, and the thought is well organized. This is a selection in which you will need to think actively every moment that you are reading it. Keep your mind steadily upon what the author is saying. The language is seductive. Do not be charmed by the magic of the words. Get the thought.

Read the article as rapidly as you can, always being sure you are understanding what the author is saying.

Time your reading of the article accurately. Are you ready to read? If so, jot down the exact time in these blanks: MINUTES _____

SECONDS _____

Now, begin to read.

ON FINDING WORDS [3]

Words can work wonders that benefit all mankind; they can create untold wickedness; they can be "wild and whirling," clear and shining, or flat and dull. Words are our obedient servants to be used as we will.

We are interested principally in the use of words in business and for everyday purposes, but they have far greater significance than that.

Such uplifting words as "I am the Light of the World" have inspired countless millions with unfaltering faith and hope; the calculated and inflaming words of demagogues and dictators have hurled nations and people into darkness and disaster.

Do we fully realize the importance, the strength and the beauty of the world of words lying open to us?

The time we live in is referred to as the Atomic Age, but we who live in it can rightly call it the Verbal Age. Few of us can escape the ever-increasing stream of spoken and written words pouring from our radios, books, newspapers, correspondence and public platforms. We are so immersed in words that often we feel like the drowning man going down for the third time—we feel as if we were sinking in a whirlpool of words. Let us defy tradition and come up again, and take a clear, calm look at all this verbiage.

[3] "On Finding Words," *The Communication of Ideas*, Monthly Letter of the Royal Bank of Canada (Montreal), April, 1952.

Our Unique Heritage

It is language that sets us off most sharply from the higher animals. Without language we should be as dogs or monkeys, and because we possess it we are human beings, capable of good and evil and outstanding intellectual achievements. Or, for its lack, we may be dismally stupid. For better and for worse, words make us the men and women we are. Words are the stones of which we built our civilization.

Gifted with language we, the ordinary people, make language, for language is nothing if not democratic. Scholars and men of learning enrich and cultivate it, but it is from the common soil that language derives its strength, nourishment and vigour. With our need for expression of new ideas language grows, and new systems of thought and new ways of living originate new words and phrases.

As was so well said by Walt Whitman, language is not "an abstract construction of the learned, or of dictionary makers, but is something arising out of the work, needs, ties, joys, affections, tastes, of long generations of humanity, and has its bases broad and low, close to the ground."

Since we, the people, are the possessors and makers of language we must look upon ourselves as inheritors of its glorious past, custodians of its present and guardians of its future. And we must use it well.

If we are truly conscious of our opportunity in this matter of language, we are better fitted to beautify and strengthen it. A writer of the last century said that language is the amber in which a thousand precious and subtle thoughts have been safely embedded and preserved, and that it has arrested ten thousand lightning flashes of genius, which, unless thus fixed and arrested, might have been as bright but would have passed and perished as quickly as the lightning.

Why do we talk or write? The purposes are many. We wish to describe objects and events, to express moods, to persuade, to please, to exhort, to explain, to make small talk, and often to lessen loneliness. And over all these lies the main reason for all our talking and writing—to transmit the ideas from our own minds to the minds of others.

Thoughts Are Words

We need words even to communicate with ourselves. Simple thoughts such as deciding what to have for dinner, whether to buy the red or the gray hat, or whether to walk or take a tram, are formulated *by* yourself *to* yourself in some arrangement of words. Every writer or speaker who ever invented a new word had to explain its meaning by means of other words which people already knew and understood.

Communication is the vital chain between ourselves and our neighbours, our business associates, the people living in the next town, the next province, the next country and on the other side of the world. Words, spoken and written, are the golden links in that chain.

The cardinal principle of good communication is understanding. There is no satisfaction or accomplishment or, to be materialistic, gain, in meaningless and muffled words given out into unreceptive and uncomprehending air.

Here lies our main responsibility as a speaker or a writer. If our communication is open to more than one interpretation, or allows the listener or reader to say to himself, "What does he mean?" then we, at the transmitting end, have failed.

That a man will respond to some words while remaining indifferent to others is a well-known fact that influences all human affairs. The power of words is bound up with the images they evoke, and is not dependent on their dictionary meaning.

It is impossible for two persons ever to have learned the same word under precisely the same circumstances, at the same time, and with the same background of experience. Just as one person can never *be* another person, no matter how closely he is bound to him mentally, physically and spiritually, so with words.

Even such a simple word as "home" conjures up quite different pictures to different people, although the basic meaning is the same. Each person takes the word into his conscious mind ringed around with his own special and personal associations. For this reason, says Stuart Chase in his book, *The Tyranny of Words*, a student of Greek and Latin classics can never get more than a part of their meaning, for he can never personally live through experiences of the culture that fashioned them.

Our Opportunity

Herein lies opportunity for the business man, the social correspondent, the public speaker, and the person who aspires to be accounted a good conversationalist. Their attention needs to be devoted to choosing words which convey accurately and vividly to the minds of others what is in their own minds.

To transmit what we have to say effectively we need, above all, to remember our audience. There is the important part of the interchange.

To reach our readers we must write with them in mind, in words *they* know and understand, in language that means something to *them*. If we are unable to do so it would be better if we laid aside our pens.

In the writing of business letters, for instance, it is essential that we study our market, the people who make it up, their likes and dislikes, their desires and demands—and then write to them in words they want, in phrases they understand. As in so many other acts of unselfishness, this sublimation of self reaps rewards.

Keeping the reader firmly in mind, and with his interests at heart, how best can we appeal to him?

The heavenly twins of better communication could well be named Simplicity and Clarity. They have been called the art of arts, the glory of expression, and the sunshine of the light of letters. Often before we have pleaded their cause.

Clear, straight thinking must be behind the words we use. If you understand the proposition well, then your natural tendency will be to explain it in understandable terms. Thinking and wording cannot be dealt with separately, for they are cause and effect.

A man must analyze, group, marshal into order and define his thoughts before they can appeal with any force to his intelligence, or be used by him so as to appeal to the intelligence of others.

Not Easy: But Worth While

To reach our readers, to maintain their attention and influence them favourably, we would do well to describe and suggest concrete, not abstract things. In the field of business writing, our words should always make it easy for the reader to picture the proposition, service or article, and its advantages and benefits.

To express one's thoughts accurately is not easy. To be precise may sometimes appear to be dangerous, and we may be tempted to prefer the safer obscurity of the abstract. But abstract words are more open to misunderstanding than concrete ones, and if we want to make our meaning plain we will avoid them. "Thou canst not adorn simplicity," said Epictetus about 2,000 years ago, and it is still a fundamental truth.

The conviction that long words, which also aid and abet obscurity, make for learning and enhance our prestige is deeply ingrained in our culture, says an article in *Scientific Monthly*. Most of us remember Hans Christian Andersen's charming fairy tale of the artificial nightin-

gale, who bore the grand title: "Chief Imperial Singer of the Bed-
chamber," and the music master who wrote five and twenty volumes
about the counterfeit bird ". . . in all the most difficult Chinese characters. Everybody said they had read and understood it, for otherwise
they would have been reckoned stupid."

What Are "Good" Words?

A struggle for life is constantly going on among the words and grammatical forms of a language. In the battle between short and long
words the former seem to be winning, and this is a healthy sign.

If the choice is between two words that convey the writer's meaning
equally well, one short and familiar and the other long and unusual, of
course the short and familiar should be preferred.

Sir Winston Churchill, an outstanding master of words, does not
hesitate to use such a word as "liquidate" rather than the simpler
"destroy," if he thinks that the less common word will be more effective
in transferring what is in his mind into his readers' minds. And C. E.
Montague says: ". . . Clear out of your mind the notion that a language is, or ought to be, a finished and immutable system in which
certain words are indefeasibly highcastes and certain other words are
doomed forever to be untouchables."

Good words are words the reader understands, whether they be short
and Saxon, or long and Latin. Usually they are the former, but we need
not feel ourselves pushed into using nothing else. The sensible thing is
to use the word that fits the case. As Mark Twain wisely said: "The
difference between the right word and the almost right word is the
difference between lightning and the lightning bug." It may mean, in
modern terms, the difference between a sale and no sale, between a
promotion and no promotion.

The right words convey the right meaning. Grammar and syntax are
not nearly so important as the choice of words. The selection of one
word rather than another may alter the whole weight and influence of
a poem, or a passage in prose, or give a sinister meaning to a passage
you intend to be a winner of friends.

Arrangement is, of course, important, but a happy sequence of choosing the right words is that they have a graceful way of arranging themselves. Sometimes it almost seems as if words have a life of their own;
that they object to careless handling, and that unruly words actually
struggle in the sentence.

Words Paint Pictures

Every word and phrase we use in our writing, whether it be in our business letters, reports, articles or speeches, is as vital as the brush stroke of an artist. To make the picture real and appealing we do not use strange or mysterious words, technical terms, exaggerations or inaccuracies. We use words that are concrete, interpretive and vivid. Words paint pictures, but there is little room for "still lifes" in our gallery.

By making patterns with words and phrases that please the ear, we affect the emotions, move our readers, and thus drive home our point. Then we are well on the way to becoming artists in words.

Metaphors and similes, if they are simple and shining, help paint the picture. The New Testament is full of profound but simple metaphors. Compare "feed my sheep" with "teach my doctrine." Does not the former convey a far more human, tender and sympathetic picture? And in the simile, from the Psalms, "They shall soon be cut down like the grass, and wither as the green herb"—do we not see the picture much more vividly than if the writer had said "They shall perish"?

Clichés, those worn-out, bleached-dry phrases, are to be avoided. Most of us use them daily in our conversation, and they do not seem particularly dead or even noticeable. In the written word they show up in all their exhaustion. Sometimes a phrase such as "break the ice" or "cry over spilt milk" does express what you wish to say in the most fitting way. But it is well to think twice before we trot out the old familiar phrase. A new one—the fruit of a little more thought—might be better. Often the old expression may have become so blunted and blurred by constant use that it doesn't cut into the mind.

Slang is another "acceptable" in conversation that has little place in writing. The place for slang is in face-to-face conversation, where it may add wit and humour, increased vivacity and intimacy to our speech. But it is better to use it sparingly, if at all, in written communications.

Words Are Beautiful

Let us look for a minute, as a collector might look lovingly at his treasures, at the beauty of words. Hawthorne spoke of "the unaccountable spell that lurks in a syllable," and though we may not all have music in our souls, we can learn to appreciate the kind of language that comes from a combination of feeling, skill and artistic usage.

It has been said that words, like precious jewels, depend upon their grouping and the choice of neighbours. They may be strange or beautiful, amusing or tragic in isolation, but they will be doubly so when an author of judgment has put them in the right company.

Make this little test. Think of any familiar verse of poetry or passage of prose—even a business letter—that you find pleasing, and then analyze your enjoyment of it. You will find that only a part of the enjoyment comes from contemplation of the situation to which it draws your attention. Much is aroused by the beauty of the words, considered solely as a pattern of sound and rhythm. But we must not become intoxicated with words as words, easy though it can be, for our writing would be robbed thereby of the clarity we are striving for. The two aims of a great artist in words must always be lucidity first and then melody.

The English Language

What a wonderful instrument our language is! It is rich, because it is omnivorous; it takes words from other tongues and assimilates them, giving them a form and character so familiar that they seem to be of native stock.

It is expressive. Take the word "greed," for example. Doesn't it give off a feeling of fatness? Hasn't the word "sublime" a shimmer and a sheen? And doesn't the word "gloom" sound dark and foreboding?

Our language is vital. It evaluates, in a broadminded way, new entrants to its huge vocabulary, and accepts or rejects them with complete fairness. It is not rigorously regimented, but truly alive and evergrowing. The advertising writer and the direct-by-mail salesman have no excuse for not being able to make their points in written words; the public speaker can find in our language all he needs in the way of words, carefully selected and skilfully assembled, to move his audience.

Enriching Your Language

How can we add to our knowledge and appreciation of our language? One important way is to enrich and enlarge our vocabulary. By acquiring all the stock of words we can, we have a basis for weighing one word against another, for rejecting a word because we know a better one. We have a rich and full treasury upon which to draw.

The more words we know the more selective we can be. It is a paradox, but perfectly true, to say that without a large vocabulary we will often use six words instead of one.

Just as we can't make new friends if we never meet anybody, so with words. To build our vocabulary we must meet new words, and to meet new words we must read, the more the better.

The business man who reads Shakespeare or a comparable author can write better business letters than the man whose sole diet is cheap fiction—and the stenographer who reads Shakespeare will do better letters and be more of a participant in the business than the stenographer whose only literary food is chit-chat.

We can think of the world of words as a great and glorious garden. Like flowers, words have scent and texture and beauty. Like trees, they have strength, and grandeur and vitality. We are the gardeners, responsible for their cultivation and their fairest blooming, their arrangement and their disposition.

Let us toil happily in this garden, sowing the seeds of thought with care, and nurturing the tender blossoms that grow from them: and let us be ruthless in uprooting the weeds that threaten to choke and kill our language.

Ours will be the harvest. Words give us beauty and sustenance and self-expression; expressions of love and feelings of duty. They enable us to convey to others the philosophy by which we would influence them.

What time is it now? MINUTES _____

SECONDS _____

What is your reading time for this selection? MINUTES _____

SECONDS _____

Now, answer the following questions. Do not refer to the article.

Comprehension quiz

1. Language is determined by
    a   scholars.
    b   the general population.
    c   writers and others who use the language extensively.
    d   the conditions of the time in which we live.

2. The author suggests that the real meaning of words
    a   is that given by the dictionary.
    b   is entirely an individual matter.

    c should be carefully studied to help us use our language effectively.

    d is the same for everyone.

3. Behind the words we use should always be

    a clear, straight thinking.

    b a full realization of the wonder that words can work.

    c the ultimate aim of selling the reader an idea.

    d a deep appreciation of the beauty and history of the English language.

4. "Thou canst not adorn simplicity," was said by

    a Aristotle.

    b Hans Christian Andersen.

    c one of the writers of the Bible.

    d Epictetus.

5. Good words, as defined by the author, are words that

    a are short and derived from Anglo-Saxon.

    b the reader understands.

    c have sprung from common, everyday speech.

    d have a picturesque quality.

6. Slang is acceptable in

    a conversation but not in writing.

    b both conversation and writing.

    c neither conversation nor writing.

    d writing but not in conversation.

7. The artist in words must be concerned first of all with

    a melody.

    b emotional content.

    c lucidity.

    d meaning.

8. We can acquire a better knowledge and appreciation of the English language by

    a avoiding clichés.

    b enlarging and enriching our vocabulary.

    c reading the great authors.

    d listening attentively to the salty speech of common folk.

9. The author feels that having a large vocabulary is likely to cause a person to be

    a selective and pointed in expressing his thoughts.

    b wordy and prolix in expressing his thoughts.

    c more profound in what he says than those with lesser vocabularies.

    d more refined in his writing and speaking.

10. The author's approach in this essay is
  a idealistic.
  b utilitarian.
  c scholarly.
  d theoretical.

How well did you comprehend what you have read? Compare your answers with those given in the Answer Key. Each correct response is worth 10 per cent.

What is your level of comprehension?   _____%

What is your speed of comprehension?   _____wpm

What is your reading index $(R \times C/100)$? _____

Reading for Speed of Comprehension—2

"What a piece of work is a man!"

That is a simple sentence, and you read it with no effort. Perhaps you remember as you read it that this is one of the famous utterances of Hamlet. Be that as it may, the reading of these seven one-syllable words is a simple, yet an amazing feat. In fact, everything that you read, that you see, hear, touch, smell, or taste, or that in any other way intrudes upon your consciousness calls for a response from that miraculous telephonic network of the body, the nervous system.

Perhaps none of the demands upon the neural mechanism is more interesting than that employed in the act of reading. The eye receives tiny, tiny wavelets of shimmering light and shadow. These fall upon receptors of the nervous system within the eye. And out of these pulsating patterns comes meaning. It is the turning of these black symbols into thoughts, memories, and knowledge and the dynamic dreams of things unborn that is the miraculous mystery of the act of reading. In all of this transformation the nervous system plays a vital role.

"Our Amazing Network of Nerves" is a piece that is highly informative and that you will thoroughly enjoy. Read it for information, but read it as rapidly as you can. It is an exciting account about a part of the piece of work that is man of which most of us know very little.

Time: MINUTES _____

    SECONDS _____

OUR AMAZING NETWORK OF NERVES [4]

by Stuart Chase

Signs and messages are constantly flowing in from the world outside through our senses, of which scientists have identified at least 20. These include, along with sight, hearing, touch, smell, and taste, a temperature sense, a muscular sense, a distance sense which is especially keen in the blind, a sense of balance—the disturbance of which makes us seasick—and so on.

Despite these sensitive receptors, we miss a great deal of what is happening. I have watched a wren, for instance, singing with all its might. Suddenly, while its small throat and mouth and every feather go on quivering, the sound stops. The song has passed into registers beyond the range of my ears.

Our skin is sensitive to vibrations up to about 1,500 per second, but beyond that we feel only a steady push. The eye misses ultraviolet rays, electric waves, X rays, cosmic rays, and the deadly gamma rays. Ultraswift movement can baffle it; above a given speed, a three-bladed electric fan appears to be a flat surface.

We can train ourselves to see more, or feel or hear more, but always far below the total range of what is there, often below what other animals can perceive. Our senses catch only hints and snatches of what nature has to show, leaving the brain to create a whole picture and attach meaning to these scattered indications.

Some events which reach us from the submicroscopic world, such as cosmic rays, are not consciously recognized at all, but the body may have to deal with them. Cosmic rays, by hitting the genes, may cause sudden biological mutations. We are drilled by about 100 cosmic rays every minute of our lives.

The senses usually see enough to adjust the organism to its environment. They perceive what the individual needs to survive—or has needed in the past—and little more. Those high notes are doubtless useful to a wren, but not to me, though I should love to hear them.

What the eyes see, the ears hear, and the fingers touch, gives our minds the shape of the ordinary or macroscopic world of the senses. Every person, due to his structure and experience, sees it a little differ-

[4] As condensed in *Science Digest* from *Power of Words*, copyright 1953, 1954, by Stuart Chase. Reprinted by permission of Harcourt, Brace and Company, Inc.

ently. What I can see up there in a tree, for instance, is nothing compared to what a bird lover will observe. Nobody knows what a given animal can see, or probably ever will except in the crudest sense; but we may be sure it is a very different view from ours, and from that of other species.

Human eyes will probably never see the atomic world which lies below the microscope world, except indirectly, as in an X-ray tube. Yet the atomic world is perhaps the most "real" of all. In it, substances as we see and feel them on the ordinary level dissolve into electric charges rushing about at something like the 186,000-mile-per-second speed of light.

We are aware of reality on three levels: normal, microscopic, and atomic. Any object—a writing table or an apple—is very different in each. Until recently, only the first level was accessible, but now science has opened up the other two.

The signs we know as sensations come in to eye, ear, skin; what happens then? All over the body are delicate receptors to decode the signs, and nerve fibers to conduct the message at some 200 miles per hour to the brain. In the eyes alone are about one million sensitive cells called cones, each connected with a nerve fiber which forwards messages concerning patterns of light and shade.

Patterns received in the ear require fewer and less intricate conductors, and in the nose very much fewer. But the sense of smell, though relatively feeble in man, is associated with deep emotions. A familiar scent can carry one back to early childhood, in a wave of excitement tinged with mystery.

The goal of evolution in developing this complex network is not, of course, to produce poetic images, but to keep the organism alive; the poetry comes later. Every animal, says Dr. J. Z. Young, requires information about changes in its environment. Also its brain needs information about internal changes—say a cramp in a leg muscle or a shift in blood chemistry. Messages from both outside and inside are carried by nerve fibers, with the aim of keeping the organism in a steady state.

Young calls the fibers which carry information to the brain *input* nerves; those carrying messages out from the brain to other parts of the body he calls *output* nerves. They are grouped in bundles, like wires in a cable, each nerve fiber carrying one faint impulse, say a simple item of information, like temperature. The interconnections, however, are exceedingly complex, with many alternate routes if one is blocked. The fibers are sometimes two feet long and average 1/1,000th of an inch in diameter.

Recent research has demonstrated how a message is carried. The impulse which travels along the nerve fiber resembles the dot of a Morse code—an electrical signal fired along the fiber in a series of bursts. A booster mechanism keeps the signal going. Just how this works is in some dispute, but physiologists agree that the nerve fiber is a chain of relay stations, many stations to the inch, constantly regenerating the signal.

Some fibers are naked, but evolution has introduced an improved model clothed in a sheath, which works about ten times as fast as the old model, with 1/10th the energy.

The nervous system has the ability to slow down output messages—which is fortunate for me at this moment. Writing would be impossible if hand and arm muscles contracted all at once. Many thousands of fibers are involved, each in control of only a small amount of muscle. Thus the writing muscles can be brought into play gradually and smoothly, not in one big jerk.

Automatic action can handle a variety of signals. Here is your small son, says Young, under the table as you write. He tickles your leg, but you are concentrating too hard to notice. A reflex makes the leg muscles move your foot a little. He tickles again with no response. About the fourth or fifth time, the nerve impulse crashes into your consciousness and you exclaim "Hey!"—causing Junior to beat a fast retreat. Your internal apparatus has made some complicated connections. So has Junior's.

There are some 10 to 15 billion nerve cells in the normal human brain. One of the latest mechanical computers has only 23,000 tubes.

The brain is the central office of the nervous system, decoding and interpreting the messages from input nerves, sending messages to the muscles over output nerves. The mathematical sum of theoretically possible interconnections between 15 billion units is something to give even Mr. Einstein pause, for it is rather more than all the molecules in the universe!

From billions of possible connections, our central office can select the right combination, often select it instantaneously. Here you are with your foot on the accelerator, approaching a signal light at a dangerous road intersection.

If the light is red, the excitation from the retina must be transmitted through the nervous system so that the cells in the motor cortex send impulses down to the leg muscles which make the throttle close.

If the light is green, impulses must go down to keep the throttle open.

The whole complicated transmission is to be handled, and your safety guaranteed, by neurons which form no conception of "red," "green," "stop light," "traffic cop," "accident," at all. Yet the system works! It works because of past experiences that have opened connections in the nervous system.

Is everything which ever happened to a person recorded somewhere in the nervous system? In 70 years everyone can theoretically receive 15 trillion separate "bits" of information to store. Dr. Ralph W. Gerard reports a bricklayer who, under hypnosis, described every bump on the top surface of a brick he had laid in a wall 20 years earlier. Can all the "bits" be tapped? Some laboratory scientists, including Young, are inclined to think so; others doubt it. The psychoanalysts have amply demonstrated that many childhood experiences are stored, and may be summoned to consciousness by appropriate techniques.

Do we know enough about the human nervous system and the brain to improve our day-to-day performance? I am confident the answer is yes. The lessons for education are dramatic. "I do not see," says Young, "why it is impossible to teach nearly everyone to follow complicated arguments, and draw correct conclusions—even by the use of elaborate mathematics."

Every normal person seems to have the equipment for a very fine performance. What most of us need is broader firsthand experience as a basis for building patterns, and more practice in evaluation.

If the physiologists are right, everyone of us creates the patterns in his brain, beginning the day he is born. The world he apprehends at any given time is shaped by those patterns. He has, moreover, the power deliberately to seek new experience, create new patterns, and even change the shape of his world. The most dramatic proof of this is what happens when the blind learn to see. By keeping at it, they can change a spinning mass of lights and colors into the normal panorama of earth and sky which the rest of us learned unconsciously in early childhood.

What time is it now? MINUTES _____

SECONDS _____

What is your reading time for this selection? MINUTES _____

SECONDS _____

Now, without referring back to the article, check the level of your comprehension with the following quiz:

Comprehension quiz

Part One

1. The reason that every person sees the world differently is
    a not known exactly.
    b that no two people have exactly the same level of eyesight.
    c the individual differences in structure and experience.
    d that some people look at the world from a poetic standpoint, while others regard it factually.
2. The basic reason for the development of the human nervous system was to
    a compete with other animals.
    b help the organism to exist.
    c help man to enjoy more fully the world around him.
    d give man greater enjoyment through his senses.
3. The author infers that man's nervous system
    a is superior to the nervous mechanisms of animals.
    b is man's most important asset.
    c has become weaker in civilized man because of the strain of civilized life.
    d has become more efficient with the passage of time.
4. The nervous system has the ability to control the speed of
    a outgoing impulses.
    b incoming impulses.
    c neither outgoing nor incoming impulses.
    d both outgoing and incoming impulses.
5. According to modern psychological thought,
    a our birth is but a sleep and a forgetting.
    b the golden days of yesteryear are gone for evermore.
    c everything we ever knew is part of us, inside.
    d there is a land of happiness which we can reach if but we will.

Part Two

This part of the quiz will test your ability to recall the facts from your own recollection of them. Fill in the blanks with the appropriate word:

1. According to scientists, we have at least _____ senses.
2. We are aware of reality on three levels: the _____, the _____, and the _____.

3. Nerve messages travel at about _____ miles per hour over neural fibers that are _____ of an inch in diameter and _____ feet long.

4. There are more interconnections possible in the brain of man than there are _____ in the _____.

5. Nerve messages are tiny bursts of _____ energy.

How well did you comprehend what you read? Check your answers against those given in the Answer Key. In Part One each correct answer is worth 10 per cent; in Part Two each blank correctly filled in is worth 5 per cent.

What is your level of comprehension?   _____%

What is your speed of comprehension?   _____wpm

What is your reading index $(R \times C/100)$? _____

Reading Habit Index

	Never	Rarely	Sometimes	Usually	Always
1. When I pick up something to read, I read in terms of paragraph-units. I look for the topic noun, main idea, and details.					
2. I notice punctuation, and try to use it as an aid toward helping me to read better.					
3. When I read I think about the thought which the author is trying to convey.					
4. I notice the words which change or emphasize the direction of the thought flow.					
5. At times other than when practicing with this book, and for the sake of extra practice, I try to read rhythmically with two or three fixations per line.					

Reading habit index score: _____

(See directions for scoring, p. 75)

Date: _____

Chapter Seven

Higher speed
with less effort

HALF A century ago motoring was different from what it is today. There used to be an old song, "Get out and get under the car." It reflected the mood of the times, when every motorist carried with him a kit of three essential items: a monkey wrench, a screwdriver, and a pump! Every man was his own garageman. Highways were narrow, grades were steep, and mud was plentiful. Automobiles were built in a fashion that was dictated by those adverse road conditions.

Today is the era of the long, curving, concrete strips—the turnpike and the superhighway. We go places with more speed and less trouble. And with the changing times has come a revolution in automotive design. This is the day of the streamlined body and the cruising gear. We have learned how to go faster and farther with greater economy and less effort.

As we have learned to drive more efficiently, so has the reader who speeds along the print lanes learned to read more efficiently. *He* uses the ideas of modern power transmission in his reading techniques: he travels at higher speed more economically.

Reading at cruising speed is similar to motoring in overdrive. You use it when conditions permit. When the road is open and the grades are gentle, when the rolling landscape lies before you and the ribbon of highway stretches out into the distance, then the motorist slips into cruising gear and glides away with effortless power and speed. Similarly, when the material is easy for the reader to understand and the facts are not too closely jammed along the throughways of print, when you would like to sit back in your chair and let your eyes cruise down the printed page with a safe assurance that you are comprehending the thought as you read, then you can read for speed with the "cruising gear" technique.

Obviously there is some of Einstein and Nietzsche, some of Eddington and John Stuart Mill that you will not want to attempt to cruise through. These are rocky, tortuous roads where the jagged obstructions of difficult ideas pierce the surface. The thoughts of authors like these are original, pioneering thoughts, and they are usually hard to handle and rough to negotiate. For that reason the books of such authors belong to the little-traveled roads of thought. He who explores them must do so in low gear for the most part, and with care and caution.

But such is not the bulk of our reading. Come what may, the cruising technique will help you in all of your reading. Once you have learned to practice it, you will find it applicable in many, many reading situations where at first thought you may consider it unusable. Patent attorneys and others whose reading is of the most meticulous and exacting type imaginable find that when they have learned to read for the thought, with minimum obstruction from the words, even *their* work is made easier and their pace is accelerated.

Now we are at a crossroads in the matter of establishing a view toward efficient reading. The way needs to be marked very clearly so that there will be no confusion in your mind at this juncture of the discussion with reference to fast, powerful reading.

Seeing versus reading

You should recognize clearly the difference between *seeing* and *reading*. We have pointed out that reading is a matter of searching for the thought that was in the mind of the author and which now lies in the meaning of the words which are before the reader. To *read* we must process the author's words; we must distill and extract from the words, as such, the nugget of thought which the author is trying to express. In the process of being written, the thoughts of the author have undergone metamorphosis: what started in the thought areas of the author's brain as notions, ideas, thoughts, concepts have come to us as a string of black symbols on a white background, irregularly grouped, and put together according to an accepted and arbitrary formula, involving rules of grammar and rhetoric, which we call by the blanket term of writing, or written communication.

At this point in the communicative process the reader comes upon the scene and meets the author's thoughts—enshrouded in words. He proceeds to reconvert these words back into their essential substance: thought. There is one thing that the efficient reader is looking for, that is, what *thought* lies beneath the printed word.

Words are important; they are not *all*-important. Yet the average reader treats them as though they were! Many people are much more conscientious about reading every *word* in a book than they are about getting every *thought* upon the page. They treat an author's words as though they were some hallowed abracadabra, the unlocking of whose mystery depends upon the degree of attention which we give to each and every one of them. And it is from this attitude toward the page that much word-by-word reading is justified and perpetuated.

One of the greatest things that any reader ever learns is that not all words are *equally* important. You recognize this fact when you send a telegram. The reader who will ever be worth his salt must keep in mind the distinction between the words that the eye *sees* and those that the mind *reads*. They do not equal each other! Like matter in the physical universe, words have a greater or lesser "meaning density" as they stand side by side in a sentence. Some prose has a high idea concentration. Other writing is much more tenuous. The words may be many; the ideas, few. Or the reverse may be the case. The skillful reader, however, spots the compactness of the thought almost as soon as his eyes alight upon the page. This is a characteristic of the printed page which he definitely looks for, and it is one of the skills of good reading to appraise the thought density of the page immediately and set one's pace of reading accordingly. But, no matter how compact the thoughts may be, every sentence that expresses these thoughts has some dead spots where the eye notices the words, but where the mind does not do any reading. Why? Because nothing is in those particular words that helps to convey or advance the thought.

Take any short paragraph, and doodle with it. With your pen or pencil, strike out all but the *essential* words. Assume that you are telegraphing the thought content of that paragraph and that all the extra wordage must be excised. Count the number of words that the paragraph contained *before* you began cutting. Count the number of essential words you have left at the conclusion of your condensation. You should be able to reduce any paragraph by 50 per cent or more. Some paragraphs you may cut severely without sacrificing the thought. Practice a little each day with your newspaper.

The paragraph which you have just read contains exactly one hundred words. Now, let's take it, and do with *it* as we have suggested that you do with any paragraph. We shall reduce it for telegraphic communication. Here are the words that your mind *reads*, even though your eyes *see* every single word in that paragraph:

TAKE ANY PARAGRAPH   DOODLE WITH IT   STRIKE OUT ALL BUT ESSENTIAL WORDS   ASSUME YOU ARE TELEGRAPHING THOUGHT   COUNT WORDS BEFORE CUTTING   COUNT AFTER CONDENSATION   REDUCE PARAGRAPH 50 PER CENT OR MORE   PRACTICE WITH NEWSPAPER

There! We have reduced the original paragraph by 68 per cent. We have used only 34 words to express the thought—or rather, to sketch it. Seen thus, the thought stands out in bolder lines and clearer outline in the mind of the reader. What has been lost is nuance, shading, and degrees of meaning. As a line drawing compares with a carefully shaded portrait, so does this condensed version compare with the fully worded paragraph.

Read for thought

What does this technique mean in terms of actual reading? First, it means that you have cut your reading load to a mere fraction of what it is for the word-by-word reader. The mental work involved in getting the meaning has dwindled incredibly. Suppose that you could reduce every sentence which you have to read by 68 per cent. A 2000-word article withers to a mere 640 words. You have shifted into a speed gear in your reading where you travel faster and with far less effort.

Second, it means that you do not see any less. Your eyes perceive many times faster than your brain apprehends. But it also means that, while *seeing* all the words, your brain learns to disregard all of them, except the key words and word combinations which speed you on your way. If, for instance, you drive through excessively heavy city traffic, there is much that you see. But that which claims your attention is only a fraction of the total traffic situation that is passing before your eyes. Let any irregularity occur anywhere in the field of your vision—let a child that is running on the sidewalk suddenly make a dash for the curb, and you are immediately conscious of him—although up to this point you may not have been aware of that child at all. He was just a part of the total visual context.

So it is with reading: when you look for the key words and phrases, you concentrate upon the main stream of the thought. So long as the thought flows smoothly, completely, and without irregularity, you move forward rapidly and smoothly. Let something out of the ordinary occur, however, and you are suddenly aware that here is a situation which demands the exercise of caution and skill. The little word "not," the adverb "only," the directional words "but" and "however" and "on the contrary"—these are the verbal signposts that should alert you to action. When they loom into your field of vision, they prove that a great deal was going on all the while on the printways that you were seeing, but perhaps that was not of such importance that you needed to give it your complete attention. You were concentrating on the thought. And that is where you *should* concentrate, if you are an expert reader until, of course, a verbal pedestrian darts out. Then, because you are seeing everything, you are prepared to meet such a verbal emergency.

Third, telegraphic reading does not mean that you have lost any of the thought content. Let us look at the whole situation very practically. In every sentence, in every paragraph, there is just so much *thought content*. You cannot augment or diminish that thought content by increasing or decreasing the number of words used to express the thought. Take the following three sentences:

It rains.
It is raining at this moment.
The clouds have opened, and their showers are watering the parched earth.

Now, the *thought* is the same in these three sentences. Each one is simply expressing the fact that it rains. Yet the first sentence expresses the thought in two words; the second sentence uses three times as much wordage to express the same idea, while the third sentence uses six times as many words to express the same thought.

Fourth, by looking for only those words which are the key words of the sentence, you are establishing a habit of rapid, economical reading which is sound both educationally and psychologically. Your eyes will travel with speed along the lines of print; but as your eyes speed, your mind idles. That is what a motorcar does when the motorist shifts into overdrive. Instead of getting the habit of trying to see and digest and comprehend and retain every word that meets your eyes, you will have formed the more efficient habit of selecting from those words that flow before your eyes the ones which convey the thought clearly and economically. And remember, good reading is dependent upon the establishing of desirable habits.

Most concepts of speeded reading presuppose that you force yourself to read faster and faster and faster. It is all a kind of dizzy whirl of acceleration. But speeded reading in the best sense is much more than this. It is learning to see rapidly, while your mind calmly, yet adroitly, notes, evaluates, and absorbs the thought. *See* all the words, but *read* only those which give you the thought which the author is attempting to convey.

Always try to be completely cognizant of what the author is saying without the clutter of all the words which he has used. He has been bound by the exigencies of formal language usage. Rules of structure in writing require more than a telegraphic representation of the thought. But the eyes of the good reader sail down the avenues of print, seeing all, but dwelling only upon the significant word and the important phrase. He forms the habit of spotting these key words and phrases a long way off, and to anticipate the turn which the thought of the author will next take. He has learned to heed the guideposts by the way. The "directional" words that we have discussed in an earlier chapter guide him in keeping track of the thought flow; the punctuation helps to keep the thought lanes cleared.

The days of the word-by-word reader are as old-fashioned as are the cars of yesteryear. We have learned in both instances that there is a better way of reaching one's destination. The long, ribbon-like lanes of print lie before you. More and more of them are laid out for you every year. They are an invitation to sit back comfortably and let your mind cruise along them. Experience this freedom of speed and fleetness of thought and you will never go back to the old low-gear way of reading every word. At first, you will have to look deliberately for the meaningful word, and be aware of the tendency to loiter. Hurry yourself at first, but only for the purpose of apprehending the next *thought*. Soon you will begin to experience a new sense of flight into the realm of the printed word. But it will take time. This new experience will come with practice. So let us begin that practice now.

Practice reading with more speed and less effort

Certain paragraphs will be listed on the next page to help you to develop the skill of reading only key words and phrases. But first, you must be able to recognize these—to *see* the significant words among all the verbal undergrowth on the page. Most paragraphs *can* be reduced in wordage nearly 50 per cent or more and still convey the full thought content.

In the designated paragraphs, take your pencil or pen and strike out all of the words which are unnecessary. Assume, for the purpose of this exercise, that you are editing each paragraph in order to telegraph it. Cut it to the bone. Use only the words of the paragraph. Do not insert any. Always go back and read over the words that you have left standing to be sure that they make sense by themselves. After you have finished deleting the unnecessary words, count the number of words you have struck from the paragraph. Then, to find your *percentage of reduction*, do the following:

1. Divide the number of words which you have struck out of the paragraph by the total number of words originally in the paragraph.
2. The quotient will be the percentage by which you have reduced the reading load of the paragraph.

After each paragraph you will find the total number of words which the paragraph contains.

Here is an example of the way in which you should handle each of the paragraphs:[1]

Every book has a skeleton hidden between its boards. Your job is to find it. A book comes to you with flesh on its bare bones and clothes over its flesh. It is all dressed up. I am not asking you to be impolite or cruel. You do not have to undress it or tear the flesh off its limbs to get at the firm structure that underlies the soft. But you must read the book with X-ray eyes, for it is an essential part of your first apprehension of any book to grasp its structure. (96 words)

[1] Mortimer J. Adler, *How to Read a Book*, p. 160, Simon and Schuster, Inc., New York, 1940.

There were 49 words struck out of the paragraph. Therefore 49/96 = 0.51 or 51 per cent. The paragraph has been reduced by 51 per cent of its original length. Now, try your hand on the paragraphs indicated in the following list:

Page	Paragraph beginning	No. words	Per cent reduction
54	Man has always had . . .	125	_____
57	Why do these . . .	100	_____
65	I hold that we are . . .	147	_____
96	History as the record . . .	101	_____
106	The purpose of punctuation . . .	62	_____
106	Where there is much . . .	83	_____
112	Try reading your . . .	138	_____
114	There is another . . .	195	_____
120	If we are truly . . .	81	_____
123	Good words are . . .	90	_____
124	Clichés, those . . .	114	_____
132	Is everything . . .	97	_____
132	If the physiologists . . .	102	_____
135	Reading at cruising . . .	125	_____
137	One of the greatest . . .	221	_____

These paragraphs were suggested merely to get you started to read telegraphically. Go on from here on your own initiative. Read your newspaper, your pocket digest in telegraphic fashion. Occasionally stop reading rapidly and take a paragraph or two and see just how far you can reduce these samples while still keeping the meaning. Practice a little each day; you will be amazed at your progress within a very short time.

Develop Your Visual Span

Take your 3- by 5-inch card again, with the arrow midway across the top edge. You have made a good beginning in widening your eye span, but the good reader will practice widening his eye span as the accomplished musician practices his scales—because it keeps him artistically in trim. Keep yourself up to par as a reader. Practice eye-span development as you would practice scales if you were a musician, or punch the bag if you were a boxer, or do any other practice activity which enhances your skill and keeps your technique from becoming rusty.

Here are some exercises such as you had in Chapter Four. Try to inch just a little beyond the record that you were able to set there.

Remember look steadfastly at the mid-point of the line of type at the place where the vertical line crosses the line of type. Don't shift your eyes. Try to push the outside vision edges farther apart.

Think now	9
Concentrate	11
Find key word	13
Words are tools	15
Heed punctuation	17
Reading is thinking	19
Look up word meanings	21
Check achievement often	23
Survey the whole page now	25
Clear thinking aids reading	27
Practice and review every day	29
There is a relationship of fact	31
Each paragraph has a main thought	33
Know how paragraphs are constructed	35

How well did you do? Each time you work at this exercise, record below the maximum span you were able to read. Give your peripheral vision a working out. *Insist* that your eyes see more. Work at this every day for a week.

stretch vision	14
study paragraphs	16
read when you read	18
word power is a help	20
when you read — think	22
work at span development	24
look for directional words	26
analyze the author's purpose	28
why did the author write this?	30
look for the paragraph beginning	32
the best readers always think fast	34
do not let your eyes slide or shift	36

Each time you work at these exercises record in the blanks below the maximum span you were able to read.

Date	*Duration of Practice* *(Minutes)*	*Maximum Span Read*
_____	_____	_____
_____	_____	_____
_____	_____	_____
_____	_____	_____
_____	_____	_____
_____	_____	_____
_____	_____	_____
_____	_____	_____
Average:	_____	_____

Refer to your previous chart of maximum span achievement in Chapter Four. Did you improve on your record there?

Reading for Speed of Comprehension—1

The article which you are about to read is packed with facts. Read to remember as many factual details as possible.

In this age, when we are talking about space platforms, trips to the moon, and interplanetary excursions, the article which you are about to read should prove very interesting and informative. It deals with the first barrier that man must cross—the barrier of atmosphere—and discusses what the trip through that barrier may entail.

Try to visualize the facts as you read them. You will want to try, also, to outdo your previous records of speed of comprehension.

Time yourself accurately. Are you ready to read? If so, jot down the exact time in these blanks: MINUTES _____

SECONDS _____

Now, begin to read.

"THIS MOST EXCELLENT CANOPY, THE AIR" [2]
by Waldemar Kaempffert

By the time World War I had ended and long-distance commercial planes had evolved out of bombers, it was predicted that some day man would rise into the stratosphere and cross the Atlantic between breakfast and luncheon. With the development of rockets the prediction has been fulfilled. Bold engineers write confidently of rocket ships which are to circulate in space among the planets. Meteorologists and physicists are sending up rockets loaded with instruments that automatically record temperatures, atmospheric pressures, moisture, electrical effects. These scientists are the Columbuses, Magellans, and da Gamas of our time. The earth's crust has been explored by adventurous and curious men who have crawled through its jungles and over its deserts, mapped its polar regions, and plumbed its oceans. The air around us is as much a part of the earth as the land and the sea. The circumnavigators of old

[2] Waldemar Kaempffert, *Explorations in Science*, Chap. 7, pp. 102–108, The Viking Press, Inc., New York, 1953.

had their successors in the scientists who are sounding the air to find the answers to questions that have long perplexed men. What lies above the fluffy clouds? How high is the blue sky? Is the air all of one piece? Where does the atmosphere end and interstellar space begin? The air is still something to marvel at, still Hamlet's "most excellent canopy," still his "brave o'erhanging firmament," still his "majestical roof fretted with golden fire."

Well into the last century it was thought that beyond 100 miles there must be a perfect vacuum. Today scientists hold otherwise. If there is no more than an atom of gas in a cubic foot of space they will still talk of an atmosphere. For this reason they will not say where the atmosphere ends. Some maintain that even at 10,000 miles there is air, though less than in the best vacuum that can be created in a laboratory. Other physicists talk of 18,000 miles. There is no outer edge, no sharp line of demarcation from outer space. Even between the stars there are particles of dust and atoms of gas.

Exploration of the atmosphere with unmanned balloons freighted with instruments which wrote down what they saw, felt, and experienced, and with radio waves that were sent up and reflected back to the earth, and inferences drawn from auroras, nacreous clouds, and the way the sound of great guns was reflected from on high during World War I, led to the conclusion that the atmosphere is constructed not of one piece but layers like an onion. Roughly, the layers may be described as follows.

First comes the troposphere or sediment in which we live and which is about five miles thick at the poles and about 10 miles thick at the equator. It is a layer of rapid changes in weather and in turbulence, a layer of storms here and calms there and of polar cold and tropic heat, a layer in which the temperature falls steadily about 1 degree Fahrenheit for every 300 feet until a low of −67 degrees Fahrenheit is reached. Eighty per cent of the air by weight is packed in the troposphere.

Above the troposphere lies the tropopause, a no man's land, a thin layer in which the temperature ceases to fall with increasing altitude.

Next comes the stratosphere, which extends from about 7 miles up to 50. This is a region of steady, gentle winds, occasional nacreous, or mother-of-pearl, clouds, and of steadily rising temperature. The sky is a brownish-black canopy, according to observers who have risen into the lower reaches in balloons and airplanes and according to skylight recorders. In the higher reaches the sun has a fierce, hard metallic glare. The pearly corona is always visible and so are the stars, even by day. The sky seems blue to us because of dust particles which scatter blue and violet rays from the sun. There is not enough dust in the stratosphere to scatter blue and violet rays. At 15 miles there are gleams of nacreous clouds—masses of ice crystals as iridescent as mother-of-pearl. Higher up are the noctilucent clouds—wraiths of dust whirled up from the troposphere, visible from the ground at sunset.

At a height of about 25 miles in the stratosphere begins the ozone layer, which extends to 40 miles, and which has the property of absorbing and holding more heat from the sun than does the air below it. This layer contains a little highly diffused ozone. On this small amount of ozone, life on earth depends for protection against the sun, for the ozone filters out an excess of solar ultraviolet radiation that would otherwise blind and kill. Too much ozone would be just as harmful.

If all ultraviolet light were cut off no vitamin D would be formed, with the result that life would again be impossible. Below the ozone layer, the solar spectrum seems to end abruptly, so that no astrophysicist on the ground can say that with his spectroscope he has ever seen all of the sun in the sense that he has seen all its light.

The ozone layer had to be postulated when it was noted that the sound of heavy gunfire is not audible 20 miles away, or 40 miles away, but booms again at 60 miles' distance. It was concluded that sound waves travel not along the surface of the earth but upward, whereupon they are deflected downward to reach spots far from the explosion. The speed of sound increases with the temperature of the transmitting air. It follows that the sound waves strike a hot roof of air aloft. But how could there be a hot roof high up? An ozone layer, suggested by the English meteorologist Dr. F. S. W. Whipple, met the requirements. Reports from V-2 rockets sent up from White Sands, New Mex., with instruments, leave no doubt that there is an ozone layer in the sky and that it cuts off much ultraviolet radiation. As we leave the ozone layer at 40 miles the temperature drops from an average of 170 degrees Fahrenheit to an average of 0 at about 50 miles, just as physicists expected.

Beyond the ozone layer there must still be a little air. At 45 miles there are signs of twilight, a phenomenon impossible in a vacuum. But what is the composition of the air? Nitrogen assuredly, and oxygen probably. Here agreement ends. For theoretical reasons some physicists hold that light gases, such as hydrogen and helium, ought to float up.

Above the stratosphere, about 60 miles above sea level, lies the lowermost layer of the ionosphere, our fourth onion-skin. Because the air is so very thin here the conditions are much the same as those in neon or argon tubes on Main Street. There are so few gas atoms that they are easily electrified by ultraviolet rays and electrons hurled out by the sun. The rays and electrons tear away outer electrons from the gas atoms. Thus partly stripped, the atoms rush about trying to capture electrons to make good their loss. In this electrically excited condition they are called "ions," meaning "travelers." They are now good conductors of electricity.

There are several layers in the ionosphere, and all serve as reflectors of radio waves. One layer reflects long waves, others reflect shorter waves. Some short radio waves pass straight through. Radio waves are invisible light waves; and like light waves they travel in straight lines. Because of the curvature of the earth we could not see at Atlantic City even the brightest beacon in London. The curvature would prevent us from transmitting and receiving radio messages around the earth, if it were not for the ionosphere. That electrical mirror in the sky reflects waves back to the earth, the earth sends them up again, and so they reach their destination. All this had to be assumed when Marconi first sent radio signals across the Atlantic Ocean. The assumption proved to be correct —another proof of the accuracy of scientific reasoning about the atmosphere.

It takes time for a signal to be sent and for its echo to be received. Radio waves travel with the speed of light—186,000 miles a second. If a signal is sent up into the sky and its echo is heard, a fraction of a second later it is easy enough to calculate where the reflection occurred. This is how the height of the various layers of the ionosphere was determined. So there is no doubt about the location of the layers. But no one knows where the ionosphere ends.

There are four ionized layers, designated by the letters D, E, F_1, and F_2. The height and electrical conductivity of these layers change from day to day, from season to season, from year to year, from place to place. Why? Because of the connection with sunspots. If there are more sunspots—an indication of solar storms, since sunspots are hurricanes of the glowing gas—there are more ultraviolet rays and more electrons to hurl at the earth. And when there are more ultraviolet rays and more electrons the auroras are more resplendent. It then becomes almost impossible to telephone or cable across the ocean. Compasses go wild because of the vagaries of terrestrial magnetism. We have, then, electrical storms on high and corresponding magnetic storms on the earth.

Temperature rises in the ionosphere, until at 80 miles it reaches an average of 212 degrees Fahrenheit, the boiling point of water, and a possible maximum of 638 degrees Fahrenheit. This is the most startling discovery of all. At the end of the last century it was supposed that above 35,000 feet the temperature of the air remained constant at −67 degrees Fahrenheit.

Why should the temperature rise in the ionosphere at a height of 80 miles? Heat manifests itself in molecular motion. At absolute zero molecules theoretically stand still. The higher the temperature the more active they are. When the temperature is very high, molecules fly off, which happens when liquids boil. It follows that something must move in the ionosphere to produce heat as hot as that of a kitchen oven. It is therefore supposed that there are cosmic dust particles in the ionosphere, and that these hold heat. There is some basis for this supposition. Faint reflections have been seen in the ionosphere—reflections of noctilucent clouds, which are believed to be aggregations of dust. No one knows how dust collected at such a height, nor whence it came. But there is no longer any doubt about the high temperature of the ionosphere because of those ghostly noctilucent clouds. If manned rocket ships attain heights of 80 miles and more—even if they never proceed to the moon— their designers will have to reckon with an average heat that can boil water and at its worst can roast a baron of beef. Professor F. A. Paneth, a leading authority on the chemistry of the atmosphere, thinks that in the uppermost reaches of the atmosphere (150 miles) a gaseous mass at 2000 degrees Fahrenheit must be assumed. If he proves to be correct formidable difficulties confront the designers and navigators of rocket ships destined to reach the moon or Mars.

In the ionosphere, earth physics (geophysics) and star physics (astrophysics) meet. For this is the region where meteors glow their brightest and into which the shimmering curtain of the aurora dips. It is a region that belongs to astrophysics because of the meteors and because of the electrons which come from the sun and produce the auroras, and that also belongs to geophysics because when auroras are at their brightest terrestrial magnetism is influenced. One meteorologist has suggested that the pressure of sunlight, which has been measured, acts on what little air there is at extreme altitudes, so that the earth has a tail like a comet. According to this view the high aurora is formed when corpuscles from the sun encounter this tail.

What lies beyond 80 miles and beyond the ionosphere? Diffuse auroras as far out as 620 miles, and meteors. Where auroras shimmer and meteors flash there must still be some air, even though there is not enough of it to carry the sound of a voice and probably less than remains in the best vacuum that can be produced in a laboratory. How far, then, does the atmosphere extend? Perhaps several thousand miles. No one knows. What is 80 miles compared with even 1000? We are much like primitive savages who stand on the shores of an ocean and wonder how far the water stretches beyond the setting sun.

What time is it now? MINUTES _____

SECONDS _____

What is your reading time for this selection? MINUTES _____

SECONDS _____

Now, without referring back to the article, answer the following questions:

Comprehension quiz

The comprehension of this article may be tested in two ways. For that reason the quiz will have two parts to it.

Part One

If you read this article correctly, you should have visualized each step that the author discussed as you read along. Visualization—seeing in your mind's eye what the author is presenting—is always an excellent aid to comprehension. Let's test your visualization of the article.

Draw a cross section of the atmosphere from the data supplied in the article. Include as much information as possible in your sketch. Draw this as if you were drawing an illustration to accompany the article.

After you have finished, compare your sketch with that in the Answer Key. Both sketches should be essentially the same.

Part Two

Each statement has four choices. Choose the one which best completes the statement according to the information given in the article.

1. The first prediction of stratosphere flight was made about
   a 1910.
   b 1920.
   c 1930.
   d 1940.

2. The belief that the atmosphere may extend not much farther than 100 miles was abandoned in the
   a seventeenth century.
   b eighteenth century.
   c nineteenth century.
   d twentieth century.

3. The author's position is that
   a the atmosphere extends upward 18,000 miles.
   b the nacreous and noctilucent clouds are on the outer fringe of the atmosphere.
   c no one knows the extent of the atmosphere.
   d the atmosphere extends to the tropopause.

4. The troposphere
   a has a constant thickness of about five miles.
   b is a low-lying sediment about 300 feet thick.
   c is a calm area beyond the storm-cloud range.
   d varies in thickness for different parts of the earth.

5. The ozone layer is in the
   a stratosphere.
   b ionosphere.
   c tropopause.
   d troposphere.

6. The existence of the ozone layer is
   a a hypothesis.
   b a theory.
   c a certainty.
   d uncertain at present.

7. Beyond the ozone layer we are sure that there is
   a oxygen.
   b helium.
   c hydrogen.
   d nitrogen.

8. The ionosphere begins 60 miles above
   a sea level.
   b the troposphere.
   c the stratosphere.
   d the tropopause.

9. Radio waves are
   a invisible light waves.
   b similar to light waves, but basically different.
   c unlike each other, depending upon wavelength
   d similar in some respects to light waves.

10. Sunspots cause
    a atmospheric storms.
    b changes in the temperature of the ionosphere.
    c changes in the height of the atmosphere.
    d changes in the ionized layers.

How comprehensively did you read? Check your answers against those given in the Answer Key. Each correct answer is worth 10 per cent.

What is your level of comprehension score? _____%

What is your speed of comprehension score? _____wpm

What is your reading index $(R \times C/100)$? _____

Reading for Speed of Comprehension—2

Thousands of words and dozens of articles have been written about the businessman's reading. The tired businessman, lugging home his bulging briefcase containing its load of words, has become the symbol of the modern executive.

Interested in this forlorn figure and his reading problem, *Fortune* magazine decided to "look over the businessman's shoulder and into his bulging briefcase." What *Fortune* saw has been, in part, condensed into the article which you are now about to read.

In this article you may find that the paragraphing is somewhat mis-leading. It may defy certain conventional rules of writing. If it does, so much the better. This very fact will test your ability as a reader.

You should read it, therefore, being on the lookout for main ideas and for facts. In some instances a cluster of paragraphs present but *one* main thought. Try to see those main thoughts as you read. Then be alert to the individual facts as they are presented to support the main ideas. You will need to apply everything that you have learned thus far to read this article well. Look for the *thought* of the author, however, and you should have no trouble.

Time: MINUTES _____

SECONDS _____

THE BUSINESSMAN AND HIS READING[3]

by Duncan Norton-Taylor

"The American executive reads at least five times as much as the ordinary citizen." Most of his reading is what he feels he has to do in connection with his business and it consumes most of his waking hours.

The typical daily pattern of the executive's reading begins with his advance on his office, his nose buried in his morning newspaper, his mind already beginning to recoil from one aspect of the job that lies ahead. Sure enough, he has scarcely landed in his office when a staggering load of printed matter begins to fall upon his desk.

This consists of trade papers, trade bulletins, company and department reports, surveys, technical data, and technical publications. It may include several Washington newsletters, commercial digests, possibly the *Wall Street Journal* or the *Journal of Commerce*, or both. What he can't get through at his desk he will stuff in a briefcase and take home.

Either during the day or on his commuting train or in the evening he will read or skim business magazines and news weeklies. The public-spirited executive will have at least one community enterprise in which he is involved. He may conscientiously try to read a bulletin or two on that.

The executive deserves sympathy, no doubt. But whether the picture of the executive mind, struggling against unconscionable odds, is a heroic picture depends in some measure on the virtue of the struggle. Is everything he tries to read worth it?

Executives themselves admit that it probably isn't. One analyst of management practices says: "Most of this reading is redundant and repetitious. And, furthermore, the executive himself is not selecting it. It is being selected for him by subordinates, other department heads,

[3] Condensed from "Why Don't Businessmen Read Books," by Duncan Norton-Taylor, *Fortune*, vol. 49, May, 1954, p. 115 and *passim*. Copyright 1954, Time, Inc.

so-called experts, secretaries, and colleagues. It includes memo after memo from clucks trying to make a record. It is incredible—the amount of junk that crosses the executive's desk.

Why does he read it all? The best answer is that he suffers from overconscientiousness or apprehension, or both. He feels that he has to "keep up" with everything in the company and the industry. He doesn't know how, or he hasn't the courage, to eliminate and select. And in the end he substitutes reading for thinking.

The ceaseless effort to ingest current facts, then, is the usual pattern of the American executive's reading habits. But it should be immediately pointed out that the stereotype does not cover everything. It does not mean that the American executive, on a trip or a vacation, does not occasionally read what he speaks of as "a good book."

It appears that executives rarely discuss books with each other. In the course of a number of interviews it was common for one executive to say of another: "I didn't know *he* read any books. Thought he read only financial reports."

The infrequency of exchange of literary confidences may be due to a lack of opportunity or just embarrassment. As one executive said: "Reading is not a part of the concept of what a businessman is supposed to be, or to be doing. The concept is of a man pressed by tangible problems that require tangible solutions. The businessman is a man of action. Reading doesn't fit into this concept."

But there are a minority of 20 per cent who could be called book readers. What are some of the books?

The two *Saturday Review of Literature* polls and the *Fortune* poll all showed that the most consistently favored books were those that dealt, either through fiction or through fact, with adventure, physical challenge, and accomplishment. If there was any noticeable recent change in this general pattern, it was an awakening interest in religious books.

It would be reasonable to assume that books dealing with the theories of economics would fix the attention of executives. Apparently they don't. Such books seem to have little more interest for them than books dealing with theories of art, theories of politics, theories of truth, and theories of power.

There may be a good reason for the low readership in books on abstract economics—namely, its forbidding and abstruse nature, which the authors do little to alleviate; their style is generally as repellent as their titles.

The "how-to" books are read extensively by junior executives and other ambitious rising personnel, which indicates certain popular convictions as to what a successful executive *should* be, and may even present a picture of what the senior executive is, since no one is under closer scrutiny by imitators and aspirants to his job.

Several general types of executive readers emerge, then. There is, first, the predominant type, the executive buried under what he considers to be his essential reading—reports, memos, digests, current news— often soothing his overwrought nerves with some overwrought, 25-cent imagery. There are those who once in a while read a "good book," but without enough enthusiasm to lead them into making a habit of it. There are those, say 20 per cent, who earnestly try to keep up with what is current and popular. And finally there are the subexecutives, studying the "how-to" books as reliable road maps to success.

The American executive is not a quiet and contemplative reader. Even momentarily escaping from his job with a book, he is a man of action, a conqueror of heights, a mover and a maker.

He reads with a kind of old wives' inquisitiveness, not with intellectual curiosity. In his reading he is frequently looking for self-justification and encouragement. He is also groping for spiritual inspiration, which suggests an encouraging aspect of his cultural side: he is basically an anxious man.

His literary interests are narrow and he is a self-confessed, not to say determined, non-intellectual. The majority of top executives almost never read drama, great fiction, the philosophers, the poets.

The executive's explanation for not reading books is that he hasn't time for them. But what his comments unwittingly suggest is that the reading he doesn't get around to is merely the reading he doesn't think is necessary to his success.

In *Democracy and Leadership* (a book, incidentally, that executives should read), Professor Irving Babbitt, of Harvard, wrote some twenty years ago: "Leaders, good or bad, there will always be." And democracy, he warned, will be judged, therefore will stand or fall, according to the quality of its leaders. Their leadership will depend, in turn, on the quality of their vision. If the managers of capitalism default, then the game will go to those extremely imaginative visionaries, the demagogues. Without any vision at all—"the people will perish," said Babbitt. "But where there is sham vision, they perish even faster."

The point that true vision can be acquired only through an earnest study of the historians and interpreters of mankind would seem to be so obvious as hardly to need making. But the analysis of what American executives do read, or neglect to read, makes it plain that the point is only honored in the breach.

What time is it now? MINUTES _____

SECONDS _____

What is your reading time for this selection? MINUTES _____

SECONDS _____

Without referring back to the text, test your level of comprehension by answering the following questions:

Comprehension quiz

Part One

Among the following ten sentences, some are statements of main ideas found in the article; others state merely supporting ideas or specific facts. Check only those items which are statements of the main ideas.

1. Executives usually take home the reading which they cannot do at the office.
2. The average executive reads five times as much as the average citizen.
3. Most businessmen read the "better books" without enthusiasm or interest.
4. The "how-to" books indicate what a successful executive should be.
5. Leaders there will always be.
6. The executive usually reads his newspaper on the way to the office.
7. Reading does not seem to fit into the executive concept.
8. The average executive reads much that is useless.
9. Few executives even attempt to keep up with what is current and popular among readers generally.
10. Executive readers are of several types.

Part Two

1. Some management analysts feel that most executive reading is _____

_____ .

2. Executives read probably much more than they would need to read be-

cause, on the whole, they suffer either from _____ or _____

_____, or both.

3. The author of this article feels that too often the average executive substitutes _____ for _____.

4. Only about _____ per cent of executives can be called book readers.

5. Contrary to reasonable assumption, the average executive has very little interest in reading books in the field of theoretical _____.

6. "How-to" books are read largely by the _____ group.

7. The American businessman sees himself largely as a man of _____

_____.

8. The author agrees with Irving Babbitt that to be a leader the American businessman needs _____ most of all.

How well did you comprehend what you have read? Check your answers against those given in the Answer Key. Each correct answer in Part One is worth 10 per cent; each blank filled correctly in Part Two is worth 5 per cent.

What is your level of comprehension?   _____%
What is your speed of comprehension?   _____wpm
What is your reading index $(R \times C/100)$? _____

Reading Habit Index

	Never	Rarely	Sometimes	Usually	Always
1. As I read a paragraph I notice the ways by which the author develops the main idea, i.e., by restatement, by example, or by contrast.					
2. I am now more aware of punctuation as an aid to more effective reading.					

Never Rarely Sometimes Usually Always

3. I try to read key words and phrases, and to dwell on the important words that convey the thought.

4. I have been employing in my thinking, in my writing, and in my speaking the new words that I have recently discovered while reading.

5. I notice references and allusions in reading that make me aware of the value of a broad, general knowledge background.

Reading habit index score: _____

(See directions for scoring, p. 75)

Date: _____

Chapter Eight

What is your
purpose in reading?

YOU DON'T just read. You read for a reason, a purpose, with a particular aim in mind. Probably no type of reading illustrates quite so well
the various purposes for which we read than does the reading of the
newspaper. As you read the paper, your purposes for reading change
almost as rapidly as you move from column to column or page to page.
On the first page, for instance, you read for information. Your purpose
is to find out what is happening in local and world affairs. Your aim is
to get the facts. Then, perhaps, you turn to the editorial page. Basically,
your purpose in reading the editorials is different from that which impelled you to read the front-page news. What you read on the editorial
page will not so much add to your information as it will condition your
thinking. The editor will present some of the implications behind the
news, some interpretations or viewpoints with regard to the front-page
news that will influence your decisions or direct your thinking. On the
editorial page you will read, not to get the facts, but rather to form an
opinion with regard to those facts.

After you have finished with the editorials, you turn elsewhere in
your paper. Your eye catches a special feature article. This article dis-

cusses ways in which school children might construct relief maps from papier-mâché. Your son is in sixth grade, and the other day he was asking you to show him how to make a relief map. For you this article is as timely as tomorrow's headlines, but you will read it differently from either the news stories of the first page or the editorials. This is a "how-to" article. Your purpose for reading it will be to understand a process and to comprehend directions.

After reading the map article you let your eyes wander across the columns to the day's installment of "The Love Affairs of Gay Lucy," a serial that you have been following in daily dribs. Again, your purpose for reading shifts. "Lucy" is an invitation to read for sheer enjoyment, to read to satisfy your curiosity and to find out what happens next to the lovelorn girl.

Thus, for each item that you read, you have a different and specific purpose. And it is your purpose that determines the *way* in which you read.

Probably more than any other single factor, the purpose for which you read determines the rate with which you read. And the experienced reader shifts from one reading rate to another, as well as from one reading skill to another, with the ease that a modern motorcar shifts from one gear to another. Reading conditions and fact congestion are additional factors that influence your rate and choice of technique in reading.

In general, impatience is one of the worst faults among readers—especially the tyro reader. They see a page of print; they pick up an item which must be read in the course of their business or professional reading. Now follows a very interesting behavior pattern. It is the pattern of the less skilled reader. The sight of black print on a white page incites in such a reader an immediate and irrepressible desire—the uncontrollable urge to begin reading. Such a reader takes no forethought, nor does he analyze his aim or purpose in his reading. Here is something that must be read; he merely strains at the leash to get going! Nor does he consider any of the obvious, essential, preliminary matters that always claim the skilled reader's attention before he roars down the highways of print with his reading throttle wide open. The inexpert reader has but one inordinate desire when he sees print: to begin to read. He throws his reading mechanism into gear before his thoughtful faculties get going. Print affects him like that.

Does it affect you like that, too? What thoughts streak through your mind when you come face to face with a page of print? What is your first impulse? Is it merely to begin to read?

Let's carry this analogy just a little further. Suppose a contractor or an engineer were to construct a building by reacting to the site where the building is to stand in the same way that the immature reader reacts to the printed page. Suppose that the contractor merely started to build on that site without plans, design, purpose, or specifications. What kind of structure would he be likely to erect? For the builder such a procedure would be unthinkable. He, or rather the architect before him, carefully defines his *purpose* for building; then he draws his plans and erects the building accordingly. He proceeds methodically and with a definite purpose and aim in view. But with the reader, how different: he artlessly plunges into print without plan or purpose, just the consuming urge to begin to read.

The skillful reader, however, follows in broad outline the same general approach as the engineer. Before he begins, he defines his purpose and aim. It may take him only a split second after he glances at the page of print to do so, but that particular split second is extremely important from the total reading standpoint. In terms of himself as the reader, he sees clearly why he is reading this particular item, and consequently he selects the particular technique of reading best fitted to accomplish that purpose.

But, specifically, what are some of the purposes which may motivate your reading? There are dozens of them. Here are some of the more generally recognized common purposes for which you may read. As you read over this list, try to think of a specific type of reading material which might be paired with each separate purpose. You may read to:

1. Comprehend the main ideas
2. Comprehend the specific facts and details
3. Understand and appreciate the organization of the author's thought
4. Understand broad, basic principles
5. Follow directions
6. Increase your fund of general knowledge
7. Determine whether the author is consistent and logical in his thinking
8. Solve a particular problem
9. Be informed upon what is going on in the world
10. Check or verify certain facts
11. Form an opinion
12. Learn what other people of other ages have said about your problem or about the basic problems of mankind

13. Evaluate and appraise certain material
14. Find out how to do something
15. Determine what the motive of the author was for writing the material you are reading
16. Form a basis for making a decision
17. Appreciate the other fellow's viewpoint
18. Form new interests or hobbies
19. Prepare yourself to substantiate your own position or to argue for or against an issue
20. Amuse yourself or get a good laugh
21. Improve your reading skills and abilities
22. Understand your own self: your physiology, your psychology
23. Develop your personality
24. Understand how to interpret graphic materials: maps, charts, tables, graphs, etc.
25. Locate where to buy it
26. Live in a make-believe world
27. Widen your range of interests
28. Locate a specific, single item of information
29. Check the correctness of another's work
30. Find out about some distant place or strange people
31. Make an intelligent choice or one choice from several alternatives
32. Give other people pleasure or information
33. Satisfy your particular mood or create a mood
34. Enjoy the pure music of language, the magic and fascination of words as words
35. Determine the meaning, the definition of a particular word or term
36. Determine how a word should be pronounced
37. Write a report or make a speech
38. Criticize, summarize, or review
39. Predict an outcome
40. Outline the thought of the author

With these forty major purposes for reading it is readily apparent that the one-purpose, and consequently the one-technique, reader is as handicapped as the one-tool mechanic. A screwdriver may be a very useful tool, but who wants to employ a mechanic who has nothing in his tool kit but a screwdriver? This may seem a ridiculous comparison, but ridiculous as it seems, it is literally true that there are untold legions of people who are trying to solve with only one approach to the page all of the varied reading situations which the whole range of reading presents. These people have never stopped to analyze *why* they are reading the material that is before their eyes. If you interrupted them to ask what was their purpose in reading this, they would look at you with incredible bewilderment. They have never thought about their purpose. Consequently, they have never thought of selecting the tool, that particular skill in reading which best fits that purpose and is best adapted for getting this particular reading job done.

Reading is thinking, and one of the things that every expert reader thinks about is the purpose that lies behind each item that he reads.

To help you define your purpose in reading

Suppose that you walk into a library or a bookshop. The titles there will immediately suggest to you certain specific purposes which you might have for reading each book. You may have several purposes for reading some books, only one purpose for others. Here is a list of titles. After each title, jot down the number or numbers of the various purposes suggested in the list of reasons for reading which have been given in this chapter.

Ageton, A. A., *Jungle Seas*
Alexander, David, *Murder Points a Finger*
Badger, G. M., *Structures and Reactions of the Aromatic Compounds*
Bakken, Henry H., *Theory of Markets and Marketing*
Barke, James, *The Well of the Silent Harp: A Novel of the Life and Loves of Robert Burns*
Bell, Henry, *We Adopted a Daughter*
Bristol, Claude M., *TNT, The Power Within You!*
Bro, M. H., *Indonesia, Land of Challenge*
Buck, Pearl, *My Several Worlds: A Personal Record*
Callahan, P. J. T., *How to Serve on a Jury*
Chase, Stuart, and Marian Tyler, *Power of Words*
Cole, G. D. H., *A History of the Socialist Thought*
Crounse, H. L., *Joyce Jackson's Guide to Dating*
Crowe, John H., *You Can Master Life*
Curti, M. E., *Probing Our Past*
Ford, J. C., *Man Takes a Drink*
Forrester, Gertrude, comp., *Occupational Literature: A Bibliography*
Gruman, Harris, *New Ways to Better Sight*
Hutschnecker, Arnold A., *Love and Hate in Human Nature*
Hyde, Margaret O., *Atoms Today and Tomorrow*
Jackson, Dan, *The Trap*

Jarrell, Randall, *Selected Poems*
Kaufman, J. J., *Collective Bargaining in the Railroad Industry*
Kelsen, Hans, *Communist Theory of Law*
Kennedy, J. F., *Profiles in Courage*
Laubach, Frank C., *Channels of Spiritual Power*
MacIver, R. M., *New Horizons in Creative Thinking*
Pearl, R. M., *How to Know the Minerals and Rocks*
Pincherle, Alberto, *Ghost at Noon*
Reischauer, E. O., *Wanted, An Asian Policy*
Roberts, H. R., *Leadership of Teen-age Groups*
Roget, P. M., *Thesaurus of the English Language*
Sandburg, Carl, *Abraham Lincoln: The Prairie Years*
Townsend, A. H., *Good Reading—A Guide to the World's Best Books*
Van Doren, Carl, *The Life of Benjamin Franklin*
Webster's New Collegiate Dictionary
White, William A., *Mechanisms of Character Formation*
Woodbury, R. M., *Statures and Weights of Children under Six Years of Age*
Yerkes, R. M., *Chimpanzees*
Zweig, S., *Balzac*

Learn to Read Rhythmically, Rapidly, and with Increased Eye Span

The following exercise is designed to help you to read rhythmically and to help you to widen your eye span. The skillful reader darts his eyes across the line in two or three sure, rapid fixations. He grasps an eyeful of print, then skips ahead to snatch another eyeful.

Read this exercise once or twice each day. Be sure you always read for meaning. But each time you read it, try to shorten your total reading time. You will need a watch with a second hand for timing yourself. Jot down the exact second when you begin and the exact second when you finish. Try to take in the whole span with one glance. Look at the midpoint of each group of words.

Discipline your eyes!

The purpose	of this drill	is to discipline
the little muscles	that move the eyes	from left to right.
Incorrect habits	of reading	have frequently caused
these muscles	to behave	in an undisciplined

and inefficient manner. Try to make   your eyes march ahead
in three   rhythmic leaps   across the line.
Try to feel   the tiny tug   on these six
little muscles   that move each eye.   You will note
that some phrases   are short   others are longer.
This is done   intentionally.   The amount
of line width   that various people   can see, differs
with the individual.   In these exercises   try to group
as one eyeful   all the words   in the unit;
look at a point   just about midway   in each word group.
At times   you will feel   as though the field
of your vision   is being stretched.   So much the better!
At other times   the phrase will be   too short.
We shall strive   for wider and wider   units as we proceed.
In that way   your eyes will grasp   more and more
at a glance.   Read this exercise   two or three times
every day   for a few days.   Try always
to cut down   on the time   that it took you
to read it   each preceding time.   You will soon get
the knack of it.   Do not let   your eyes "skid"
or "slide"   when you look   at a phrase.
Look at it   "amidships."   Give it a strong,
fleeting glance.   See it all   in one look;
then be off   to see the next   and the next,
and so on   to the very end   of the exercise.
And now,   how long   did it take you
to read this?   Put your time   in the blank below.

Seconds

 Each time you repeat this exercise, record your time. Try 1. _____
to show a definite record of improvement by shortening the 2. _____
time it takes you to read this. 3. _____

  4. _____
  5. _____
  6. _____
  7. _____
  8. _____
  9. _____
  10. _____
Average time: _____

Reading for Speed of Comprehension—1

The article which you are about to read will give you a glimpse of the role of chemistry in modern living.

Try to understand what the author is saying. Follow his line of thought. He makes a complex subject amazingly easy to understand. You will want to read for a thorough understanding of the article and to get the facts, but you will also want to read as rapidly as possible. You are out to beat your previous record of speed of comprehension.

Time now? MINUTES _____

SECONDS _____

Now, begin to read.

ARCHITECTS OF THE MOLECULE [1]

by James E. Payne

In primitive times, men used nature as they found it. They lived in caves. They ate what nature provided. They wore the ill-smelling pelts of animals for warmth. They changed little or nothing.

But as time passed men found that it was possible to improve natural substances. They shaped stone with stone. They found fire, preserved it, learned to create it and put it to use.

They discovered that the juices of certain plants and herbs could cure their fever; that other juices boiled from the bark of trees had a wonderful effect on animal hides, making them pliant, long-lasting. They found that certain rocks would melt and yield a strange substance that could be made into axes and knives better than chipped stone; that certain grass seeds ground, mixed with water and baked, made food for the cold, hard winter.

Necessity drove them to experiment. To survive, men had to think— and their thoughts were growing bolder. But men were still a hundred thousand years away from the concepts that nature could be torn apart, that air was not merely something to be breathed, that most natural substances were composed of building blocks that could be separated and recombined.

[1] James E. Payne, "Architects of the Molecule," *Steelways*, published by the American Iron and Steel Institute, August, 1953, pp. 1–5.

But time passed, and the concept was formed, and a wonderful thought it was: that the building blocks are atoms, joined in molecules according to nature's laws, yielding the structure of things as they appear to us.

Early chemical experiments isolating oxygen and hydrogen, revealing the omnipresence of carbon in growing things, demonstrating that an everyday substance such as table salt is really a placid union of an active metal and a pungent gas—these experiments destroyed the picture of the world men had known, and revealed an exciting new world to their mind's eye.

In the old "reality" the world had been like a stage setting complete with earth and plants and water and sky; a setting for a play of hardship and privation—never enough food, enough clothing or shelter. Then, suddenly, the chemist began minutely examining the set, uncovering the infinitesimal building blocks that could be shaped and changed in a bewildering variety of ways to provide more and better food, clothing and shelter, as well as a million and one other satisfactions ranging from the conquest of disease to the manufacture of better toys to amuse the young.

For the first time men with this specialized knowledge, these "chemists" who had come of age out of a childhood of alchemy and philosophy, could ask the question "Why?" about the mysteries of the physical world and slowly find the answers. The primitive man had asked "What?" and "Where?" and "When?" Little by little he added "How?" to his questioning as he began to manipulate his environment to improve it. But only when he could ask "Why?" did his mastery begin.

One by one the answers led man to the building blocks themselves: the elements. In laborious experiments he weighed them, studied their power of attraction, learned how they combine. His laboratory tools were growing better, his methods more precise; but his mind was improving most of all. Disciplined by the scientific method, his mind was learning to see the invisible, manipulate the intangible, construct the known out of the yet unknown.

To see some of the workings of his mind, let us look at one of the problems he solved in the recent past. When he first asked himself "Why?" about fibers, the chemist tried to fit all that he knew about fibers into his picture of the molecular world. He knew that a fiber must be long and flexible so that it can be twisted into yarn. He knew that it must be strong, to resist wear and breaking. It should be elastic, to give and stretch with the movements of the body. Why did some fibers possess these characteristics while others did not? Could he build synthetic fibers better than nature's own?

With the test tube, the microscope, his growing shelf of reagents and the exquisite tool of mathematics, he began to feel his way into the mystery. Moving slowly from the unknown into the known, the chemist ferreted out one by one the identity of the elements—the atoms—that made up the molecules of which fibers are composed.

Always, whatever the fiber, he found carbon the universal building block. Hydrogen, oxygen, nitrogen and sometimes sulphur betrayed their presence to his probing tools. In delicate experiments he found that individual fibers could be broken down into hundreds, thousands of molecules; that individual molecules could be broken down into groupings of atoms; that, in a given fiber, these breaks occurred in the same order, with the same end products, *indicating a repetitive pattern of structure.*

Time was passing, but a chemist's world is the molecule where time has little meaning. What does it matter that the "chemist" was a hundred men or a thousand? That the experiments stretched out over twenty years or thirty? According to the chemist's clock the fiber was a fiber in the morning, an unknown molecular structure of known elements at noon, and a known pattern of beautifully linked carbon chains by the time he closed his eyes for sleep at midnight.

For the chemist could not afford to be in a hurry. Even the raw materials for making true synthetic fibers could only be guessed at. As the child crawls before it walks, the chemist first set about improving on natural fibers. He tore down the gross structure of the cellulose in wool and cotton, put the purified cellulose into solution, then spun out the "natural" carbon chains into new fibers that were in many ways better than the old. This was rayon, first of the new wonder fibers that were to be, in one way or in many, better than the best that nature could provide.

By the chemist's clock, the hour hand had scarcely moved before the "Why?" of fibers had to be answered even more fully. Why are some fibers stronger than others? Reaching again into the mystery, he probed for the atoms that link one molecule to the next in the chain. He sought out the weak points and began the search for other atoms or groups of atoms that could replace these weak links and hold with a stronger grip. Then he made a brilliant guess.

What would happen if he built a chain from thousands of molecules, each with atoms at one end which would have a strong affinity for the atoms at the other end?

More seconds ticked away, more hundreds of experiments were completed. The right molecules were found, having the right atoms at each end; the most effective conditions were determined—and the chemist dipped a stirring rod into a pale liquid and drew out something new under the sun: a true synthetic fiber. He found that it would stretch up to a point, then suddenly grow strong and elastic. Soon ways had been found to make it even stronger, to spin it into greater and greater lengths, to twist it into yarn, to weave it into cloth ranging from transparent stockings to heavy silk-like material for parachutes. By the use of chemicals that could be derived in part from coal, oil or corn cobs the chemist had entered into partnership with nature in the creation of fibers.

During this period the question "Why?" was literally reverberating through the laboratories of the world. Not only fibers, but films and plastics emerged first as answers, then as products to satisfy our needs. For the first time men could make synthetic materials in the form of sheets or films for wrapping, protecting, displaying. For the first time they could make plastics that in many ways could rival metal and wood or stone. Films were developed that were so versatile they would permit the passage of moisture, yet block the passage of air. Plastics took their place not only in the form of everyday bowls, bottles and toys, but also in a wide variety of industrial uses ranging from gears and bearings to frames and shells and tubing.

The success of the chemist is due in part to his ability to dissolve certain substances in others. Many solids, for example, dissolve readily in liquids found in nature. Sugar and many salts dissolve readily in water. But what of fats and tars? The alchemist sought a universal solvent; the chemist was wiser and sought only specific solvents for specific solids. Yet, as the complexity of compounds grew, the search for solvents made the problem of the alchemist seem like child's play. With all our chemical knowledge, one of the well known new synthetic fibers was delayed for a considerable period by the search for a satisfactory solvent.

Little by little the mystery of solvents is being cleared away. "Like dissolves like" was the old rule of thumb evolved in a hundred laboratories, but often like did *not* dissolve like, and again the chemist had to ask "Why?" The answer, now partially understood, is shrouded in mathematical symbols, but it is something like this.

Think of a solid substance made up of molecules labeled "A." Think of a liquid made up of molecules labeled "B." All of the "A" molecules attract each other. All of the "B" molecules attract each other. Now drop a lump of "A" into a beakerful of "B."

If the attraction between *either* "A" and "A," or "B" and "B" is *greater* than the attraction between "A" and "B" molecules, the solid will not dissolve in the liquid. But if the attraction between "A" and "B" *is* greater, the "B's" will literally pull the "A's" out of their seemingly solid structure, and surround them. Heat and agitation also help—anything to loosen the hold that the "A" molecules have on each other.

The chemist is still working in the dark in his search for solvents, but his success can be measured in the thousands of chemical processes which, at one stage or another, depend on his ability to dissolve one substance in another. Solvents are essential to the manufacture of drugs and pharmaceuticals. Without solvents we would have no paints, no modern laundries, no synthetic fibers or plastics.

Nearby in the mysterious regions of the chemist's world lies another problem with the same fundamental simplicity, and the same maddening practical complexity. The metals which, on another level, are keys to our civilization, occur usually as ores in which the metal is frequently only a part of a chemical compound or physical mixture of various minerals. To refine the metals it is necessary to separate them from the unwanted substances to which they are physically or chemically bound.

One of the commonly used methods is to crush the ore, grind it to powder, then remove the unwanted parts by literally floating them away —or, in some instances, by floating away the ore. The problem is to achieve *selective* flotation.

At this point the chemist enters the picture. Let's label the wanted particles "A," and the unwanted particles "B," and see how his mind works.

He first discovers that "A" particles have a strong affinity for a particular substance, let's say an oil, but that "B" particles do not attract that oil. When he treats the mixture of "A" and "B" particles with the oil it coats "A" particles in a thin, tenacious film, but does not coat "B" particles.

He then places the treated particles in a vessel containing water, adds a chemical to create froth, bubbles air into the mixture, stirs it violently, and a small miracle happens. The oil-covered "A" particles hook onto the air bubbles as though they were balloonists making an ascension, and the air bubbles carry their passengers to the top of the water where they can be skimmed off. The "B" particles stay down in the water, to be discarded.

Such thoughts as these seem simple, but they have a profound effect on our standard of living. By using such processes we can salvage millions of tons of low grade ores.

The debt of the metallurgist to the chemist is very great. Without chemistry there would be no steel industry as we know it, no aluminum or titanium, no electrolytic tin lines. In the steel industry, alone, the chemist has greatly increased the output and quality of the products of blast furnace and open hearth; he has worked out the high speed techniques for descaling and degreasing steel, developed lacquers and bonding agents for finishes, found ways to process chemical coproducts of the mills. Hardly a phase of steelmaking or fabrication has not benefited from the chemist's inquisitive mind.

But perhaps the greatest contributions the chemist has made to our civilization lie still deeper in the mystery of the molecule and the atom: how the chemist is using his ever increasing knowledge to capture the spectrum of color in dyes, how he has come to the aid of the farmer with better fertilizers, insecticides and weed killers, and how he has recently brought about changes in the soil itself.

What time is it now? MINUTES _____

SECONDS _____

What is your reading time for this selection? MINUTES _____

SECONDS _____

Now, answer the following questions. Do not refer back to the article.

Comprehension quiz

Each of the following statements has four choices. Select the choice which best completes the statement in accordance with what the author says in the article.

1. The building blocks with which chemists work are
   a fibers.
   b molecules.
   c atoms.
   d solvents.

2. According to the author, man's mastery of his environment began when he asked the question
   a what?
   b when?
   c how?
   d why?

3. The building block found in all fibers is
   a sulphur.
   b nitrogen.
   c cellulose.
   d carbon.

4. In any given fiber
   a the chemist always finds oxygen, hydrogen, nitrogen, sulphur.
   b each molecule must be long so that the fibers can be twisted into yarn.
   c the structural pattern is always constant.
   d the structural pattern depends upon the shape of the molecules.

5. The author implies that
   a time is very important to the chemist.
   b chemists frequently develop a new fiber within the span of a working day.
   c chemists frequently have to work overtime to complete their building of carbon chains.
   d in the chemists' world time has little meaning.

6. Chemists have devised plastic films that
   a would prevent moisture from passing through them, yet permit air to pass through.
   b would permit passage of moisture yet prevent the passage of air.
   c permit neither air nor moisture to pass through them.
   d are used as air filters.

7. In part, the quest of the modern chemist is for
   a specific solvents.
   b a universal solvent.
   c a substance that will dissolve in any solvent.
   d a substance that will not dissolve in any solvent.

8. The author says that
   a we have found in the laboratory the answer to the mystery of solvents.
   b solvents are no mystery: the rule is, "like simply dissolves like."
   c solvents are not fully understood.
   d solvents are always liquids.

9. Solution depends upon
   a like molecules having a greater attraction for each other than for anything else.
   b unlike molecules having a greater attraction for each other than each has for his own kind.
   c the breaking down of molecules by heat and agitation.
   d having sufficient liquid so that the solid molecules have room to dissolve.

10. Selective flotation is a method used in
   a creating strong fibers.
   b refining metals.
   c removing already dissolved substances from the solution.
   d the manufacture of plastics.

How well did you comprehend what you have read? Check your answers with those given in the Answer Key. Each correct answer is worth 10 per cent.

What is your level of comprehension?   _____%

What is your speed of comprehension?   _____wpm

What is your reading index $(R \times C/100)$? _____

Reading for Speed of Comprehension—2

Many of us have forgotten Robert Louis Stevenson's lines:
   Politeness is to do and say
   The kindest things in the kindest way.
But the application of the idea in business and in personal relationships sometimes brings big dividends. A little thoughtfulness invested in the common words of everyday speech may have effects that stretch beyond the imagination.
   In the article you are about to read, a psychologist discusses the wis-

dom and value of thoughtfully chosen words. The article is easy to read. Read it for its wisdom and for its information.

Time: MINUTES _____

    SECONDS _____

TASTE THAT WORD! [2]

by Donald A. Laird

Long ago and in all innocence Bernard M. Baruch made an unwise choice of a single word. Its cost to him was a possible partnership with J. P. Morgan, to the great financier millions of possible profit. Discussing a deal he had proposed to the banker, young Baruch deprecated the risk involved by saying that Morgan had taken bigger gambles. Detesting the common gambler, Morgan took icy umbrage at the unmeant implication and dismissed both caller and deal.

A fluent and literate person, as the world today well knows, Bernard Baruch might easily have said, had he first "tasted" the resented word for possible unpleasant connotations, "You have faced greater risks, Mr. Morgan."

Do you "taste" your words on your mental tongue before you speak them, and savor them to see if they'll sound sweet or bitter to the hearer?

Words too hastily chosen may build walls beyond scaling between people, make enemies of friends. Lord Chesterfield, master of the *mot juste,* wrote his son: "For 40 years I have never spoken one single word without giving at least one moment's time to consider whether it was a good one or a bad one." Chesterfield well knew the worth of testing words against one's "inner ear."

Dr. Hulsey Cason, the psychologist, analyzing the sources of irritation in hundreds of individuals, learned that nothing annoys people quite as much as people, and that we are most irksome to others through our conversational ineptitudes.

Apparently the most costly of all physical handicaps is a careless or an ignorant or unbridled tongue.

Does a limited vocabulary excuse our conversational blunders? By no

[2] Condensed from Donald A. Laird, "Taste That Word," *The Rotarian,* January, 1954, pp. 15, 52.

means. Experts in Basic English maintain that we need command only about 1,000 words to make whatever we have to say understandable.

Yet, if you are a typical American, your vocabulary totals about 12,000 words. If you have spent two years in college, your speaking vocabulary should contain another 2,000 words. A wizard with words, such as Woodrow Wilson was, may fluently use as many as 110,000 of the 600,000 words to be found in the unabridged dictionaries.

We understand far more words than we use, too. The average person can grasp the meaning of four times the number of words in his speaking vocabulary. This lopsided ability with words makes us far better listeners than talkers, better at taking in than at giving out, which explains why we can so easily and often get in trouble if we fail to "taste" our words before we speak them.

Whether our vocabularies be great or small, only a minor proportion of the words we know are irritating in themselves, even if we speak in a friendly and pleasant manner. But the few really grating words or phrases that exist, especially if used in a hostile, critical, or domineering way, can lead to social or business suicide.

Yet even derogatory terms may be given a flattering connotation in the right circumstances. When old friends meet, one may exclaim, "Why, Frank, you old baboon!" and win a delighted grin from Frank. But unless you know Frank intimately don't try calling him a baboon; his reaction might be in keeping with the violent nature that makes a baboon one of the most dangerous of beasts.

The mother who calls her baby a "little monkey" is saying that it is the most adorable of infants. You, however, may apply the same term to the child only at the risk of her undying dislike.

Owen Wister in *The Virginian* capsuled the technique of making the normally resented term palatable in the phrase, "When you call me that, *smile!*" But the safest of conversational techniques is to avoid all words or terms or phrases that can only be redeemed by close friendship or a disarming smile.

It is safer to be consistently kindly in your conversation than to risk misunderstanding for the sake of being thought a wit. And the first step toward increasing your conversational skill is *decreasing* your vocabulary. Weed out the words and phrases, discard the speech mannerisms that are likely to stir avoidance reactions in a great many people.

Use fewer words, with better judgment of their possible effect on others. Play safe with phrases that build bridges rather than walls between people.

What time is it now? MINUTES _____

SECONDS _____

How long did it take you to read this selection?   MINUTES _____

SECONDS _____

Now, test your comprehension of what you have read by answering the following questions. Do not refer back to the article.

Comprehension quiz

Fill in the blanks with the appropriate words:

1. Dr. Cason found that nothing annoyed people quite so much as _____

   _____.

2. The most costly of all physical handicaps is a careless _____.

3. Basic English experts maintain that we need only about _____ words to express what we have to say.

4. The vocabulary of the typical American totals about _____ words.

5. We _____ far more words than we _____.

6. Only a very few words are _____ in themselves.

7. Owen Wister suggested a _____ may make an otherwise resented term more palatable.

8. The first step in increasing your conversational skill is to _____ your vocabulary.

9. The author advises using better _____ with the words that we do use.

How well did you comprehend what you have read? Check your answers against those given in the Answer Key. Each correct answer is worth 10 per cent.

What is your level of comprehension? _____%

What is your speed of comprehension? _____wpm

What is your reading index $(R \times C/100)$? _____

Reading Habit Index

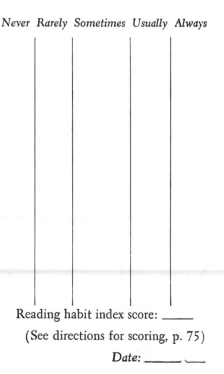

Never Rarely Sometimes Usually Always

1. In my own mind I have a well-defined purpose in reading any particular item.
2. I vary my reading rate and reading techniques according to the purpose for which I am reading.
3. If I meet an unfamiliar word in reading, I try to derive its meaning from the context. Failing that, I look it up in a dictionary.
4. I visualize when I read, i.e., I form mental pictures or concepts in an attempt to understand the thought clearly.
5. I try to find the main idea in paragraphs as I read them.

Reading habit index score: _____

(See directions for scoring, p. 75)

Date: _____ ____

Chapter Nine

Skimming–
key to rapid reading

Contrary to the popular notion, skimming is not just glancing down the page. Instead, skimming is a well-defined reading skill: a highly selective process of looking at a page so that the reader is able to grasp quickly that for which he seeks. Skimming is of two types:

1. In skimming *for the main idea*, the reader largely neglects details, concentrating on the main ideas. He is interested only in the principal points, the high lights of the thought which the writer is attempting to convey. And he knows that a piece of writing is more easily comprehended if the reader skims it first.
2. In the second type of skimming, the reader looks for a particular fact, a single item, a given detail. Such skimming is skimming *for details*.

But in any event, the topflight reader does not rely upon mere chance. He knows where to look to find quickly, and with the least margin of error, exactly what he wants. It is this knowing *how* and *where* to look that distinguishes the first-class reader from the dawdler. The eyes of the expert reader move down the page with swift, unerring skill. And as soon as they alight upon a paragraph, they strike at the heart of that paragraph—at the object of their search—with the deadly aim of a cobra. It

178

may be that the reader is trying to see as many main ideas as he can in the briefest space of time. If such is the case, he keeps himself free from the underbrush of trivia and detail so that he may concentrate more effectively upon the main line of the author's thought.

Skimming: step by step

Skimming is not a mere hit-or-miss procedure; it is a well-defined skill of reading. Because of its supreme importance in efficient reading, this technique should be carefully "spelled out" step by step. That is what this chapter proposes to do.

The skimming technique has essentially two principal phases:

1. The surveying, or inspecting of the material to be read: just simply knowing *what* to look for and looking for it on the page before you
2. The actual reading to discover the sequence of the main thoughts and the way in which these are structured into the whole

A mistaken impression exists among many readers with regard to skimming. They seem to feel that it is always an end in itself; that "speed" in reading means merely skimming the surface. You must be very careful not to get the wrong idea with reference to skimming.

Skimming is merely a tool for the reader. Like any tool it is to be employed when it is needed to accomplish a certain result. And the expert reader employs it frequently, but always purposefully. He realizes that, like any tool, skimming is a method of extracting ideas from the pages of print; it is a means to an end. Depending upon his purpose, the expert reader will decide how he will use the skimming technique.

Skimming *may* be an end in itself, or it may be only the first step in a chain reaction which will blast the reading structure wide apart so that the meaning will fall out more readily. It is frequently used to "soften up" the chapter or the article preparatory to the digesting of it more completely for facts or details. It is usually wise to skim any article first. Get over the entire article. See the parts in relation to the whole. Use the skimming technique as a means of sifting out that to which you need to give only cursory attention and that which you may wish to consider at greater length and with more care. Used intelligently, the technique of skimming is one of the most useful tools for "cracking" the printed page. But whatever else it may be, it is not a haphazard method, to be employed at random and without purpose. Neither is it a cure-all for every reading situation nor a royal road to speed alone.

On the other hand, skimming *is* the master key to rapid and efficient reading. It is the first step toward laying hold in the most complete, orderly and systematic manner of the thought that is cloistered within the printed word.

Skimming implies a psychological attitude toward the material to be read. The reader must try to see whatever he is reading as an entity—a whole in relation to its various parts. It means surveying, inspecting topographical features, and noting typographical aids. Certain mathematical problems can be solved by inspection. This means simply that the mathematician looks at the problem until the structure and the relationship of the parts is apparent. Many reading situations can be solved the same way. But most readers never look before they leap! Their first impulse is to dive headlong into the text; they are impelled by an uncontrollable desire, the moment their eyes behold a page of print, to do nothing else but begin to read. And begin they do, with the first sentence of the first paragraph, nibbling away at each succeeding sentence, looking neither to the right nor to the left, but continuing unto the end, like the little mouse who thought he would eat his way through the cheese—and became lost in doing it. Some readers also, because of the same approach, get into trouble.

"Eyes they have, but they do not see," is a saying that may well apply to most readers. On every page the author, the editor, and the printer have cooperated to make the task of the reader easier. Each page of print has behind it a long history of effort, thought, and careful preparation. A book is a miracle of planning and thoughtful purpose for one reason only, that it may be the more easily read. Yet, readers, as a general rule, bypass the efforts of the writer, the editor, and the printer; and rare, indeed, is the reader who makes *full* use of all the aids that lie patent and manifest before his eyes.

Look!

Have you ever noticed a surveyor at work? He is interested in only a few items, but they are the key considerations to the further use of the land. He wants to know the length of the land and the width of it. He spots out significant points and locates the marks that define the tract as a whole. The surveyor is not interested in detail: a square foot here or a certain spot there. His view is broader and his purpose more general. But his work is basic. Further use of the tract depends upon the survey.

Surveying reading material is akin to surveying the land. The surveyor in either case gets much of his information by sheer observation. But it is most important that the surveyor knows *what* to look for and *how* to look for it. Accordingly, when your eyes alight upon any piece of reading matter, you should be consciously looking for certain specific things:

1. *Look at the Whole Page First!* See it objectively. This means that you must get away from it that you may see it whole. Now, in speaking of getting away from the page, we are referring basically to a psychological detachment rather than a physical act. Until you get the habit, however, of *psychologically* viewing the whole page, try a simple aid that may help you. As a first act of skimming, hold for a moment at arm's length whatever you intend to read. Look at it. Notice that it looks somewhat different to you from out there. You see the high lights of the page that you would otherwise overlook at closer range. The typographical features stand out: title, by-line, subdivisions, section headings, paragraphing, italics, bold face, and other features of the page are there, clearly seen from your more detached point of view. The author and the editor placed all these visual aids there to expedite your reading. At arm's length you will see them—clearly and unmistakably. Soon you will not need to push the page away; you will see all these features in a split second at the normal reading distance, but at the moment your greatest need is to do one thing: to form a new reading habit—the habit of seeing the whole page first. Certainly you would not read at that distance. But you are not reading at this moment. You, like the surveyor, are merely looking.

2. *Look at the Title.* Think of its implications. Focus your attention upon the most important word in the title. Looking at titles correctly is a skill in itself. The author puts a title at the head of what you read to tell you at a glance what the entire piece is all about. Here in a few words he sketches for you the whole domain of your reading.

In looking at the title, isolate the *one thing* about which the author is writing. By means of the title determine the focal point of the author's thinking. This will be the axis of your reading: the point around which all your thinking will revolve as you read.

For example, an article appeared entitled, "The Facts about IQ

Tests." [1] Now where is the "focal point" in this title? Many readers looking at this title would proceed to read the article on the nebulous assumption that the author was writing "something" about intelligence tests. And that is true, so far as it goes. The trouble lies in the fact that such an assumption does not go far enough. The person who begins to read with no better mental focus than this did not look at the title with the discrimination that characterizes a master reader.

While the article deals with the generic area of IQ tests, that area is so vast that a library of books might be written on the various phases of it. This article is not about IQ tests indiscriminately. This article is about one matter only: *facts*—those particular facts relating to IQ tests which the author has selected for you, the reader. When you read the article, then, there is one thing that you are expecting the author to present—fact, fact, fact!

And that is precisely what the author does present. The opening section of the article deals with the facts incident to the growing use of intelligence tests. He then gives the factual background relating to the manner in which IQ tests were originated and developed, and finally the author presents factual answers to eight questions generally asked about IQ tests.

Let's take a book instead of an article. Here is one titled *Responsibilities of Business Leadership*.[2] What is the author going to discuss in this book—business leadership? That is not what the title indicates. The title indicates that the book will be principally about one thing, responsibilities. Look at the Table of Contents; it confirms the focal point of emphasis as proclaimed by the title: the chapter headings are "Businessmen's Responsibilities to the Public," "Businessmen's Responsibilities to Employees," "Businessmen's Responsibilities to Government," and the book goes on to tell of businessmen's *responsibilities* to consumers, stockholders, and the world at large, so that when you read this book, you will be reading basically about one phase of business leadership—its responsibilities.

It is as important for the reader to find the focal point of emphasis in the title of what he is going to read as it is for the physicist to find the focal point of light in the lens he proposes to use. Learn to look at

---

[1] Bruce Bliven, "The Facts about IQ Tests," condensed in *The Reader's Digest*, Vol. 64, No. 385, May, 1954, pp. 126–130.

[2] Harwood F. Merrill, ed., *The Responsibilities of Business Leadership*, Harvard University Press, Cambridge, Mass., 1948.

the title before you begin to read. Say to yourself, "What *one* dominant emphasis is the author likely to stress in this generic area about which he is writing?" You must not be too naive to realize, however, that some authors use titles merely as red flags to attract your attention. When you become skilled in looking at titles, you will become skilled in recognizing a fake when you see one. The principal reason for looking at a title with the discrimination of an experienced reader is to orient yourself, to discover the thought axis, that pivotal point of emphasis around which the whole piece of reading is likely to revolve.

3. *Look for Subdivisions.* Frequently the author, the editor, and the printer have helped you to see the skeleton of the thought by subdividing the text, inserting subdivision headings and section titles. In such cases a mere flipping of the pages with the index finger will frequently give you the bird's-eye view that you need in order to appreciate the thought structure of the article.

Here, for example, is a chapter from a book on habit formation. The chapter is entitled "Habits That Bring You Success . . . Failure." [3]

All right, let's start cold. Let us assume that you have never seen the book from which this chapter is cited. Suppose that you were asked to take your pencil and your note pad and to jot down what you *think* might be in that chapter. You would suddenly have a sinking feeling that you were simply "at sea" so far as the content of that chapter, which you had never seen, was concerned. There are so many things that the authors might say, so many lines of thought that they could develop, that the very prospect of trying to guess what the authors did say is bewildering and confusing.

Actually, however, if you were reading this book, there would be no need for you to be so hopelessly adrift without a sense of thought content and direction of its trend. The authors have given you the thought content in their subtitles. Let me flip through the book for you from p. 11 to p. 87, and here is what we find:

Attitudes toward Work

> Do you like your work?
> Find the work you want
> Or change your attitude toward the work you have

---

[3] From *Make Your Habits Work for You*, copyright, 1952, by Adele de Leeuw and Cateau de Leeuw; Farrar, Straus and Cudahy, Inc., pp. 11–87.

Or find an interest in the work you have
Make your work a challenge
How do you feel about responsibility?
How do you feel about your superiors?
How do you feel about your subordinates?

Chart I
   How to analyze yourself
   How to improve yourself

Approach to Work
   Do you work too long? Or too hard?
   Do you work enough?
   Conservation of energy
   Make the most of the abilities you have
   How do you handle your good and bad points?
   How about human interest and human relations in your **work?**
   What is your working temperament?

Chart II
   How to analyze yourself
   How to improve yourself

Methods of Work
   Make your habits work for you
   Concentration
   Rhythm of work
   The open mind

Chart III
   How to analyze yourself
   How to improve yourself

Thus, by simply thumbing through the book, you are able to construct fairly well just about what the authors will say in those 76 pages. The organization of the thought is very simple. There are three main areas of the authors' thinking: (1) attitudes toward work, (2) approach to work, and (3) methods of work. At the end of each of these principal divisions, the authors give an analysis-improvement chart that centers about the discussion of that particular topic.

One of your greatest aids in reading, therefore, is an index finger, properly used. It helps you to get an over-all picture of the organization of the material in a way that nothing else can. The sight of the first subdivision, or section head, should be a clue to the alert reader that the index-finger technique is in order. Flip over the pages until you come to the next subtopic, and the next, and the next. By means of the index finger, you can look down on the broad outlines of the work as you can do in no other way. Use it!

4. *Look for Graphic Aids.* Reading matter is illustrated with all manner of graphic helps of one sort or another. They are placed there for only one reason: to make the reading of the page easier for *you*. Pictures are sometimes literally worth a thousand words, but even though they are plainly before the reader's eyes, most people have to *look* for these graphic helps or they will never see them.

Notice the abundance of graphic helps of one sort or another that fill the pages of the material that you read. The best of readers gather from pictures, maps, graphs, drawings, or diagrams a wealth of material in a single glance—and often without reading a single word. Look! That's frequently all you need to do. In each graphic portrayal information of some sort is being spread before your eyes. Sometimes the graphic aid tells the whole story which the accompanying words merely repeat; sometimes these aids are merely supplementary to the text and help the reader to visualize the situation more clearly. But whatever their purpose, a mere glance at the visual aids in connection with a cursory inspection of the text may give you much advance information on the ideas and thought areas that lie within the text.

5. *Look at the Paragraphs.* Just look at them: their size. Are they big blocks of print—or small? These are the cells of thought within the body of the text. To the reader these thought cells of print are as important as are tissue cells to the histologist. Each of these paragraph units represents a basic structure. Each, according to its form, will determine what the characteristics of the corporate whole will be. The reader who really knows *what* to look for on the printed page will immediately be aware of the type of paragraph which the page presents. Why is this so? It is so, because from the mere shape and observational structure of the paragraph the reader will be able to tell how the thought will behave. The paragraph is a thought unit; it is, therefore, one of the most important elements for the reader to observe closely. Several chapters have been devoted to the technique of reading paragraphs. But for the purpose of the discussion in this chapter it is sufficient to recall that if the paragraphs are long and apparently well developed, one might expect that the author will present a main thought and then will expand and elaborate upon it, turning it over and exploring all of its phases and

implications; or he will show the reader by example, parallel statements, and contrast what that thought means in terms of its several manifestations. Shorter, more numerous paragraphs indicate, on the other hand, that the reader may expect the author to toss out ideas less fully blown and certainly not so well developed in terms of showing the fullest implications of the central idea. The very shape of the paragraph upon the page will tell you much: large and bulky, the thought looms large in all its rounded fullness; squat and skimpy, the thought is slender, skimpy, meager, thin. Size up the paragraph, and you'll know how the author will spread his thoughts upon the page.

6. *Look for the Arrangement of Facts within the Paragraphs.* Look—see if you can determine how the author is presenting his ideas within the paragraphs. Is he thinking chronologically, statistically, or logically? Do the facts meet your eye under a neat "first, second, third" arrangement; are there dates, or facts and figures? Is the prose informal and rambling or closely knit and forbiddingly formal? These are important matters to observe when you take a split second to glance at a paragraph.

7. *Look for a Broad, Basic Plan.* Try to discern the thought areas. In the factual article, paragraphs cluster together to form topical "islands," which develop one phase, or area, of the topic; then, the author will leave that and proceed in a following cluster of paragraphs to discuss another phase, and so he moves through his discussion by dealing with various areas of it. Try to discover what the area is which the author is discussing, and how many such areas there are in the article as a whole. It is possible to learn to do this very adeptly if you practice looking for the structuralization of the whole article. As you survey the article, preliminary to reading it, keep asking yourself two questions as you face each page:

1. What is the author talking about on *this* page; i.e., with what particular phase, part, or portion of the general subject is the author now dealing?
2. Is this the same subject that he was discussing, or the same area of the subject that he was discussing, on the previous page? These questions will tend to direct your thinking, and they will tend also to emphasize the shift from one thought area to another.

8. *Look for the Author's Purpose in Writing What You Are Reading.* Why did the author write this? This is a question, the answer to which

you should be seeking as you survey the material prior to reading it. The author will betray his purpose in many ways: the tone of his writing, the style he uses, the vocabulary he employs, the order in which he presents his thoughts. All these are clues to the author's purpose in writing what you propose to read. One point is important to remember: authors do not just write. They always have a reason for writing what you read. It may be simply to inform, or to share with you an experience which the author had; it may be to argue a point, to persuade you to adopt a certain course of action, to give directions, or simply to entertain. Whatever the purpose, the author had one. Of that you may be sure. You will be able to read more intelligently if you can define the author's purpose and keep this purpose in mind as you read.

9. *Define Your Own Purpose in Reading.* What are *your* reasons for reading this? When you have answered that question, you will have determined the matter which will dictate the rate at which you will want to read this article. How fast or how thoroughly you read depends largely upon what you wish to have as the end result of your reading. Upon inspection, if this is an article of which you should have a general idea as to its main points and content, so that by reading it you will be able to discuss its subject matter in general over the luncheon table, then a rapid speed rate will be the one that you will use.

On the other hand, if complete absorption is your aim, if you wish to know thoroughly what the article contains, then you will proceed more slowly and carefully. When you absorb the total power of the material you are reading, you must compensate for this added power by slower pace. One does not read Kant's *On Pure Reason* as he reads James Thurber. Everything depends upon your purpose in reading; define that and these other factors resolve themselves. And your purpose will be apparent after you have looked at the article, but before you begin to read.

10. *Look at Your Watch.* Consider the piece you are going to read; decide upon the end result you want from your reading; estimate roughly the number of words, or figure how long it will take you to read a page, and note how many pages there are. Set a pace for yourself. Have a reading deadline, and try to beat it. If you have looked at the preceding nine items in this list carefully you should know a great deal about the piece of writing you are going to read. When a motorist starts out for a trip, he estimates roughly how long it will take him. Readers should do the

same before they begin to read. Only by so doing will you increase your speed and improve your comprehension.

How long should it take you to survey the material and look at the ten preceding items? Not more than 30 seconds. Every piece of writing is the better read for its having been surveyed first. Always include the time for surveying the piece in the time it takes you to read an article. Thirty seconds spent in getting your feet on the ground with reference to the material you are going to read is a wise investment of time. In these seconds you are providing yourself with potential reading horse-power that will give you the superperformance necessary to drive you smoothly, quickly, and surely through the remainder of the time you spend upon the material you are reading. The survey time is well spent; do not underestimate the importance of it.

After the survey, of course, you are ready to read.

Read!

Up to this time you have been merely looking. Certain facts were self-evident. These you looked for. What was not so apparent was the sequence of the author's thoughts. To get this you need to read. In the skimming technique you are interested in only the principal points which the author is presenting, as these march along, orderly and sequentially, in long columns of dignified print.

The reader should think of himself as a kind of reviewer upon a parade-stand, before whose eyes the ranks of facts go filing by. In skimming you want to see the whole parade, every paragraph contingent of it, and you want to see at a glance what these contingents are.

Thus, as an observer, you are interested in the groups of facts which comprise the paragraph. And in each paragraph you are looking for the leader of the facts—the main idea.

Where will you find it?

For the most part the leading thought in each paragraph is clearly expressed and obviously apparent. It is contained in the sentence that is known as the topic, or leading, sentence. It is only occasionally that you will encounter a paragraph without a leading sentence. In such cases you will need to coin one as you read.

For the moment, however, we will disregard the unexpressed-topic-sentence paragraph. This has been considered in Chapter Four. Furthermore, this is a not-too-frequently-encountered type of structure, and for that reason failure to consider it here will not materially affect your learning of the skimming technique.

There remains, then, the type of paragraph which has a topic sentence contained somewhere within it. But where?

From this point on we will proceed in our discussion upon generalizations based upon mathematical chance and upon the facts of human psychology. Our writing reflects our thinking. Most of us think according to a pattern similar to this: We get an idea; we state it; we explain or elaborate upon it, and sometimes we restate the idea again in a kind of final summary after we have finished presenting all the details. Listen to random conversation. Note whether the persons talking do not usually utter a statement and then proceed to explain that statement or to tell the implications that arise from it. Writers follow essentially the same pattern. This means that human psychology simply casts most of our paragraphs into a main-idea-and-supporting-details type of verbal structure.

Sometimes, however, you will find a person who thinks in terms of particulars. The details come first. He spreads them out in fine array. Fact, by fact, by fact he communicates his thought, and then he brings all these details together in a final master statement. Such a mind puts the punch line last.

There are very few minds who put it in the middle. This is not a popular style, because it is not the way most of us think.

Formula for skimming

Now, from all these facts, let us build a rule-of-thumb formula for skimming. You are the reviewer of the paragraph parade. You are interested only in the flow of thought that will represent the onward, relentless march of ideas in the piece. Up to this time you have seen the parade in perspective, and you have looked at it from ten separate vantage points. Now you are ready to see the ideas go by at closer range. Where will you find them? Combine mathematical chance and human psychology, and the following procedure is a generally safe one to follow:

Trial Procedure 1
Read only the first sentence of each paragraph straight through the article. When you come to a place where there seems to be a missing link in the thought continuity, try Procedure 2.

Trial Procedure 2

When a break does occur, frequently the sentence that does not seem to fit into the thought parade contains a word that refers back to something stated previously upon which your out-of-step sentence depends. The most common of these reference words are "this," "that," "these," or "those." When you see these verbal fingers pointing backward over the ground that has already been covered, return immediately to the paragraph that precedes the one in which the out-of-step sentence appears and read the final sentence of that previous paragraph. You will usually find there the missing link of thought that will bridge the gap and give meaning to the sentence that was obscure at first reading.

Trial Procedure 3

If still there is no continuity of thought, then search the paragraph for a *medial* placement of the topic sentence; or,

Trial Procedure 4

If you still find that the thought parade has come to a halt, suspect that here you are dealing with a paragraph *without* a topic sentence; and from a rapid inspection of its details, you must coin a topic statement, a leading sentence, to get the thoughts on the page marching through your mind again.

From experience you will find that Steps 3 and 4 are seldom used, but they are important to keep in mind, in case the first two suggestions fail to bring results.

But no rule of thumb, no formula, no packaged directions can take the place of the experience that comes with practice. As you skim, you will learn to skim. The skilled reader, like the champion swimmer, learns much from practice. Do not expect that you will read this chapter and become, thereby, a master skimmer. That is as foolhardy as expecting that by reading a book on swimming you will be able to swim the Channel.

In skimming concentrate always on one thing: the onward, steady march of thought. Skimming is a surface coverage of the material to be read, but its purpose is to connect the principal thoughts of the author into a progressive unbroken chain of thought.

It is like a bird skimming the surface of a lake. Watch him as he swoops across it, dipping into it only at those points where he is rewarded for his effort by a morsel of food. So it is in skimming, you touch the page of print only at those points where you will be rewarded to the greatest degree for your effort. But the bird knows *where* to look for the mosquito and the gnat. The reader will do well to imitate the bird. Learn *where* to look in the rank and file of paragraphs for the leading thoughts. Practice will do more than anything else to help you.

When you pick up a page of print, apply the ten "look" procedures immediately. Follow these with as many of the "read" procedures as you need to use to forge the chain of thought.

How Quickly and Accurately Can You See?

One of the important skills of reading is the ability to see quickly a specific item of information among a context of similar information. This is a skill in reading that can be developed to a high degree of efficiency. You use it when you refer to a dictionary, when you consult an encyclopedia, or any reference work or compilation, to find or confirm a particular fact.

The skill of locating specific information quickly and accurately can help you in many, many ways. In the exercise you are about to do, you will be given a phrase of two words. You will also be given a designated page on which that phrase appears. Look at the phrase *only once*. Train yourself to look at data, information, references only once. Look at the number of the page where the phrase is found *only once*. Then, as rapidly as possible, turn to the page, let your eye scan it, looking for the specific phrase. As soon as you locate it, write down the word *before*, and the word *following* the phrase. You will time yourself. Here is an example:

Phrase	Page	Word before	Word after
up quite	121	conjures	different

When you are ready to begin, write down the time: MINUTES _____

SECONDS _____

Phrase	Page	Word before	Word after
infinitely more	70	_____	_____
too short	70	_____	_____
then you	70	_____	_____
who wish	71	_____	_____
through factories	71	_____	_____
very well	71	_____	_____
do anything	71	_____	_____

Phrase	Page	Word before	Word after
skill and	71	_____	____ _____
almost sinful	72	_____	_____
find men	72	_____	_____

What time is it now?   MINUTES _____

SECONDS _____

How long did it take you?   MINUTES _____

SECONDS _____

Application of the techniques of skimming

In the foregoing pages you have been told exactly how to proceed in skimming an article. It is very important at this point that you know precisely what to do, so that if you need to review any of the material in the discussion, do it now. Be sure you understand thoroughly the procedure under both the "Look" and the "Read" sections. After you begin the following test of your ability to skim, do not refer back to any part of the discussion.

Now here is what you do:

1. Take no longer than 45 seconds to survey the article that follows. Put into practice as many of the suggestions as you possibly can, which were outlined in the part of the discussion dealing with the survey of the article. So that you may give the article your undivided attention, it may be better to have another person time you for this part of the test. Instruct him to allow you exactly 45 seconds from the time you begin surveying the article until he stops you. After 45 seconds, stop and turn to Part One of the comprehension quiz.

2. After you have taken as much time as you need to answer the questions in Part One (you do *not* time yourself while answering the questions), turn back immediately to the beginning of the article and skim it again, this time trying to get only the main idea of each paragraph with whatever additional facts you may be able to see. *Begin timing yourself as soon as you begin to read this the second time* and time the interval during which you are reading to find the main ideas. Enter the time immediately where told to do so. Then follow directions.

You will first apply the survey techniques (for 45 seconds). Are you ready? Time: MINUTES _____

SECONDS _____

HOW TO GET AN IDEA ACROSS [4]

by Robert P. Cort

The Problem

Getting ideas across is the paramount problem of a host of people—of the executive writing memos or leading a conference, of the supervisor giving orders, of the job trainer, the salesman, the advertiser, the educator, the lawyer, the reporter, etc. In fact, anybody who must rely on the written or spoken word to achieve results is effective only to the extent that his ideas enter, influence, and stick in the mind of the recipient or learner.

This is far from being the simple process that many people suppose it to be. The average human mind resists change, resists new habits, new ideas. Usually, it will accept novelty only when it is utterly convinced. The status quo is quite comfortable, thank you, so go peddle your ideas somewhere else!

The problem is often complicated by the fact that, while the idea-sender understands perfectly what he is trying to get across, he is so wrapped up in, so sold on, the content of his idea, that he isn't concerned with the technique of transmission. As a result he fails to put it over.

Who Is to Blame?

When an idea has failed of its mark, the receiver is often the one to be blamed. The teacher blames the dunce. The foreman blames the "dumb" employee, as well as the employment office that did the hiring. The executive blames his staff. It is like blaming the catcher for the wildness of the pitcher.

"Blame" is a harsh, futile word to use anyway. Instead, let's use "responsibility for lack of success." So, *when an idea has failed to enter the mind of the receiver, the responsibility for lack of success lies with the sender.* This is the fundamental principle of all idea-sending. Salesmen and advertisers accept this principle without question. Why shouldn't the teacher, the supervisor, and the job trainer accept it?

To be sure, some of the causes for failure to transmit the idea may lodge with the receiver. But it is the sender's responsibility to determine in advance, if possible, all potential causes of failure and to tune his transmission for optimum reception.

[4] Robert P. Cort, "How to Get an Idea Across," *Personnel*, July, 1951.

Comparison to Television

Communication of ideas between people can very aptly be compared to television. For a person to communicate an idea, he must literally send the image that is in his own mind to the screen of the learner's mind. This image may be the visualization of some manual skill, or the concept of a word meaning, or the recall of some observed situation.

For communication to take place, three things are essential. The receiver must be tuned for reception, the transmitter must be tuned for sending, and you must select the best wave length. Later we shall discuss some of the sender's and receiver's chief difficulties which must be overcome for good reception.

Prepare the Idea

Before you send a major idea or group of ideas, you should first analyze and organize your material. You must decide (*a*) What is the whole? (*b*) What are the main parts? (*c*) What details should be fitted into the structure?

A. *What Is the Whole?* Careful selection of an accurate title to describe the whole is most important. Is the title clear and simple? Does it define as well as restrict the meaning? A training film entitled, "The ABC of G" is a nice, catchy title, but what does it mean? Is it a VD film on gonorrhea? No, it is about gravitational pull on airplane pilots. Why not say so? The film called "Stowaways" is about food handling on shipboard. Why not call a spade a spade?

B. *Selection of the Main Parts.* The learner's first grasp of a new situation is a crude impression of it as a whole. The main parts show him the simplified whole or structure and enable him to get the important relationships clearly in mind first. Then he has no trouble fitting in the details where they belong.

Thus the structure must be presented to the receiver *early in the game*. A book does it in the table of contents. A newspaper story does it in its sub-headlines.

Structure, or the crude whole, can often be shown graphically. If possible, boil your ideas down to a single page chart. Then explain the chart in 10 or 20 pages of your best prose. But don't be surprised if people like and understand your chart much better than they like your deathless prose.

C. *Fitting in the Details.* Now you are ready to nail the siding to the structure, but first you must assemble your materials—the details.

Use the Reporter's Bible—Who, When, Where, Why, What, How— as a check list, to be sure you have studied the matter thoroughly from every angle.

Then, using standard outline form, arrange your facts in some logical order, in accordance with the logic of the particular situation. This could be chronological, numerical, alphabetical, directional (clockwise, left to right), from concrete example to the induced rule, from the promulgated rule to the concrete examples, etc.

When you are finished, check your outline. Is it logical? Is it complete? Are some items overcrowded? Have you listed sub-items *a* to *y* (25 in all) under a single item? That is too many. Group them logically into three to five categories. The human mind will have difficulty comprehending those 25 sub-items. After regrouping, it will be much simpler.

How Many Ideas at a Time?

If you wanted to master European history since 1815, would you sit down and read a 700-page textbook on the subject in four or five sittings? Certainly in a single reading of the textbook, the average person would not master this complicated subject, even if his motives for wanting to do so were the strongest.

Receiving ideas is like biting and chewing food. Too big a chunk of roast beef will choke you. Small pieces, thoroughly chewed and swallowed one at a time, are easily digested and absorbed into the system. So it is with ideas. How small the chunk of ideas should be will vary with the capacity of the recipient. Generally speaking, the chapter in a textbook has been set up as a logical unit. Each unit should be mastered one at a time—i.e., presented, applied, tested, reviewed and retested before going on to the next unit. All this is time-consuming and you must plan accordingly. It is well to remember that, since big chunks of ideas rapidly presented will only confuse, it is better to move too slowly than too fast. You may run the risk of boring some, but this is better than confusing the majority.

Expressing Your Ideas

Ideas have to be couched in clear simple English if they are to get across. This problem is probably as old as civilization itself.

Why people speak and write in an involved way is subject to conjecture. Perhaps it is because they subconsciously want to impress others with their erudition. For example: The home economist from the state university was giving a cooking demonstration to a group of farm women. "Take an egg and carefully perforate the basal end," she said. "Duplicate the process at the apex. Then applying the lips to one of the apertures, by forcibly exhaling the breath, discharge the shell of its contents." Eighty-five year old Aunt Cissie turned to a neighbor. "Beats all how different these new-fangled ways is," she whispered. "When I was a gal, we just poked a hole in each end—and blowed!"

Rudolf Flesch would call Aunt Cissie's comment Shirt Sleeve English. He says that commercial houses are using Shirt Sleeve English more and more in their correspondence today. Flesch's two books, *The Art of Plain Talk* and *The Art of Readable Writing*, are well worth close study. In bare essence, his three main principles in writing to be understood are: Keep your sentences short; make many references to people in your writing, avoid the longer words of Latin derivation, such as "incomprehensible," "retroactive," etc.

Whether words are long or short, you are always faced with the problem of what they mean to the receiver. Stuart Chase asked 53 different people for their definitions of "fascism" and got 53 different answers. The word "scab" means one thing to the union man, another to the picket line-crosser who needs a job, another to the industrialist, still another to the boy with a skinned shin—all with different emotional responses. An important message to be put over in Shirt Sleeve English should be checked by as many average people as possible against the query—"What does it mean to you? Tell it in your own words." Only by some such sort of test can you determine whether you have selected the right words to convey your meaning.

The Avenues of Learning

With the idea analyzed, organized, and couched in clear, simple English, how do you go about transmitting it to the screen of the learner's mind? You do it through the "avenues of learning" as they have been called. These are the five senses, and a combination of two or more senses should always be used. The two most useful ones are *seeing* and *hearing*. Together, they are pretty effective. Hearing alone is relatively ineffective.

You have heard the expressions, "in one ear and out the other," "one picture is worth a thousand words." These all point up the weakness of the spoken word. To be sure, a Billy Sunday or a Hitler could work up a crowd to an emotional frenzy, but we are talking about rational ideas that you expect to stick in the receiver's mind.

The visual sense, when measured alone, rates 87 per cent effective as an avenue of learning, with hearing only 7 per cent and the other senses splitting up the remaining 6 per cent. This fact shows the importance of graphic portrayal of ideas. In instruction, the blackboard is your basic tool, as important in its way to human progress as the invention of the wheel. The blackboard has five major advantages: (1) it appeals to the visual sense; (2) it is utterly flexible; (3) it prevents the instructor from going too fast; (4) it can readily show the relationships among your ideas; (5) it serves as a review device. Graphic charts can be as effective as a blackboard, but the sender must be careful he doesn't sail through them too fast for comprehension.

What Are the Sender's Chief Difficulties?

If the sender accepts his "responsibility for lack of success," he will want to recognize his own difficulties so that he can strive to overcome them. The main one probably arises from the fact that he *is* so expert in his subject. Thus, *he fails to see the subject from the learner's point of view*. Hence, the importance of analyzing and organizing the idea or chunk of ideas.

A second difficulty is in *having enough patience with the slow learner*. A concomitant of this is *keeping the quick learner interested*. It is most important to gauge the ability of the learner and adjust your rate of transmission, choice of vocabulary, etc., accordingly.

A third difficulty is in *finding the right appeal to motivate the instruction*. The best appeal is *self*-interest, but there are other effective ones. Remember, "The man convinced against his will remaineth unconvinced still."

A fourth—*judging the learner's interest and response*—is not easy. It can often be read on his face or judged by his asking of questions. It cannot be judged by asking him, "Do you understand this? Do you have any questions?" The invariable answers to these are *yes* and *no*, respectively—and they will tell you nothing as to the comprehension of the learner.

Finally, the idea-sender must always be ready and willing to scrap his beautiful plan if it is not suited to the receiver, and *adapt his instruction to the needs of the learner*. This hurts, but it must be done or confusion will result.

What Are the Receiver's Chief Difficulties?

The receiver also has difficulties which, if not circumvented, create mental blocks. The chief one is psychological. "Holy smokes. They are putting me on the spot! I have to take a test and it goes into my record. I am too old (or too something) for these new-fangled ideas!"

The answer is motivation. Also, pointing out that a test, or an interview, or a questionnaire is less a measurement of the receiver than it is a measurement of the sender. In fact, the sender is the one who is on the spot, providing you accept the principle that responsibility for lack of success rests with him.

Usually, a test, when graded with a per cent, is used to determine how much a learner has learned. When the missed questions are also tabulated—i.e., two persons missed question one, six missed question two, and so on—then, a test becomes what it should be, a diagnosis of the mistakes of the sender. It points the way to effective reviews and reminds the conscientious sender that he must analyze and improve his transmission for the next group.

A second difficulty is the lack of related background information or manual skills needed to learn complex operations. This sometimes becomes a problem of individual guidance—of steering the receiver into channels where he will succeed, perhaps through a re-assignment, or it may involve adapting your original plan to meet the needs of the receiver.

The Four Steps in Sending an Idea

To get an idea over, the sender must first prepare the receiver, then present the idea, then help him apply it until a habit is started, and finally check the success of the sending. These are the four steps made famous in the Training Within Industry program of World War II. They were developed for instructing a learner in a "job"—i.e., a piece of work that a skilled instructor can dash off in from two to three minutes. Anything more than three minutes tends to be too big a chunk for the receiver to take in as a single unit.

The Four Steps are applicable not only to teaching a job *but in all cases where you are trying to send an idea.* In the teaching profession, they are known as the Five Steps but are essentially the same as outlined below:

The Four-step Method

The Four "Steps"	*How Each Is Accomplished*
1. *Preparation:* *Prepare* learner to receive new experience.	1. Put learner at *ease*. 2. Tell him the *title* of job. 3. Explain *purpose* of the job. 4. Explain *why he* has been selected to learn. 5. Help him relate his *past experiences* to the job.

2. *Presentation:*
 Set *pattern* in his mind.
	1. *Introduce* him to tools, materials, equipment and trade terms.
	 2. *Demonstrate* the job, *explaining* each step slowly and clearly.
	 3. Review with him what he should know up to this point:
	    Title of job.
	    Purpose of job.
	    Steps to be taken.

3. *Application:* Help him form *habit*.	1. Supervise *his* doing of the job. 2. Question him on *weak* and *key* points. 3. Have him repeat until he has developed the *manual skills* and/ or *habits of thought*.
4. *Test:* Check the *success* of *your* instruction.	1. Have him do the job *alone*. 2. Inspect the job against *standards* of performance. 3. Discuss with him *where he goes from here*, whether to production work or new learning experiences.

The Four Steps are applicable in sending or selling any idea, whether you are an instructor, salesman, executive, reporter, etc. Are you trying to sell an idea to your boss? Then you must *prepare* him to receive your idea. The timing here may be especially important. You must *present* the idea to him. You must help him while he *applies* the idea until it becomes a habit. Finally, you must *check the success* of your sending. And if the idea has failed to enter his mind, *you* are at fault. Perhaps it was the timing, or the idea wasn't analyzed and organized properly. Or you didn't use the Four Steps. Whatever it was, don't "blame" the boss. It's your own fault.

Learning by Doing—Application

Learning takes place when habits are being formed. Since this is so, then the most important of the Four Steps is Number Three, Application. This step should be controlled and supervised with the greatest of care. It is generally the longest of the steps, because it is *learning by doing under supervision.*

Very often, it is a step that is omitted completely. An executive holds a conference to explain a new supervisory procedure. Everybody nods his head in unison and agrees it is a fine idea. But old habits are not changed. There has been no application of the new idea, and there has been no test or follow-up. This time the boss has failed.

Your boss may be an excellent speaker. He may also be an expert at writing clear, concise English. But unless he insists on application and the follow-up phase or test, he isn't putting across his ideas. After all, the proof of the cooking is in the eating, and not in whether the chef mixed the ingredients with a grand flourish.

Conclusion

Getting across ideas makes up more than 50 per cent of the working day of all executives and most supervisors. These are the people who accomplish things through others. If valuable ideas, conceived in good will, are successfully gotten over, it should mean an end to misunderstanding and all the end results of misunderstanding—spoilage, grievances, absenteeism, emotional upsets, etc. In this sense, getting across ideas is the essence of good employee relations and of good management.

Comprehension quiz   Part One

(To be answered after surveying the article for only 45 seconds)

What time is it now? MINUTES _____

SECONDS _____

Without referring to the article, answer the following questions.

1. From the title of the article, what is the "focal point" of the author's thought? What one, central thing is the author discussing in this article?

   _____

2. What does a survey of the article reveal with respect to the author's pattern of thinking?

   _____

3. Is there a summary or résumé anywhere within the article which gives you a condensation of the article?

   _____

4. Is there any "outline" immediately observable when you survey the article rapidly?

   _____

5. Where is it in the article?

   _____

6. How does the author emphasize certain ideas?

   _____

7. Is the style of this article
   a informal?
   b scholarly?
   c humorous?
   d dignified?

8. Aside from the period and the comma, what other marks of punctuation did the author use freely throughout the article?

   _____

9. What can you tell about the audience for whom this article was intended: were they a specialized group of people (executives, supervisors, job trainers, etc.), or is this article suited for general reading and would it have an appeal for the average reader?

_____

10. What was the author's purpose in writing this article?

_____

Now, go back to the article and apply all the techniques suggested under the "reading" phase of skimming. When you have finished with the article, answer the questions in Part Two of this comprehension quiz.

Time your reading of this second time over the article. What time is it now? MINUTES _____

SECONDS _____

Part Two

What time is it? MINUTES _____

SECONDS _____

By subtracting the time you have just entered from the time you noted at the very end of Part One *and adding 45 seconds,* you will have the total skimming time for this article. What is it? What is the total time you spent in skimming the article? MINUTES _____

SECONDS _____

How Well Did You Comprehend the Main Ideas?

Now that you have skimmed this article, you should have the main ideas of the author clearly in mind. Test yourself. Do not refer to the article while taking the test.

1. The author compares communication of ideas between people to
   a a catcher and a pitcher in a ball game.
   b an avenue of learning.
   c television.
   d shirt-sleeve English.

2. In selecting a title for an idea which you wish to present, you select one that

    a gets attention.
    b describes the whole.
    c is informative.
    d is worded simply, yet forcefully.

3. The learner's first grasp of a new situation is
    a a crude impression of it as a whole.
    b the visualization of the outline.
    c a vague impression of details.
    d a clear recognition of the logic behind the author's reasoning.

4. The author suggests that fitting in the details calls for use of
    a graphs to show the structure of the article.
    b an accurate title.
    c the Reporter's Bible.
    d the standard outline form.

5. Receiving ideas is like
    a tuning in a radio.
    b biting and chewing food.
    c a cooking lesson.
    d an executive conference.

6. The author says that whether words are long or short, the final problem is always
    a how well they express the author's thought.
    b how vivid they are to the imagination of the reader.
    c what emotional content they have.
    d what they mean to the receiver.

7. The "avenues of learning" are
    a the five senses.
    b seeing and hearing.
    c the blackboard and graphic charts.
    d shirt-sleeve English and a common vocabulary.

8. The effectiveness of the visual sense when measured alone is
    a 7 or 8 per cent.
    b 67 per cent.
    c 78 per cent.
    d 87 per cent.

9. A step that is very often omitted in getting an idea across is
    a learning by doing under supervision.
    b explaining the purpose of the job to the employee.
    c reviewing what the learner should know about the firm.
    d discussing with the employee "where he goes" after his training.

10. Getting across ideas
    a is an art in itself.
    b is applied psychology in the most practical sense of the term.
    c helps to make supervisors excellent speakers and writers.
    d takes more than half of the working day of all executives and most supervisors.

How effectively did you skim? Check your answers with those given in the Answer Key. There are twenty questions in all. Each question is worth 5 per cent.

What is your level of comprehension?   _____%

What is your speed of skimming? [5]   _____wpm

What is your reading index ($R \times C/100$)? _____

Reading Habit Index

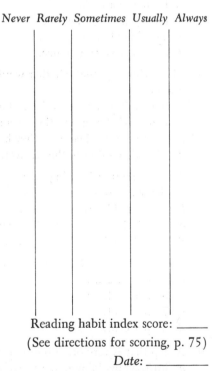

                                         Never Rarely Sometimes Usually Always

1. I survey an article *before* I actually read it, i.e., I apply the look-before-you-read techniques as outlined in this chapter.
2. I employ skimming as one step, at least, in practically all types of reading.
3. Before I begin to read, I look carefully at the title to find its focal point.
4. I am alert to the function which punctuation plays in aiding me to read better.
5. When I read I immediately notice any guide, or directional words, that indicate a change in the thought flow.

Reading habit index score: _____
(See directions for scoring, p. 75)
Date: _____

[5] Your rate may be exceptionally high in this exercise. Bear in mind that you were not attempting to read every word—instead, you were skimming, looking only for principal thoughts and main ideas

Chapter Ten

Reading
to follow directions

B Y CRACKEY, I kin git lost goin' nowhere!" exclaimed the old New
England farmer in confessing his inability to follow the directions
of the crossroads signpost.

That old New England farmer has plenty of company. Most of us
have trouble in following directions.

In fact, one of the specific skills of reading, which is much more
commonly employed than is generally recognized, is the skill of reading
for the purpose of following directions. Think of the innumerable occasions every day which demand skill in reading directions. The simplest
form of this type of reading probably is the crossroads signpost, with its
weather-beaten arrow pointing off across the hills to Centerville, 5 miles
away. From this lonely and lowly beginning, direction reading spirals
upward in our modern, complex world. Tommy reads directions to find
out how to assemble his model airplane or balsa kite. His father reads
directions—to learn how to assemble the precut furniture or an outdoor
fireplace. Mother reads directions before baking a cake or making a new
dessert. Sister studies the directions and lays out the tissue-paper parts
before she cuts the material to make a new dress. Whether it is at the

office or on the job, whether you buy a bottle of patent medicine with "directions inside" or pore over the meaning of Federal regulations and tax directives, the problem is still the same. One fact stands out: for all of these circumstances one reading skill is required—the ability to read for the purpose of following directions.

This skill is an approach to reading that requires a synthesis of many basic skills and techniques. These have been emphasized in previous chapters.

In reading to follow directions we come probably to one of the few situations where a slower, more deliberate type of reading may be necessary. At times the reader may have felt that this book was posited upon the proposition that all reading should be fast reading. Nothing could be farther from the fact. Readers generally do not measure up to their potential in either speed or comprehension most of the time. But there has never been any suggestion that a slower, more careful, more deliberate approach should not be employed if the purpose of the reader seemed to dictate that such deceleration of rate was more desirable or more in keeping with the type of material or the purpose for which it was being read.

When reading to follow directions, the sequential order in which the facts are presented is more important than in almost any other type of reading. In the usual arrangement of the data each step depends upon the successful understanding of the step preceding. For that reason such words as "first," "then," "after this," "now," and so forth are the guiding words encountered particularly in this type of reading. These words usually indicate the beginning of a new step in the directive process: *First*, you do this; *then*, you do that; *after which* you complete a third operation—and so the directions go. There is a logical, steplike arrangement of the thought, set in the order in which the operations are to be carried out.

Because there is a definite order in the presentation of such material and because the relationship between the various steps must constantly be kept in mind and understood as you read, this type of reading may require a slower and more conservative pace. You may also have to re-read more than usual. Do not be unduly concerned, therefore, if your rate declines somewhat and you note yourself making more regressions than normal for this exacting type of material, especially in the early stages of learning to read to follow directions. Try, however, to increase your rate and to decrease regressive tendencies as you improve your skill in reading to follow directions.

Steps in reading to follow directions

1. *Look for the Directions.* This is the first step in following directions, namely, to find them! It is amazing how many persons never see the directions that the author places before their eyes. The number of college students each year is legion who fail even to *see* the directions on their tests and examinations. Adults buy items and then rush into using them without so much as looking for the directions that they know must be somewhere close by. A woman blew the roof off of her house the other day and put herself in the hospital because she was using a dry cleaner under conditions which the directions expressly forbade. A glance at the side of the can could have saved a perfectly good roof, four walls, and some of the lady in question.

2. *Put Your Preconceived Notions Away.* This is a corollary to the preceding point. Many people read directions with their minds already made up before they begin to read. They *know* how it should be done, but they'll look at the directions anyway. It's a sort of behavioristic conventionality, an old and gentle custom to look at directions, even though you *know* beforehand that they will add nothing to what you know already, that *you* can't possibly be wrong, and you don't intend to heed them anyway. And so, with psychologically watertight doors between your own thoughts and your reading processes you look, but you do not read.

When I was in college, the psychology department always gave one true-false test in which the directions at the head of the test explicitly read: "If the statement is true, mark an *F* in the blank before the statement; if it is false, mark a *T*." Everybody invariably missed the road, and then argued with the professor because he had given a "trick" question. There was absolutely no trick about it, except the trick of putting away your preconceived notions and simply reading the instructions and following them.

3. *Read through the Directions Rapidly at First.* Directions should be read the first time carefully and completely, but also rapidly. Look for the final goal toward which the whole set of directions is tending. To get the over-all view is very important. Skim first; orient yourself to

the *whole* situation. Of course, you will want to read again, more carefully, the steplike progression of points that lead to the final goal, but as you do so, it will help immeasurably to have the final goal in mind. See that goal, therefore, early in the process with unmistakable clarity.

4. *Try to Understand the Logic of Each Step.* A characteristic of directions is that each step follows every other in logical sequence. First, this; then, that; and after that, a third thing: that is the formula. Try to see how each operation hinges on the one before it and how that, in turn, serves as a preparation for what is to follow.

5. *Visualize the Critical Points.* See the steps as you read them. Imaginatively live the experience. Try to see yourself doing exactly what the words are telling you to do. Note especially the *critical* points. If the directions tell you to turn left two blocks and then right, there are three critical points where you might err: you must be sure the *first* turn is to the *left* (critical point 1); then, after proceeding *two blocks* (critical point 2), you turn to the *right* (critical point 3).

6. *Note Especially the Key Words.* In Chapter Seven you learned how to read key words and phrases. You need this skill especially in the reading of directions. Scale down the wordage, and keep a sharp eye open for the key words. For example, suppose the following directions concerning the dilution of sulphuric acid were given:

Pour the sulphuric acid slowly into the water, never reverse the process by pouring the water into the acid.

The key words to remember are these:

POUR ACID SLOWLY INTO WATER, NEVER REVERSE

Remember that, and you have remembered everything. From the 19 words of the original, you read only seven—slightly more than one-third —but that was the vital, all-important third!

7. *Review the Steps in a Final Summing Up.* Finally, read the directions again, rapidly, noting in a kind of last-look technique every turn of the thought, every change in direction at a critical point. Note the key words and essential data. Keep an eye always open for the directional words which are the signposts at the crossroads of the thought: *now, then, after that, lastly.* Visualize the whole process again as you go over it. Try to wrap up the package in your own thinking as a complete and compact whole—a power-packed bundle of directions. Know precisely what is to be done, how, when, and under what conditions. A final review will help to fix all this in your mind.

Reading directions successfully is one of the specific skills of reading. To read directions well means approaching the printed page with a definite purpose and a specific technique. There are seven steps in the process. Practice them incessantly until you become a master at reading and comprehending directions.

The exercises that follow will give you an opportunity to test your skill.

Test your skill at reading to follow directions

In this section you will find a number of exercises to be read for the express purpose of following directions. Remember the hints which were given to you in the discussion. If you feel that you need to refresh your memory on these main points, go back now to re-read them. You should have the main points clearly in mind.

Do the exercises in this fashion:

1. Read the directions in any way which you feel is the most efficient way to read the particular set of directions with which you are dealing at the time.
2. When you have finished reading that set of directions, and are directed to do so, turn to the section following the directions, and you will there test your comprehension in reading to follow directions.
3. Time yourself in reading each of these selections. The word-count and formula for computing your rate will be given with each selection. You may expect that you will do this type of reading at a generally slower rate than has been your usual pace.

TO BOIL EGGS (HARD OR SOFT) [1]

Time: MINUTES _____

  SECONDS _____

1. Have eggs room temperature to prevent cracking.
2. Cover eggs in saucepan with cold water. Heat until water boils.
3. Remove from heat. Cover pan. Let stand off the heat until eggs are cooked.

[1] Adapted from *Betty Crocker's Picture Cook Book*, p. 252, copyright, 1950, General Mills, Inc., reprinted with permission of the publishers, McGraw-Hill Book Company, Inc.

4. Allow 2 to 4 minutes for soft-cooked eggs; 23 to 25 minutes for hard-cooked eggs.

Time: MINUTES _____

       SECONDS _____

Reading time: SECONDS _____

Total words: 49

Turn to the comprehension questions at the end of this section of directions.

To find your rate of reading:

$$\frac{49 \times 60}{\text{reading time in seconds}} = \text{wpm}$$

HOW DO I GET TO CITY HALL?

Time: MINUTES _____

       SECONDS _____

A tourist drove into Centerville and asked a policeman stationed at Center Square how to get to City Hall. The policeman gave him the following directions:

Drive down this street immediately ahead of you. This is Main Street, running south. Proceed five blocks on Main Street, to the intersection of Washington Street. Turn left on Washington Street and proceed east four blocks. At that point you will enter a traffic circle, which has a fountain in the center of it. Drive around the traffic circle, to the right, not quite three-quarters of the distance around the circle from the point at which you entered. A street will emerge from the circle at this point, leaving the circle at an angle to the street on which you entered. This is Conway Street. Proceed along Conway Street two blocks. At this point you will come to a fork. Take the right-hand street at the fork. You are still on Conway Street. Drive two blocks to High Street. Turn right on High Street, one block to the intersection of Federal and High Streets. City Hall is on the northwest corner of Federal and High Streets.

Time: MINUTES _____

       SECONDS _____

Reading time in seconds: SECONDS _____

Total words: 192

Turn to the comprehension questions at the end of this section.
To find your rate:

$$\frac{169 \times 60}{\text{reading time in seconds}} = \text{wpm}$$

HOW TO GIVE YOUR MONEY AWAY

Time: MINUTES _____

SECONDS _____

If you're doing any estate planning, consider this: It may be sounder
—financially—to give property to your heirs while you're living than to
will it to them at death. Here's why:

Properly planned, gifts may cost nothing in taxes.

But even if they do cost some gift tax, the bill may be far less than
an estate tax bill.

A gift gives your heirs the full amount of what you intend them to
get. For when you make a gift, you do not pay any taxes; on an estate,
the taxes usually come out before the heirs get their share.

Here's how much difference there can be between willing and giving:

A man has an estate of $300,000. His choice is whether to give his
family $100,000 or will it to them.

If he dies without making the gifts, his estate includes the $100,000
and the estate tax is boosted by $12,700. But if he gives the money to
his sons and daughters—assuming that he makes "split" gifts with his
wife, that they have made no prior gifts, and that the cash is spread
around the family—the tax might be as little as $500.

One catch to this: If the man made the gifts and then died within
three years, his estate would have to prove the gifts weren't made "in
contemplation of death" to avoid the estate tax. Otherwise, the government would tax the money at estate-tax rates.

Just what is the gift tax and when does it apply?

The tax is Federal (12 states also levy on gifts) and is based on a table
of rates ranging from 2¼% to 57¾%. Generally, it applies only to gifts
of $3,000 or more to any one person or organization in any one year.
(But remember: Any gift of a "future interest" is taxable; "future
interest" is too complicated to spell out here.)

If you give more than $3,000 to a person in a year, you have to file a
gift tax return by the following April 15. But that doesn't necessarily

mean you'll have to pay a tax. By planning gifts carefully to take advantage of exclusions and deductions, you can give as much as $66,000 to one person in a year—completely tax free.

Here are the main rules that ought to be considered in planning any big giving:

The law allows a $3,000 exclusion each year for each donee.

On top of the annual $3,000 exclusions, you have a lifetime exemption of $30,000 in gifts. This applies just once to your entire life; you can use it all in one year or spread it over several years. (A man decides to give away, say, 20 gifts of property—each worth $4,500—to 20 different relatives. His gifts, $90,000 less his 20 annual exclusions equal to $60,000 come out to $30,000 and thus he pays nothing.)

Gifts can be "split" with your wife. Thus both of you could use up your lifetime exemptions ($60,000), take two annual exclusions ($6,000), and give your son $66,000 in one year, tax free.

Gifts to your wife are only half-taxed. Say that you gave her $10,000. Taking out the annual exclusion of $3,000 leaves $7,000. But the law figures your gift to be $2,000. It deducts half of the initial gift from what is left after the exclusion. This is called a marital deduction.

Gifts to bona fide charities are not taxed at all.

Time: MINUTES _____

      SECONDS _____

Reading time: SECONDS _____
Total words: 578
Turn to the comprehension questions at the end of this section.
To figure your rate:

$$\frac{578 \times 60}{\text{reading time in seconds}} = \text{wpm}$$

CAN YOU DO THIS?

Time: MINUTES _____

      SECONDS _____

Do not attempt to pencil or trace any of the following lines. Merely read the directions; then turn to the comprehension questions at the back of this section.

From a circle, a line is drawn tangent to the circle, but opposite to your relationship to the circle. This line is AX. The point where it is tangent to the circle is T. From T another line is constructed at 90° to AX, which does not enter the circle. This line is TC. Another line begins at A and terminates at S, passing entirely through the circle. From X to S another line is drawn.

Time: MINUTES _____

SECONDS _____

Reading time: SECONDS _____

Total words: 104

Turn to the comprehension questions at the end of this section.

To find your rate of reading:

$$\frac{104 \times 60}{\text{reading time in seconds}} = \text{wpm}$$

CONCENTRATE! [2]

You will need a pencil, before reading this.

Time: MINUTES _____

SECONDS _____

Work out this set of directions as you go along. You may read them over first, if you so desire, but it will add to your total reading time. Note your time only after you have actually followed each direction. If you follow directions carefully, you will change the name of a magazine to something else, which is very unlike a magazine, indeed!

1. Write in a line the letters of the word, "Red Book." This is to be written as one word.
2. If there are less than five vowels, place a t at the beginning of the line and insert a c after the last o.
3. If the first four letters do not spell a word, change the b to ch.
4. If there is an odd number of letters, strike out the middle letter.
5. Place a w before the fourth letter.
6. If the first three letters do not spell a word, insert a u before the last c.
7. Change the r to h and insert the double letter between the w and the d.

Time: MINUTES _____

SECONDS _____

[2] Adapted from *The Reader's Digest* (Educational Edition) September, 1951, p. 4-E.

Reading time: SECONDS _____
Total words: 181
The answer to this set of directions will be found in the Answer Key.
To find your rate of reading:

$$\frac{181 \times 60}{\text{reading time in seconds}} = \text{wpm}$$

Comprehension quiz

How Efficiently Could You Follow Directions for Boiling Eggs?

Check which of the following procedures are *not* correct:

1. Have eggs at room temperature before cooking.
2. Boil eggs in a saucepan.
3. Boil eggs 24 minutes for hard-cooked eggs.
4. Cover eggs in saucepan with warm water to prevent cracking.
5. Cover pan while boiling water.
6. Start eggs in cold water.
7. Have water boiling 2 to 4 minutes before putting eggs in.
8. For soft-cooked eggs, have water boiling, cook eggs 2 to 4 minutes.

How Efficiently Could You Follow Directions to Get to City Hall?

Draw a map of the route which the policeman outlined, marking all the points along the way which he mentioned as critical points.

*How Efficiently Could You Follow Directions
on How to Give Your Money Away?*

1. By enumerating the steps 1, 2, 3, 4, and so on, show how you can give as much as $66,000 to one person in a year—completely tax-free.
2. The author gives you directions how to give $10,000 to your wife and be taxed on a basis of only $2000. Show how he arrives at $2000 as the figure on which the calculation of the tax is based.

*How Efficiently Could You Follow the Directions
on "Can You Do This?"*

1. Draw the figure as described.
2. What geometrical figure is formed when you connect X and S?

How Efficiently Could You Follow Directions in "Concentrate!"?

Refer to the Answer Key for the correct answer to this exercise.

Measure Your Rapid-perception Span

Get out your card that you used for rapid perception in **Chapter Six**. We are going to do some more rapid-perception reading. Last time you had a space 1½ inches between the guide arrows. This represented a potential span of about 24 letters in width. Widen the horizontal bar to 2 inches, flanked by the two arrows. Practice with this. See if you cannot widen that eye span. Below are blanks for record of what you do.

	Phrase seen	*Type units*		*Phrase seen*	*Type units*
1.	_____	____	1.	_____	____
2.	_____	____	2.	_____	____
3.	_____	____	3.	_____	____
4.	_____	____	4.	_____	____
5.	_____	____	5.	_____	____
6.	_____	____	6.	_____	____
7.	_____	____	7.	_____	____
8.	_____	____	8.	_____	____
9.	_____	____	9.	_____	____
10.	_____	____	10.	_____	____

No. correct _____   No. correct _____

Av. type units _____   Av. type units _____

	Phrase seen	*Type units*		*Phrase seen*	*Type units*
1.	_____	____	1.	_____	____
2.	_____	____	2.	_____	____
3.	_____	____	3.	_____	____
4.	_____	____	4.	_____	____
5.	_____	____	5.	_____	____
6.	_____	____	6.	_____	____

	Type		*Type*
Phrase seen	*units*	*Phrase seen*	*units*
7. _____ ____		7. _____ ____	
8. _____ ____		8. _____ ____	
9. _____ ____		9. _____ ____	
10. _____ ____		10. _____ ____	

No. correct _____   No. correct _____

Av. type units _____   Av. type units _____

Compare your achievement on this perception exercise with your achievement previously. Refer to your former record in Chapter Six.

Reading for Speed of Comprehension—1

Television—particularly color television—underscores probably more than ever our need to know something about the sensations of light and color. The article which you are about to read for speed of comprehension deals with this significant subject and was written by one of the most distinguished physicists of our time, particularly in the area of optical physics.

Read to break your former records of speed of comprehension. Be alert as you read to get the facts, so that you may keep your level of comprehension at a high point of achievement. Time yourself accurately.

Time: MINUTES _____

SECONDS _____

THE SENSATIONS OF LIGHT AND COLOUR [3]

by Sir C. V. Raman

Amongst the means which Nature has provided for us to enable us to become conscious of our surroundings, the sensations of light and colour occupy a position of supreme importance. The sun by day and the stars by night are the power plants from which flow the streams of

[3] Sir C. V. Raman, *The New Physics*, Chap. 6, pp. 35–42, Philosophical Library, Inc., New York, 1951.

light which illuminate our surroundings. Not content with these natural sources, man likewise seeks to turn night into day by exercising his ingenuity and providing himself with artificial sources of light of various kinds. The radiations from the sun play a far greater role in our lives than merely enabling us to see our surroundings. . . . No wonder, from the earliest times, the tremendous outpouring of energy from the sun has filled mankind with awe and made it the subject of adoration. The source of all that energy has naturally been one of the greatest problems of science.

The first real step towards an understanding of the nature of light is taken when we analyse light by means of a spectroscope. This instrument spreads out the light of the sun into a band of colours traversed by a great number of dark lines. The colours in this band or spectrum, as it is called, vary continuously from one end to the other. The trained eye can easily appreciate fifty or even a hundred distinct tints in traversing the solar spectrum from the extreme violet to the extreme red end.

The spectroscope thus teaches us that the physical entity which we perceive as white light is essentially composite in its nature. To enable the characters of light to be defined in a precise way, we must consider the narrowest possible strip of the spectrum, which we may call monochromatic light. This is conveniently provided for us in the emission from certain gases and metallic vapours when excited by an electric discharge. The sodium vapour and the mercury vapour lamps which are now a feature of the street lighting in our great cities are seen on examination through a spectroscope to emit a small number of distinct monochromatic rays or sharp bright lines in the spectrum.

Various physical experiments, some of which are very simple, show that monochromatic light in its travel through space can be pictured as wave motion with a definite wavelength and frequency. The velocity of light in free space is the same as that of the electromagnetic waves sent out by radio stations. This by itself is sufficient proof that what we call light is essentially electromagnetic radiation, its wavelength being different from point to point in the visible spectrum, but everywhere only a minute fraction of the wavelength of even the shortest waves used in radio transmission. The physical basis of colour is thus the difference in wavelength and frequency of the electromagnetic waves corresponding to the different monochromatic rays in the spectrum. The wavelength of visible light diminishes from about 7,000 to about 4,000

Angstrom units as we pass from the red to the violet end of the spectrum. An Angstrom unit is a hundred-millionth part of a centimetre.

Light is thus revealed to us as a minute strip in the whole tremendous possible range of wavelengths of electromagnetic radiation. It is natural to ask, "Why is it that we are able to perceive only this highly restricted part of the electromagnetic spectrum as light?" The answer to this question is, I think, to be found in a study of the radiations of the sun which is our principal luminary. An examination of the nature of solar radiation shows that its spectrum extends well beyond the visible region both towards the longer and shorter wavelengths; such extension, however, is restricted on either side by absorption in the earth's atmosphere. The distribution of the solar energy within the spectrum is determined by what is called the effective temperature of the surface of the sun which is about 5,500° C. If one draws the energy curve of the heat radiations from a body at that temperature, one finds that it rises fairly rapidly with decreasing wavelengths and reaches a peak at a wavelength of about 5,500 Angstrom units and then drops very steeply for shorter wavelengths.

If one were to draw a curve of the sensitivity of the human eye as dependent on the wavelength of the incident radiation for equal energies, one would find that the maximum sensitivity falls approximately at a wavelength of 5,500 Angstrom units. This coincidence between the wavelengths of maximum sensitiveness of the human eye and of maximum energy in the solar spectrum can hardly be considered accidental. If it is an accident, it certainly is a most remarkable coincidence. Indeed, it seems much more reasonable to suppose that the development of our visual sense during the long course of biological evolution has been such as to make the fullest possible use of the actual optical environment provided by the radiations of our sun.

Not merely are we conscious of light, but we also find ourselves in a position to obtain a reasonably accurate idea of our surroundings by means of our vision. Particularly remarkable is the fact that we get a three-dimensional picture of our surroundings and that we can at will fix our attention on any desired object either far or near. These powers rest on the constitution of the human eye as an optical instrument capable of forming a focussed image on the sensitive screen at its back known as the retina. Our stereoscopic sense of three-dimensional vision is possible because we possess two eyes and the retinal images formed by them are slightly different. It is really wonderful, when we come to think of it, that though two distinct pictures of the external world are formed on the retinae of our two eyes, we do not see double and are conscious only of a single external world. The perfect way in which we are able to direct our vision on any object either far or near and thereby scrutinise it in all its detail is also a remarkable example of how the structure of the organs of vision adapts itself to the demands made upon it.

One of the most remarkable features of our power of vision is its ability to adapt itself to the wide range of brightness in our surroundings. When we pass from the bright glare of sunshine in the open air to the dimly lit interior of a building, the intensity of illumination may fall by a factor of a million to one. If the eye is embarrassed by such a sudden drop in the intensity, it is only for a little while. Soon it adapts itself to the feeble illumination. After a long enough rest in the dark, objects that were invisible at first may appear insupportably bright. Under favourable conditions the sensitivity of the human eye is indeed amazing.

If the world we live in were just made up of whites and greys and blacks, it would indeed be a very dull world. Our capacity to appreciate differences in colour adds enormously to the pleasure with which we are conscious of our surroundings. As mentioned earlier, the physical basis of colour is the difference in wavelength and frequency corresponding to the different parts of the solar spectrum. But this statement covers but a very small part of our experience in regard to the actual sensations of colour. It is a question of great interest why a comparatively small change of wavelength or frequency should produce such profoundly different sensations in the human eye. We may also wonder what the physiological mechanism is which enables the eye to be conscious of such differences. In this connection it is very noteworthy that in actual practice we are but rarely concerned with the monochromatic tints of the spectrum. An object may appear vividly coloured, but on examination by a spectroscope may show all the colours of the spectrum. The blue colour of the sky is a typical illustration. Colour regarded as sensation is generally the result of a distribution of intensity in the spectrum different from that found in standard white light.

The study of colour regarded as physiological sensation is a subject of great interest. It is also of much practical importance. As typical examples of the striking facts met with in the study of colour, we may mention the following: The colour of yellow light may be counterfeited by mixing spectral red and spectral green. White light may be counterfeited by mixing spectral yellow and spectral violet in a hundred to one ratio. Every known hue can be counterfeited by the appropriate mixture of three primary or spectral colours, one red, one green and one blue or violet. The wavelengths of the colours chosen as primary can be varied to a considerable extent and they may also be broad spectral bands instead of monochromatic rays.

No account of light and colour is complete which does not consider the visual phenomena coming under the general descriptions of illusion and visual fatigue. These play a great part in the sensations experienced by us when we view variously illuminated or coloured objects. They also play an important part in determining the effects known as contrast, visual harmony and clash which arise when different colours are placed adjacent to each other and play a vital part in visual aesthetics.

Some mention must also be made of the interesting condition known as colour blindness which afflicts some unfortunate individuals and prevents them from recognising differences of colour which are patent to normal sighted persons. To be colour-blind may be dangerous in certain types of employment. That is one of the reasons why its study has received much attention. It is also of interest as it throws some light on the phenomena of normal colour vision.

Of recent years, many exact studies have been made of the reactions of the eye to light. Attempts have also been made to translate the actual facts of vision into a theory of visual processes and sensations. Such theories largely rest on the known structure of the retina and the presence in it of certain hypothetical coloured materials which absorb the light falling on them and undergo certain temporary chemical changes. It is a fact that a coloured substance called visual purple can be extracted from the rods of the retina of the higher animals and that a solution of visual purple is bleached by strong light. It is this fact which forms the starting point of some of the newer theories of physiological optics.

What time is it now?   MINUTES _____

SECONDS _____

What is your reading time for this selection? MINUTES _____

SECONDS _____

Without referring back to the article, take the following test.

Comprehension quiz

This is a test of your knowledge of the facts which you have read. It is a test of the familiar true-false type. Each statement will belong to one of three categories: *true, false,* or *not mentioned.* Place the letter *F* before the statement if it is true; a *T* before the statement if it is false, and a 0 before the statement if it has not been mentioned in the article.

1 _____ The colors of the solar spectrum do not vary from end to end.
2 _____ The human eye can distinguish several hundred tints in the solar spectrum.
3 _____ Monochromatic light is the narrowest strip of spectral light possible.
4 _____ Monochromatic light is best secured by analyzing a strip of sunlight.
5 _____ A spectroscope measures intensity of light.
6 _____ Monochromatic light is marked by sharp, bright lines in the spectrum.
7 _____ The frequency of light waves in free space is the same as that of radio waves.
8 _____ Light is composed of a spectrum of distinct colors from red to violet.
9 _____ Color blindness is hereditary.
10 _____ We see light only between 4000 and 7000 angstroms.
11 _____ The light that we see is a small part of a much larger electromagnetic spectrum.
12 _____ The maximum sensitivity of the eye corresponds to the angstrom equivalent of the effective temperature of the sun.
13 _____ Stereoscopic vision is possible because our two eyes are slightly out of focus.
14 _____ Human vision has a wide latitude of intensity adaptation.
15 _____ The author is of the opinion that the coincidence between the solar and angstrom wavelength medians is a result of evolutionary factors.
16 _____ Most of the color that we see is monochromatic color.
17 _____ Yellow light is a fusion of spectral red and spectral yellow.
18 _____ Visual purple is resident in the retinal rods.
19 _____ Strong light intensifies visual purple.
20 _____ Light reacting too intensely upon the eye is the cause of poor vision.

Check your answers against those given in the Answer Key. Each correct answer is worth 5 per cent.

What is your level of comprehension?   _____%

What is your speed of comprehension?   _____wpm

What is your reading index $(R \times C/100)$? _____

Reading for Speed of Comprehension—2

At no time in the world's history have maps been used by more people and for more purposes than in the present day. Captains who pilot the ships that sail the seven seas and navigators who fly the airways of the world are never without their maps. But the map is not alone for those who sail to faraway ports and distant lands. The family goes off for a vacation, and a road map charts their course and destination.

The world has grown small and intimate. Countries and cities that were once indistinct realms, uncharted and unknown, are the hot spots of today's news and the determiners of tomorrow's history. Modern man cannot live without a map.

Because of the importance of the map in our daily living, the following article should be especially interesting to all of us. It traces the development of map-making from Ptolemy, the first of the map makers, to photogrammetry, the most modern method of charting the face of the earth.

Read it as rapidly as you can, at the same time getting the facts of the article.

Time: MINUTES _____

SECONDS _____

MAP-MAKING

from Ptolemy to Photogrammetry [4]

It is late in the afternoon. Two weary hikers trudge down a lonely, rutted road in search of some assurance—a familiar oak, a brook, an advertisement plastered on the side of a barn—that they are on the right path. Suddenly one of the hikers spies a farmer working in a cornfield and calls him over to ask the way. The farmer picks up a stick and traces

[4] *Aramco World*, vol. 6, October, 1955, pp. 2–5.

in the dirt at their feet a rough outline of the local road system. The hikers thank their guide and continue down the lane, certain now that the next fork on the right will lead them straight into town.

Man has been likened to an ant in a rug: he knows the exact nature of the fiber around him, but the overall design is beyond his vision. Human beings were able to draw maps, at first using only a stick and the ground, long before they ever discovered writing. In the beginning this ability was often a matter of sheer survival, as when it became necessary to mark out a route leading to more rewarding hunting grounds or to locate possible break-through points of enemy attacks. Later, man's insatiable curiosity about the planet he lived on, combined with his adventurous spirit and growing technical skill, was responsible for increasingly accurate and useful maps, until today there is very little of the earth's surface left which has not been reproduced through the art and science of cartography.

A map has been defined as a conventionalized picture of the earth's surface pattern. Someone once declared that a modern cartographer must be 50% geographer, 30% artist, 10% mathematician and 10% everything else. Every map-maker throughout history has had to be part artist and part scientist, but not always in the same proportions. Maps turned out by the ancient Greeks, for example, were no great works of art, but they did show strongly the influence of the scientific mind at work. Their superior talents in the field of mathematics helped the Greeks to decide that the earth was sphere-shaped, and to establish such sophisticated cartographic concepts as latitude and longitude, the poles, the Equator and the Tropics of Capricorn and Cancer.

The Romans were more inclined to think of maps in terms of their practical worth, and found them most useful as aids in planning distant military campaigns and in administering their vast domains. They disregarded the carefully worked out distortions found on earlier Greek maps and reverted to the old disk shape of the Ionian geographers, with the Roman Empire itself covering more than four-fifths of the area shown. Although the idea of "north, south, east and west" is as old as map-making, the practice of placing north at the top of maps became general only in comparatively recent times. Roman cartographers located eastern regions, or what was then thought of as the Orient, topmost on all of their maps, a custom which has given us our term, "orientation."

It was natural that the Arabs, who excelled in such subjects as astronomy, arithmetic and geometry, should turn out some highly skilled cartographers. Every good Moslem has always prayed five times a day facing in the direction of Mecca, so each follower of Mohammed possessed an inherent sense of direction from earliest childhood. The Islamic religion strongly influenced the design of early maps made by the Arabs, who always located Mecca, the center and most important place in their world, near the top.

Such was the genius of Greek cartographers that their innovations stood as the most advanced in the field until some time around 1500. Then, suddenly, vast improvements came in rapid succession within a matter of a few years. There were three major reasons behind that period which later historians talk about as the "renaissance of maps." The first was the rediscovery of Ptolemy's complete *Geographia*, a detailed treatise of Greek map-making which had been preserved in part by the Arabs through the Middle Ages. Using Ptolemy's maps as prime source material, 16th century cartographers were able to incorporate into them important corrections based on further research since his day.

The second event which so profoundly affected map-making was the invention of printing. Before this, each copy of each map had to be drafted by hand, so the use of maps was necessarily limited to very few people—heads of state, military leaders and the like—who had a special reason for needing them. With the introduction of printing and engraving, maps could be reproduced by the thousands from a single plate, bringing costs of the finished product down to a fraction of what they had been, and knowledge of the then-known world was made available to the common man.

It is an odd coincidence in the story of maps that the first terrestrial globe was constructed by a Nurenberg cartographer named Martin Behaim in 1492, the same year that Christopher Columbus landed for the first time on American shores. The great discoveries made by Columbus and those who followed him gave map-making its third great impetus. Geographical conceptions changed more rapidly in the first quarter of the 16th century than they ever had either before or since. The earliest map to show the two Western Hemisphere continents clearly separated from Asia was prepared in 1507 by the Alsatian Martin Waldseemuller, the first cartographer to write the word "America" over those land masses which came to be known as the New World. Diego Ribero's 1529 map of the world, laid out in a flat plane, looks remarkably like the world maps of today.

The earth as seen by a map-maker is covered by a network of evenly spaced horizontal and vertical lines, by the use of which we can locate and refer to any point on our globe. This system of parallels and meridians, first established by the Greeks in the Fifth Century, B.C. is the most fundamental principle of cartography. The Greeks thought of the world as being oblong in shape—twice as wide across as up and down—and that is why we refer to the east-and-west direction as *longitude* and north-and-south as *latitude*.

The *prime meridian* is a north-south line connecting the two poles. Looking down on it, we begin to count everything to the left of this line as being in the *western* longitudes and everything to the right as the *eastern* longitudes. . . . Since there is no natural law that dictates the location of the prime meridian, this all-important cartographic line has been moved from one point on the globe to another throughout the history of map-making. Ptolemy established it near the legendary Fortunate Isles, which we now think might have been the Canary Islands off Africa, the western limit of the then-known world. Dutch and English cartographers of the 17th century moved it farther west, in the vicinity of the Azores. With the growing national consciousness of the 18th century each country boosted its own capital for the honor, and for a time Paris, London, Lisbon, Madrid and even Philadelphia and Washington were points through which the prime meridian passed. The prestige of the British Admiralty, which reckoned its longitudes from the Greenwich Observatory near London, was the deciding factor in settling on a permanent prime meridian site, and all cartographic calculations are now made on the basis of the meridian marked "Zero" passing straight through Greenwich, England.

The general physical appearance of the earth's surface has been stabilized, for all practical purposes, ever since the Ice Age, and man has been measuring and plotting its features from the time a nameless Babylonian mounted the first map on a stone tablet back in 2500 B.C. Still, the work of the map-maker continues apace, trying to keep up with an ever growing demand for knowledge about our planet, and the minute changes it is constantly undergoing. Daily information flows into the offices of the big map publishers which must be incorporated into new editions of every work they produce, whether it is a thick new atlas or a road map of the State of Rhode Island. . . . Communities such as abandoned mining towns sometimes cease to exist, and cartographers, keeping abreast of the times, take a blue pencil and literally wipe them off the map.

The publishers of maps have editors on their staffs just as magazines and newspapers do, and their duties parallel those of their colleagues in the periodical field: deciding what facts should be included or left out and designing a product which is easy to understand and attractive to look at. Such factors as typography are constantly undergoing changes to improve a map's readability, and the colors of maps are being scrutinized for purposes of increasing clarity and improving appearance. Some time ago commercial map publishers began using Gothic type for their place-names and a deeper, more vivid blue to set bodies of water off from land areas.

Whenever there is a special need for information about an area on which little is known, map-makers move in to chart that region, often starting from the beginning. . . . One of the initial steps in this procedure is the taking of thousands of photographs of the entire area from an airplane flying at approximately 30,000 feet on carefully worked out lines of flight.

The exact positions on land are fixed by astronomical calculations and ground measurements so that the control points on the ground can be identified on the photographs. Since adjacent photographs overlap at least 60% in line of flight and 30% between flights, common control points can be lined up with considerable precision. In the cartographic laboratory trained experts transfer each control indicated on the aerial photographs to big map boards. Using a stereoscope to bring out the hills, valleys and plains, the photogrammetrist can see the terrain in relief as shown on the pictures. They then outline the topographical features in ink and crayon right on the photograph before transferring these delineations to the map board itself with the aid of an instrument called a sketch master. The form-lines on the map boards are next inked by the cartographic draftsman to picture the terrain as nearly like the photograph as possible. Relief areas are shown by shading done by drawing numerous short lines. This technique is called hachuring.

Finally, roads, villages and other features created by man are added and place-names are lettered in before photo-copies of the resulting maps are made.

Photogrammetry has turned out to be the most efficient, accurate and economical method yet devised for mapping areas in months which formerly would have required years. By this means, instead of peering over the narrow ground like the myopic ant, man can now look down and see this earth as the birds do.

What time is it now? MINUTES _____

SECONDS _____

What is your reading time? MINUTES _____

SECONDS _____

Without referring back to the article, answer the following questions:

Comprehension quiz

1. The map of the farmer resembled, more than anything else, the maps made by
   a the Babylonians.
   b the Greeks.
   c the Arabs.
   d races earlier than any of these.

2. The Greek map-maker was
   a more of an artist than a scientist.
   b more of a scientist than an artist.
   c neither artist nor scientist.
   d influenced strongly by astronomy and geometry.

3. The Romans
   a improved on Greek maps.
   b used maps modeled after those of the Ionians.
   c first used the north-south-east-west idea in their maps.
   d decided that the earth was spherical.

4. The early maps made by the Arabs showed the influence of
   a the Greeks.
   b the Romans.
   c Mohammedanism.
   d none of these.

5. The first cartographer to write "America" over the land masses of the New World was
   a Christopher Columbus.
   b Martin Waldseemuller.
   c Martin Behaim.
   d Diego Ribero.

6. The system of parallels and meridians was devised by the _____.

7. Geographical conceptions changed more rapidly in the first quarter of the _____ century than either before or since.

8. The Greeks thought of the world as being _____ in shape.

9. Relief areas are shaded by drawing numerous short lines; this is called

_____.

10. The most efficient, accurate method for making maps is known as

_____.

How well did you comprehend what you have read? Check your answers with the Answer Key. Each correct answer is worth 10 per cent.

What is your level of comprehension?   _____%

What is your speed of comprehension?   _____wpm

What is your reading index (R × C/100)? _____

Reading Habit Index

Never Rarely Sometimes Usually Always

1. I use the survey technique in reading so that I may get a skeletonized preview of the thought.

2. I am aware that my mind is reading only certain key words, although I am sure I am seeing all the words.

3. I notice words that indicate a change in the flow of thought.

4. I regard each sentence as a part of a larger whole—each sentence a current, or countercurrent, in the stream of thought —a functionally important unit of the paragraph.

5. I am paragraph-conscious.

Reading habit index score: _____
(See directions for scoring, p. 75)
Date: _____

Chapter Eleven

How to remember
what you read

"THE TROUBLE with me is that I can't remember what I've read!"
So that's your trouble? You feel that much of what you read flies
away as soon as your eyes leave the print. One consolation is yours: you
have much company among your fellows and kinsmen along the road
of print. Yet, this need not be so. In the normal individual there is really
no valid reason why people cannot remember what they've read.

Remembering isn't some strange art. It is not some gift of Fortune;
it is not some mysterious mental attribute that some people have, while
others have it not. It is a skill that can be developed, like reading itself.
You remember because you actively do something to help yourself
remember. The memory process doesn't merely mean becoming a
human storage battery. It is more than the hoarding of facts and figures.
It is the faculty of appreciating facts and their relationship to each other,
figures and their meaning and interpretation with reference to pertinent
fact. The way *not* to remember is to think of remembering as some
Herculean task or superhuman feat. The skill of accurate recall is, like
any other skill, capable of development. But, that you may the better
understand how to proceed in developing it, a few simple rules may be
of help.

Steps in remembering what you read

1. *Approach the Page with a Positive Purpose.* Do you pick up an item to be read simply *knowing* that you will not retain the details and the facts? If so, the chances are that you will not be disappointed. The old saw that we get pretty much what we look for holds for reading as it does for most other situations of life. Many people simply "accept the fact"—that's their phrase for graceful, but unconditional surrender—that they cannot remember what they have read. And, in consequence, they don't.

Remembering begins with your own psychological outlook. Are you capable of coming to the page in a highly hopeful and expectant mood? The will to recall is your greatest initial asset. It is with such a psychology that the achievement of remembering what you read begins. This may not *seem* important, it is true, but it may make a great deal of difference in the net result of your achievement. Don't underestimate the power of a positive purpose in setting the stage for remembering what you've read.

2. *Survey Before You Select.* You must select only those facts that are worth remembering. Remembering is a discriminative process, based upon an evaluation of what is most worth while. Take time to look around. Here is where the skimming technique should be used.

Too many readers start attempting to remember before they know whether what they have decided upon is worth the effort that they are putting into it. Many an author has summarized for his readers the important facts at the end of the article, or he has pointed them out in boldface type or section division, but the reader is so intent in trying to remember what he reads that he grabs the first fact in sight and proceeds mentally to salt it down. Because it is a fact, such readers feel that it must be an *important* fact. Some students study like this. They arm themselves with a pencil and sally forth to underline their texts. When they finish, practically every word is underlined!

To such readers *every* fact is important. If they are to remember anything, they must remember everything. And so, like the indiscriminate woodsman, they start chopping at the first tree they see. Whether it be a sapling or a giant of the forest, they know not; nor do they care. To the woodsman it is the first tree; to the inexpert reader it is the first fact. Both fall upon their find with the same uncritical zeal.

Take your time. Apply all of the suggestions made in the chapter on skimming. Spy out the land, the length of it and the breadth of it, and size up the inhabitants thereof. You may be surprised what you will see.

3. *Facts of a Feather Flock Together.* Like bees, facts swarm. Within the subdivisions of the material you are reading, you will find swarms of facts with a generic "common denominator" which binds them together. In common parlance we call these "related" facts. It is only natural that this should be so. Each paragraph has a central idea. Following the main ideas are facts, a string of them, that support the main idea, explain it, and give it meaning. Facts are the bricks within the larger structure.

Try to see facts, therefore, as *units of information* within the larger framework. This viewpoint groups the factual material for easier remembering. Don't attempt to remember each fact as a "fact" in isolation; relate it to its proper place within the greater whole. Not all facts are equally important. There are principal facts and supporting facts, and all the facts are integrated by means of a factual *pattern* into the larger common whole. Facts are gregarious. You will find them in the company of each other. Seldom are they found alone, and they are usually found also in the custody of a main idea—a principal fact.

4. *Perceive if Possible How the Facts Are Packed.* When you read, look for the way the facts are packed. The container is the paragraph. But within the paragraph there are certain conventional styles of fact packaging.

One of these is the straight *chronological* arrangement. Facts are frequently reported in the paragraph in a natural time-sequence arrangement, one following the other as they might happen in point of time.

Then, there is the *logical* arrangement. That is, presenting the facts as they logically relate to each other. Action and reaction, cause and effect, circumstance and reason for the circumstance—all these are relationships with respect to the logic of the situation. Reasoning and logic dictate this pattern of fact arrangement.

Sometimes facts are contrasty in quality. They are arranged alongside each other in a paragraph in a kind of *contrast-comparison* arrangement.

However the author may arrange them, the smart reader will look at the paragraph in an attempt to discover the pattern by which they are packed. By so doing, the reader may be helped in remembering the facts as they first appeared to him when, lifting the lid of the paragraph, he saw them neatly arranged in groups. Therefore, it is wise to perceive, if possible, the way in which the facts are presented.

5. *Quiz Yourself with Questions.* When you find that you are surrounded with facts, don't do anything rash. Stop to think. Settle certain things in your own mind before you dash headlong into doing anything. Reading for accurate recall is a strenuous mental process. Take it easy until you have certain matters settled in your own thinking.

For example, ask yourself: *Why* is the author presenting these facts, anyway? Have you attempted to see the author's idea as a complete thought structure? Can you visualize the place which each fact occupies in the structure as a whole? Is it important that you try to remember *all* the facts? If not, what facts *are* important? *Why* do you want to remember these facts, anyway? Is there any method by which you can make the recalling of these facts easy for yourself?

With respect to this last question, do you recall a certain gentleman, Roy G. Biv? Perhaps your mind may hark back to the days when you studied the colors of the spectrum. You may remember that your instructor suggested that by remembering the name of the certain acrostical personage you would never again have trouble in reciting all the hues of the spectrum in their proper order from red to violet. He suggested that you acquaint yourself with Red, orange, yellow, Green, Blue, indigo, violet. Take the initial letter of the name of each color, and you form the acrostic. Occasionally it is possible to remember other facts in similar fashion.

All the questions proposed above, and others like them, should buzz around in your head as you begin to read. They should serve to bring the whole factual picture into sharp focus in your own mind. They should serve as aids in helping you to define the purpose for which you are reading.

Obviously each reading situation presents a different purpose from the point of view of the reader. In this book, for instance, you read the longer selections at the end of each chapter for the purpose of testing your skill in reading more rapidly and recalling details more accurately than you have done previously. You want to beat your own record. But when you read a directive on the job, or at the office; when you read a set of directions in a do-it-yourself kit, or when you read a professional journal or a newspaper, you have other purposes in mind. To bring your purpose for reading and for remembering into clear focus, quiz yourself with critical questions before you begin to read.

6. *Read, Reflect, and Recall.* Now you are ready to read. You know what you are looking for; and, having thus established your purpose, you will try to accomplish it by reading with it in mind. But navigators do not settle upon a destination and then strike out, leaving their charts and instruments behind. Any navigator who hopes to arrive checks and rechecks his course again and again en route. It may take him but an instant, but by so doing he knows that he is "on the beam." He knows he is flying toward his destination.

Now, what is your destination? It is to remember what you have read. You should, therefore, check your bearings as you fly through the domain of print. After you have finished a paragraph, with the speed of lightning, let your mind flash back over it; note the main idea again; summarize in a split second the facts that the author presented to support his statement or prove his point. This split-second review will do much to set the facts in your own mind before you go on to pile more data upon the undigested mental material which you already have on hand.

It may help you to focus upon the facts to read the topic sentence and, immediately upon reading it, to pause momentarily to ask yourself the question, "What does that mean?" or "Why?" Then, read to find the answer to your question. The psychology behind this little help is that we find what we look for. When you read a topic sentence—which is a generalization—and then you ask yourself, "What does that mean?" you are, from that point forward looking for facts to answer the unresolved question which is lingering in your mind. By approaching the paragraph in an interrogatory frame of mind, and leaving it with a last lightning glance you have very literally assaulted the facts both coming and going. Such treatment of the paragraphs should help you considerably in remembering what you've read.

7. *Practice Recall Persistently.* Use every occasion to improve your powers of recalling specific data accurately. There are thousands of opportunities every day that can be utilized for building a better mental recall. Addresses, telephone numbers, names of people to whom you have been introduced, bits of information from here and there—these are all excellent situations to test your faculties of remembering and recall.

One of the best aids to factual recall is the daily newspaper. Pick up the paper and read a paragraph, or a couple of paragraphs. Turn the paper face down. With a note pad, list in a 1, 2, 3 fashion *all* the facts that you can remember from the item which you have just read.

Then go back to your news story, and with your pencil check off in the story itself, point for point, the facts as you have listed them on your note pad. Out of the total number of facts in the news story—which number you might consider as 100 per cent—figure the percentage of facts which you recalled correctly.

If there were 8 facts in the paragraph, and you listed 6 of them on your note pad, your comprehension factor would be 75 per cent. This will be a rather accurate index as to your power to recall facts accurately, it will measure your recall ability—in other words, your reading comprehension of factual data. Repeat this exercise again and again.

A variant of the above exercise may be helpful in strengthening your recall ability. Take a certain width of column from a magazine or a book and measure 1, 2, 3, or as many inches down the column as you think is a sizable block of print that you can handle. The density of the factual data will dictate somewhat your selection length. Read this. Then take your note pad and, with the material turned face down, try to recall as much of the data as possible. Go back; check against the material read, again to determine your per cent of accurate recall.

On the same article, try to increase the number of inches in the block of type that you choose as a selection. Try also allowing a lapse of time between reading the material and recalling the facts. Stretch these dimensional factors *both* ways. For instance, you read a two-inch sample and recall six out of the seven facts presented. You therefore have an 86 per cent comprehension of what you have read.

Now read another two-inch sample taken from another part of the same article. Allow a five-minute time lapse before you attempt to jot down any of the facts by way of recall. Think of something else during the intervening five minutes. When the five minutes are up, take your note pad and repeat the exercise as described above.

Practice these exercises for fifteen minutes or more each day. Keep your scores. The exercises following this discussion will help you to get started in this technique. Keep up this practice on your own initiative. You will be surprised what perseverance, skill, hard work, and will can accomplish in improving your recall ability within a relatively short time.

Now, let's get started on the problem of finding out how efficiently you recall the data which you have read.

Practice remembering what you have read

To practice remembering what you have read, use the following paragraphs in this manner:

1. Read the paragraph carefully and attentively, reading as rapidly as possible, yet trying to note *all* the details.
2. Jot down the time when you begin and when you have finished reading each paragraph.
3. Close the book. (You might want to slip a piece of paper in the book at the page where you were reading.) Take your note pad, and listing 1, 2, 3, etc., jot down as many of the *facts* in the paragraph you have just read as you can recall. After you have finished jotting down the facts you can recall, refer to the paragraph, checking off your facts with the corresponding ones in the paragraph. Aim to be able to check off every fact in the paragraph.

Here is an example of a paragraph with the facts marked: [1]

Some 9000 stars can be seen with the unaided eye over all the	*Fact one*
earth throughout the year, but only some 2500 to 3000 at any	*Fact two*
one time in any one place. They range from the sixth magnitude	*Fact three*
to the first magnitude, and the first magnitude stars are 100	*Fact four*
times as bright as the faintest stars that we can see.	

There are four facts in that paragraph. If this were one of the paragraphs designated in the following list, you would read it, close the book, jot down the facts, and then go back to the paragraph to check off, fact for fact, those which you have been able to remember.

After each indication in the following list is the word count for the paragraph. Keep an accurate record of the length of time *in seconds* that it takes you to read each paragraph. Figure your rate of reading for each paragraph by multiplying the number of words in the paragraph by 60. Divide into this product your reading time in seconds to get your reading rate in words per minute. This expresses it mathematically:

$$\frac{\text{words in paragraph} \times 60}{\text{reading time in seconds}} = \text{wpm}$$

[1] H. J. Barnhard, D. A. Bennett, and H. S. Rice, *New Handbook of the Heavens*, p. 21, McGraw-Hill Book Company, Inc., New York, 1948.

It will be better for you to begin with shorter paragraphs. When you score 100 per cent in the suggested procedure, then try this variation:

1. Read the first paragraph, observing Steps 1 and 2 above.
2. Read a second paragraph, observing Steps 1 and 2 above.
3. Perform Step 3 for the first paragraph, without referring to it before jotting down details.
4. Perform Step 3 for second paragraph, also without referring to the text before attempting recall.
5. Check comprehensiveness of your recall for both paragraphs.
6. Repeat this procedure with another two paragraphs.

Strive constantly for longer paragraphs and a longer lapse of time between reading and recall. As soon as you become proficient in the variation above, try reading *three* paragraphs before attempting recall.

Here is a list of a few of the shorter paragraphs in this text that are suitable for this type of practice. All are taken from the early pages of the book. It is suggested that you work through the book *systematically*, rather than select passages at random. *Make* yourself remember more and *more*.

Page	Paragraph beginning	Word count
2	A great deal . . .	49
2	But you, too . . .	41
7	Coming into vogue . . .	72
9	When you read, *read* . . .	62
9	Before beginning . . .	38
9	When you come upon . . .	71
9	Put new skills . . .	78
11	But why as a college . . .	113
11	Let us go back . . .	111
12	Termination of instruction . . .	101

Learn to Read Rhythmically, Rapidly, and with Increased Eye Span

You have had exercises in previous chapters designed to improve your eye span and to encourage you to read rhythmically. The span in this exercise will be just a little wider than that of previous exercises. Try to take it all in one fixation. Look at the midpoint of each phrase.

I LIKE SCIENCE FICTION [2]

by John M. Cory

Man's writing explores a spectrum of ideas
extending from fact at one end to pure fantasy at the other.
Toward the middle band of this spectrum of thought
is the rapidly expanding rainbow of imaginative science.
Science, broadly defined, is that which is known.
Imaginative science projects this one step further
in the spectrum of ideas to include that which is known
to be possible. It takes facts and, in the term
of the mathematician, it *extrapolates* from these facts
to their possible consequences. In form, the literature
of imaginative science may be a kind of nonfiction
in which there is emphasis upon facts and extrapolations
without the framework of a story; or it may be fiction
with a novel or short story incorporating the
scientific speculation.

Not all science fiction writers agree on such matters
as definition, classification, educational values and standards.
After all, we must admit that science fiction is
still young and, for the most part considerably unstandardized.
By the same token, it is vigorous and stimulating
and full of surprises. What writers and readers
do agree on is that science fiction is fun.
That should be an invitation enough for anyone.

Seconds

Each time you repeat this exercise, record your time in
seconds. Try to show a definite record of improvement.
Swing your eyes faster and faster down the page. Be sure that
you *see* the whole of each fixation; be sure that you *get the*
thought as you read.

1. _____
2. _____
3. _____
4. _____
5. _____
6. _____
7. _____
8. _____
9. _____
10. _____

Average time: _____

[2] John M. Cory, "I Like Science Fiction" (adapted), The New York Public Library *Branch Library Book News*, vol. 30, October, 1953, p. 111.

Reading for Speed of Comprehension—1

The article which you are about to read discusses a number of practical ways in which your memory can be improved. Read this article to see how rapidly you can comprehend the author's ideas. Try to see his whole discussion as a unit. Read this with the thought that if you were called upon to discuss it after you had finished reading it, you could talk about it from the standpoint of an integrated whole.

Read to break your former record of speed of comprehension. Get the facts, and also see the master plan by which the author has them organized. Be sensitive to the relationship of one fact to another.

Time: MINUTES _____

        SECONDS _____

CAN MEMORY BE IMPROVED? [3]

by Joseph Mayer

To answer this question and ascertain how memory can be strengthened, if at all, it is first necessary to clarify several related issues, chief among them being why we lose memory or become forgetful.

The word "forget," which means the opposite of "get" as applied to the mind, is of almost no help in such a clarification. It is a completely neutral term and indicates merely a passive inability to remember. When you become "forgetful," however, and fail repeatedly to recall important events, something *positive* has happened to the memory. To grow "forgetful" is to develop a deficiency, to lose a power previously possessed.

The word "disremember," is somewhat better for clarification. Though little used today except in slang or in fun, it carries that positive significance I wish to convey—the idea of something disabling or disorganizing the memory, literally disfiguring it and thus destroying its effectiveness. This is the clue to the main cause of progressive forgetfulness.

Many people unwittingly develop a tendency to disfigure a memory pattern. This may be caused by fear, worry, "toying" with or questioning a memory image, lack of confidence in one's ability to remember. If the

---

[3] Condensed from Joseph Mayer, "Can Memory Be Improved?" *Hygeia*, vol. 26, March, 1948, pp. 176–177, 222, and April, 1948, pp. 254–255, 291–292.

disfigurement is only partial and occasional, one may get a ludicrous result, as when Mrs. Malaprop is reported to have said that she went to the ball dressed like Cinderella while her escort came dressed in the *garbage* of a monk! If the disfigurement is complete the result is to blur the memory image so that nothing definite comes up in attempts at recall.

A simple illustration will show how such disfigurement occurs. A friend gives you a telephone number, "Main 1234." Later you want to recall it, but instead of accepting what comes up in the mind, you say to yourself, "maybe it is Main 4321 or 2143." What have you done? You have stamped over the original proper impression, "1234," several other impressions—until what comes up is "Main blur blur blur blur." In protecting your memory, Rule No. 1 is *never guess at or foolishly toy with a memory image. If you are not sure, verify it at once.*

Thus far we have assumed that you received a proper memory image in the first place, but right here certain important general factors enter the picture. If you have never been aware of an incident even though it has occurred, you cannot consciously recall it. If you have received a false or muddled impression, the memory image will be false or muddled. Rule No. 2 is that *in order to have an accurate memory recall, one must have an accurate impression to begin with.*

We now turn more definitely to the problem of improving the memory. If we assume that Rules No. 1 and 2 are being faithfully followed— that care is being taken to secure accurate impressions and to avoid guesswork and distorted images in efforts at recall—what, in addition, is required? Rule No. 3 may at first seem rather elementary. It is simply a matter of *accurate repetition* until the physical dexterity or mental exercise or a combination of the two has been mastered and the reactions become a matter of habit.

I say Rule No. 3 is simple, but that is so only provided the first two rules are being scrupulously adhered to, which implies also that fears and worries and distrust in one's ability are being resolutely pushed aside. It is the failure to follow the first two rules which accounts for most memory lapses. The third rule is nevertheless important since it provides that positive exercise through which memory is strengthened and assurance in one's ability to memorize is renewed or built up. A few illustrations will demonstrate how these rules can be applied to particular situations.

1. *Telephone Numbers.* If you have developed trouble recalling

'phone numbers or have always had difficulty, the following brief exercise should prove helpful. Get a small book, with alphabetical tabs, to carry in purse or pocket. Write names and addresses and telephone numbers in the book. Put down the numbers carefully. Keep adding entries as occasion warrants and carry the book with you.

As a memory exercise, copy from the book on a piece of paper (that can be readily folded and kept in the book) about a half dozen names and 'phone numbers in which you are most interested—name on one line and number underneath. Go over these four or five times in an evening or other convenient time, carefully repeating name and number aloud while looking at the sheet. Do not guess or try to "reason" anything out. Now cover everything on the sheet except the first name. Wait to see if the telephone number comes to mind. If nothing comes up, uncover the number and repeat it aloud. Follow the same procedure for each pair of names and numbers. Then start over again. But remember the first two rules—do not worry or guess or lose patience.

Repeat this exercise ten minutes a day for several days. Soon you will recognize the telephone number as you uncover it. You'll say to yourself, "Of course that is it!" Next, the number will come to mind as you look at the person's name. When that happens you will come to feel completely sure. If at any time you temporarily lose this feeling of certainty, look up the number again, *without delay or further attempts at recall.* It is in such moments of temporary uncertainty that disfiguration of the memory image takes place. If "toying" with an image has become a habit with you, it may take some effort to break the habit.

By faithfully following for a week the simple exercise indicated above you will be surprised not only at your renewed ability to remember a few telephone numbers but also at the new confidence you feel in yourself. Should the image become dim after a lapse of time, as it often does, consult your book at once. There is nothing wrong in this, for memory patterns usually require fairly frequent recall to keep the images sharp and distinct.

2. *Names and Faces.* If you have difficulty remembering names, your trouble may be primarily with Rule 2. You may find it hard to get a correct mental impression in the first place. Someone is introduced to you and names are exchanged, but all you get is a jumble or only half a name to which you add a tailpiece of your own! Have you not sometimes admired the man who. when he is introduced, will face you down,

say he is sorry but he didn't catch the name, and make you spell it out for him? You would like to be able to do that yourself. Well, you will have to learn to do it—or something a bit less "bold"—if you wish to remember names more readily, for you must get the correct name in the beginning in order to have a proper recall later on.

An exchange of cards is a useful device. If your visitor hasn't a card, give him one of your own and ask him to write his name and address on it. After he leaves, jot a note on the card indicating something of the circumstances of your meeting. Keep these cards handy and go over them frequently, recalling events of the meetings and what the various people look like.

Failure to remember faces may be traced to a similar difficulty—you may have a habit of averting the eyes and not really seeing what your visitor looks like when you meet him (a habit it is well to break, for more than one reason)—or it may be that your visual perceptions in general need strengthening. A good exercise for this purpose is to devote a few minutes daily to visualizing a scene that can be verified and that has recently occurred. For example: You are sitting alone in a room waiting for someone. Look around; then close your eyes and try to visualize the various objects; now look again and see what you have missed. Your first attempts with such an exercise may be rather disappointing, but sufficiently repeated it is certain to sharpen your visual perceptions and to strengthen your ability to remember faces.

3. *Attention.* To be sure, there is such a condition as *general* inattention, which may have a number of causes—from poor physical health at one end to a definite psychoneurosis at the other. But normally, if one has fallen into the habit of letting the attention wander and there is nothing else amiss, one or two simple exercises should be sufficient to correct the difficulty. It of course stands to reason that unless one is able to concentrate to some extent, one becomes fuzzy about everything, including the memory.

One thing to do is to find some simple mental interest and focus on it for a half hour daily—say, a game of solitaire or a simple crossword puzzle, if nothing better. But the inattentive person going through such an exercise must do it deliberately, constantly fighting the tendency of the mind to wander. If the person has become interested in strengthening his memory, the exercises already suggested with respect to names, faces and telephone numbers will be even more helpful in steadying his attention. Another exercise is to set aside a convenient time each day when the wandering mind is, so to speak, caught hold of and forced to recite details of its meanderings for a brief period that has just passed. Try to recall what has gone through the mind in the past half hour. What has interrupted or given a new direction to the train of thought? Could the interruptions have been avoided? A repeated focusing of attention on recent mental events and giving them a deliberate examination will not only make one more generally alert but will also ferret out the causes of one's mental wandering and thus assist in correcting it.

4. *Adult Memory and Learning.* It is well known that as a rule adults find it harder to memorize and to learn than children do. This is especially true where the higher reasoning faculties are not primarily involved —as in learning poetry and language and such skills as skating and bicycle riding. Why is this true and is it necessarily true?

Notable exceptions demonstrate that the rule does not apply universally, but of course there might still be a kind of mental deterioration setting in soon after adolescence which makes the rule apply by and large. Some such general belief is apparently widespread and as part of it is the idea that as one outgrows childhood one begins to lose an inherent power—to memorize and to learn—which he previously possessed. There is probably no more erroneous notion than this. At the same time there are certain tendencies, already touched upon, which help to give the notion its wide currency.

Any inherent powers man possesses to memorize and to learn grow stronger, not weaker, throughout the years of normal health and strength unless he develops habits of guessing, worry and lack of confidence which obstruct the free exercise of those powers.

As with adult learning, so with adult memory. If you can overcome your acquired inhibitions and habits of guessing, memory should be easier for the adult than for the child.

5. *Language and Science.* Picking up a new language is primarily a matter of memory. With science and mathematics the question is essentially one of reasoning. Now these two mental processes are in one very important respect diametrically opposed. Memory requires complete faith; doubt and question applied to a memory image will tend to disfigure if not destroy it. Reason assumes a doubtful and questioning attitude at every turn. Thus one can readily develop memory at the expense of reasoning or reason at the expense of memory, especially if a strong bent in one direction or the other shows itself at an early age and the student is never taught the important distinction just indicated.

A full recognition, however, of the necessity for exercising faith where memory is concerned and question where reasoning is involved, enables one to develop both faculties at the same time. Here lies probably the most neglected area in our educational system.

It will be noted that no mention was made of mnemonic or artificial memory systems based upon arbitrary associations of ideas—as, for example, changing numbers into letters, then building words and sentences out of the letters, and later on employing the coded words and sentences to recall the numbers.

If one wishes to prepare some parlor tricks or has a business or professional reason for linking and recalling lists of unrelated names or numbers or events, there are mnemonic means to such ends, provided one's memory is already good and that the three memory rules continue to be utilized. These pages have been primarily concerned with the rational improvement of *normal* memory, for which purpose a conscientious application of the three rules is all that is ordinarily required.

What time is it now? MINUTES _____

SECONDS _____

What is your reading time for this selection? MINUTES _____

SECONDS _____

Comprehension quiz

Multiple choice, true and false, and other tests of comprehension of that general type lay emphasis upon remembering specific details and isolated facts. Comprehension, however, embraces much more than that. Another type of comprehension test is that which tests how adequately the reader has been able to see what he has read in its larger outline. That is the type of comprehension test this one is.

Below is a skeleton outline of the article which you have just read. Fill in the outline.

I. _____

A. _____

B. _____

C. _____

II. _____

   A. _____

   B. _____

   C. _____

   D. _____

   E. _____

Check your outline against the one given in the Answer Key. While there may be a difference in wording, the two outlines should be substantially the same.

There were 10 blanks to be filled in. Each blank is worth 10 per cent.

What is your level of comprehension?   _____%

What is your speed of comprehension?   _____wpm

What is your reading index $(R \times C/100)$? _____

Reading for Speed of Comprehension—2

Here is an essay in political philosophy that evaluates democracy in the light of modern trends and contemporary thinking. What role that is distinctive and unique does democracy play in a rapidly changing world? What is the future of democracy? These are the questions that Benedetto Croce, one of the truly great minds of our age, attempts to answer in the essay that follows.

Read this essay as rapidly as possible, always being careful to understand fully what the author is saying; but, having once comprehended it, push on to get the next thought and the next. Concentrate on the thought, but keep going.

Time: MINUTES _____

      SECONDS _____

THE FUTURE OF DEMOCRACY [4]

by Benedetto Croce

People are always asking, Do you think that the world is moving toward an authoritarian system of government? Do you think that

[4] Benedetto Croce, "The Future of Democracy," *The New Republic*, vol. 131, 1954, pp. 100–101 (40th Anniversary Issue).

philosophy is moving toward a new anti-idealistic realism? Do you think that art is moving toward futurism or dadaism or "hermitism"? and so on.

I call this kind of question "meteorological"; it is like asking, "Do you think that it is going to rain today? Had I better take my umbrella?"

But moral, intellectual, esthetic and political problems are not things outside ourselves, like rain or fine weather; they are within ourselves and for that reason there is no sense in asking what is more or less likely to happen. We need solely to make up our own minds and to act, each one according to his understanding and his capacity.

You will permit me also to state that, among the insults today offered to liberty, none seems to me more gross than that implied in the question whether the liberal system is to be preferred to the authoritarian system.

It reminds me of the story of a man who went to a friend and said: "I was given a slap in the face today, what do you advise me to do about it?" and the friend replied, "Why, if it was given to you, keep it." It is evident that a man who asks advice about his personal dignity has already actually renounced it.

The choice between liberty and suppression of liberty is not on the same plane as a choice between things of different values, one of which may reasonably be preferred to the other—the first means human dignity and civilization, the second the debasing of men until they are either a flock to be led to pasture, or captured, trained animals in a cage.

Coming to our own times I see the future that liberty promises always as a beacon; I do not see any light in the future promised by authoritarianism. In the past, under the forms of theocracy, of monarchy, or of oligarchy, authority had at least a background of religious mystery. Modern humanistic thought has dissipated the mystery, replacing it by simple humanitarian ideals.

But authoritarianism in our times, in those we see looming ahead, is irreligious and materialistic, despite its pretenses and rhetoric, and comes down to a brutal rule of violence over people who are prevented from seeing and knowing what is going on, and who are forced to submit to leadership and give unquestioning obedience to it.

To lend glamor to this obedience by associating it with the noble and the heroic, it is usually called military discipline, which has been extended, or should be extended, to the whole of society. But military discipline has its function only as one aspect of the social order. If instead of being contained within the society, it is itself the containing body or is co-extensive with society, it can no longer be called military discipline, but is a general process of fostering universal stupidity. An artist with the face of a corporal, a scientist with that of a sergeant, a politician who waits for his orders and blindly carries them out, is no longer an artist, a scientist or a politician, but an imbecile.

We see it also as a phase of mental decadence that the political problem is now usually presented in terms of "the masses," and what is suitable "for the masses." "Masses" are not, as people seem to believe, something new in history; they have always existed, smaller than today, to be sure, since the proportions of society as a whole were smaller, but of the same nature and with the same spirit, the same threat, the same peril.

Sound political sense has never regarded the masses as the directing force of society, but has always delegated this directive function to a class which was not economic in its basis of selection, but political; one capable of governing. The problem concerns therefore not the masses but the governing class. Here too the evil, if evil there be, is in ourselves, and in ourselves alone is the remedy. It is vain to look for it elsewhere.

Liberalism should be at one and the same time the friend and the foe of democracy. It should be its friend, because the governing class is fluid, and its efforts are applied to increasing its membership and its following to choosing them more carefully, and thus democracy implies an administration that provides at the same time an education of the governed for governing. But liberalism must be the foe of democracy when the latter tends to substitute mere numbers or quantity for quality, because by so doing democracy is preparing the way for demagoguery, and, quite unintentionally, for dictatorship and tyranny and its own destruction.

A practical corollary for men of good will: to work unremittingly under whatever conditions prevail, with every means at hand, and continuously, to work for the preservation and strengthening of the liberal spirit, seeking the most suitable means, but always those that lead to the end in view and not to its abandonment or its replacement by other ends.

A man who works for an ideal finds in that ideal his hope and his joy. And yet his human flesh may perhaps look for comfort in some more specific aspiration. And this too he can have, if he considers that, under the present conditions of the world, the reserve of intellectual and moral force is still enormous, and that civil liberties have been preserved in great and powerful nations. These will withstand the perils to which they are exposed and will serve as signal flares for general recovery and resumption of progress.

But supposing we assume that the worst will happen. The worst that can be envisaged is that the struggle which is today tearing the world asunder will culminate in the complete rout of liberty and the triumph of authoritarianism, or as it is now called, "totalitarianism," even in the countries which have up to this time remained immune.

Well, then, freedom will succumb, to be sure, but with the certainty that the processes of acquiring it will have to begin all over again, and that, in order to begin again, people will resume the efforts which for the time being have failed to win victory, but which will win it in days to come.

In this sense, and not in that of obedience, in this knowing how to suffer death for a greater life, the task of humanity is in truth inspired by a military and a heroic spirit.

Can we suppose that our affairs will be in safer hands if we give *carte blanche* to others to manage them as they see fit, without the interested persons being able to intervene, to object, or even to ask questions?

Here, too, an anecdote comes to mind, that of the king of Illyria in Daudet's *Les Rois en Exil* who renounces his throne to live blissfully as a private individual with a woman. When he triumphantly announces to her that he has done so, she laughs in his face, "Jobard, va!" (you poor simpleton) and walks out.

What time is it now? MINUTES _____

SECONDS _____

What is your reading time for this selection? MINUTES _____

SECONDS _____

Now without referring back to the article for any purpose whatsoever, answer the following questions:

Comprehension quiz

1. The author recommends
   a   group thinking.
   b   individualistic thinking and action.
   c   a questioning attitude.
   d   thinking in terms of the worst that might happen.

2. The author's position is that
   a   the free man has no alternative in the modern world but to accept insults.
   b   authoritarianism is all right as long as it does not mean totalitarianism.
   c   all free people need to be curbed by authority, hence governments are instituted among men.
   d   the difference between liberty and authoritarianism is not a difference of gradations but a difference of extremes.

3. Military discipline in a democratic society
   a   is a general process for fostering universal stupidity.
   b   should be coextensive with society.
   c   should be contained within society.
   d   is an inevitable result of the democratic process.

4. Presenting the political problem in terms of the masses is a sign of
   a   mental decadence.
   b   a recognition that the masses are the directing force in society.
   c   an acknowledgment that the masses are politically a threat and a peril to democracy.
   d   being interested in the greatest good for the greatest number.

5. When a democracy emphasizes quantity at the expense of quality, it
   a   becomes even more democratic.
   b   changes from a democratic to a liberal state.
   c   sows the seeds of its own destruction.
   d   provides a greater opportunity for a greater number of its people.

6. The author believes that men should work unremittingly for the
   a   liberal spirit.
   b   cause of peace.
   c   future of democracy.
   d   abolition of totalitarianism.

7. The author sees in the democratic nations
   a an antidote for authoritarianism.
   b hope for the masses.
   c a liberalism which is the hope of the future.
   d an enormous reserve of intellectual and moral force that will serve as an inspiration for future progress.

8. If western democracy should succumb to the forces of totalitarianism, the author predicts that this would be
   a the complete rout of liberty.
   b the final triumph for authoritarianism.
   c a mere interim in the ultimate triumph of the democratic way of life.
   d merely the inevitable result of the trend of our times.

9. The author endorses
   a Lincoln's concept "that government of the people, by the people, for the people shall not perish from the earth."
   b Jefferson's idea that "all men are created equal, that they are endowed . . . with certain unalienable rights . . . that to secure these rights, governments are instituted among men."
   c Webster's view, "liberty and union, now and forever, one and inseparable."
   d the pronouncement of the Charter of the United Nations, "to reaffirm faith in fundamental human rights . . . and in nations large and small."

10. The directing force of society has been
    a the masses.
    b democracy.
    c totalitarianism.
    d the governing class.

How well did you comprehend what you have read? Check your answers against those given in the Answer Key. Each correct answer is worth 10 per cent.

What is your level of comprehension?   _____%

What is your speed of comprehension?   _____wpm

What is your reading index $(R \times C/100)$? _____

Reading Habit Index

Never   Rarely   Sometimes   Usually   Always

1. When I read I am aware that a paragraph usually contains a statement of the main idea, and I look for such statement.
2. As I read I try new techniques to get the thought from the printed page quickly.
3. I read as I drive, with varying rates of speed, depending upon reading conditions.
4. I "flash back" over the paragraph after I have read it to summarize in my own thinking the material I have read.
5. I read most paragraphs in a basically questioning, or interrogatory, frame of mind, looking for answers as I read.

Reading habit index score: _____
(See directions for scoring, p. 75)
Date: _____

Chapter Twelve

Why did the author write this?

AUTHORS are very practical people. They write as they do largely because of you, the reader. Whether you realize it or not, they have their eye on you constantly. You, and others like you, are the imaginary ghosts, the disembodied spirits that float in the background of the author's mind as he writes, and he calls you his "public." Employing another phrase of the writing craft, he says that he is "writing for a market." From the standpoint of the reader, therefore, you should recognize clearly the motives of the author.

Every craftsman sees you in the light of his own particular trade. The writer is no exception. He sees you essentially as a human being with a bundle of reactions who will respond, puppetlike, to the words which he will put before your eyes. One of the first laws of journalism is to slant the story to the prospective reader.

The type of reading which demands that the reader inspect the author's motives and *evaluate* them is called *critical* reading. Critical reading is reading at its very best. It is skillful, efficient reading—plus. In many places we have said that the important thing in all reading is to understand the thought of the author. By inference, therefore, one might think that the role of the reader is merely receptive. This is not so. "Reading is thinking." Only as the reader thinks, actively and aggressively, along with the author does he *really* read.

The reader must bring something *to* the page, instead of expecting merely to take everything *from* it. He must cease from being only a passive participant and actively join with the author in thinking about the subject under discussion. Critical reading demands that the reader have his eyes wide open for subtle nuances of meaning, for implications that lurk behind the words, and for the long shadows of the author's ulterior motive.

Nor does this mean that the reader will disregard the author's line of thought and substitute his own. Reading critically is not an opportunity to read into the text what is not there, or to use the author's words simply as a springboard from which to depart into the realm of the reader's own bias.

Too many readers never let the *author* speak. They begin reading with their minds made up. They have predetermined what the author *should* say. They finish, confirmed in their own thinking that the author *has said* precisely what they predestined that he should. Such people work on the "I-told-you-so, I-knew-it" philosophy. During the whole time in which they were *looking at the words* (for, to be sure, they were not *reading!*), they were so occupied with their own ideas that they had no time to comprehend those of the author. Such an instance is, of course, an exaggerated example, but it smacks of commonplace behavior, with the difference one of degree only.

The first rule for critical reading, therefore, is *know what the author is saying*. There will be plenty of time later for your own thinking. You may, of course, not agree with what the author says, nor may you be able to see things in the same way that he does. He may, in fact, attack your most cherished beliefs; but even that is no excuse for refusing to hear him and to weigh his words with a fair and open mind.

No reader is a skillful reader until he knows exactly what he has read. And until you *have* understood clearly and exactly the thought of the author—no matter how bizarre or revolutionary that thought may be— you have no right to make up your mind about his writing. In good reading every man should have the right to be heard. Prejudice means to *pre-judge*; that is, to make up your mind before you have ascertained the facts. Don't be stampeded. Beware of your own prejudices. Read with an open mind.

Judge, rather, *as* you read the facts. This is evaluation; this is critical reading. In such reading you judge the idea from a position totally outside of the idea itself. The evaluative or critical reader is aware of two separate acts taking place almost simultaneously. As his mind is recording the author's thought, he is at the same time comparing, analyzing, evaluating, and forming opinions about that thought or about the statements of facts which the author is making.

This means that to read critically you must have a broad background of general, factual knowledge. Let us suppose that you are reading an article dealing with certain economic conditions. To appraise that article correctly, to make any kind of evaluation of it you will need a background of fact, probably from American or world history, a knowledge of current events, of elementary economics, of banking, of business, and related fields.

A common type of critical reading is that which is done by the critic or reviewer who appraises new books, plays, and music. These critics are specialists in the area in which they review. By bringing their total knowledge of the field to bear upon a particular book, for instance, they evaluate its worth as a creative piece of literature or a contribution to a specific area of factual knowledge.

The role of the professional critic amply points up the importance of a broad background of general knowledge for the critical reader. But every reader is a critic to some degree. Whenever a person makes up his mind about something which he has read, he engages in critical appraisal. Sometimes this is done with the knowledge that he already has. By means of it he judges how well the new presentation fits into the general pattern of fundamental facts relating to the subject. At other times the reader must judge on the basis of his feelings, his likes and dislikes, his own response to the writer's presentation, and his innate sense of artistic balance and proportion. This latter approach is reserved for evaluating the less factual and more creative forms of literature.

For these very reasons, reading critically is one of the most difficult phases of all reading. It demands a sensitive awareness of what the author is saying and also what he is *implying*. It means staying on the beam of the author's thought, but at the same time it means the ability to see where that beam is leading and to determine whether the direction is consistent with logic, common sense, and the already prevailing knowledge in the field. Critical reading demands that the reader appraise the author's appeals, evaluate his techniques, weigh his judgment, and test his reasoning by standards of logical reasoning and by an unimpassioned interpretation of the facts as they are presented.

To what do writers appeal?

What are some of these appeals, some of these techniques to which readers should be alert? Let us look at several of the principal ones.

1. *The Appeal to the Pocketbook.* This appeal is at the root of all writing done in the name of advertising. Much political news writing is also aimed at an appeal to the reader's pocketbook: news of what Congress is doing, or planning to do, in the matter of cutting or raising taxes, reforms to save taxpayers' money, swindles and graft in government, what the new candidate plans to do to economize and balance the budget, and a thousand other situations, examples of which may be found on every front page of the nation's newspapers. The "how-to-do-it-yourself" books and magazine articles bid you save the strain on your pocketbook by doing yourself what otherwise you would pay another to do for you.

Much of the writing, likewise, in the homemaking sections of the magazines and newspapers: how to make tasty dishes from dreary leftovers, budgeting by buying cheaper cuts of meat, suggestions for saving pennies here and there in the day's routine doings—all of these hints are aimed at plugging the leaks in the family budget. The writer of such material has only one purpose in view—to get the reader's attention by appealing to his need to economize.

2. *The Appeal to Egotism.* Every person likes to think that in one respect or another he is the most important person on the face of the earth. He thinks well of himself, and he likes others to think well of him. He delights in your suggestion that he has fastidious tastes; he takes pride in your telling him that he is a discriminating judge of fine values. Such personal qualities set him off from his fellows. It makes him "important."

A man reads a book on *How to Know and Choose Antiques.* He will know, after reading it, the difference, for instance, between the severer Sheraton and the more ornate Hepplewhite. Such knowledge will give him prestige. He can now speak "with authority" about antiques. His possession of knowledge that his neighbors do not have gives him personal satisfaction. Or, instead of antiques, it may be gardens or violins, books or postage stamps.

3. *The Appeal to Curiosity.* A tremendous amount of reading material has been produced because of man's insatiable curiosity. All factual prose, any piece of writing which satisfies man's intellectual curiosity, has come into being because of its basic appeal to a curious, questioning creature.

You look up at the stars, and you wonder about the shape and the dimensions of the universe, how the stars came to be, and what will be their end. In that case, certain writers have written books which will appeal to your curiosity: Eddington, Einstein, Hoyle, Jeans, and Gaposchkin—and there are dozens of others.

Or, perhaps, you wonder about the American past. If so, other writers —Charles and Mary Beard, Allan Nevins, Henry Steele Commager, Arthur Schlesinger, and others—have written that which will appeal to your curiosity.

Curiosity also takes other forms. It is a natural thing to be curious about the doings of others. We take pleasure in learning about the trivia of each other's lives. Listen to most conversation. Witness the content of the newspaper column, the metropolitan daily as well as the small-town weekly. Countless inches—*miles* would be a more accurate measure —of American newsprint is dedicated each day to the idle chitchat of who goes where, who gets married, who have babies, who was seen with whom, and so on and on to the last syllable of recorded time!

4. *The Appeal to the Need of Sharing Experiences.* Few people like to live totally alone. They need someone to share with them the happenings of their lives. When there is no one else, then a book must suffice. The girl in a strange city and the wife on the western ranch are both lonely souls. They resort to love stories and stereotyped radio serials. When we cannot live actually, we must live vicariously. Authors know this. That is the reason why newspapers and magazines print the serials that millions read. For the same reason shipwrecks, wars, adventure make good reading. Success and Horatio Alger stories will always have a market; those who have succeeded will read them, and also those who have failed.

5. *The Appeal to the Supernatural, the Mysterious, and the Unreal.* From the tales of Edgar Allan Poe to the latest account of flying saucers and visitors from outer space, we have been intrigued by the supernatural, the mysterious and the unreal. Pick any newsstand, and look over the number of periodicals dealing with science fiction. You'll be

amazed at how many of them there are. This is mute testimony to our interest in the superhuman and hyperphysical.

Literature has been studded in every period with such novels as *Frankenstein*, such gothic tales as *The Mysteries of Udolpho*. Whodunits and science thrillers have taken the place of these old, creaking prototypes, but the motives for writing them and the appeal to the reader are perennially the same.

6. *The Appeal to the Sense of the Beautiful, the Artistic, the Esthetic.* This is one of the strongest appeals of every salesman. He calls to your attention the lines, the color, the beauty of the item which he has for sale. Because a thing of beauty can be a joy forever, millions of dollars are spent each year for beauty alone. Look through the advertisements in any magazine and note the emphasis on beauty as a selling point. Writers also appeal to the sense of beauty in their readers by colorful and picturesque descriptions.

7. *The Appeal to Religious, Spiritual, and Moral Values.* Man is interested in the better side of his nature. Among the titles on the best-seller list, there is at least one which is basically concerned with the values of the higher and better way of life. The appeal to justice and fair play, to tolerance, to kindliness, and to help for others—these are all variations of the theme of applied religious values.

These have been the basic appeals. Let us look now at some of the techniques for influencing the reader's mind.

Techniques of the appeal

You will do well to approach a critical reading situation with certain "yardstick questions" by which you may be able to get a more accurate measure of the item which you are reading:

1. Who is the author? Is he competent to write on this subject?
2. Do *you* know enough about this area of knowledge to make any sort of competent judgment with regard to the facts the author presents?
3. Does the author think straight and play fair? Does he give both sides of the issue, or is he indulging in salesmanship and propaganda?

The last of these questions deals with the whole matter of influencing others. This practice has been variously labeled salesmanship, propaganda, persuasion, and deception. It usually deals in a readily recognizable set of wares. The verbal jugglers who sell these tricks pass them off in attractive wrappings with plenty of verbal frills.

The Institute for Propaganda Analysis some years ago tore off the wrapping, and under the glitter of a wordy exterior they found this assortment of doubtful items. These are standard techniques for influencing the thinking of the reader. The critical reader will recognize any one of them as soon as he encounters it.[1]

1. Name-calling
2. Glittering generality
3. Transfer
4. Testimonial
5. Plain folks
6. Card stacking
7. Band wagon

These are the principal tricks of the trade. They are methods of tricking the naive and deceiving the gullible. Let us move in for a close-up and inspect these several items more closely.

Name-calling

Most of us enjoy vicariously the pleasure of name-calling. Look at this advertisement. Its appeal lies in the fact that it employs the technique of name-calling.

Don't be an old grouch! Who loves a Sour Puss? Take Vita Drops. Two Vita Drops a day make you feel wonderful. They put that old smile back on the face! *Stop* being a Sourball. Take Vita Drops today.

And there is, of course, accompanying the advertisement, the picture of a miserable old grouch.

That is the same low-grade humorous approach that so often characterizes the comic strips. The visions of Old Sourball give us a quiet sense of superiority. At least *we* are not an old lemon-face—thank goodness for that—although at times we do *feel* the way this fellow looks. Maybe Vita Drops *would* be good for us. Name-calling is an extremely subtle technique. See how it operates? Maybe Vita Drops *would* be good for us!

[1] This list of techniques is reprinted from Alfred McClung Lee and Elizabeth Briant Lee, *The Fine Art of Propaganda*, p. 23, Harcourt, Brace and Company, Inc., New York, 1939.

Glittering Generality

Everybody will be riding in a new, fashionable Jack Rabbit convertible this year!

Everybody? That word is mighty general! And won't you feel lonesome—unutterably lonesome—and out of place, if you're poking along in your old, eight-cylinder hard top wheezer instead of riding in a luxurious new Jack Rabbit convertible this spring? Think about it, and shudder.

What power of appeal and compulsion the glittering generalization has! And glittering generalizations are sneaky things. They get by even the most watchful eyes at times. They sneak into our consciousness and do their damage by being concealed in such innocuous, Trojan-horse phrases as, "Everybody knows that . . . ," "It's an accepted fact that . . . ," and by the way of the simple, unqualified statement.

Transfer

The scene: a swank executive suite
Properties: a spacious desk and red leather chair (unoccupied) behind the desk
The caption says: "Picture yourself in this chair tomorrow!"

Then the rest of the text proceeds to convince you that by taking Bright Boy Correspondence Courses you will be laying steppingstones straight to that chair. It is really dangerous to look too long at that picture, or to read that advertisement too intently. If you do, you really *will* see yourself sitting right in that chair behind that desk.

That is the power of the appeal to transfer. The imagine-yourself-in-his-place technique is widely used and is often presented much more subtly. For instance, there is the "wouldn't-you-like-to-own-a-home-like-this-one" approach. Then you are told how easy it is to live in this Fall Apart ranch house. You pay only $100 a month for the next fifty years—and it is yours!

Testimonial

I have never been so popular in all my life before. Popularity began when I switched to Sparkle Smile Tooth Paste.

People, well-known and unknown, great and small, are represented by the testimonial. Some testimonials are by stars of stage, screen, and television; others are by obscure and unknown "J.Q.P., Anywhere, U.S.A." Testimonials are used to sell everything from soap to nuts.

Usually testimonials are of two types: the paid testimonials of the well-known great, and the simple words of the average man. Neither is too dependable. The one says what he has been paid to say; the other may be attributing to the product more than is due that product. J.Q.P. may forget, for instance, that he joined a hiking club about the same time that he began using Sparkle Smile, and that the popularity he attributes to the tooth paste is due to the new friends he met in the club rather than because of the wonderful effects of Sparkle Smile.

Plain Folks

We all like to be plain and folksy. There is something in our democracy that makes of plain folks, appealing folks. Take, for instance, the disarming appeal of the following:

AN INVITATION
to Mr. and Mrs. Average American

Come into our store today. You'll find our clerks are just plain, folksy people like yourself. They like to talk to you about your household problems, and they appreciate the need to stretch the budget of the average family. They'll try to help you stretch it as far as possible—but they'll see to it that you always get quality first.

Card Stacking

Card stacking is a technique that is used to influence the reader by selecting only those facts or falsehoods, logical or illogical statements, which will present the best or worst possible case for an idea, a person, or a product. Political speeches employ this formula. You meet it frequently in advertising:

There is NO other answer! Do not be fooled. There is only *one* way to save money on your fuel bill. Polar Bear Storm Windows—that's it—Polar Bear! Polar Bear Storm Windows will save you many times their cost, and they're really very inexpensive. You can try everything else—thousands of others have—and they have found out only *one* thing: Polar Bear is the *only* answer.

You actually *feel* yourself saving money the first week that you have Polar Bear installed. It's true!

That is card stacking! Questions and arguments are anticipated and answered *before* they arise. The aces are all in one hand.

Band Wagon

Sunshine Pass is the most popular skiing resort in America. All of your friends will be there over the holiday, and many of America's famous personalities, too. Come to Sunshine Pass for a holiday that you will never forget. And, if you don't ski, come anyway. You'll have a wonderful time, and you'll be where all America is enjoying itself.

The human animal is fundamentally gregarious; he wants to be where everybody else is. Many a little boy has been heartbroken when all his little friends have gone to the picnic or the circus and he has had to stay home. Many a little boy grown to manhood has exhibited the same reaction when he thinks the crowd is on the band wagon and it will roll on without him. We do not like to think that we are being left behind. The very thought of it disturbs many of us deeply. Conjure up thoughts of being left behind in the mind of your reader, and there is a fairly good chance that you will get action from him.

Rudolf Flesch, however, in his book, *The Art of Clear Thinking,*[2] suggests that practically all of these appeals may be unmasked with two simple formulas: "So what?" and "Specify." For example:

Gopher Brand is a nationally advertised product (So what?). Chefs (Specify) in the foremost hotels (Specify) serve Gopher Brand with pride (So what?). When you are having special guests (Specify), why don't you serve Gopher Brand, too (So what?)?

While the point has been amply implied in all that has been said, there is another pitfall for which the critical reader should be alert. That is verbiage with a high emotional charge. One highly emotionally charged word can be as devastating as an atomic bomb. Some types of journalism employ the vocabulary of emotionalism to achieve an effect and to appeal to a certain group of readers. Consider this example:

After *shilly-shallying* for a while, the *shifty-eyed thug glared* at the judge and *blurted* out, "All right, I'll talk!"

[2] Rudolf Flesch, *The Art of Clear Thinking*, p. 69 ff., Harper & Brothers, New York, 1951.

The critical reader should also be alert for the nebulous abstraction. The weatherman sometimes speaks of a "violent disturbance" when he means specifically a hurricane; we may refer to one as having "social indiscretion" when we do not want to be so blunt as to say that he eats his pie with his knife. The discriminating reader will sense whether the author should have been clear, sharp, and exact—in a word, specific —or whether he is the better artist with words for throwing over the thought the veil of haziness, of abstraction. The reader must decide whether the portrait is better for having some diffusion, or whether the author should have dealt in clear, sharp images. There is a place for both techniques. The critical reader will decide which is the more appropriate in any given instance.

So, then, critical reading is probably the most exacting, the most refined of all types of reading. The reader must add the personal factor, discriminating taste, and appropriateness in all things. It is the reader's total reaction as a reader to the thought of the author which is important.

Critical reading is reading—plus! It is those plus factors with which this chapter has been concerned.

Are you capable of being a critical reader?

Being an expert critical reader demands an emotional stability that many people have difficulty in acquiring. Some writers may be congenial to your way of thinking, while others may irritate you by what they say. Ardent Democrats find it difficult to read without prejudice the campaign speeches of their Republican opponents. Republicans, by the same token, cannot read the product of Democratic pens.

One leading banking economist that I know found it almost impossible to read a rather superficial and in some places inaccurate account of business conditions by another analyst. He kept protesting that, "This is all rot; I don't agree with him anyway." Obviously such an approach to the printed page is more of a demonstration of personal pyrotechnics than any attempt to understand what the man was saying —faulty in places as it may have been.

This is one of the most common dangers and pitfalls of critical reading. Remember that reading is reading—it is never an excuse for you to vent your own spleen. When you read, read. Find out what the other person is saying. This is your first obligation as a reader. Even though you heartily disagree with your author, that is no excuse for refusing to hear him.

The man of broad understanding and mental maturity listens to all comers and then thinks independently and for himself. Every man ought to be capable of reading *El Koran* and the *Sayings of Confucius*. This does not mean that he should expect to agree with everything that he finds therein. But he will at least know what they contain and be able the better to appreciate the Islamic and the Oriental mind.

There are two ways of meeting another person's viewpoints in print: one is to burn the books that contain the views with which you disagree or to ban them from being read; the other is to exhibit toward these views the true spirit of American concept of freedom, in acknowledging that every person has the right to be heard in his own behalf. But the expert reader should be skillful enough to evaluate, after a full and impartial hearing, what he deems to be valid and what he concludes on good substance of thought to be unsound. But first and foremost, the accomplished reader should at least *know* what the other person has to say, and be able to understand *why* he is saying it. Such a reader is a critical reader. In a world of confused issues and misrepresented truth, readers of this type are greatly to be desired.

How critically do you read?

On the following pages are some selections with which you can test your ability to read critically. Find in magazines and newspapers additional examples of writing which require critical techniques of reading. Analyze them. Advertisements, speeches, editorials, and syndicated columns should provide you with rewarding material.

Indicate your reactions to each of the selections as follows:

1. In the margin of each selection identify the basic appeal to the reader which the author is making. You may find more than one appeal in each selection; if so, note each new appeal as it appears.
2. Place also in the margin in a small circle a number corresponding to the number of the standard technique which is being used to influence the thinking of the reader. (The seven techniques are listed on p. 257.)
3. Employ the Flesch method for unmasking the technique used by the writer to influence the reader. After the statement which needs clarification, or is questionable, insert a caret ($_\wedge$) and between the lines write, "So what?" or "Specify," whichever fits the case.

4. Mark with a plus sign (+) any words which have a high emotional charge.
5. Mark with a minus sign (−) any fuzzy, inexact, nebulous words.
6. There may also be fallacies in reasoning: conclusions which do not logically follow from the facts as given by the author. If such logical fallacies occur, point them out with the comment "Illogical," written in the margin, and underline the statement in question.

Executive-Line

. . . in your choice of decorator colors
. . . 46 smartly-styled models, efficiently designed
. . . and sturdily built for a business lifetime of wear.

Picture in your own office this smart Executive-Line, finished in Pine Frost Green! Or you can have it in Gray, Suede Brown, Autumn Haze, Glen Green or Manila Tan—with harmonizing Veltouch or Textouch writing top.

These are the decorator colors in which E-L now offers modern metal desks. They bring freshness and new life into any office. They convert drab monotone clerical areas into interesting inspiring places to work.

As for the E-L desk itself it incorporates too many new *exclusive* features to name here. But of this you may be sure: It has everything you'd expect in a much costlier desk . . . plus some exclusive features you won't find even in far more expensive desks. This metal desk can't split or warp, its drawers will never stick, its solidly-welded joints can't come loose. Year after year, from the day you buy an E-L desk it will be as handsome as it is today

There's an E-L Executive-Line for every office job . . . 46 models . . and the best way to choose is to see them for yourself at your nearest E-L dealer or factory branch showroom.[3]

What Makes You Believe a Letter Is Important . . .
even before you read it?

You open an envelope, glance at the letter and let it drop into the waste basket. Why? You open a second envelope, glance at the letter and lean back to read. Why?

It couldn't be the words as you did not have time to read them. The truth is, you got an impression . . . a favorable impression from the excellent design of the letterhead and the feel and appearance of the paper.

[3] Advertisement appearing in *Newsweek*, vol. 45, March 28, 1955, p. 43. Adapted, reprinted with permission.

Yes, fine rag paper does have a positive psychological effect. In your own life you have your baptismal record, diplomas from school, awards you have won, war bonds, the title to your home and so on.

Today, when you handle a firm, crisp sheet of rag paper you unconsciously feel that this piece of paper is important too, and you stop and examine it.[4]

They'll Grumble, Yet—They'll Fight for the Boss!

Newspaper men and their radio contemporaries are individuals of responsibility. Many have arrived at their present positions by virtue of good college educations and considerable experience covering various fields of human endeavor. Others started from scratch and without benefit of much formal schooling have attained responsible posts in their respective fields. They are citizens of the community and interested in the welfare of their neighborhoods just as you and I are. They work for a living just as your employees do. They grouse and gripe about the treatment they receive from their employers, the owners of the newspapers and radio stations. But their comment is worse than their feeling. Let anyone else criticize their boss and more often than not they will fight at the drop of a hat, just as your employees would do for you if you would only take them into your confidence and let them know what is going on and the reasons why.[5]

Today it's only
Half a Loaf . . .

Yesterday's dime bought a loaf of bread; today it buys you only half a loaf.

Yesterday's dollars that paid for a house and furniture, linens, silver, today have barely half as much buy in them. And the limits of fire insurance you bought to protect your investment in house and furnishings at yesterday's values are only half a protection today.

Half a loaf, to be sure, is better than none; and so is half enough insurance. But buying less fire insurance than today's values demand is false economy.

With building and furnishing costs soaring, chances are that if you haven't increased your insurance limits apace, fire would find you tragically underinsured. Why not have your local agent help you determine your requirements—today? [6]

[4] Advertisement of Neenah Paper Co., appearing in *Printing Magazine*, vol. 78, September, 1954, p. 16. Condensed and reprinted with permission of the advertiser.

[5] James W. Irwin, "Industry Muffs the Ball," speech delivered before the Industrial Relations Association of Chicago, January 6, 1953, in *Vital Speeches of the Day*, February 1, 1953, p. 241.

[6] Advertisement appearing in *Banking*, vol. 45, December, 1952, p. 81.

Gain This Valuable Asset

One of the best things that could happen to your business this year is to have a great many more people tell their friends how fine your product is.

Undoubtedly you enjoy an enviable reputation right now, but your business, like every business, can enjoy additional prosperity through more *word-of-mouth* advertising. This particular kind of promotion is potent and profitable, a highly valuable asset in these competitive days.

Put People on the Right Track

It is essential, however, to make sure that people say the right things about your product. Misstatements, errors, half-truths passed along from one person to another are damaging to your sales and your reputation.

So put people on the right track with facts in print, in booklets, bulletins, brochures, broadsides, folders, reports, manuals, catalogs . . .

Your Ally—A Good Printer

Your most helpful partner in the planning and production of effective selling . . . is a good printer. Let him show you examples of quality printing. The result will be finer printed pieces for your business, produced with less effort on your part—and with economy.[7]

How Quickly and Accurately Can You See?

In Chapter Nine you tried your skill at seeing quickly and accurately an item of information hidden within a context of similar information. As your total skill in reading improves, your individual skills should also improve. The skill of seeing a specific item within a context is the skill of scanning. Do the following exercise, timing yourself carefully. When you have completed the exercise, figure out how long it has taken you, and then compare your achievement on this exercise with that on p. 192.

What time is it now? MINUTES _____

SECONDS _____

Phrase	Page	Word before	Word after
made it	217	_____	_____
this band	217	_____	_____
spreads out	217	_____	_____
free space	217	_____	_____

[7] Advertisement appearing in *The Saturday Evening Post*, January 15, 1955, p. 87.

Phrase	Page	Word before	Word after
both towards	218	_____	_____
eye as	218	_____	_____
it, that	219	_____	_____
is its	219	_____	_____
is the	219	_____	_____
of much	219	_____	_____

What time is it now? MINUTES _____

SECONDS _____

How long did it take you? MINUTES _____

SECONDS _____

How long did it take you previously (page 192)?

Reading for Speed of Comprehension—1

The article which you are about to read will discuss what reading really is. The author enunciates many of the ideas which you have already read in this text, but he says them differently from the way in which you have already met them. You will need to be mentally alert as you read this selection. Keep saying to yourself—as always—what *idea*, what *thought* is the author trying to make clear? Look for thought. After you have finished this, you should be able to explain to a child in fifth or sixth grade just what the author says—in your own words, of course, and simple enough for the child to understand readily what you are attempting to tell him.

This is a good criterion of comprehension. Always say to yourself, after you have read some particularly difficult piece of writing: "Could I explain this to a ten- or eleven-year-old child?" Try it. The ideas—even in Plato—are relatively simple. If you can communicate them, simply, to others, you have *comprehended* them yourself.

Time: MINUTES _____

SECONDS _____

THE READING OF "READING" [8]

by Mortimer Adler

One obvious fact shows the existence of a wide range of degrees in ability to read. It is that reading begins in the primary grades and runs through every level of the educational system. Reading is the first of the three R's. It is the first because we have to learn to read in order to learn by reading. Since what we have to learn, as we ascend in our education, becomes more difficult or complex, we must improve our ability to read proportionately.

Literacy is everywhere the primary mark of education, but it has many degrees, from a grammar-school diploma, or even less, up to a bachelor's degree or a Ph.D. But, in his recent commentary on American democracy, called *Of Human Freedom*, Jacques Barzun cautions us not to be misled by the boast that we have the most literate population in the world. "Literacy in this sense is not education; it is not even 'knowing how to read' in the sense of taking in quickly and correctly the message of the printed page, to say nothing of exercising a critical judgment upon it."

Supposedly, *gradations* in reading go along with *graduations* from one educational level to another. In the light of what we know about American education today, that supposition is not well founded. In France it is still true that the candidate for the doctor's degree must show an ability to read sufficient to admit him to that higher circle of literacy. What the French call *explication de texte* is an art which must be practiced at every educational level and in which improvement must be made before one moves up the scale. But in this country there is often little discernible difference between the *explication* which a high-school student would give and one by a college senior or even a doctoral candidate. When the task is to read a book, the high-school students and college freshmen are often better, if only because they are less thoroughly spoiled by bad habits.

The fact that there is something wrong with American education, so far as reading is concerned, means only that the gradations have become obscure for us, not that they do not exist. Our task is to remove that

[8] From *How to Read a Book*, copyright 1940, by Mortimer Adler; reprinted by permission of the publishers, Simon and Schuster, Inc., pp. 20–32.

obscurity. To make the distinction in grades of reading sharper, we must define the criteria of better and worse.

What are the criteria? . . . We say that one man is a better reader than another if he can read more difficult material. Anyone would agree, if Jones is able to read only such things as newspapers and magazines, whereas Brown can read the best current nonfiction books such as Einstein and Infeld's *Evolution of Physics* or Hogben's *Mathematics for the Millions*, that Brown has more ability than Jones. Among readers at the Jones level, further discrimination may be made between those who cannot rise above the tabloids and those who can master *The New York Times*. Between the Jones group and the Brown group, there are still others measured by the better and worse magazines, better and worse current fiction, or by nonfiction books of a more popular nature than Einstein or Hogben, such as Gunther's *Inside Europe* or Heiser's *An American Doctor's Odyssey*. And better than Brown is the man who can read Euclid and Descartes as well as Hogben, or Galileo and Newton as well as Einstein and Infeld's discussion of them.

The first criterion is an obvious one. In many fields we measure a man's skill by the difficulty of the task he can perform. The accuracy of such measurement depends, of course, on the independent precision with which we can grade the tasks in difficulty. We would be moving in circles if we said, for instance, that the more difficult book is one which only the better reader can master. That is true, but not helpful. In order to understand what makes some books more difficult to read than others, we would have to know what demands they make on the skill of the reader. If we knew that, we would know what distinguishes better and worse readers. In other words, the difficulty of the reading matter is a convenient, objective sign of degrees of reading ability, but it does not tell us what the difference is in the reader, so far as his skill is concerned.

The first criterion has some use, nevertheless, to whatever extent it is true that the more difficult a book is the fewer readers it will have at any given time. There is some truth in this, because it is generally the case that, as one mounts the scale of excellence in any skill, the number of practitioners diminishes: the higher, the fewer. Counting noses, therefore, gives us some independent indication of whether one thing is more difficult to read than another. We can construct a crude scale and measure men accordingly. In a sense, that is the way all the scales, which employ reading tests made by the educational psychologists, are constructed.

The second criterion takes us further, but is harder to state. I have already suggested the distinction between active and passive reading. Strictly, all reading is active. What we call passive is simply less active. Reading is better or worse according as it is more or less active. And one reader is better than another in proportion as he is capable of a greater range of activity in reading. In order to explain this point, I must first be sure that you understand why I say that, strictly speaking, there is no absolutely passive reading. It only seems that way in contrast to more active reading.

No one doubts that writing and speaking are active undertakings, in which the writer or speaker is clearly doing something. Many people seem to think, however, that reading and listening are entirely passive. No work need be done. They think of reading and listening as *receiving* communication from someone who is actively *giving* it. So far they are right, but then they make the error of supposing that receiving communication is like receiving a blow, or a legacy, or a judgment from the court. . . .

Given the same thing to read, one man reads it better than another, first, by reading it more actively, and second, by performing each of the acts involved more successfully. These two things are related. Reading is a complex activity, just as writing is. It consists of a large number of separate acts, all of which must be performed in a good reading. Hence, the man who can perform more of these various acts is better able to read. . . .

Most of us do not know what the limits of our comprehension are. We have never tried our powers to the full. It is my honest belief that *almost all of the great books in every field are within the grasp of all normally intelligent men*, on the condition, of course, that they acquire skill necessary for reading them and make the effort. Of course, those more favored by birth will reach the goal more readily, but the race is not always to the swift.

There are several minor points here which you must observe. It is possible to be mistaken in your judgment of something you are reading. You may think you understand it, and be content with what you get from an effortless reading, whereas, in fact, much may have escaped you. The first maxim of sound practice is an old one: the beginning of wisdom is a just appraisal of one's ignorance. So the beginning of reading as a conscious effort to understand is an accurate perception of the line between what is intelligible and what is not.

I have seen many students read a difficult book just as if they were reading the sports page. Sometimes I would ask at the beginning of a class if they had any questions about the text, if there was anything they did not understand. Their silence answered in the negative. At the end of two hours during which they could not answer the simplest questions leading to an interpretation of the book, they would admit their deficiency in a puzzled way. They were puzzled because they were quite honest in their belief that they had read the text. They had, indeed, but not in the right way.

If they had allowed themselves to be puzzled *while* reading, instead of after the class was over; if they had encouraged themselves to note the things they did not understand, instead of putting such matters immediately out of mind, almost in shame and embarrassment, they might have discovered that the book in front of them was different from their usual diet.

Let me summarize now the distinction between these two types of reading. We shall have to consider both because the line between what is readable in one way and what must be read in the other is often hazy. To whatever extent we can keep the two kinds of reading distinct, we can use the word "reading" in two distinct senses.

The first sense is the one in which we speak of ourselves as reading newspapers, magazines, or anything else which, according to our skill and talents, is at once thoroughly intelligible to us. Such things may increase the store of information we remember, but they cannot improve our understanding, for our understanding was equal to them before we started. Otherwise, we would have felt the shock of puzzlement and perplexity which comes from getting in over our depth—that is, if we were both alert and honest.

The second sense is the one in which I would say a man has to read something that at first he does not completely understand. Here the thing to be read is initially better than the reader. The writer is communicating something which can increase the reader's understanding. Such communication between unequals must be possible, or else one man could never learn from another, either through speech or writing. Here by "learning" I mean understanding more, not remembering more information which has the same degree of intelligibility as other information you already possess.

There is clearly no difficulty about getting new information in the course of reading if, as I say, the novel facts are of the same sort as those you already know, so far as their intelligibility goes. Thus, a man who knows some of the facts of American history and understands them in a certain light can readily acquire by reading, in the first sense, more such facts and understand them in the same light. But suppose he is reading a history which seeks not merely to give him some more facts but to throw a new and, perhaps, more profound light on all the facts he knows. Suppose there is a greater understanding here than he possesses before he starts to read. If he can manage to acquire that greater understanding, he is reading in the second sense. He has literally elevated himself by his own activity, though indirectly, of course, this was made possible by the writer who had something to teach him.

What are the conditions under which this kind of reading takes place? There are two. In the first place, there is initial inequality in understanding. The writer must be superior to the reader, and his book must convey in readable form the insights he possesses and his potential readers lack. In the second place, the reader must be able to overcome this inequality in some degree, seldom perhaps fully, but always approaching equality with the writer. To the extent that equality is approached, the communication is perfectly consummated.

In short, we can learn only from our betters. We must know who they are and how to learn from them. The man who has this sort of knowledge possesses the art of reading in the sense with which I am especially concerned. Everyone probably has some ability to read in this way. But all of us, without exception, can learn to read better and gradually gain more by our efforts through applying them to more rewarding materials.

What time is it now? MINUTES _____

SECONDS _____

What is your reading time for this selection? MINUTES _____

SECONDS _____

Without referring to the article, take the following test.

Comprehension quiz *Part One*

1. Improvement in reading ability is necessary for the person who expects to get an education because

    a reading is the first of the three Rs.

    b there is more to read than ever before.

    c as what we have to learn becomes more difficult, we must improve proportionately in our ability to read.

    d we are the most literate population in the world.

2. The author says that reading is one's ability to
    a get the facts from the printed page.
    b vary the technique of reading according to the purpose for which he is reading.
    c get mental concepts from visual symbols.
    d unfold competently, as a prerequisite for promotion to the next educational level, the meaning of the text.

3. So far as reading is concerned, in American education,
    a a person may graduate without actually having progressed.
    b graduation is *prima facie* evidence of achievement.
    c we are not clear on the relationship between progress and educational achievement.
    d we do not have a clear sense of the values of gradation.

4. That which makes one book more difficult to read than another is the
    a background which the reader has for understanding what he is reading.
    b increased demands made by the more difficult book on the skill of the reader.
    c need which the reader has in reading a particular book.
    d number of people who read any particular book.

5. The author thinks that reading
    a is active.
    b like listening is a passive activity.
    c is active or passive according to the purpose and mood of the reader.
    d is strictly speaking a skill and is, therefore, neither active nor passive.

6. The author thinks that the great books are
    a so difficult that few people read them.
    b known in broad outline to many, but actually read by a few.
    c well within the grasp of all normally intelligent people.
    d largely neglected because they were written so many years ago.

7. People frequently have trouble with reading because they
    a do not have adequate reading skills.
    b do not recognize the fact that different skills are employed for different levels of difficulty.

 c center their reading too much upon light reading as, for example, the sports page, comics, and similar chitchat.

 d do not know when they are having trouble.

8. The author says that

 a it is a salutary sign if you are at times puzzled while reading.

 b it is well to read the newspaper rapidly.

 c as a general rule, most college students know how to read.

 d most Americans are poor readers.

9. If the reader is to acquire greater understanding through reading, the author and the reader must be, initially,

 a of the same viewpoint.

 b of different viewpoints.

 c unequal in understanding.

 d equal in understanding.

10. "Reading," according to the author, means reading

 a widely all sorts of printed material.

 b more quickly and with greater comprehension.

 c that which may be somewhat beyond our ability to understand.

 d that which is readily comprehended.

Part Two

Now try in 100 to 200 words to write a summary statement of what reading really is, so that a ten-year-old child may understand clearly what you are trying to say.

How well did you comprehend what you have read? Check your answers against those given in the Answer Key. Each correct answer is worth 10 per cent.

What is your level of comprehension? _____%

What is your speed of comprehension? _____wpm

What is your reading index $(R \times C/100)$? _____

Reading for Speed of Comprehension—2

In a strange way we have categorized living. Certain values we seem to feel are not native to certain areas. Culture and cultural values we would normally consider to belong to a world less rough-and-tumble than that of business and everyday affairs. Culture is a plant which should be seen in the halls of colleges and in ivory towers, not in a bank or an office building.

It is both interesting and highly significant that the article which you are about to read, "A Culture for Today," is a message from the *Monthly Letter* of the Royal Bank of Canada. Perhaps it is one of the indications of a more liberal, more inclusive view of business toward all the values of living. But whatever it may mean, it is superb good sense for any person who wishes to live up to his greatest potential in our modern world.

Read this to get the thought, the position of the author.

Time: MINUTES _____

SECONDS _____

A CULTURE FOR TODAY [9]

Some persons think culture is something one has, rather than something one is. Others think of culture as being divided, as culture of the cultured, culture of the masses, culture of the educated, culture of the cloistered, and so on. To still others culture is fragmented into music, poetry, sculpture, painting, and many other arts and crafts.

A culture for today will take into account our material resources, our scientific knowledge, our religious practices, our family and social systems and our government: the practical things of life as well as the graces. Culture is a pattern of all these and the other ingredients of living expressing the present day life force of our people.

We can't be "cultured" now and again, when we get specially fixed up for it. Culture is a constant state of becoming. We have not yet (and we are glad of it) reached our fullest development in art, religion, education, and intellectual growth.

If we are to endure as a nation of consequence, our cultural progress cannot be looked upon as something incidental, something that takes second place in importance to any of its ingredients.

One of the fascinating things about culture is that it is indefinable. It partakes too much of the spirit of a people to be put in wordy chains.

Attempts to analyse the ultimates of life like faith, love, patriotism,

[9] Adapted from "A Culture for Canada," *Monthly Letter* of the Royal Bank of Canada (Montreal), September, 1954.

religion and beauty always fail, because these components of culture cannot be reduced to terms lower than themselves.

Culture cannot be accepted as a fixed code by which to live. It is not stagnant, but dynamic. It gives us wide realms to explore. There would be nothing noble about culture if we could say: "This is it; this is our absolute and accepted scale of culture; by this we shall live." Culture is not, as some conceive it, an eternal resting on a throne to which we have been elevated by our forefathers, but it is something to be hourly achieved and realized at the very peril of losing it.

Culture is the outcome of our social experience. It includes invention and discovery, the accumulated results of human effort, our philosophical explanations of thought and action, the institutions we have devised to make society a working reality, our sentiments and attitudes. All the past of humanity enters into it, as well as the more recent contributions of the people of all nations.

There must, however, be some fundamental features in culture—features of which art, music, sculpture, literature, philosophy, science, family life, and social custom are some of the symbols.

Basic to a lasting culture is the search for truth. Culture is opposed to bigotry, and no one has a right to call himself cultured who cannot listen to both sides of an argument, who refuses to tolerate things merely because they are distasteful to him personally.

Intelligence is a part of culture. When we start to understand the meaning, purpose and conditions of life we are at the beginning of intelligence. We develop in cultural intelligence in the degree in which we use it and accept responsibility for consequences.

Intelligence restrains our innate violent and unsocial impulses, prompts us to seek higher than animal pleasures, and gives us the ability to see things in their proper connections. At the same time, while enabling us to learn all about the sun and the atmosphere and the earth, it leaves us free to enjoy the radiance of the sunset.

Intelligence of this sort does not depend upon formal education. It is not at all rare to come upon comparatively unlettered people who have struck profound depths of thought and have reached the poetry of things. And there are highly educated people, capable of performing clever antics with their minds, who have no deep sense of the worthwhileness of living.

Much of culture is simply unbroken tradition. Each of us is born into a society with a more or less fixed system of relationships. From the immemorial past have come down to us ways of getting a livelihood and approved patterns of family and social conduct.

Without the starting point provided by these traditions, development would be inconceivable. The culture of today rests upon the preservation of the accomplishments of all who have gone before us, and the culture of tomorrow depends upon what we of today add to that heritage, not so much in the way of habits and customs, but in ways of thinking.

By far the most important channel of transmission of culture is the family. The meagre furniture of a native hut becomes immensely significant because it is grouped around the hearth, symbol of the intimate personal relationship of family life.

The general stock of ideas, prejudices and sentiments picked up by the hearthside impinge on thought and actions throughout life. Statesmen and financiers, educators and artisans, men and women in all activities of life are influenced in their decisions and actions by the intangibles absorbed in home life.

Cultured people are distinguished by the superiority of their thoughts, their enjoyment of beauty, their effort to improve themselves and their environment, and their willingness to look at something new.

Of all these qualities none is more vital to culture than the last. A person, however well-informed, is not cultured unless he can look at a thought or an event or a belief from at least two sides. To enjoy life perfectly a man must be free from taboos, prudery, superstition and prejudice. He will recognize all degrees of shadings between those who agree with him and the people who don't.

Perhaps the best recipe for culture is just to have the courage to be what we are. We must be free intellectually to deal with whatever comes our way. Our lives, individually, are links in the chain, and what we do has national and universal significance.

No one need live meanly except by choice. Those who overvalue physical comforts, the material things of the world, and ease of work, are living a sparse cultural existence, and cannot be rated high in an appraisement of civilization. There is no need to live the rigorous life of our forefathers, but if we banish it from memory we are depriving ourselves of the best, most logical and most thrilling base for our culture.

We are seeking a harmony of culture that will bind together four qualities: truth, beauty, adventure and art; and this harmony, exclusive as it is of egotism, self-seeking and immediacy, can be attained onlv as a process of growth extended in time.

What time is it now? MINUTES _____

SECONDS _____

What is your reading time for this selection? MINUTES _____

SECONDS _____

Now, answer the following questions. Do not refer back to the article.

Comprehension quiz *Part One*

1. The author believes that culture is
   a a synthesis of many ingredients.
   b a product of our civilized way of life.
   c a finished product with each age.
   d an absolute scale of values.

2. We cannot analyze culture because it is
   a transitory.
   b indefinable.
   c a national heritage.
   d incidental.

3. The author thinks of intelligence as
   a the end product of a formal education.
   b an appreciation of art, literature, music, and similar artistic and intellectual values.
   c the ability to discern the meaning and worthwhileness of living.
   d the mind of man and its limitless capabilities.

4. The author feels that the most important channel of transmission of culture is
   a education.
   b an enlightened populace.
   c the family.
   d democratic government.

5. The main thesis of the author is that culture is
   a innate.
   b a summary of the habits and customs of a people.
   c a code of values inherited from the past.
   d an evolutionary process.

Part Two

Fill in *one word* in each blank to complete the thought of the sentence in accordance with the statement which the author has made in the text.

1. Much of culture is simply _____.

2. No one need live meanly except by _____.

3. If we are to endure as a nation of consequence, our cultural progress cannot be looked upon as something _____.

4. Culture is opposed to _____.

5. Culture is the outcome of social _____.

How well did you comprehend what you have read? Check your answers against those given in the Answer Key. Each correct answer is worth 10 per cent.

What is your level of comprehension?　　_____%

What is your speed of comprehension?　　_____wpm

What is your reading index (R × C/100)? _____

A Midway Summary of Your Reading Skills

So far in this book we have discussed the contents of a beginner's kit of techniques for better reading. We shall take up more specialized approaches and types of reading in the remainder of the book. Following is a list of reading skills and techniques which you should be using at this point with ease and facility. Each one has been discussed fully in the book thus far; in each skill you have had specific practice. How many of these skills and techniques do you use purposefully and specifically to handle a given reading situation? Why not put a check mark before those techniques that you have *not* been using as extensively as you know you should? Try to find many occasions each day to use the checked skills. Here are the basic skills of reading:

1. *Skimming for main ideas* will help you to get a general, over-all view of the material you are going to read, to get a broad outline of the author's thought, and to understand the main ideas which the author presents.

2. *Skimming for details and isolated facts* will help you to locate a single fact or item of information from among the context.
3. *Reading a paragraph* will help you to crack the paragraph so that you are able to find the main idea and to see how that idea has been developed and unfolded, so that you may see it in full bloom.
4. *Discerning the flow of thought within the paragraph* will make you sensitive to the thought and what it is doing, sentence by sentence, in the course of its development.
5. *Using the punctuation as an aid in getting the meaning* can help you to speed and streamline your reading by using punctuation as an aid to grasping quickly the meaning of the author.
6. *Reading key words and phrases* will aid you in getting the meaning more quickly by concentrating upon those particular words which are especially important in conveying the thought.
7. *Defining your own purpose in reading* will aid you in selecting the approach and technique best suited to accomplish the end for which you are reading and to do this with the greatest economy of time and effort.
8. *Remembering what you read* is a skill which is generally referred to as "comprehension." You should be able to recall accurately and in an organized manner the content of your reading.
9. *Following directions* is a skill which will aid you in many reading situations requiring a step-by-step performance.
10. *Discovering the author's purpose* is a phase of critical reading which will help you to define your own purpose more clearly.

These are the basic tools of a master reader, but it will take months of diligent use until you become adept at using the particular tool or tools—the particular skill or skills—necessary to handle a specific reading situation efficiently and effortlessly.

How many items did you *not* check? Count each of these 10 per cent; the total is your reading habit index score for this chapter: ____%

Chapter Thirteen

Readability as an aid to better reading

Is it easy or difficult to read?"

You have instinctively asked yourself that question almost as many times as you have picked up something that you proposed to read.

How can you tell whether it is easy or not? And if you find reading that is either difficult or easy, what are the factors that make it so? These are questions that are germane to the task of every reader.

For many years the experts have tackled the problem of the level of difficulty. They wanted an answer that was more than guesswork on the part of each individual as he came successively to each new reading situation. They wanted a formula, spelled out in terms of logic and mathematics. Their work has been beset by many obstacles, but the expert reader should know its implications and appreciate its values. Knowledge of readability factors can make your reading easier, as knowledge of road conditions can make your trip more enjoyable and, at the difficult spots, less of an unpleasant surprise.

Both reading and writing belong to the larger area of the communication skills. Because of the complexity of the world in which we live, it is very important that the communication lanes be kept open and functioning at a high level of efficiency. What you have to say should be said with the least amount of loss at both the sending and the receiving end—the writing should be clear, the reading easy. Giant corporations find that the more simply they phrase their ideas, the easier it is for their employees, their customers, and their correspondents to understand what they are saying. Insurance companies at times must explain simply and explicitly some of the knotty problems relating to policies and payments. This must be done in the language of the layman rather than in the jargon of business. In one firm the handbooks which purported to explain the firm's policies, regulations, and procedures to its personnel were written in language that a college graduate would have had to furrow his brow and scratch his head to comprehend. The employees for whom these manuals were intended had an average reading ability of sixth grade to high school!

We are, as a result of the readability emphasis, becoming more conscious of reading ease than ever before; despite that, enough difficult reading is still stalking about for the average reader to be alert and quick to recognize it and to know *why* such reading is difficult and what to do about it, once he spots it.

Perhaps here a brief historical detour will bring the whole readability situation into clearer focus. Let us look back to the 1920s and the 1930s. The whole idea of measuring ease of reading stems from the efforts of certain educators to provide an answer to certain questions arising out of the making of children's textbooks, especially readers at the grade-school level. There was a need to evaluate the reading difficulty and the grade level of these texts. All sorts of plans and approaches were proposed. Out of these early attempts came the Winnetka formula, the Lorge formula, and the Gray-Leary scale to determine what makes a book readable.

Following these pioneer efforts to formulate a readability approach, Rudolf Flesch, in his Ph. D. thesis, *Marks of a Readable Style,* and later in *The Art of Plain Talk,* proposed his original readability formula. Soon after this Edgar Dale and Jeanne Chall proposed an alternate approach to that outlined by Flesch. Meanwhile, Flesch had amended his formula and simplified it. This revision is the Flesch formula now in general use.

The readability bug was buzzing. Here and there people in industry, in business, and in education were putting the new readability ideas to the practical test. A whole new literature sprang up in the professional journals: a literature that discussed the pros and cons of readability, that proposed and counterproposed changes and modifications in the original structure of the earlier formulas.

Simplification was demanded. General Motors Corporation attacked the problem with a plastic dial-and-scale gadget called a "Reading Ease Calculator," on which you dial up the number of sentences in 100 words and read down the scale to the proper number of syllables in 100 words and the reading level of the sample being tested is shown in a color band ranging from very easy to very hard. This device General Motors used in studying the problem of readability in their thirty-five house organs and other materials distributed to employees by the corporation.

Robert Gunning, of Gunning Research Associates, has proposed an idea similar to the Flesch plan in his "Fog Index Formula." Others also have offered suggestions for simplification and revision of the original readability plans.

If the reader can appraise the level of difficulty of the material he is reading, he can better come to grips with it. The more the reader is enlightened and prepared, the better reader he is likely to be. Here, for example, is a particular journal, a book, or a specific type of reading which you must read. If you can predict its probable difficulty, especially if it lies in the difficult–very difficult zone, the better you can meet the storm of words when they threaten to engulf you. By being forewarned, you can batten down the hatches and get ready for a rough time. And skillful sailors know how to handle their craft in a storm as well as they know how to sail it over a placid sea. The reader and the sailor have much in common. Each needs to know how to negotiate the stormy areas skillfully. Let us look at two of the simplest methods of determining readability. The first of these is by means of a readability score developed by Rudolf Flesch.

To measure the readability ("reading ease" and "human interest") of a piece of writing, go through the following steps: [1]

1. Take samples: take enough to make a fair test (3 to 5 of an article, 25 to 30 of a book). Go strictly by numerical scheme: for instance, take every third paragraph or every other page. Each sample should start at the beginning of a paragraph.
2. Count each word in the sample up to 100. Count contractions and hyphenated words as one word. Count as words numbers or letters separated by space.

[1] Condensed from Rudolf Flesch, "A New Readability Yardstick," *Journal of Applied Psychology,* vol. 32 (1948), pp. 228–230.

3. Count the syllables in each 100-word sample. If in doubt about syllabication rules, use any good dictionary. Syllabify symbols according to the way they are normally read aloud: % and $, two syllables; 1918, four syllables.
4. Figure average sentence length per 100 words. Find sentence ending nearest to the 100-word mark. Count the number of sentences up to that point. Divide the number of sentences into the aggregate number of words in those sentences. Follow units of thought rather than punctuation: usually sentences are marked off by periods; but sometimes they are marked off by colons or semicolons—like this one.
5. Figure the number of "personal words" per 100 words in the samples. "Personal words" are (*a*) all personal pronouns except the neuter pronouns and those pronouns referring to things rather than persons, (*b*) all words having masculine or feminine natural gender (*girl, father, actress*) but not common-gender nouns (*teacher, employee, asssitant*)— count singular and plural forms—and (*c*) the group words *people* (with plural verb) and *folks*.
6. Figure the number of "personal sentences" per 100 sentences in the piece of writing, or in all the samples combined. Personal sentences are (*a*) spoken sentences, marked by quotation marks or "speech tags" (*he said, he replied*), (*b*) questions, commands, requests, and other sentences addressed directly to the reader, (*c*) exclamations, and (*d*) grammatically incomplete sentences whose full meaning has to be inferred from the context. If the sentence fits two or more of these categories, count it as belonging to only one of them. Divide the number of these "personal sentences" by the total number of sentences you found in Step 4.
7. Find your reading ease (RE) score by inserting the number of syllables per 100 words (word length, *wl*) and the average sentence length (*sl*) in the following formula:

$$RE = 206.835 - 0.846\,wl - 1.015\,sl$$

The reading ease score will put your piece of writing on a scale between 0 (practically unreadable) and 100 (easy for any literate person).
8. Find your human interest (HI) score by inserting the percentage of "personal words" (*pw*) and the percentage of "personal sentences" (*ps*) in the following formula:

$$HI = 3.635\,pw + 0.314\,ps$$

The "human interest" score will put your piece of writing on a scale between 0 (no human interest) and 100 (full of human interest).

In applying the formulas, remember that Formula A measures *length* and Formula B measures *percentages*. Here are tables to guide you in interpreting the "reading ease" and "human interest" scores:

READING EASE SCORES

Reading ease score	Description of style	Type of magazine	wl	sl
0–30	Very difficult	Scientific	192 or more	29 or more
30–50	Difficult	Academic	167	25
50–60	Fairly difficult	Quality	155	21
60–70	Standard	Digests	147	17
70–80	Fairly easy	Slick fiction	139	14
80–90	Easy	Pulp fiction	131	11
90–100	Very easy	Comics	123 or less	8 or less

HUMAN INTEREST SCORES

Human interest score	Description of style	Typical magazine	pw, per cent	ps, per cent
0–10	Dull	Scientific	2 or less	0
10–20	Mildly interesting	Trade	4	5
20–40	Interesting	Digests	7	15
40–60	Highly interesting	*New Yorker*	11	32
60–100	Dramatic	Fiction	17 or more	58 or more

Robert Gunning has also devised a "readability formula," which he calls the Fog Index.[2] Readability is ascertained in three simple steps.

To find the Fog Index of a passage:

1. Jot down the number of words in successive sentences. If the piece is long, you may wish to take several samples of 100 words, spaced evenly through it. If you do, stop the sentence count with the sentence which ends nearest the 100-word total. Divide the total number of words in the passage by the number of sentences. This gives the average sentence length of the passage.

2. Count the number of words of three syllables or more per 100 words. Don't count the words (1) that are capitalized, (2) that are combinations of short easy words (like "bookkeeper" and "butterfly"), (3) that are verb forms made three syllables by adding -ed or -es (like "created"

[2] Robert Gunning, *The Technique of Clear Writing*, pp. 36–38, McGraw-Hill Book Company, Inc., New York, 1952.

or "trespasses"). This gives you the percentage of hard words in the passage.

3. To get the Fog Index, total the two factors just counted and multiply by 0.4.

Gunning then tests the following paragraph from *The Summing Up* by W. Somerset Maugham:

I have never had much patience with the writers who claim from the reader an effort to *understand* their meaning. You have only to go to the great *philosophers* to see that it is *possible* to express with *lucidity* the most subtle *reflections*. You may find it *difficult* to *understand* the thought of Hume, and if you have no *philosophical* training its *implications* will doubtless escape you; but no one with any *education* at all can fail to *understand* *exactly* what the meaning of each sentence is. Few people have written English with more grace than *Berkeley*. There are two sorts of *obscurity* you will find in writers. One is due to *negligence* and the other to *wilfulness*.

The number of words in the sentences of this passage is as follows: 20–23–11–13–20–10–11–10. (Note that the third sentence is actually three complete thoughts linked by a comma, in one instance, and a semicolon in the other. These should be counted as separate sentences.) The total number of words in the passage is 118. This figure divided by 8 (the number of sentences) gives the average sentence length: 11.5 words.

The words of three syllables or more are italicized in the above passage. There are 15 of them, or 12.7 per cent.

Adding the average sentence length and percentage of polysyllables gives 27.2. And this multiplied by 0.4 results in the Fog Index of 10.9, about the level of *Harper's*.

The following table compares the Fog Index with reading levels by grade and by magazine:

Fog Index	Reading level by grade	By magazine
17	College graduate	No popular magazine
16	College senior	this difficult. Professional
15	College junior	journals, scientific and
14	College sophomore	technical writing, fall
13	College freshman	here.
Danger line		

	Fog Index	Reading level by grade	By magazine
	12	High school senior	*The Atlantic*
	11	High school junior	*Harper's*
Easy-reading range:	10	High school sophomore	*Time*
	9	High school freshman	*Reader's Digest*
	8	Eighth grade	*Ladies' Home Journal*
	7	Seventh grade	*True Confessions*
	6	Sixth grade	Comics

Now, what does all this mean for the reader? How can he use this information for his own best interests in learning how to read better?

Primarily, it means two things:

1. It gives the reader a glimpse behind the scenes. It helps him to understand more fully the factors that enter into reading from the standpoint of ease of reading and consequently its relationship to speed and ease of comprehension.
2. It prepares him to estimate, in the split-second interval when his eyes appraise the page of print, what the approximate readability level of that page is likely to be.

We have discussed in Chapter Two what should take place the instant that an experienced reader's eyes fall upon the page. A chain reaction should result; things should begin to pop in his thinking. Questions should come streaming into his mind. Mentally he should react to that page of print spontaneously and instinctively. Among the many other things that he will be looking for, he should be looking at the page in an attempt to evaluate its level of difficulty. Every reader should go into combat with the printed word knowing something about the general nature of the adversary. And the seasoned reader, like the experienced physician, can tell much by straight observation.

Readability formulas measure reading difficulty on two principal assumptions:

1. The longer the sentence, the more difficult it is to read.
2. The longer the words, the more difficult the reading of the selection as a whole is likely to be.

From the standpoint of the efficient reader, it is desirable for him to appraise word length and sentence length as soon as his gaze meets the page. By so doing, and remembering the factors by which readability is determined, he may make a tentative prognosis of the difficulty of his reading. In reading as in battle, forewarned is forearmed. It is amazing how quickly readers learn to estimate the approximate difficulty of the material they are about to read once they actually begin looking for certain aspects of readability. They go into battle with their eyes open. But there is more to readability than the reading formulas.

While various objective methods of evaluating readability have helped to underline the need for some criterion of reading ease, none of these formulas are the *complete* answer to the question, "How readable is it?" The mature reader should know about such attempts, however, and use them in any way that will help him to simplify his reading and diagnose the problems which face him. Because he *is* a mature reader, he should be acquainted with all the methods which have been proposed toward making reading easier. But even formulas leave much to be desired.

One of the weaknesses of relying only upon the formula approach lies in the fact that all the factors conditioning the reading-ease score are not purely objective. The reader himself, for instance, is still the most important factor in the whole reading process; and every reader is a highly subjective organism.

Again, writing is neither so easy, nor reading so simple that the counting of a few syllables or the framing of a set of brief sentences will eliminate the basic, mutual problem of both writer and reader—that of clear, unmistakable communication of thought from one to the other.

At least three other factors enter into readability and the ease with which the reader gets the meaning from the page: (1) an adequate vocabulary, (2) skill in understanding the structure of the sentence and the paragraph, and (3) the ability to translate *instantaneously* into clear, easily understood equivalents any word groups in which none of the individual words may be troublesome but, when taken as a unit, combine to form phrases whose meaning may be obscure. These three factors will now be discussed at greater length.

The readability formulas are postulated upon the belief that one-syllable words are the easiest to understand and that the more syllables a word contains, the more difficult the word is likely to be. Within limits this, of course, is true. But let's give this theory a practical test.

Here are 20 words; they are all words of one syllable. Theoretically, they should keep the readability indicator pointing to the "very easy" end of the scale. How many of these words are simple for you to understand? Do you know the meaning of each, clearly and unmistakably? Try your skill on this simple test. Any one of these 20 words you might meet in your everyday reading. Or you might meet all of them; it's possible. They were gathered out of newspapers, magazines, advertisements, and general reading material. Here they are:

1. apt: *a* likely   *b* similar   *c* tense   *d* fascinated
2. beige: *a* light brown   *b* light purple   *c* light green   *d* light blue
3. bode: *a* reside   *b* conceal   *c* contemplate   *d* portend
4. brook: *a* crush   *b* tolerate   *c* cross   *d* forbid
5. churl: *a* vegetable   *b* monster   *c* rustic   *d* utensil
6. crux: *a* critical point   *b* hard shell   *c* prop   *d* small bottle
7. crypt: *a* edge   *b* cradle   *c* mud   *d* vault
8. deem.   *a* reduce   *b* think   *c* point   *d* dub
9. dour: *a* sullen   *b* dull   *c* dark   *d* old
10. fain: *a* straight   *b* counterfeit   *c* showy   *d* well-pleased
11. flag: *a* arouse   *b* whip   *c* weaken   *d* defeat
12. foil: *a* defeat   *b* foist   *c* oppose   *d* work
13. gaunt: *a* ghostly   *b* medieval   *c* tall   *d* emaciated
14. irk: *a* labor   *b* annoy   *c* dye   *d* augur
15. limn: *a* branch   *b* portray   *c* hobble   *d* straighten
16. moot: *a* fastened   *b* sad   *c* unlikely   *d* debatable
17. roil: *a* turn   *b* disturb   *c* heat   *d* surround
18. svelte: *a* slender   *b* elegant   *c* quiet   *d* sweet
19. tome: *a* hat   *b* note   *c* book   *d* giant
20. tort: *a* wrongful act   *b* trunk of the body   *c* punishment   *d* twisting motion

How well did you do? Turn to the Answer Key to find out. What was your score on these words that are supposed to make reading easy?

In the initial evaluation tests of this book, an attempt was made to indicate your word power and vocabulary potential. Inadequate word power may stall any reader in comparatively easy prose. That is one of the reasons a third-grade child finds only frustration in trying to read a sixth-grade reader. For the mature reader a comparable situation exists, a little further along the scale. To read prose at any level, a certain basic vocabulary is a must. For this reason provision has been made in the closing pages of this book for you to improve your vocabulary. You should unhesitatingly know the meaning of every word given in those lists. You should also know the meaning of each prefix, root, and suffix. Word power and reading efficiency go hand in hand.

Again, prose which seems unreadable to one person may give another little or no trouble at all. This is, in part, because the second reader may be able to see the structure of what he is reading better than the first. He sees how it is put together; how the whole organism of thought behaves under the web and network of words. He can unravel the sentence and the paragraph with greater skill and less effort.

The efficient reader recognizes that each sentence is made up of at least one part and sometimes two parts. Those two parts may be equal in importance or, as very frequently happens, one part may be more important and the other less so. Knowledge of all these facts of grammar and of the mechanics of expression helps the reader immeasurably. The good reader has his grammar and his knowledge of punctuation and of the paragraph at his finger tips as the engineer has his basic physics or the physician his anatomy always ready when he needs it. We have discussed in earlier chapters the role of the paragraph and the relation of punctuation to better reading.

Many sentences are not nearly so difficult as they may at first appear. Below, for instance, is an example. By all readability criteria it should be very difficult indeed. The Flesch formula places it high in the "very difficult" classification. It contains 33 words, 61 syllables. The Gunning Fog Index indicates that this is a sentence for graduate students to wrestle with, and the G-M Calculator insists that it is "very hard."

Look at it. Find the main statement; let the punctuation aid you in getting the meaning. See how easy the reading of this really is: [3]

If expenditures for consumer durables and housing level off—due to stagnant or falling real incomes, dwindling savings, and a restriction of consumer credit—a downward chain reaction may overtake the entire economy.

What happens in the thinking of the expert reader when he suddenly chances upon such a sentence in his reading? Well, what happens is largely subconscious. Even the reader would probably not be aware that what we are here trying to get into slow motion has really happened. But this is it:

[3] *Maintaining Prosperity*, A Report by the Committee on Economic Policy, Congress of Industrial Organizations, Washington, D.C., July, 1953, p. 22.

First, as he whips along down the page and comes to the word, "If," with a capital letter, he is subconsciously aware (1) that another complete thought is about to be presented (the capital letter tells him that) and (2) that the thought will not be presented until later in the sentence (his sense of grammatical structure will tell him that the "if" introduces a group of words that will condition, or modify, the main idea yet to be presented). So that, psychologically, the reader's attitude at this point will be one of expectancy. He is awaiting the coming of the idea that he knows, sooner or later, is sure to fall within his span of vision. Then he comes to the dash. There is further delay; the new idea cannot arrive now until the parenthetical "aside" is completed, indicated again by another dash. Then, finally, having all of these dangling conditions teetering in his mind, he comes upon the solid statement of the main thought, which he has been anticipating since his eyes fell upon the first words of the sentence.

The seasoned reader does all this in a flash. Like a chess-player who sees a whole line of strategy in a single move, the reader frequently senses the whole structural situation from the sight of a single word. Sentences beginning with "if," "when," "because," "although," and similar words, are blaring announcements to the alert reader that the main thoughts in such sentences will come only after a condition has been enunciated, a reason given, an exception or a qualifying clause stated.

It is not within the scope of this book to teach the reader the fundamentals of grammar that he will need to read up to his maximum level of efficiency. If, however, at this point, he recognizes that he needs to review the fundamentals of grammar and the mechanics of English expression, he will be wise indeed to do so.

Going back to the example above, it is the last nine words that express the main thought of the sentence. And what does the whole sentence mean? It means, simply, that we are likely to have a depression if money becomes tight and we stop buying.

That brings up the third intangible to reading ease that cannot be estimated by word count or sentence length; namely, the ability to put into one's own words the gist of the thought of the author. Reading is a translation process. Basically, reading thoughts expressed in a foreign language and translating those thoughts into English is no different from reading in English and translating the thoughts into your own words. The ability to translate what you read into your own words is one of the best and most searching tests of comprehension.

We witness very often that some people can do this with remarkable ease in their own special field of endeavor. The physician, for instance, can explain with amazing ease and clarity the meaning of the words in a medical journal which the layman would find practically unreadable. For the doctor the readability of the article poses no problem at all. The same words that he reads so easily bring you to a complete halt. The lawyer, the scientist, and the engineer are equally adept in reading the literature of their own special fields. This is because of the fact that words which the average person uses commonly with one meaning have taken on a very specialized meaning in certain areas. "Choke" means one thing to the man in the street; it means something quite different to the electronics engineer.

Even more complex becomes the matter of reading when simple words combine to convey ideas entirely different from the meaning which either word, taken by itself and combined with the meaning of the other word, might convey. For instance, the meaning of the word "real" is perfectly obvious; so is the meaning of the word "income." Now put those two words together and talk about "falling real incomes," as we have in the sentence quoted above, and what happens? Familiar words suddenly take on a new, unfamiliar meaning, and they have a strange, difficult appearance when we meet them on the page.

Look at the situation from the viewpoint of someone learning English. His word concepts are much the same as those of the average reader. A word usually has one concept, occasionally two, or perhaps even three. A vest is a piece of clothing; interest is money paid for the use of other money. What does the foreigner, or the average reader, for that matter, make of the phrase "vested interests"?

Let's make a test at this point. Jot down following the phrases what each means to you:

1. active duty _____

2. real action _____

3. bird blind _____

4. black light _____

5. wide gutters _____

6. shortstop bath _____

7. water glass _____

8. creep strength _____

9. flash point _____

10. turtle deck _____

Turn to the Answer Key to see how many of these you had correct.

From what we have pointed out in this chapter, it should be apparent that readability is a great deal more than a matter of a slide rule, a word-and-syllable count, and multiplication constants. These alone may not encompass the factors which make reading either difficult or easy to comprehend, or which make the same piece of prose difficult for one person and easy for another.

How readable is it—for you?

We have emphasized in the discussion of this chapter that readability is not an absolute factor. Every person must determine *for himself* whether a selection is difficult or easy to read. He may be guided in his decision by the criteria outlined in this chapter. There are five of these:

1. Average word length
2. Average sentence length
3. Vocabulary
4. Structure
5. Idiomatic expressions and word clusters with specialized meanings

In each of the selections indicated for readability analysis:

1. Compute the readability level by the Flesch and the Gunning formulas.
2. Analyze the selection from the standpoint of the subjective factors: vocabulary, structure, and word groups.
3. Finally, evaluate the difficulty of the selection according to *your own estimate,* by placing it in one of the following categories: very easy, easy, fairly easy, standard, fairly difficult, difficult, very difficult.

Jot the information in the margin opposite the sample you have tested. Take several readability samples from the selections which you have read. Evaluate them according to the three procedures outlined above. Here are suitable selections:

1. Test I, pp. 23–26
2. Test II, pp. 27–30
3. Test III, pp. 32–34
4. Homo Sapiens, pp. 95–99
5. On Finding Words, pp. 119–126
6. This Most Excellent Canopy, the Air, pp. 145–150
7. The Businessman and His Reading, pp. 153–156
8. How to Get an Idea Across, pp. 193–200
9. The Sensations of Light and Colour, pp. 216–220
10. The Future of Democracy, pp. 244–247

Measure Your Rapid-perception Span

Get out the card that you used for rapid perception in Chapter Six and in Chapter Ten. We are going to do some more rapid-perception reading. Last time you had a space of 2 inches between the arrows. Widen the bar for this practice to 2¼ inches. Practice with this. Try to see the whole line of print within this 2¼-inch span. Below are blanks to record what you achieve.

Phrase seen	Type units	Phrase seen	Type units
1. _____	_____	1. _____	_____
2. _____	_____	2. _____	_____
3. _____	_____	3. _____	_____
4. _____	_____	4. _____	_____
5. _____	_____	5. _____	_____
6. _____	_____	6. _____	_____
7. _____	_____	7. _____	_____
8. _____	_____	8. _____	_____
9. _____	_____	9. _____	_____
10. _____	_____	10. _____	_____

No. correct _____

Av. type units _____

No. correct _____

Av. type units _____

Phrase seen	Type units	Phrase seen	Type units
1. _____	____	1. _____	____
2. _____	____	2. _____	____
3. _____	____	3. _____	____
4. _____	____	4. _____	____
5. _____	____	5. _____	____
6. _____	____	6. _____	____
7. _____	____	7. _____	____
8. _____	____	8. _____	____
9. _____	____	9. _____	____
10. _____	____	10. _____	____

No. correct _____   No. correct _____

Av. type units _____   Av. type units _____

Compare your achievement on this perception exercise with your achievements previously. Refer to your former records in Chapters Six and Ten.

Reading for Speed of Comprehension—1

Are you one of those people who have every good intention in the world of reading the things you would like to read but are constantly excusing yourself for not reading because, you say, you do not have the time to read? Aren't we all more or less like that? Louis Shores, who is Dean of the School of Library Training and Service at the Florida State University, has suggested a solution to the problem of not having time to read in the article which follows.

Read it with an eye open for everything: facts, main ideas, subsidiary ideas, structure, implications, and whatever else you might see or think about as you read. Try to get *total* comprehension in reading this very readable article.

Time: MINUTES _____

SECONDS _____

FINDING TIME TO READ [4]

by Louis Shores

If you are an average reader, you can read an average book at the rate of 300 words a minute. You cannot maintain that average, however, unless you read regularly every day. Nor can you attain that speed with "hard" books in science, mathematics, agriculture, business, or any subject that is new to you.

The chances are you will never attempt that speed with poetry or want to race through some passages in fiction over which you wish to linger. But for most novels, biographies and books about travel, hobbies or personal interests, if you are an average reader, you should have no trouble at all absorbing meaning and pleasure out of 300 printed words every 60 seconds.

Statistics are not always practicable, but consider these: If the average reader can read 300 words a minute of average reading, then in 15 minutes he can read 4,500 words. Multiplied by seven, the days of the week, the product is 31,500. Another multiplication by four, the weeks of the month, makes 126,000. And final multiplication by 12, the months of the year, results in a grand total of 1,512,000 words. That is the total number of words of average reading an average reader can do in just 15 minutes a day for one year.

Books vary in length from 60,000 to 100,000 words. The average is about 75,000 words. In one year of average reading by an average reader for 15 minutes a day, 20 books will be read. That's a lot of books. It is four times the number read by public-library borrowers in America. And yet it is easily possible.

One of the greatest of all modern physicians was Sir William Osler, who taught at Johns Hopkins Medical School. He finished his teaching days at Oxford University. Many of the outstanding physicians of today were his students. Nearly all the practicing doctors of today were brought up on his medical textbooks. Among his many remarkable contributions to medicine are his notes on how people die.

His greatness is attributed by his biographers and critics not alone to

[4] Louis Shores, "Finding Time to Read," *The Wonderful World of Books*, Alfred Stefferud, editor, pp. 106–108. Copyright, 1952, by Alfred Stefferud, published jointly by The New American Library of World Literature, Inc., and Houghton Mifflin Company.

his profound medical knowledge and insight, but also to his broad general education, for he was a very cultured man. He was interested in what men have done and thought throughout the ages. And he knew that the only way to find out what the best experiences of the race had been was to read what people had written.

But Osler's problem was the same as everyone else's, only more so. He was a busy physician, a teacher of physicians and a medical-research specialist. There was no time in a 24-hour day that did not rightly belong to one of these three occupations, except the few hours for sleep and meals.

Osler arrived at his solution early. He would read the last 15 minutes before he went to sleep. If bedtime was set for 11 P.M. he read from 11 to 11:15. If research kept him up to 2 A.M., he read from 2 to 2:15. Over a very long lifetime, Osler never broke the rule. We have evidence that after a while, he simply could not fall asleep until he had done his 15 minutes of reading.

In his lifetime, Osler read a significant library of books. Just do a mental calculation for half a century of 15-minute reading periods daily and see how many books you get. Consider what a range of interests and variety of subjects are possible in one lifetime!

Osler read widely outside of his medical specialty. Indeed, he developed from this 15-minute reading habit an avocational specialty to balance his vocational specialization. Among scholars in English literature, Osler is known as an authority on Sir Thomas Browne, 17th-century English prose master, and Osler's collection of Sir Thomas's works is considered one of the best anywhere.

A great many more things could be said about Osler's contribution to medical research, to the reform of medical teaching, to the introduction of modern clinical methods. But the important point is that he answered supremely well for himself the question all of us who live a busy life must answer: How can I find time to read?

The answer may not be the last 15 minutes before you go to sleep. It may be 15 minutes a day at some other time. In the busiest of calendars there is probably more than one 15-minute period tucked away somewhere still unassigned. I've seen some curious solutions to the problem of finding time for reading.

During Army days in the last year of the war, I discovered a Pfc. in my squadron who seemed unusually well-read. I checked in his 201 file and found a remarkable civilian and military biography. His four years of service included two overseas, all meritorious but without heroics. Had all of his recommendations for promotion gone through, he would have had not only his commission, but probably the rank of captain.

But here he was, still a private first-class—because, despite the military emphasis on education, efficiency, loyalty and all other criteria for determining promotion, accident plays a most important part. Every time this Pfc. had been recommended for promotion, except once, he had been transferred, or come up against a table of organization limitations, or a new change in regulations or a superior officer who had filled out the forms incorrectly. And so he had remained a Pfc., and had taken his reward in reading. The amount he did in the Army was prodigious.

I was curious about his method. And one day, before I asked him, I found a partial answer. Every day the enlisted men put in an hour of drill and formations. During that time at least one fairly long period of rest was called. Imagine my surprise on my first visit to the drill field when, at the command "rest!" I saw one man in the line pull out a paper pocket-book and begin to read, standing up.

When I talked with him, I found that from boyhood he had developed the habit of carrying a little book from which he read every minute he was not doing something else. He found a book especially useful and relaxing during the periods of waiting which all of us experience daily— waiting for meals, buses, doctors, hair cuts, telephone calls, dates, performances to begin, or something to happen. There were his 15 minutes a day, or more. There were his 20 books a year—1,000 in a lifetime.

No universal formula can be prescribed. Each of us must find our own 15-minute period each day. It is better if it is regular. Then all additional spare minutes are so many bonuses. And, believe me, the opportunity for reading-bonuses are many and unexpected. On a recent night an uninvited guest turned up to make five for bridge. I had the kind of paper-book at hand to make being the fifth at bridge a pleasure.

The only requirement is the will to read. With it you can find the 15 minutes no matter how busy the day. And you must have the book at hand. Not even seconds of your 15 minutes must be wasted starting to read. Set that book out in advance. Put it into your pocket when you dress. Put another beside your bed. Place one in your bathroom. Keep one near your dining table.

You can't escape reading 15 minutes a day, and that means you will read half a book a week, two books a month, 20 a year and 1,000 or more in a reading lifetime. Surely, that is an easy way to become well-read.

What time is it now? MINUTES _____

SECONDS _____

What is your reading time for this selection? MINUTES _____

SECONDS _____

Without referring back to the article, answer the following questions.

Comprehension quiz   *Part One*

This is a completion type of examination. Fill in the words which are missing, according to what was said in the text.

1. The author says that the average adult reads _____ words per minute.

2. The average book is _____ words in length.

3. The average public library borrower reads _____ books a year.

4. Sir William Osler collected the works of _____.

5. With fifteen minutes of reading time a day the average reader could read _____ books a year.

6. All the minutes in excess of fifteen minutes a day that a person spends in reading, the author considers as a reading _____.

Part Two

1. The author implies that your rate of reading
   a is unimportant as long as you read fifteen minutes a day.
   b will vary with your physical well being.
   c will vary in direct proportion to the difficulty of the material.
   d will vary in inverse proportion to the difficulty of the material.

2. The author implies that you should read
   a not more than fifteen minutes a day.
   b at least fifteen minutes a day.
   c as much as you can and not bother about the number of minutes a day that you read.
   d for fifteen minutes before you go to sleep.

3. The implication of the article is that
   a reading is best when it covers many areas of knowledge.
   b physicians and surgeons should read before retiring.
   c soldiers have more time for reading than most of us.
   d if you are going to be widely read, you must read for fifteen minutes a day for fifty years.

4. The one basic requirement that is mentioned is to
   a set aside at least fifteen consecutive minutes at the same time each day for reading.
   b have many books lying around the house so that you can get them easily.
   c have the will and determination to read.
   d make reading a lifelong habit.

How well did you comprehend what you read? Check your answers against those given in the Answer Key. Each correct answer is worth 10 per cent.

What is your level of comprehension?   _____%

What is your speed of comprehension?   _____wpm

What is your reading index $(R \times C/100)$? _____

Reading for Speed of Comprehension—2

Time: MINUTES _____

       SECONDS _____

RELIGIOUS MOTIVES IN BUSINESS [5]

A lot of people think that business is grubby, greedy, money-mad, materialistic and without ideals. True, portions of it are and some people engaged in it are, but the merely sordid facts do not tell the full story, and those who limit their view to the sorrier aspects may miss the vision of the whole.

You hear people talk of "public service." They want to serve humanity. What they usually mean is that they would like to go into one of

[5] "Religious Motives in Business," from *Changing Times*, the Kiplinger Magazine, August, 1954, pp. 43–46.

the professions, such as the ministry, or teaching, or medicine, or government. They seldom include business as a field or a method of service. This is particularly true of young college graduates, full of ideals, who say they aren't interested in going into business or making money (as if business and money were synonymous). They only want to serve humanity (as if this were the antithesis of business). You may even hear young people decry the "profit motive" (as if such a motive were ignoble) without stopping to examine the fruits of the profit motive.

There is something screwy about these lofty ideas and good intentions. What's wrong is that they are too limited. The holders of them lack knowledge of what business really is, and they also may lack imagination about the world of today and the integral part that business plays in all operations of it.

What this discussion aims at suggesting is that . . .

. . . Business is as good a way of serving God and humanity as anything else, and it contains a wider range of opportunities for such service than almost anything else.

. . . The motives that lie deep down in much business, even if not in all business, are motives for human service with religious overtones.

. . . The religious portions of the motives are not advertised, are not worn on the lapel for all to see, because the average business person has a great fear of being considered a hypocrite, and would turn and run like the wind to avoid being regarded as sanctimonious.

. . . Motives which are religious at their roots, even if not on the surface, dominate a great deal of business conduct and business ethics. The religious approach has become so much of a habit that its real nature is sometimes obscured.

. . . The progress of religion as a motive in business has had its ups and down through the centuries, but for the past half century, which covers the lives of most of us, it has been on an up. Not as yet as high as it might be, nevertheless moving upward.

Those are assertions based on observations of our times. Not every one of them is provable by the array of fact upon fact, and some of them are open to attack from the cynic or the skeptic. Any person of such a mind can cite examples of immoral and irreligious conduct and practices, and these may all be true, yet such exceptions do not necessarily destroy the general observations.

Just What Is "Business"?

For a moment let's take a look at business and see what it is. Essentially it is a way of getting a job done. Originally jobs were done largely by individuals, but the jobs grew more complex and the individual had to have helpers. Thus arose employers who employed one or two or half a dozen or even fifty helpers.

But most business today is done through a setup known as the corporation. It is really a sort of cooperative method of getting a job done. There are owners and managers and submanagers and counselors and employes, and the miracle about them all is that they work more or less smoothly together and in a spirit which is essentially cooperative. The frictions are publicized more than the smooth cooperation, and so have more weight in the public mind than they deserve.

What drives these businesses? Oh yes, they want to make money for the owners, the managers, the entrepreneurs. This is the "profit motive." It is not only the goad, the driving force; it is also the automatic trimmer of useless or badly conceived enterprises, for a business that does an unwanted job or a poor job passes out. It fails, and the failure trims oui system of expensive deadwood. So the profit-and-loss system under which we operate has its excellent uses, both to stimulate activity and to rid us of the needless.

Now ask who is in business, and you find that most of us are in business, on the inside of it, looking to it for our incomes or else dependent on it to supply our needs. Most of us could not lead normal lives for one hour without the aid of things which come to us through the channels of business. It is apparent, therefore, that the greatest servant of all is what we call business.

The man who heads up a business, or the men—for there are usually a number of them—are very important people, for they influence pretty much the destinies of people who work with them and they contribute heavily to the well-being of their customers. They have great power for giving good, bad or indifferent service to humanity.

And what do they work for? Well, partly they work for money, except that money itself is a symbol, a measure. It is good for the purchase of things. What people in business really work for is advancement and success, just like everyone else, and this goes beyond money. They also want to be recognized in the community, like everyone else. And, under all these surface motives, they want to do good jobs, honest jobs. If they succeed, they gain money, advancement, recognition, and that other thing which is so desired by all of us—inner satisfaction.

It is at this point that religious motives enter. Every meditative man knows in his heart that material success is not enough, that money alone is no full reward and cannot be relied upon for permanent happiness. There is the groping for spiritual success, too, and this groping enters into a multitude of decisions that are made hourly or daily by a host of men in business, at the top and down the line. Sometimes it is conscious, but oftener it is subconscious, hardly recognized at the time the decisions are made. It is a sort of religious atmosphere, regardless of whether or not it is so labeled.

How Business Morals Grew

As said before, the proof of these assertions is hard to lay your hands upon in a tangible way, but there are many pointers.

In the very earliest period of American history there was a close relation between business and religion. The early settlers left the Old World because they believed that religion should be a personal way of life, not a separate ritual performed by the church. Religion did not require a man merely to attend church. In those days, religion required that a man be thrifty, sober, industrious and frugal. It was sinful to be lazy, frivolous, extravagant or wasteful. The religious man worked hard and saved his money. These savings over the years provided the capital that was to settle the West and expand commerce and industry.

John Wesley said that religion makes a man frugal, frugality begets wealth, and wealth makes a man indifferent to religion. And so it often worked out in the 1800's. The country expanded and business prospered, and with prosperity came a new doctrine—laissez-faire. The best possible world would be achieved, said its advocates, by letting each individual do what he pleased with the least possible interference from church or state. Religion became a once-a-week affair. Religion was for Sunday; business ran the rest of the week.

In the last half of the nineteenth century, especially in the 70's, 80's and 90's, business rules were pretty much based on the idea of dog eat dog. Ruthlessness was condoned as "good business." To the strong went the victory and success. A certain amount of cheating was secretly admired. Shrewdness was respected, even though it sometimes involved cutting corners on strict probity. Employers sweated their employes without too much human compassion, for "business was business."

Eventually the tide turned again. It is hard to say that the turn occurred at any specific time. Perhaps the spirit of Theodore Roosevelt contributed to the idea of business decorum. Certainly the ideas of Woodrow Wilson brought forth laws and systems to curb business brigandage, especially in the realm of banking and finance. The 20's made their contribution. There was the congressional commission to investigate and reform, if possible, the expensive systems of distribution.

There were the famous Brookings reports which set people to thinking along these lines: Pay as high wages as possible so as to help make a mass market for industry. Don't hire and fire indiscriminately. Remember that employes are the nation's customers directly or indirectly. Great production is dependent on great consumption, so let there be wide distribution of income, and that will make good business. This was not radical doctrine, but it appeared as such in the 20's.

Actually, it was merely a formalization of the earlier ideas of Henry Ford, who shocked orthodox businessmen by raising wages to unheard-of levels and cutting prices at the expense of dividends so his workers could buy the products of his factories.

Depression and New Deal

Then came the depression. This sounded the death knell of laissez-faire. The New Deal, supported by the majority of people and many businessmen, was almost a spiritual rebirth in terms of humanitarianism operating through political agencies.

True, many of the New Deal reforms were shoved through over the opposition of business. There was vigorous opposition to the Securities and Exchange Act; there was balking at social security and unemployment compensation. But deep down, most businessmen soon granted that the changes were for the best. For proof, try to find a responsible corporate executive today who would seriously propose repealing the laws regulating the securities markets or those establishing social security.

Two more things which are distinctly of this world and not religious have contributed to the practice of liberality on the part of business, especially toward employes. One is the steep income tax, and the other is the rise of labor unions.

Once upon a time, before the days of heavy income tax, if the owner-operator of a business could hold down wages and save a dollar on his payroll, he got to keep the dollar himself. It was that simple.

Nowadays government taxes away about half of the dollar that shows up at the end of the year as income, leaving roughly 50 cents. And if the owner-operator takes this 50 cents for himself, the government takes away a good portion of it in further taxes, the amount often running to two thirds or three fourths, depending on how high his income is. Thus the incentive for making money is lessened because the government-partner takes such a large thick slice. Consequently there is less resistance to wage raising than there would be if there were not such high taxes. The taxes are a sort of prod to liberal motives. Furthermore, the rise of big-scale philanthropy through foundations is largely a product of estate taxes, death taxes. To avoid taxes after death, a man gives away a portion of his wealth for worthy causes. The motive is a mixture of tax avoidance and humanitarianism, and it is impossible to determine how much of each.

The unions, too, enforce higher pay, the wider distribution of income, the wider enjoyment of the profits of business and other benefits. Those who run business may or may not be willing and glad to do these things, but the fact is that they must, for the unions prescribe. Here again the motives of businessmen are probably a mixture.

Nevertheless, over and above the pressures from high taxes and strong unions on the nerve of liberality, it is true that businessmen are more concerned with the welfare of their employes and of people generally than they were even a generation ago. It has become orthodox to think in terms of mass welfare, although half a century ago it was none of the businessman's business. If he had thought and talked humanitarianism, he would have been regarded as soft-headed and queer. The improvement is conspicuous, and it comes from good motives, not merely from compulsion.

A Businessman's Creed

The steel industry 60 or 70 years ago gained a notorious record for being tough and ruthless. It saw some of the bloodiest strikes in U.S. history. So when the top boss of a big, modern steel company writes a book and endeavors to set forth what he believes in, it is worth noting. Here are some excerpts from *Freedom's Faith* by Clarence Randall, chairman of the board of Inland Steel.

"Almost without exception the men whom the world calls great have found their tasks tolerable only because deep down inside they have believed they were part of a greater whole, and that life had depth and meaning beyond that which they were able to comprehend.

"I believe this to be predominately true of businessmen. A man may, of course, make a great deal of money under our system and believe in nothing. When that happens, he will usually be found in some activity where he can work and live to himself, neither requiring the support of an important segment of the public who can know him personally, nor receiving a vote of confidence from organized groups. Like a wolverine, he follows the trap lines of free enterprise, profiting from the efforts of others, but never sharing their sacrifices.

"But wherever men are chosen by others for positions of trust and responsibility, you will find with convincing frequency that they are men who possess in some form a compelling religious belief. Sometimes their faith is so intimate and personal that they do not even associate it with formal worship, but there is an infallible relationship, in my opinion, between the fact that they hold fast in all situations to some belief which is fundamental in their lives, and the fact that they are where they are. No experience is more moving than to come to admire a man in some other business than your own for the honesty of his purposes and the inspiring quality of what he says and writes, and then on closer acquaintance to find that he and you share the same religious concepts."

Does This Case Make Sense?

You may wonder whether all this makes a convincing case for the presence of religious motives in business.

If you choose to regard the examples cited as indicators of mere morality or business ethics, or if you wish to regard them as humanitarian, although not necessarily religious, well, perhaps you are right. But a great teacher, on whom the Christian religion was founded, did not separate godliness from humanitarianism. He said,

"Inasmuch as ye have done it unto one of the least of these my brethren, ye have done it unto me."

Motives can never be weighed and appraised absolutely, or slipped into neat pigeonholes. But in the case of business motives, it is obvious that some of them go beyond the bounds of what is required by mere good business or the desire for profits. They stem from something deep down—an urge for the general welfare of people. They spring from ideals and from goodness for goodness' sake, and this is the realm of religion.

What time is it now? MINUTES _____

SECONDS _____

What is your reading time for this selection? MINUTES _____

SECONDS _____

Now, test your level of comprehension by answering the following questions. Do not refer back to the article.

Comprehension quiz

1. The author thinks that the view that business is grubby, money-mad, greedy, and materialistic is
   a a realistic statement of the situation.
   b a partial view of the situation.
   c the viewpoint of those who hate business.
   d a challenge to religion.

2. The author feels that most young people with idealistic viewpoints, who are primarily interested in serving humanity,
   a will find little satisfaction or reward in a business career.
   b are unsuited for business because of their idealism.
   c confuse essential issues.
   d lack facts and imagination.

3. Underlying all the surface motives of most business leaders is a deep, sincere desire to
   a show a profit above all else.
   b do a good honest job.
   c make other people's lives easier.
   d advance and succeed by their own initiative.

4. A close relation between business and religion has been
   a the result of a desire to make more money.
   b a part of our philosophy from the very earliest period of American history.
   c an antidote, for the most part, for the pioneer spirit of rugged individualism.
   d of relatively recent development.

5. Henry Ford was
   a a very religious man.

 b an astute businessman who paid good wages to his best workmen in order to keep them.

 c a pioneer in labor relations and wage-scale increases.

 d one of the first big business executives to read the Brookings Report and put its recommendations into effect.

6. The New Deal

 a was basically a political program aimed at getting more votes for the Democratic party.

 b fell just short of being a spiritual rebirth.

 c was a substitute for *laissez faire*.

 d was the fulfillment of the ideas of Woodrow Wilson.

7. The author sees high government taxes as

 a a necessary evil of our modern economy.

 b an aid in giving the worker a higher standard of living.

 c a benefit to labor unions.

 d a sign of the times.

8. Clarence Randall, chairman of the board of Inland Steel, feels that a compelling religious belief has a relationship to the

 a attainment of positions of trust and responsibility.

 b kind of work a person does.

 c acceptance a person receives from organized groups in the modern social structure.

 d admiration one has for his colleague's achievements and accomplishments.

9. The author feels that religious motives in business spring from

 a a desire to serve the present age.

 b a desire to live up to the conventional requirements of ethical business practice.

 c ideals and goodness for goodness' sake.

 d the individual businessman's own creed and dogma.

10. The author takes the position that

 a business really has more cynics and skeptics in its ranks than it likes to admit.

 b on the whole there is much more religion in business than is ordinarily recognized.

 c business exploits religion for the purpose of keeping face.

 d idealism is incidental; business is primarily interested in its own advancement.

How well did you comprehend what you have read? Check your

answers with those given in the Answer Key. Each correct answer is worth 10 per cent.

What is your level of comprehension?   _____%

What is your speed of comprehension?   _____wpm

What is your reading index $(R \times C/100)$? _____

Reading Habit Index

Never Rarely Sometimes Usually Always

1. I am aware of paragraphs and their characteristics: length, structure, vocabulary, and readability.

2. As I begin to read, I have clearly in mind the purpose for which I am reading, and I read in keeping with that purpose, regulating my speed accordingly.

3. More than ever, I look for the key words and phrases. I have learned to read with higher speed and less effort.

4. I have made skimming a habit with my reading procedures. Usually I skim an article prior to reading it more carefully.

5. I try to discern why the author wrote what I am reading.

Reading habit index score: _____
(See directions for scoring, p. 75)
Date: _____

Chapter Fourteen

How to read a newspaper

WHETHER you get your quota of news dangling on a strap en route to or from your work, or get an eyeful by peeking over the other fellow's shoulder, or consume your sheet in the beslippered luxury of your easy chair—one fact remains: most Americans *do* read the newspaper.

And the newspaper can be a daily challenge to you as a reader. It can bring out the best that you have in you, as you pit your puny strength against this Gargantua of the fourth estate. Every edition can provide you with ample opportunity to put your *total* reading skills to work.

Obviously, none of us reads every word of every issue. The presses are prodigal with the news. Every day the reader has more—much more —than he knows what to do with. His interest rises and falls, ebbs and flows, as he roams the paper from column to column.

How shall he deal with these never-ending ribbons of print that roll ceaselessly day after day from the platens of the presses to his morning breakfast table or his office desk?

There are ways. Every reader can make his newspaper his servant. Instead, all too often he has become its slave. The newspaper is a challenge and an opportunity to help you develop your reading skills and your perceptual techniques. By using it thus, you will also get the news and get it better than you otherwise would. Let's suggest a few ways in which your newspaper can help you daily to develop your reading habits.

Total mobilization of reading skills

In reading your daily paper, put your *total* reading skills to work in dealing with it. This means that you will need to read with imagination and resourcefulness. Remember the basic skills of reading, and make them pay off when you read the news. What are these skills? How may they be employed in reading your paper and perfecting your techniques? Here are some suggestions:

1. *Use Your Newspaper to Practice Skimming.* Let's face it—there's too much in every daily sheet. You can't read all of it. Here's where you *must* make up your mind; there is no alternative left. If you are going to get over the daily sheet, you *must* skim. But remember, skimming isn't a hop-skip-and-jump procedure. It is a rapid reduction of what you read to basic, essential fact; it is *selective* reading.

In skimming the newspaper some of your ideas gleaned from the previous chapter on skimming will have to be modified to suit the newspaper milieu. In the first place, there is little paragraph structure, as such, in the news story. Each paragraph is but a sentence or two in length. Usually these sentences are packed with fact. Supercharged with data, they are production-line pieces, all pretty much the same, without character, or personality.

A news office is a busy, bustling, get-things-done sort of place, operating to the incessant din of teletype machines, and hovering over it is the odor of printer's ink. The newspaper game on the whole is a noisy game. News is born to the clack and clatter of the typewriter, set to the jingle of the linotype, printed to the rumble of the press, and sold under the blatant and raucous cry of the newsboy.

When the reader picks up the sheet, the clamor still continues. The banner headlines scream at him the most urgent story of the day. Streaming across the columns in usually 72 point or more, the banner lines are out to get some action from the reader. His eye sweeps across the big, black letters and lands in the column farthest to the right, where bank after bank of secondary headlines summarize and give the gist of the principal happenings of the event.

Finally, the eye of the reader settles down, crosses the date line, and begins the reading of the story itself. He has done a lot of skimming up to this point. The editors have helped him to do it. There is much that he knows about the happening, even though he has not read a single word of the story itself. That's the purpose of the headlines, to help the reader to skim.

Now he gets to the story itself. There's the first "paragraph." It is always an account of "who, what, when, where, why, and how" of the event. All the essential information that he will need to read the rest of the story is given in those few lines of the opening paragraph. It is, in fact, an outline for what follows. Every news story has two main parts, the "lead" paragraph, which summarizes the story, and the "body," which is an elaboration of the lead. In the body, the news drama unfolds in all of its detail, the points are expanded and dwelt upon at some length.

Most news stories are written in chronological sequence. The reader should keep this in mind. One thing happens, then another, and another, and another.

Note for example the following account of a disaster which occurred on Main Street of Home Town, U.S.A.:

WILD MILK TANKER CRASHES, 3 KILLED [1]

Truck Speeds Down-Hill Out of Control at Home Town—10 Hurt 13 Vehicles Smashed

HOME TOWN, U.S.A. July 21—A fifteen-ton milk tank trailer-truck hurtled down a hill here out of control this afternoon, rammed a smaller truck from behind, and caused a spectacular multiple crash in which three persons died and ten were injured.

Analysis
The lead paragraph contains 3 points:

Point 1. Milk tanker goes wild.

Point 2. Other vehicles involved.

Point 3. Persons killed and injured

Altogether, thirteen vehicles figured in the disaster.

Expansion: Point 2

The tanker lost its braking power on the slopes of Route 17, which becomes North Main Street in this village, gateway to the Upstate vacation area. Home Town was thronged with week-end shoppers from near-by resorts when the chain accident started at 2:05 P.M.

Expansion: Point 1

Suggestion of Point 3

Suggestion of Point 2

[1] Adapted from an account in *The New York Times*, July 25, 1954, p. 1.

Southbound, accelerating at a deadly rate, its horn blaring frantically, the run-away tanker hit the vehicle ahead with an impact sufficient to telescope two parked cars like opera hats.

A northbound jeep, striving vainly to avert disaster, ended up on the west side of the street with the tanker, both jammed between a half-toppled telegraph pole and the wall of an old house. One of those killed was a woman pedestrian, pinned between the jeep and the pole, in a tangle of twisted steel and shattered glass.

Flames Attract Crowd
Flames seethed from the massive vehicle—filled with milk that was later condemned and pumped out—attracting practically the entire population of the village.

A plan to have Route 17 bypass Home Town has been in the blueprint stage for several years. The accident was regarded as sure to spur a move to get action on the project.

The tanker ultimately came to rest about 100 yards north of the center of the community, where Main Street intersects with West Street in the heart of the business section.

Although differing in details, the crash was strikingly similar to the one at nearby Neighborville, a little more than three years ago.

In the previous accident a trailer truck laden with bottled gas went out of control on a mountainous stretch on Route 17. It ripped up a line of eleven cars, killing four persons and injuring sixteen.

Those who were victims of this afternoon's crash were:

[Here follows list of names and addresses.]

Analysis
Further expansion: Point 1

Further expansion: Point 2

Further expansion: Point 2

Points 1 and 2

Further expansion: Point 3

Further expansion: Point 1

Ancillary material: Strictly, has nothing to do with the accident itself.

Further expansion: Point 1

Ancillary material: Although a parallel situation, this has nothing to do with the accident at Home Town.

Further expansion: Point 3

This is only one article, but it is typical of thousands that appear on the pages of the nation's newspapers every day in the year. From this article the eyes of the reader roam up and down the packed aisles of print that tell of happenings great and small. Some of these items he merely notes, and then moves on; others he pauses to read more carefully, as his interest dictates.

In any event he should know briefly what the master pattern of each news story is. News stories, in contrast to editorials, are written in the pattern of an inverted pyramid. The big end, the important facts in the news comes first. Then the story starts to dwindle. Less and less significant material is presented until, at the end, the story holds interest for the reader only if he happens to have the most intimate knowledge of the situation or the actors concerned.

To take the milk-tanker tragedy again, the story would actually look something like this in terms of data importance:

WILD MILK TANKER CRASHES—THREE KILLED

Fifteen-ton tanker hurtled down hill out of control, rammed other vehicles, three persons killed, ten others injured. Thirteen cars involved in the disaster.

> Tanker lost braking power on slope entering town. Town was thronged with week-end shoppers. Horn blaring, it roared down Main Street. Hit one car; telescoped others. Jeep jammed, pole toppled, woman killed, debris and wreckage.

>> Flames attack crowd. By-pass planned. Accident may spur action.
>> This crash similar to the one at Neighborville three years ago.
>> Summary of that crash.
>> Dead and injured.

And so, the first technique of reading that you should always practice with your newspaper is the technique of skimming. You may recall that in the chapter on skimming these words were written, ". . . and in skimming you touch the page only at those points where, by so doing, you will be rewarded to the greatest degree for your effort. Learn *where* to look . . . for the leading thoughts."

These words apply to reading your newspaper. Skim it. Keep in mind the characteristic structure of the news story. It will help you to know where to look for what you want. That is all that skimming is. Next, we shall suggest a specialized use of skimming, that is, skimming to locate a specific item of information. Applying both of these skimming skills, that is, skimming for the main facts and skimming for the specific facts, should help you to consume your newspaper with the skill of an expert.

2. *Use Your Newspaper to Skim for Specific Details.* It is not enough to skim for the broad, general idea only. Sometimes in our reading we need to spot the specific fact, the isolated item of information. In many reading situations you have need to scrutinize the page for a particular detail. In skimming of this type, the same visual and psychological process takes place that occurs when you stand upon the brow of a hill and look for a certain landmark in the broad panorama of landscape that stretches out before you. You look for a particular point of interest, perhaps a certain building in a distant village, or a church steeple on a far hill. In any event, you are scrutinizing the landscape for one definite point of interest.

The reader frequently does exactly the same thing with his page of print. An extremely important skill of reading, therefore, is this ability to locate quickly and unerringly any particular fact out of the context of surrounding data. Every reader uses this skill when he consults an encyclopedia to verify or locate an item of information. He uses it whenever he looks for a single statement among a mass of statements. In business, in industry, in executive positions, in the professions, in school, in almost every walk of life, this is a skill that we use far more often than we are aware.

For that reason it is important that you master this technique of skimming. Use your newspaper to do it. Every day take a few minutes to skim for certain specific facts. Do it this way: Take a fact that is announced in the headline. Select just *one* item of information. For example, in the milk-trailer tragedy story, which was printed earlier in this chapter, the third line in the subhead announced, "13 Vehicles Smashed." *There* is your fact. But exactly where *in the article itself* is this fact mentioned? See how quickly you can find it. In doing this, you will skim down over the column, not reading for connected thought, but intent on searching for only one item: the fact that thirteen vehicles were involved in the disaster. If you are skillful, you will *see the fact immediately* in the second paragraph of the story.

Try this technique with your newspaper for a few minutes each day. Select a detail. Then, by your watch, see how many seconds it takes you to locate the fact itself in the body of the news story. You will be surprised how this practice will give you an eye for the facts. You will also be surprised to find the way in which the skill which you develop as a result of this simple technique will pay off at the office, in the library, in countless other places in your reading in helping you to find quickly and accurately the particular fact for which you are searching.

There is another particularly effective way of employing the skimming technique in finding specific details. Take your newspaper, and begin to read any article of considerable length, reading the lead paragraphs only. Then, select the particular facts about which you would like to know more. Skim the article to find this information. This is selective reading, and it can help you speed down the long, narrow lanes of newsprint with plenty of reading horsepower.

3. *Use Your Paper to Improve Your Eye Span.* We have emphasized the importance of a wide eye span to more effective reading. The more visual material you can scoop up at one fleeting glance, the more rapid your reading is likely to be. He who nibbles at the page in visual tidbits reads slowly, largely because he *does* take visual tidbits. He feeds his eyes piecemeal, hence his eyes feed his mind piecemeal, and the result is piecemeal reading—a fragmentary thought pattern which it is difficult for the individual to synthesize into an integrated whole.

Practice a little each day with your newspaper on improving your visual span. Try looking straight down the middle of the roadway of print. With *one* fixation, look at the middle word in each line down the column. At the same time try to read with the "corners" of your eyes the words that recede from your field of visual acuity on either side. This is not an easy exercise, and will be discouraging at first. You will be tempted to give up, but persevere. By the end of one week, with 10 minutes of solid practice each day, you will be aware that you are actually seeing more. You will have demanded that your peripheral vision wake up, and you will indeed find it beginning to do so.

Sometimes the reader is helped by taking a ruler and drawing a line from top to bottom, down the middle of the column. This serves as a quick point of fixation for each line of print. Where the vertical line crosses the line of print, there focus your eyes quickly, and keep them there unswervingly. Do not permit them to slide or slip. Do not sneak side glances, but fixate at the midpoint and look with the corners of your eyes. Try it. Read one rather lengthy article in your newspaper each day in this manner. Then read it again—in the same way. It is for practice only, at first; but in a little while you will be making one fixation per line as a regular feature of your reading habits when you pick up your newspaper.

4. *Use Your Newspaper to Help You Remember Details.* This is a brief reminder of a technique that we suggested earlier in this book. You will find it described on pp. 233–234. Refer to it now. Keep your note pad close by when you read your paper. Lacking a note pad, use the margins—top, bottom—and the blank spaces within and around the advertisements. Your paper is expendable; mark it up, use it as a daily workbook to help you improve your ability to remember ever more clearly and accurately the details of what you have read.

5. *Use Your Newspaper to Practice Reading Key Words and Phrases.* That is what headlines are—key words and phrases that give you the gist of the news. Spot the significant word, grab it, and get on down the column.

Take this account of an earthquake in South America: [2]

THREE INJURED IN ANDES QUAKE

by Associated Press

SANTIAGO, CHILE, July 23.—Three persons were injured by falling walls in Coquimbo early today when a sharp earthquake rocked the central zone country. The earth shocks were felt in other cities, but no other damage or injuries were reported.

The quake was also felt in Buenos Aires and the observatory there said the epicenter was probably in the Andes between Argentina and Chile.

Sixty words, that. How many did *you* read? Your *mind* should have picked up something like this, as your eyes ran over the words:

THREE INJURED ANDES QUAKE

Santiago, Chile . . . Three injured . . . falling walls . . . Coquimbo . . . earthquake rocked central zone . . . Shocks felt . . . other cities, no damage or injuries . . . Felt in Buenos Aires . . . epicenter probably . . . Andes between Argentina and Chile.

Thirty-four words *that*—headline, date line, and all! And you have cut your reading load, the actual verbiage that your mind must process, by 43 per cent.

6. *Use Your Newspaper to Develop Skill in Critical Reading.* Now we turn from the news columns to another part of the paper: the edi-

[2] Adapted from an Associated Press news release, in the *New York World-Telegram and Sun*, July 23, 1954, p. 1.

torial. This may be the material that is found on the editorial page proper, or the same type of material which is found in the writings of certain columnists who review, interpret, and comment upon matters of general interest to the reader.

Editorials differ from news stories in several ways. One of the most important differences is, of course, in their structural organization. Whereas the news story begins with the broad-base statement of the five Ws and then proceeds to paragraphs of lesser and lesser importance, the editorial reverses that pattern. The editor begins by a recital of facts, usually facts with which you are already familiar. He reviews a situation to bring all the pertinent facts afresh to the reader's attention. Then he proposes his solution, or bids for the reader's support. This type of writing bids for reader reaction.

From a reading standpoint, the editorial page is an excellent place to try to discern the motive behind the writing. When you attempt to do this, you are reading critically. Ask yourself, "Why did the editor write this? What was his real purpose?" He may be just chatting with you; he may be explaining or attempting to show certain implications of some happening in the news; he may be celebrating an occasion, an anniversary, or an event; he may be attempting to mold public opinion; or he may be simply reflecting what other people are thinking and saying about a matter of common concern. As a reader, however, you should not be deceived. Editorials have many forms and purposes. Read the editorials critically. Analyze your author in terms of his appeal and his motive for addressing the reader.

7. *Use Your Newspaper to Make Your Reading Time Count.* Don't just "read the paper." Set a schedule for the reading of your entire paper. Be specific with the time allotments and give each department of the paper its proper and reasonable time. Plan to get over the entire issue within the time budget that you have set.

The *New York Herald Tribune* in a little booklet [3] whose purpose is to help the *Tribune's* readers get the most out of their newspaper suggests one way of making the most of a half-hour spent with a metropolitan newspaper. The plan is as follows:

a. *The Bird's-Eye View* (3 minutes). Start by getting a comprehensive idea of the paper's content for the day. This you can do by skimming the front-page headlines, and by using the paper's index to glean the main

[3] "How to Get the Most Out of Your Newspaper," pp. 15–16, published by the *New York Herald Tribune*, 1952.

news on the inside pages. This preliminary survey—including a hasty reading of the top news stories in which you have compelling interest—can be compressed into 3 minutes.

b. *The Day's Big News* (12 minutes). You should spend at least 12 minutes of your precious half-hour on general news—local, national, and international. As you read, try to see the world in one piece and the news trends as part of a pattern. (NOTE: Newspaper advertising—"the ads" are also big news and demand your daily attention. You'll probably want to do your armchair shopping within this period, too.)

c. *What Does It All Mean?* (5 minutes) Now you want the comment of the skilled interpreters to unravel the news and help you with your own opinions. So you read the columnists whose job it is to assign meanings to events *and* you turn to the editorial page where the newspaper itself interprets the news and takes its stand on the major issues of the day—also where readers like yourself air their views in letters to the editor.

For this valuable interpretative reading, you should allow at least 5 minutes. (This, frankly, is where our plan starts popping at the seams! Interpretation and comment really deserve more attention than this scant time period.)

d. *Ten—Taken to Taste* (10 minutes). Having read the main news and comment, you may now feel free to pursue the interests closest to your heart. You may wish to spend most of your remaining time on the sports pages—the women's pages—the financial section—the society columns—the book reviews—or giving the ads a closer perusal. You may prefer to relax with an entertaining columnist, and the comics.

This is the part of newspaper reading that's almost pure enjoyment; a kind of reading dessert. However, if you make it a part of a well-balanced meal, you will get a sharper, fairer picture of what goes on in the world each day, rather than just in your own province of interest.

Choose for Facts and Fun

To repeat, this is one minimum package for reading a newspaper. You may be satisfied with other good methods. This brings up an important point.

Newspaper reading is meant to be enjoyable as well as profitable. Nobody can be branded as an intellectual outcast because he likes the funnies or dashes for further details when the headlines proclaim "Movie Star Shoots Husband." Nor will anyone contest the right of the oat-grower to turn first to the price of oats, since oats are closer to him than all the seeds of discord sown that day across the globe.

But . . . and it's a BUT in big letters . . . you can get more out of your paper if you explore beyond your own personal brand of oats. If you're choosing your newspaper discriminatingly—if you're applying a little more thought to the way you're reading it—you're getting all the cake plus the vitamins, the fun plus the facts.

When you have the facts, you'll never be at sea in a serious discussion. You'll know where you stand on important issues. You'll think straighter on crucial decisions, be able to vote more intelligently. People will enjoy talking to you to get your opinions.

Yes, all these lie within the pages of your good newspaper . . . if you make the most of it.

8. *Use Your Newspaper to Increase Your Word Power.* By the very nature of its language the newspaper will, for the most part, display a vocabulary which is simple, vital, and commonplace, yet to the observant reader, the newspaper *can* be a source of a daily quota of words which are new, unfamiliar, or little used by the reader to express his own thoughts.

The front page of one large city daily yielded the following words for one day:

log jam	scuttle
futile	predicate (verb)
dupe	caravel
capstone	invincible
mace	fiscal
analogous	maligned

You can use your paper to increase your word power by having an eye open for the words that you recognize as not being a part of your active vocabulary. Encircle them. Some days there will be many of them; other days there may be few or none. Try this circle-the-word technique by using one day the front page, another day the editorial page, and at other times the financial pages, the women's page, the sports page, or the weekly magazine supplement. Having ferreted out these words, put them to work in your conversation, in your writing, in your thinking. Make them help to carry the burden of your own thoughts into the minds of others.

In connection with using the newspaper for increasing word power, do not overlook the benefits to be gained from the daily working of the crossword puzzle.

9. *Use the Newspaper to Improve Your General-knowledge Background.* "The great modern newspaper is a university in print." It was

William Lyon Phelps who said that the alert, active, interested mind should find every page of the newspaper fascinating.

We have emphasized the importance of your general knowledge quotient to rapid, efficient reading. The more you know, the better you read. Be alert, therefore, to the breadth of the horizon of human knowledge which the newspaper encompasses. One needs only to thumb through one volume of *The New York Times* Index to realize how diversified and encyclopedic are the articles that appear in one of the newspapers of the present day.

History, science, archaeology, geography, politics, economics, government, domestic problems, home economics, photography, psychology, poetry, astronomy, hobbies, famous quotations, health and hygiene, books, music, art, famous people. . . . We might go on ad infinitum. The daily newspaper carries information about all of these areas. Anyone can be well read and liberally educated by being a diligent and earnest student in the University of the Fourth Estate.

The newspaper is a daily challenge to the reader—it is a challenge and an opportunity. Here is a chance to mobilize your reading skills, to bring to play upon one area of your daily reading, in one way or another, all the skills that will make you a better reader generally. Your newspaper is your daily opportunity to improve your total reading ability. Use it as such.

Use your newspaper as suggested

The discussion of this chapter has been employed largely with practical suggestions. You have been given ideas and plans for using your newspaper to best advantage in the development of your reading skills.

Heretofore, in each chapter we have suggested a visual development exercise and lists of words to improve your vocabulary. And this has been good. But the point has come where you should be aware of these items as a skilled reader.

Put into practice, therefore, each day, for the next week the suggestions for using your newspaper to the best advantage.

1. Set a time and a schedule for reading your paper. Use either the schedule suggested in this chapter or one of your own devising, but in any event, read your paper according to a definite plan and schedule.
2. Practice the span-development exercises with your newspaper, as suggested.

3. Keep on the lookout for new words, or unfamiliar words, in the columns of your paper. Encircle each one that you find. After you have finished reading the paper each day, list these words in the space provided in this chapter for them.

4. Practice reading only the key words and phrases in the news stories. See how rapidly you can read and still get the details of the story.

5. Time your reading of one or two news articles each day. Estimate your speed of comprehension in the following way: Measure one inch of newspaper column, count the words in that one-inch sample. Repeat this at some other place in the article. Average these two word counts. Measure the number of inches in the entire story and multiply by the words per inch. This will give you the words in the article. If you then convert your reading time to seconds, and use the following formula, you will have a very accurate estimate of the words per minute that you read. Do this each day. Keep a record of your rate.

$$\frac{\text{words in article} \times 60}{\text{time in seconds}} = \text{wpm}$$

6. Check your comprehension by using the method described in this chapter and in the chapter "How to Remember What You Read." Actually work out your comprehension on a percentage basis. If you do several articles, average the comprehension factors and record the averages in the blanks provided here for that purpose.

7. Keep your eyes open for allusions or references that may make demands on your general knowledge or, if they are unfamiliar, jot them down in the blanks in this chapter and employ them to raise your general-knowledge quotient just a little higher.

Word power

	New word	Part of speech	Derivation: originally meant	Present meaning
1.				
2.				
3.				
4.				
5.				
6.				

New word	Part of speech	Derivation: originally meant	Present meaning
7.			
8.			
9.			
10.			
11.			
12.			
13.			
14.			
15.			
16.			
17.			
18.			
19.			
20.			
21.			

Speed and level of comprehension

Article read	Date	Estimated rate	Estimated comprehension
1.			
2.			
3.			
4.			
5.			
6.			
7.			
8			
9.			
10.			

Article read	Date	Estimated rate	Estimated comprehension
11.			
12.			
13.			
14.			
15.			
16.			
17.			
18.			
19.			
20.			
21.			

(The above blank is based upon the reading of three articles a day, for one week.)

General-background knowledge

From reading the newspaper this week, I picked up the following useful items of information:

1.

2.

3.

4.

5.

6.

7.

8.

9.

10.

11.

12.

13.

14.

15.

16.

17.

18.

19.

20.

21.

Reading for Speed of Comprehension—1

Here is a brief article about news and newspapers. You will want to read it for speed of comprehension. This is easy reading. Because of that you should be able to read it rapidly and with a high level of comprehension.

Time: MINUTES _____

SECONDS _____

THE NEWS [4]

by John J. Floherty

No matter how important or extensive a news event may be it can at best constitute only a part of the contents of the newspaper. No story has ever been important enough to entirely crowd out local, sports, financial or social news. Even the columnists have their say, though pages be devoted to the death of a king, a presidential election or a sensational trial. Then, too, the wheels of business must be kept turning in the advertising pages, even if the clash of war makes all else seem to be of secondary importance.

[4] Reprinted by permission of the J. B. Lippincott Company, from *Your Daily Newspaper*, by John J. Floherty, Chap. 3, pp. 21–28. Copyright, 1938, by John J. Floherty.

The complexities of the newspaper business, for after all it is a business, are sometimes baffling. While speed is a first essential, accuracy, authenticity and meticulous precision in timing and operation are fundamentals of newspaper production.

The word "Newspaper" is one of the most descriptive in our language. It connotes simply *a paper that contains news.* The word "news" itself means in substance *"things or events that are new."* There is scarcely a language on the globe that does not contain some equivalent for "What is new?" "What's the news?" or "Any news?" When the French say "Comment ça va?" they are merely saying "How goes it?" just as we do. And if that is not asking for news, what is?

This universal news hunger is one of the most ancient of human traits. The bards of old were but itinerant newsmen who set their news to music, for the entertainment and enlightenment of groups of listeners. Down through the ages all peoples, civilized and uncivilized, had their news vendors who, under the guise of oracles, priests, magicians, astrologers and medicine men spread the news, or call it gossip if you will, of the tribes or peoples among whom they roamed.

These nomadic news mongers held much of their influence over their listeners through their knowledge of the men and events of the tribes beyond the horizon.

As word-of-mouth news gave way to printed news, this influence grew steadily. Toward the end of the eighteenth century Edmund Burke in his speech before Parliament classed the influence of the press with that of the Lords, the Clergy and the Commons, the three estates of the realm, and called it the Fourth Estate, a term that is used to this day.

Modern newspaper publishing is among the most highly organized and complex of our industries. More than forty million Americans buy its product daily and insist that it be as fresh as the morning milk. When news becomes stale it is no longer news and so it ceases to exist. This ephemeral quality of news makes it imperative that it be gathered and published and placed in the hands of the reader in a minimum of time.

The publisher must have a reasonable profit on his investment. This would not be possible if the paper were devoted exclusively to news. The revenue from its sale is far below the cost of producing it. In order to increase this revenue, the publisher must of necessity sell a certain amount of space in his paper to advertisers at a price that is based on the circulation of the paper. Since circulation is built mostly on reader interest, the publisher stimulates this interest by introducing a wide range of material that will appeal to the greatest possible number of readers. This material is divided into three broad divisions. They are News, Service and Entertainment.

The first encompasses the news, activities in the fields of literature, art, music, theater, sports, finance, business, society and editorial comment which is but the elucidation of the news.

The second division gives information and advice to the reader on home economics, fashions, cookery, care of children, medical advice, etc. Here also may be included the advertising which is considered by many readers as a most valuable service.

The third and lighter phase includes fiction, poetry, humor and comics, which, strange as it may seem, have the most universal appeal of all newspaper features. One syndicate has its daily and weekly comic strips, as they are called, translated into thirty-seven languages.

News, however, is the one indispensable ingredient of the newspaper. No matter how scintillating its features or how profound its editorials, it fails unless it gives news that is fresh and accurate to its readers.

To get this news the world must be combed to its farthest and most inaccessible places. An army of 25,000 men and women hunt day and night in their never-ending search for it. With eyes and ears focused on the passing scene, they record its most delicate lights and shadows. No news item is so small that it may be overlooked and none is so great that it may not be probed for its last bit of information.

These men and women of the press live their lives under a tension that would snap the nerves of most people. The world boils around them like a witch's brew. What is on top today is tomorrow at the bottom of the cauldron. The pronouncement of a ruler may change the destiny of an empire. Loose words spoken in a tavern brawl may be the prologue of the speaker's violent end. A trinket bought with illicit funds sets the stage for the downfall of an otherwise respectable absconder.

The world scatters broadcast the seeds of the news. The newsmen harvest it when it is ripe and in full ear.

The *New York Herald Tribune,* during the past year, received from its foreign sources alone more than 13,000,000 words of which but 6,000,000 were used, while from domestic sources uncounted millions poured across the editorial desks, some to be used as news, but most of them to be swept aside like shavings from a carpenter's bench.

A correspondent in Tokio sits at his desk each morning and calls his paper in New York by radio telephone. Without the waste of a syllable he transmits the news of the preceding twenty-four hours. He receives instructions, suggestions and not infrequently a special assignment from his editor on the other side of the earth. Although it is nine in the morning in Tokio it is seven o'clock on the preceding evening in New York.

Transmission tolls to a Metropolitan daily run in excess of a quarter of a million dollars annually.

Not all the news is secured by professional newsmen. Many valuable stories come from remote spots on the globe through the alertness of the representatives of commercial concerns who visit these far-away places. A sewing-machine salesman in the interior of China may stumble on a story. He phones or telegraphs it or sends it by messenger to the nearest newspaper or news service office.

Throughout the United States in towns, small and large, in villages and hamlets, the larger newspapers have correspondents who report the happenings in these communities. Should a story of major importance break or be imminent, those points are immediately covered by staff reporters.

News is as much of a commodity as is sugar or silk or cotton. It is, however, the most perishable of all commodities. It cannot be warehoused or stored. It deteriorates from its first moment of life. That is why the gathering and sending of news and its preparation for publication, its printing and its delivery to the ultimate reader are carried on at a pace that makes men older than their years, but keeps them alive and alert long beyond their time.

At first glance it may seem that luck plays an important role in the gathering of news. Nothing could be farther from the truth. Not one news event in a thousand occurs unexpectedly when a reporter is on the spot. A kind of sixth sense known as the "nose for news" is, however, possessed by some reporters. These men and women frequently set out on a trail slender as a gossamer thread and return triumphantly with the story not through any psychological endowment, but rather through strict adherence to the soundest principles of the profession of news-gathering. They are the Dr. Mayos, the Thomas Edisons and the Madame Curies of the newspaper world.

A great part of the news as it appears each day is closely related to, and is really a part of news that has already been printed. A Presidential campaign for instance is a source of unlimited copy for months in advance of the election and for weeks afterward. A sensational trial or the bickerings of nations sometimes fill columns day after day for long periods.

Reporters who cover these events work under direction from the editorial desk. One may be assigned to do interviews, another to general observation and still another to track down a rumor. Few are entirely free to send in only what they see fit. Without editorial direction some phases of the story would be over-reported while others would be inadequately covered.

When a big story breaks, and excitement grips the newspaper office, the bustle of reporters sometimes suggests the apparently aimless scurrying of a swarm of ants. As a matter of fact every last one of them is doing a specific job on specific instructions from a hardboiled editor. In spite of the appearance of hectic bustle there is as much precision and order in every move as if it were a game of chess.

The people of the United States are particularly news conscious. To them a half-told news story is futile. It makes them feel they have been cheated or what is worse, deceived. The frank completeness of the news in the American press has contributed much toward the maintenance of our National unity. The turbulence and unrest of the peoples of many of the great nations of the world may well be attributed to ignorance of their national affairs resulting from highly censored news, garbled news or no news at all.

What time is it now? MINUTES _____
                      SECONDS _____

What is your reading time for this selection? MINUTES _____
                                               SECONDS _____

Now, test your level of comprehension by answering the following questions. Do not refer back to the article.

Comprehension quiz   *Part One*

In the early chapters of this book you learned that the good reader always is aware of the main ideas of an author, and relates the details to these main ideas. Let's find out whether you have been aware of the author's main ideas as you have read.

Below is a group of statements, some are principal ideas, some are subsidiary ideas. Check those which are statements of main ideas.

1. News, however important it may be, is but one part of a newspaper.
2. One syndicated comic strip is translated into 37 different languages.
3. The pronouncement of a ruler may change the destiny of an empire.
4. Hunger for news is one of the most ancient of human traits.
5. A sewing-machine salesman in China may stumble on a news story.
6. News is a commodity.
7. The people of the United States are particularly news-conscious.
8. When news becomes stale, it is no longer news and ceases to exist.
9. The world must be combed to get the news.
10. Some reporters have a "nose for news."

Part Two

Here is an acid test of your comprehension. If you have checked the correct items in Part One, you now have a list of some of the main ideas in the selection.

In Chapter Eleven and in the chapter discussion which you have just finished reading, we suggested a technique for remembering details. (Refer to pp. 233–234.) Now, do this to test your comprehension:

1. Write down a main idea from the list above.
2. Then, beneath the main idea, enumerate, 1, 2, 3, 4, etc., and jot down each detail which you can recall which the author employed in "developing" his idea in the article.
3. See if you can supply the details to each of the five main ideas given in the list above.

Part Three

1. Newsgathering is
   a luck.
   b a psychological endowment.
   c a profession based on well-established principles and procedures.
   d a profession where intuition plays a major role.

2. Much of the news as it appears each day is
   a news that has already been printed.
   b about the fourth estate.
   c first-time news.
   d syndicated.

3. The bards of old held much of their influence over their listeners by their
   a singing.
   b entertainment feats.
   c magic, fortune telling, and astrology.
   d knowledge of distant peoples and events.

4. The author suggests that the amount used of the foreign news that pours into a large metropolitan daily in a year is
   a one-quarter.
   b one-tenth.
   c half.
   d all of it.

5. The full, complete coverage of the American press has
   a made Americans the best-informed people on earth.
   b done much to save us from communism.
   c contributed much toward our leadership in world affairs.
   d contributed substantially toward our national unity.

How well did you comprehend what you have read? Check your answers with the Answer Key. Score only Parts One and Three of this test. Each correct answer is worth 10 per cent.

What is your level of comprehension?   _____%

What is your speed of comprehension?   _____wpm

What is your reading index $(R \times C/100)$? _____

Reading Habit Index

	Never	Rarely	Sometimes	Usually	Always
1. I regress much less now than formerly.					
2. If someone hands me a page and asks me to read it, I glance quickly over the page, noting the paragraphing and any other significant facts, and then I read it selectively.					
3. When reading a new book, I read or skim the preface and table of contents.					

Never Rarely Sometimes Usually Always

4. I read a newspaper according to the suggestions which have been made in this chapter.

5 While reading, I am in an interrogatory frame of mind.

Reading habit index score: _____

(See directions for scoring, p. 75)

Date: _____

Chapter Fifteen

Graphs, maps, charts, and other visual aids

T HE OLD saying that a picture is worth a thousand words is still true. A glance at a graph, a map, a chart, or an illustration may convey more information in one instant than columns and columns of words. These visual helps make reading easier. They convey more quickly, and in many cases more adequately, the facts which the author thinks are worthy of highlighting. And they present such facts dramatically and with an economy of space. A wavering line, unequal bars, shaded portions upon a map, or numerical data arranged neatly in parallel columns may portray quickly the significant facts which the author has been discussing.

The expert reader makes use of all these aids as soon as he glances at the page. Ofttimes before he reads the printed word, he will "read" the graphic helps. Thus, by noting the title, the legend, the scale of values, and considering thoughtfully the information portrayed, he can often bypass hundreds of unnecessary words of explanation.

As the reader thinks of all the various types of graphic aids which assist him in getting the meaning off the page faster, he must also realize that in a characteristic way each graphic aid is especially suited to the presentation of a particular type of information.

There are some types of information, for instance, that maps can illustrate better than graphs. Maps are employed particularly where area information is to be shown. Routes and locations are within the special province of the map. It would be impossible, for example, to show routes in any other way than by means of maps.

Graphs, on the other hand, are of greatest service when the author wishes to present data involving relationships or interrelationships of a two-factorial, or dimensional, sort. Even the more purely pictorial representations—drawings, diagrams, and illustrations—are helpful in showing cross sections, over-all plan, or magnified details.

The organization chart is helpful in appreciating the various echelons of authority and the relation of department to department, or unit to unit, within a business firm or other organizational setup. Flow charts are similar to organizational charts in that they show the progress of an article through the various processes of manufacture from raw material to finished product. Finally, there is the tabulation of numerical facts and statistical data.

Each of these graphic types has certain unique features; each is a medium in its own right for presenting data in a particular way to the mind of the reader. We shall take up each of these graphic devices separately, inspecting them as aids in making the reader's task easier.

Tabulations

Tabulations are a means of setting forth certain data, usually of a numerical nature, that might also be expressed in other ways. In some respects tabulations are midway between the factual paragraph and the more purely graphic forms of presentation. In many respects tabulations are like graphs. In fact, they are graphs in evolution. Every graph begins from an array of tabulated data. In tabulations trends are not as readily apparent as they are in graphs, largely because of the nonpictorial quality of tabulated data.

In reading tabulations, note the heading of each column and each row of figures. Like graphs, each item in a tabulation is stationed at a crossroads of a two-dimensional relationship. Read tabulated data, therefore, with reference to the position that the information occupies. The horizontal axis represents one dimension of the fact, while the vertical axis represents the other. Every item is, therefore, unique.

Moreover, in reading tabulations, you must be aware of a three-dimensional relationship. There is the third relationship of the unit to the whole. Any one item assumes significance in terms of its place among all the items. The reader who reads tabulations well must have a consummate sense of trend and tendency, of the unit in relation to the whole, so that he may be able to see where any particular fact fits into the over-all tabular framework.

Take, for example, the following tabulation of speeds and levels of comprehension showing the weekly averages of five individuals in a reading-improvement group:

RECORD OF READING IMPROVEMENT

| Name | *Weekly Averages* | | | | | | |
	1	2	3	4	5	6	7
J. A.	258	328	360	408	430	392	456
	76%	79%	80%	83%	86%	88%	89%
H. D.	240	268	332	354	397	417	410
	80%	78%	82%	83%	81%	83%	85%
E. F.	225	268	288	312	336	389	450
	70%	72%	73%	77%	75%	79%	80%
J. L.	266	274	316	354	418	460	505
	78%	84%	84%	87%	86%	87%	86%
R. M.	328	360	365	408	415	436	465
	86%	84%	86%	87%	88%	87%	90%

By looking *down* each column, we may appraise the reading level of the group for any one week. We may also observe that this is a fairly homogeneous group. By reading *across*, we may discover certain facts about the various individuals in the group. We may observe how each has progressed with relation to his own achievement.

By comparing the horizontal rows of figures we may observe that certain members of the group gained relatively more in one factor than in the other. By looking over the tabulation as a whole certain other facts are spotlighted: the lowest and highest initial and terminal speeds and levels of comprehension, the averages in each factor for the group as a whole for any particular week, or for the entire period.

An averaging of each column would help to bring this out more clearly. The addition of reading indexes for each entry would aid in appraisal of the net gains more easily.

In a tabulation it is not so easy to see extremes and means as it is in a graph. In certain respects, however, tabulations are of particular value. They enable us to check the accuracy with which the author has interpreted his data. We may calculate directly from the facts to verify the author's findings or to form conclusions of our own. Tables of information are also of value because of the accuracy of their data. With graphs it is frequently impossible to pinpoint these values precisely, because many times a point on a graph is merely a relative position between two grid lines.

Graphs

Graphs as a means of factual presentation have become popular only within the history of our republic. One of the earliest books to employ charts and graphs is the *Statistical Account of the United States of America*, translated out of the French by William Playfair and bearing a London publication imprint of 1805. This book was inscribed to Thomas Jefferson and dealt with the industry, commerce, and finance of the United States.

William Playfair was the pioneer in the development of graphic methods for the general reader. Until recently he has been relatively unknown, and his work unappreciated. In his *Inquiry* (1805), however, he laid down the basic maxim of the graphic method. "Whatever can be expressed in numbers," he declared, "may be expressed by lines." This is the axiom upon which all graphs are constructed.

But the very fact that graphs are the embodiment of numerical values and relationships puts them in a category by themselves. They should always be read with care and considerable skill. Mathematical values are unique: they are not only abstract; they are also complex. Numerical language is never so simple as it may seem.

In reading to get the meaning, for instance, we may have trouble in understanding completely the meaning of the simple sentence, "Two boys had six apples." Exactly what does that sentence mean? From an interpretative standpoint we have expressed a set of relationships which need clarification before we can comprehend the meaning. Did each boy have three apples? Did one boy have two apples, and the other four apples; or was it a one-and-five distribution?

Now, suppose that there are ten boys, and that we know just how many apples each boy had. We could graph that, and the reader could *see* the quantitative relationship. The boy who had the most apples would be represented by the "peak" of the graph; the lad with the least number, by the deepest "valley."

But while this seems to be so very obvious and simple that it would appear that anyone could readily learn to "read" graphs, this is not always so. Any graph may be a booby trap, and the careful reader stays wide awake when dealing with them. Graphs have a charm, a witchery about them that can be very deceptive. The complexity of a numerical fact becomes disarmingly naive when it is depicted in graceful curves and pointed profiles.

Graphic language is dynamic and dramatic. It has appeal—plus. For that very reason it is dangerous. Graphs can present facts vividly, persuasively, unescapably. They will be remembered when the words that accompany them will be forgotten. And in the hands of the unscrupulous they may lie as readily as they may tell the truth. They look so simple, so frank, so appealing that the careless readers are often fooled by them. They underestimate their power of persuasion.

Of all types of graphs, line graphs are those probably most frequently encountered. These are constructed upon a grid with ordinate and

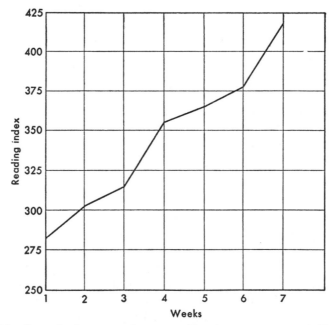

Fig. 15.1　Record of progress in net reading improvement as indicated by average weekly reading indexes.

abscissa values. The data to be plotted is located, as dictated by its own value, at a point which corresponds spatially on the graph to the numerical value of the item plotted. These locations are then connected, and a graph of progress results. Here are two examples of such graphs. Each one represents a record of progress in net reading efficiency as indicated by the reading indexes of the respective reader being plotted. Which graph shows the most progress? Put a check mark above the graph that you select.

Which one did you select? Could you give your reasons for your choice? Actually, it matters little which graph you selected. Both graphs represent the same data. If you will refer to the table on p. 334, you will see that all that we did was to take the record of R. M., work out the reading index for each entry, and plot it on the graphs above. But notice where the difference lies; it is in the left-hand scale units. In Figure 15.1 the distance between the horizontals represents 25 points of improvement; in the second scale the same distance represents 100 improvement points. No wonder the record in Figure 15.1 seems to show four times as much improvement as that in Figure 15.2.

Of all of man's devices for deception by telling the absolute truth,

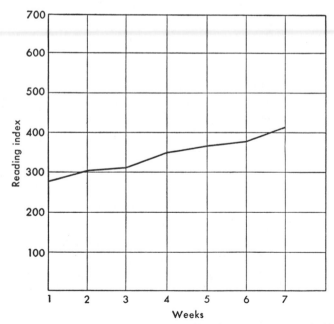

Fig. 15.2 Record of progress in net reading improvement as indicated by average weekly reading indexes.

nothing is quite so effective as the simple line graph in the hands of the inexperienced reader.

But not all graphical representations are simple line graphs. They have taken on a variety of forms, usually with the purpose of dressing up the presentation, giving it more "eye appeal," making it more dynamic and compelling, clarifying the facts, and helping the reader to lay hold of them more readily and more comprehensively.

Next to the line graph, the bar graph is used widely in emphasizing differences between two situations. The method of direct comparison is employed. Had we cast the two graphs above into bar-graph form, we should have had to employ a single scale for comparison and the identity of the two records would have been immediately seen.

There are many variants of these basic types of graphs. You will frequently come across three-dimensional graphs, pictograms, and pie or circle charts such as are used to show the distribution of the taxpayer's dollar.

Whatever their form, the basic purpose of each of these types of representation is the same: to present data so that one picture may take the place of many words, to help the reader to see the facts more clearly. Facts will always be more meaningful if they can be visualized. Graphic aids help the reader to see the abstract, to visualize the invisible.

Charts

Charts are frequently used to show the structure, organization, subordination and relation of one part to the whole. They emphasize organization and structure especially. For example, Figure 15.3 is a chart which shows the place of the personnel director in a manufacturing plant.

Let us suppose that a personnel problem has arisen in the Highland plant which should have the attention of the personnel director. A glance at the chart will show that such matter should be referred by the superintendent of the Highland plant to the superintendent of manufacturing personnel, who will refer it to the supervisor of production, who will refer it directly to the personnel director.

Another form of the organizational chart is the process, or action-flow, chart. This type of representation is particularly helpful in showing how gasoline is made, how a rubber tire is manufactured, or how a bill becomes a law. Sometimes in many processes there are a number of alternatives, and a word description of the process is involved and difficult to follow. In such cases a flow chart clarifies the whole situation and gives the reader a stepwise picture of exactly what happens at each stage of the process.

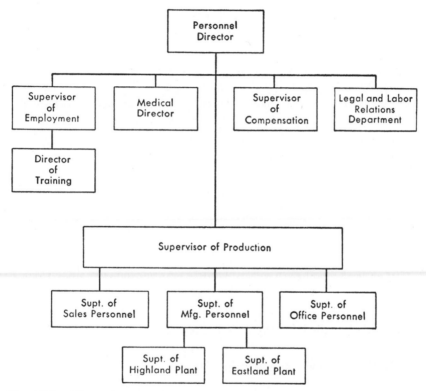

Fig. 15.3 Chart showing the structural organization of a manufacturing company.

Maps

Maps are employed especially where area information is to be shown. Through a map, presentation of the facts of size, area, route, location and territorial relationships are indicated precisely. In many cases it would be almost impossible to describe the information as accurately in words that can be shown easily by means of a map. Try, for instance, to describe the location and extent of the bituminous coal deposits in the United States, or the principal corn-producing areas of the world, and you will suddenly realize the total inadequacy of words for such a task. And even if you were able to do it, you would ultimately drive your reader to a map so that he might see what you were talking about!

By looking at a map critically, we can make certain judgments and generalizations. We see the size of a particular area in relation to the much larger size of the state, or the country, or the continental land area, and we can see the proximity of given areas to each other, and to other natural features; oceans, navigable rivers, and mountainous terrain.

Maps may employ many devices to make the information they bear more meaningful. Some maps are shaded, some are peppered with dot locations, and some, where the dots represent numerical values, by dot-density areas. Sometimes the size of the dot varies with the magnitude of the factor represented. Sometimes there are geometric symbols or diverse markings—squares, triangles, stars, dots of various magnitudes, and other symbols—for whose interpretation one must refer to the legend. Maps with pictographs are becoming increasingly popular. They have more appeal; they convey their message more quickly. Sometimes to show principal routes and their relative importance by means of width of line, flow maps are used.

But as with graphs, charts, and other graphic helps, a map has but one excuse for being—to convey information accurately, quickly, and better than any other means because the information which it contains is particularly suited for expression through this particular medium.

Illustrations, drawings, and miscellaneous aids

Finally, there are the photographs, drawings, illustrations, and similar visual aids which illuminate the text and make the reading of it easier. Little need be said about pictures and photographs. They are so common and so self-contained that the average reader needs no explanation as to their use or value in the column or on the page.

Drawings are usually employed to supplement an explanation. We describe an electronic circuit and supplement our description with a schematic or pictorial diagram. We explain how to build a table and then supplement our explanation with a detail drawing to show just how the joints of the table are mitered and joined, or how some other detail is handled.

These illustrations are common enough and present no problem of interpretation. They are, nevertheless, short cuts for the reader who wants to get the facts and ideas behind the print and to get them as quickly and accurately as possible.

No illustrative device escapes the eye of the skillful reader. Sometimes by means of a single graphic presentation he can bypass inches of explanatory material. At other times he may want to check his own interpretation of the visual help with the explanation which the author gives of it. A third time, he may want to study very carefully the author's words and compare point by point what the author says with what the visual aid portrays.

How each reader will use the visual helps on the printed page depends upon the same factors that will determine his handling of the printed words themselves; namely, the purpose and end for which he reads. But any reader can become a better reader if he is adept at "reading" the graphic additions that accompany the print itself.

Comprehension tests on your ability to read graphical materials

The following statements are either true or they are false in terms of the material presented in the graphic presentation. If they are true, put a T before the statement; if they are false, put an F before the statement.

Map (Figure 15.4): Nonfarm Employment

1 _____ The greatest increase in nonfarm employment has been in the large industrial areas of the North and East: the New England, Middle Atlantic, and East North Central states.

2 _____ There has been a moderate increase (20 to 30 per cent) in non-farm employment in North Dakota, South Dakota, Minnesota, Nebraska, Kansas, Iowa, and Missouri.

3 _____ There has been more gain in nonfarm employment in the East South Central states (Alabama, Mississippi, Tennessee, Kentucky) than in all the New England and Middle Atlantic states combined.

4 _____ The greatest increase in nonfarm employment was in the Mountain states region.

5 _____ The smallest gain in nonfarm employment was in the large mid-western farm areas, a fact which is quite understandable.

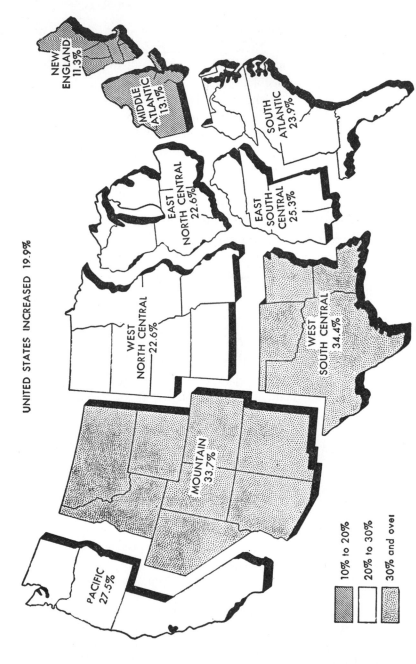

UNITED STATES INCREASED 19.9%

NEW ENGLAND 11.3%

MIDDLE ATLANTIC 13.1%

SOUTH ATLANTIC 23.9%

EAST NORTH CENTRAL 22.6%

EAST SOUTH CENTRAL 25.3%

WEST NORTH CENTRAL 22.6%

WEST SOUTH CENTRAL 34.4%

MOUNTAIN 33.7%

PACIFIC 27.5%

10% to 20%

20% to 30%

30% and over

Fig. 15.4 Nonfarm employment by geographic regions, per cent increases, 1946–1953. ("Road Maps of Industry," No. 979, Oct. 1, 1954, copyright, 1954, by The Conference Board.)

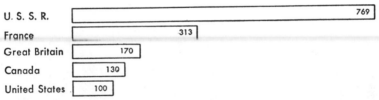

Minutes of Working Time Required to Buy Various Foods

	United States	Canada	Great Britain	France	U. S. S. R.
Bread (1 Pound)	6	6	6	9	19
Butter (1 Pound)	31	39	37	169	373
Milk (Fresh) (1 Quart)	8	9	15	20	52
Eggs (1 Dozen)	22	29	66	96	291
Potatoes (1 Pound)	2	2	3	9	11
Coffee (1 Pound)	33	53	66	159	694
Sugar (1 Pound)	4	6	9	25	122

Index of Amount of Work Required to Buy Food Basket

U. S. S. R.	769
France	313
Great Britain	170
Canada	130
United States	100

Fig. 15.5 What food costs in work time—United States and four other countries. ("Road Maps of Industry," No. 798, April 13, 1951, copyright, 1951, by The Conference Board.)

Chart and Bar Graph (Figure 15.5): What Food Costs

1 _____ Assuming comparable wage and price conditions in the U.S.S.R. as in the United States, if a man worked around the clock without cessation, he would be able to maintain only slightly more than 50 per cent of our standard of living.

2 _____ On the whole it is cheaper to live in Canada than in the United States.

3 _____ The average Britisher works nearly twice as long as the average citizen of the United States in order to maintain the same buying power.

4 _____ Among all of the staples listed, the cheapest in terms of work time is potatoes.

5 _____ Assuming a 40-hour work-week to be standard for the average American, to maintain a comparable buying power the average Frenchman would have to work more than 120 hours a week.

Pie or Section Graph (Figure 15.6): The American Public

1 _____ Most Americans of all ages live in small towns.

2 _____ The retired and unemployed of all ages far outnumber the employed in America.

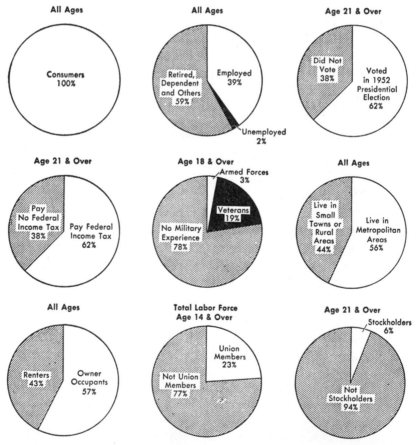

Fig. 15.6 The American public viewed in its different aspects. ("Road Maps of Industry," No. 959, May 14, 1954, copyright, 1954, by The Conference Board.)

3 _____ Nearly one-third of the American public pay no Federal income tax.

4 _____ The majority of Americans of all ages are living in rented premises.

5 _____ Almost as many Americans own or are buying their own homes as live in metropolitan areas.

6 _____ There are three times as many veterans in the United States as there are stockholders in privately owned corporations, but there are twice as many stockholders as men in the armed forces.

7 _____ There are twice as many in the armed forces as there are unemployed.

8 _____ The majority of the American labor force are nonunion workers.

9 _____ There are twice as many Americans of all ages who are renters as live in small towns or rural areas.

10 _____ Twenty-three per cent more people pay income tax than are employed.

Map and Sectional Graph (Figure 15.7): Major Sources of Income

1 _____ The manufacturing income payments of the Central States area is the largest in the country.

2 _____ The highest government income payments are in the Southeast area.

3 _____ The manufacturing income payments of the Far West are about the same as those in the Southeast area.

4 _____ Every other section has a higher agricultural income payment than the New England area.

5 _____ The highest trade and service income is in the Middle East area.

Line Graphs (Figures 15.8–15.11): Smoking

1 _____ Smokers who smoke only cigarettes lead all other groups in incidence of deaths.

2 _____ Cigar smokers seem less susceptible to coronary artery disease than any other group.

3 _____ From 62 to 69 years of age there are fewer deaths of coronary artery disease in pipe smokers than in those who have never smoked.

4 _____ Among cigar smokers there is a high climb in death rate from cancer between ages 55 and 60.

5 _____ At 50 years of age more people die from cancer among those who have never smoked than among those who have.

6 _____ From the standpoint of cancer deaths at age 50, there seems to

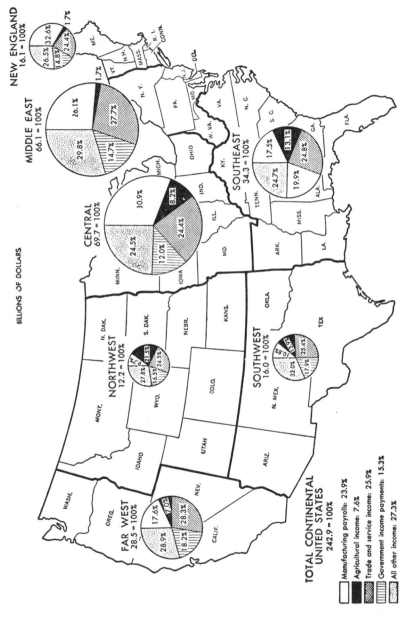

BILLIONS OF DOLLARS

NEW ENGLAND
16.1 = 100%
26.5% 14.8% 32.6% 24.4% 1.7%

MIDDLE EAST
66.1 = 100%
1.7% 26.1% 27.7% 14.7% 29.8%

CENTRAL
69.7 = 100%
30.9% 8.2% 24.4% 12.0% 24.5%

SOUTHEAST
34.3 = 100%
17.5% 13.1% 24.8% 19.9% 24.7%

NORTHWEST
12.2 = 100%
27.8% 21.5% 24.5% 16.5% 9.7%

SOUTHWEST
16.0 = 100%
32.0% 25.4% 17.9% 19.8%

FAR WEST
28.5 = 100%
28.9% 7.0% 28.3% 18.2% 17.6%

TOTAL CONTINENTAL
UNITED STATES
242.9 = 100%

☐ Manufacturing payrolls: 23.9%

■ Agricultural income: 7.6%

▨ Trade and service income: 25.9%

▥ Government income payments: 15.3%

░ All other income: 27.3%

Fig. 15.7 Major sources of income payments by regions, United States, 1951. ("Road Maps of Industry," No. 872, Sept. 12, 1952, copyright, 1952, by The Conference Board.)

be little difference whether a person smokes cigarettes, cigars, or a pipe.

7 _____ The nonsmokers have always a better chance to live.

8 _____ If you must smoke, smoke a pipe.

9 _____ Age 60 is the beginning of a much higher incidence of deaths because of smoking.

10 _____ In an over-all picture there is really very little difference in death rate between nonsmokers and pipe smokers.

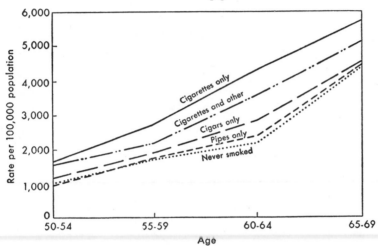

Fig. 15.8 Total death rates by smoking history and by age.

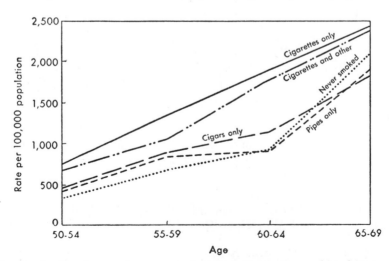

Fig. 15.9 Death rates from coronary artery disease by smoking history and by age. (*By permission, Journal of the American Medical Association,* Aug. 7, 1954.)

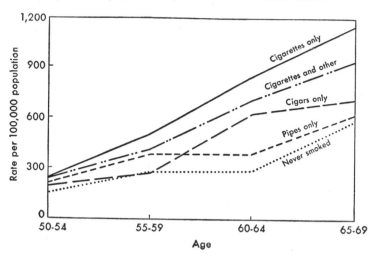

Fig. 15.10   Death rates from cancer (all sites) by smoking history and by age.

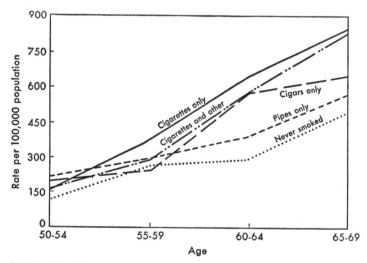

Fig. 15.11   Death rates from cancer (exclusive of lung) by smoking history and by age. (*By permission, Journal of the American Medical Association, Aug. 7, 1954.*)

How Accurately Do You See—How Long Can You Remember What You Have Seen?

This is a perception-memory exercise, in which you will use the index of this book. Many people have difficulty in remembering a reference long enough to look it up accurately. In this exercise, do the following:

1. Look up in the index of this book, the word in the left-hand column below.
2. Turn to the page or pages to which you are referred. If it is a multiple reference, keep *all* the page references in mind. Do not go back to look up anything in the index a second time.
3. After you have read the reference or references completely, then turn back to this page and list opposite the word that you have looked up the page number or numbers in the order in which they were given in the index.

Look up this word   *Page references given in index (in order)*

Fixation   _____

Ophthalmograph   _____

Key words   _____

Cliché   _____

Directional words   _____

Newspaper   _____

Purpose   _____

Flesch, Rudolf   _____

Eye movement   _____

Vocabulary   _____

Repeat this exercise with words of your own choosing from the index. Jot down a list of ten words from the index. Then proceed as in this exercise.

How Quickly and Accurately Can You See?

Several times, during the course of these visual exercises, you have practiced the skill of skimming for a specific detail. Time yourself accurately on this exercise. You will be asked to skim a specific pair of pages for a single item of information. As soon as you find the information requested, jot it down in the blank provided for that purpose, and go on immediately to the next item. Work as rapidly and accurately as possible.

What time is it now? MINUTES _____

SECONDS _____

Find the word which completes the meaning, and write it in the blank. The pages where the answers are to be found are indicated in parentheses, immediately following the statement.

1. Basically, we read to _____. (6)

2. The movements of the eyes are controlled by _____ small, but powerful muscles. (16)

3. Man, at a critical moment in his development began to invent _____. (33)

4. That _____ is a cue for the reader. (51)

5. There is no time for _____. (66)

6. This is sheer _____. (71)

7. This group of words is a very real _____. (78)

8. Every _____ has many degrees of contrast. (83)

9. We _____ all the time. (95)

10. What _____ would he use? (112)

11. The former seem to be _____. (123)

12. The whole complicated transmission is to be handled by _____. (132)

13. _____ upon the main stream. (139)

14. You will become skilled in recognizing a _____. (183)

15. They are pretty _____. (196)

What time is it now? MINUTES _____

                     SECONDS _____

How long did it take you? MINUTES _____

                     SECONDS _____

Turn to the Answer Key to check the accuracy of your answers.

What was your *average* scanning time? MINUTES _____

                     SECONDS _____

(You should be able to find the above items at an average of about 10 seconds for each item).

What was your per cent of accuracy? _____%

Reading for Speed of Comprehension

Darrell Huff, who wrote the following article, is also the author of a highly entertaining and enlightening book, *How to Lie With Statistics* (W. W. Norton & Company, Inc., New York, 1954). The following essay is very helpful in pointing out that "statistical jokers" may lie before your very eyes, and you will not see them! Read to understand the principles that Mr. Huff is explaining.

Time: MINUTES _____

SECONDS _____

HOW TO SPOT STATISTICAL JOKERS [1]

by Darrell Huff

Are wages keeping up with profits and the cost of living? Are you inviting lung cancer when you light a cigarette? Are we in the early stages of a depression without knowing it? Will toothache abandon you if there's fluorine in your drinking water or the latest miracle ingredient in your toothpaste?

Answers to such real and important questions as these lie hidden in the stream of statistics that assails all of us every day. There's no doubt that we have reached the age that H. G. Wells long ago foresaw: "Statistical thinking will one day be as necessary for efficient citizenship as the ability to read and write."

But what do the figures mean—all those little averages, percentages, percentiles, trends, norms, correlations, significances? What do they say, perhaps? No, it can't be as simple as that. One interpreter will hand down one meaning today and another will come along tomorrow and prove something quite different from the same data.

In the end the consumer of statistics—which is to say each of us— must reach his own decisions as wary as though buying a used car. We can't all be statisticians (or mechanics) but there are many statistical tricks and pitfalls that anyone can readily learn to spot. They are as revealing of phoniness as a worn-out brake pedal under an odometer brazenly reading two thousand miles. For instance—

[1] Darrell Huff, "How to Spot Statistical Jokers," *The New York Times Magazine,* August 22, 1954 pp. 13, 43.

The Unspecified Average

Read that the average income of employes in the place you work is $4,509 a year and you seem to have been told something precise and meaningful. There's the figure right down to the dollar—and an average is an average, isn't it?

That it's not. The word average covers mean, median, and sometimes other things. For some data they're about the same, and for some, including incomes, they are miles apart. The *mean* income of ninety people is their total take divided by ninety. But if the same ninety have a *median* income of $4,509, this indicates that half of them received less than that and half more. A few very high incomes will boost a mean average a good deal and make conditions look much better than they are. They won't affect a median so much, so that is the kind of average most revealing when incomes are in question.

When you see a median income given, as with Bureau of Census figures, you are getting a reasonably good picture of conditions. When you see a mean, you can guess that it has made incomes look a good deal better than they are. And when you see an "average" of unspecified nature, you can suspect that there's a cheery liar of a mean hiding behind it.

The Biased Sample

This is another highly prevalent statistical joker. Statisticians, who are as able and honest as any other group, spend most of their lives fighting it. It comes in two popular varieties: the sample that is biased from the beginning, and the one that develops its bias as it goes along.

The famous Literary Digest poll remains the archetype of the first. The enormous sample of ten million voters who agreed it would be Landon two to one came from lists of Digest and telephone subscribers. Such a sample is likely to be biased in at least one direction: wealthier than most. Given a year like 1936 when economic status seems to have had a good deal to do with voting, such a sample is badly biased.

The self-biasing sample is even trickier. For an extreme example, imagine what would happen if you sent, to a purely random sample of your fellow-citizens, a questionnaire that included this query: "Do you like to answer questionnaires?" Add up the returns and you'll probably be able to announce that an overwhelming majority of "a typical cross-section of the population" asserts affection for the things. What has happened, of course, is that those whose answer would have been "No" have eliminated themselves from the survey by flinging it into the nearest waste basket.

It was a self-biasing sample rather like this hypothetical one that led to a news story saying, "The average Yaleman, Class of '24, makes $25,111 a year." Aside from being ridiculously precise, this average is boosted by being just what you think it is—a mean rather than a median. On top of that, it has built into it the self-biasing quality common to many mail surveys. That is, it has taken into account only those members of the class whose addresses are still known and who are sufficiently proud of their incomes to reveal them to their classmates. Those poor little lambs who have lost their economic way are not added in.

The Improbably Precise Figure

This is another giveaway worth watching for. Anything based on a survey or other form of sampling procedure has a known statistical error in it, along with other and unknown possibilities of error. Spurious precision is a way of covering this up. If the Yale average had any meaning at all, it would more properly have been expressed as "about $25,000," since at best it could not have been considered accurate down to that last $111. But it's a good deal more impressive the other way, isn't it?

Likewise such a popular item as the I.Q. A child who is scored 110 is not necessarily brighter, even within the limited meaning of such a test, than the one rated at 108. The average error (called "probable error") of the Stanford-Binet, one of the best of such tests, is given as 3 per cent.

The Inadequate Sample

All sorts of fascinating chicanery is produced by this means. Flip a coin six times and what will you get? (I just tried it and got heads five times.) You may get a fifty-fifty result, and you may not. But flip it a thousand times and you can depend on getting approximately the normal expectation of half heads. Test a new toothpaste on six people and you may find a "remarkable reduction in dental caries!" even though the stuff is worthless. If you don't get the result you want, test another group. By the time you've done this a few times you're practically sure to get a favorable result.

Watch out, then, for reports relying on a tiny sample unless accompanied by a statistician's statement of significance. Good evidence on some things can be amassed with a handful of cases but more often it takes hundreds to mean anything. A polio vaccine was once tested on 450 children before anyone stopped to consider this factor. The incidence of paralytic polio is so low that meaningful results can be obtained only when the cases are in the tens of thousands, a fact taken into account in the 1954 work.

Correlations

These produce a great part of our statistical reading matter. They become misleading when cause-and-effect are read into them without evidence. College graduates make more money than other people. True, apparently. Therefore, if you send your son to college you'll increase his chances of making money. Not proved. Maybe the same traits (ambition, brains, capital) that make a boy likely to go to college are the ones that would have made him more prosperous than most folks anyway.

Therein lies one of the biggest questions about the research reports on correlation between smoking and death from heart disease or lung cancer. There seems to be good evidence that the two go together—but has the one necessarily caused the other? Still to be eliminated are many possibilities including this one: may not smoking appeal most strongly to persons of a temperament that predisposes to these ailments?

Which is not to say, of course, that the published conclusions are false or that smoking is harmless. But it remains true that although the deaths are real, the cause is still a matter of speculation. This cause-and-effect relationship may turn out to be a true one or it may some day join the lovely correlation once established between cancer and milk drinking.

It was shown that cancer was increasing in New England, Minnesota, Wisconsin, and Switzerland, where a lot of milk is produced and consumed, but remaining rare in Ceylon, where milk is scarce. Milk-drinking English women were shown to have some kinds of cancer eighteen times as frequently as Japanese women, who seldom drank milk. It sounded pretty significant but all it really meant was that areas in one group have populations with longer life spans than in the other. Cancer, predominantly a disease of middle life, has little chance to attack where people die young.

The Gee-whiz Graphs

Watching these go by is a sport to be recommended to anyone interested in looking a phony statistic in the eye. The shape of a graph is supposed to give a quick picture of some statistical fact. Don't bet on it. Chart a trend in graphic fashion and usually you will get a modest-looking rise; things like wages and costs and sales and populations generally change slowly. To give the indicating line a more spectacular appearance you have only to stretch your chart upward, putting more space between the lines.

The trouble with this is that it produces a very tall and thin chart, a suspicious-looking thing and awkward on a printed page. So chop off the bottom, leaving only the area in which the moving line is found. The result is that any slight rise becomes a hop from the bottom to the top; 1 per cent can look like a hundred or a thousand. Moral: In reading any graph in which the bottom line isn't zero, look not so much at what's there as what's not.

Even more deceptive is an unfortunately common version of the pictorial graph in which values are represented by little men or cows or moneybags. If a hundred dollars is portrayed by one moneybag and four hundred by four just like it, then you have a proper and honest graph. But it is all too usual to represent that second quantity by a single moneybag, too, making it four times as tall as the first.

What's wrong with that? Well, a bag four times as high is also four times as wide and so it covers sixteen times as much area on the page. And since it is a picture of a three-dimensional object it actually indicates a bag four times four times four times as big as the first one. An increase of four to one has been made to look like sixty-four to one, as fine a piece of exaggeration as you could ask for.

Semantic Tricks

Blend these with statistics and you have the phoniest figures of them all. The formula is: when you can't prove what you want to prove, demonstrate something else and then pretend they're the same thing.

To peddle a nostrum as a cold cure, have an "independent laboratory" testify to how many unspecified germs it will kill in a test tube. To prove young car drivers dangerous, give the figures showing them involved in more accidents than elderly ones; to hang responsibility on older drivers, give figures on accidents per million miles driven. To exaggerate dangers of train travel cite "fatalities chargeable to railroads" but don't mention that more than 90 per cent who died were either riding the rods or in automobiles that met trains at crossings.

If you'll read with an eye alert to statistical mishandling, you'll come upon many splendid specimens to add to these. You won't learn any more by reading with a skeptical eye, but you'll do something that is perhaps many times better. You'll avoid learning a remarkable lot that isn't so.

What time is it now? MINUTES _____

SECONDS _____

What is your reading time for this selection? MINUTES _____

SECONDS _____

Without referring back to the selection, answer the following questions.

Comprehension quiz

1. The average American owns one car, is a father of two children, lives in a one-and-a-half-story house, situated on 1.3 acres of land. (Find six statistical jokers in this statement.)
2. One out of every two smokers prefer El Ropo Cigars. (Find two statistical jokers in this statement.)
3. The average traffic violator is between twenty-one and twenty-five years old, a skilled or semiskilled worker, with average intelligence, respect for the law, a normal personality, and a good sense of humor. This is the picture that emerged from a survey of 300 motorists with multiple violation records in Los Angeles, made by four University of California scientists . . . The 300 cases interviewed racked up 1,774 violations in a year, such as violating traffic lights, speeding, and failure to yield right of way.[2] (Find at least five statistical jokers.)
4. The following statement and graph are published to advertise the superiority of Town Talk as a newspaper.

[2] Science Digest, vol. 37, April, 1955, p. 35.

Town Talk is a superior newspaper!

Town Talk has almost twice as many readers as its nearest rival. Read *Town Talk* for the best in news!

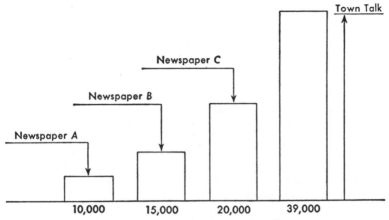

Fig. 15.12   Certified paid subscribers.

(Find in this advertisement four statistical jokers.)

5. The following is a tabulation of some basic body measurements of average seventeen-year-olds: [3]

	Boys	Girls
Weight	138.3 lb.	119.0 lb.
Height	5′ 8.2″	5′ 3.6″
Leg length	31.7″	28.9″
Arm length	29.8″	27.4″
Hand length	7.6″	7.0″
Foot length	10.1″	9.5″

From this chart we might well conclude that seventeen-year-old girls are smaller than seventeen-year-old boys. (Find at least three statistical jokers in this presentation.)

Check your answers against those given in the Answer Key. Each correct answer is worth 5 per cent.

What is your level of comprehension?   _____%

What is your speed of comprehension?   _____wpm

What is your reading index (R × C/100)? _____

[3] *Science Digest*, vol. 36, November, 1954, p. 61.

Reading Habit Index

Never Rarely Sometimes Usually Always

1. After I have been reading for a while, I stop reading for a few moments and rest my eyes by looking at some distant object.

2. I usually notice a distinctive style, or flavor, of the writing.

3. I make it a practice to skim articles, usually before I read them.

4. In reading more difficult material, after reading a paragraph or a section, I summarize the material I have just read in a momentary flash-back review.

5. I consider every reading situation an opportunity to improve my reading skills, and I try to apply the techniques of efficient reading every time I read.

Reading habit index score: _____

(See directions for scoring, p. 75)

Date: _____

Chapter Sixteen

Meeting the reading demands of business

I N THE course of a day's reading, the average businessman reads a great many types of material: letters, memos, regulations, policy changes, procedures, recommendations, code rulings and revisions, and handwritten notations and comments. Each of these types of reading presents a situation which is in some respects unique.

There are also many little obstacles which conspire to lower the reading efficiency of the man behind the desk. Most of the time he is unaware of these brakes on his progress, but they tend to make *his* reading task a somewhat more fatiguing and more difficult one than that of the ordinary reader, whose reading is largely confined to books, magazines, and newspapers.

Broadly speaking, the businessman's reading problems stem largely from the type of material that crosses his desk. These problems are:

1. Problems arising from the presentation of the material to the *eye* of the reader.
2. Problems arising from the presentation of the material to the *mind* of the reader.

When the man behind the desk sees his reading difficulties under

359

one of these two broad headings, he will be the better able to cope with them.

First, there are those deterrents to effective reading that arise from the visual factors of the material itself. From an over-all standpoint the reading of printer's type is undoubtedly optimal. At the opposite end of the desirability scale are the notes, memorandums, and comments that are hastily scrawled in longhand. Between these two extremes lie many gradations of reading material: Mimeograph, Multigraph, offset, typewritten, carbon, hectograph, and many others. The man behind the desk must read many of these types of reproduction in the daily load of paper work.

This book has largely been concerned with the general techniques of getting the thought quickly and accurately from the *printed* page. But at the office there is much that must be read that does not come off the printing press. This fact alone means more reading time and additional fatigue.

Look closely at these two short type specimens:

This is printed in the same type face that is used in this book. Do you notice how easy it is to read? Your eyes move smoothly and effortlessly across the lines of print.

    This is set in typewriter face. You can see the dif-
ference immediately. How about reading it? Can you
read this with equal ease and speed, or is there just a
suggestion of the feeling that you are "fighting your
way" along the line. Perhaps you notice by this time
that there is a slight resistance in reading this.

Which of those samples of type would you choose for a book the length of this one? Can you imagine how difficult, how fatiguing it would be to read this book if it were set in typewriter face? Why is this so? The answer lies in the difference between printer's type and typewriter face.

In printer's type the construction of each letter, with its gentle curves, its gradation of thickness and thinness of line, and its distribution of mass and weight, gives it a pleasing proportion and elegant distinction. With typewriter face, there are no subtle gradations, no shift of mass and weight. Each character is flat, thin, lifeless.

Visibility is another factor which materially affects reading efficiency. For ease of reading, sharp, jet-black characters on white, nongloss paper are optimal. Hold a typewritten letter beside a page of this book. Compare the intensity of contrast between the characters on the printed page and those on the typewritten page. But there is yet another difference: the sharpness of the outline of the individual letters. Type has a clear, crisp profile. Typewritten characters, looked at through even a small-power magnifier, are fuzzy, ragged in outline, and spindly in design.

At best, the reading of typewritten material is a decided handicap. Research has shown that both reading speed and visual span are reduced in the reading of typewritten or stencil-duplicated materials. Compared with the reading of a type face used in books and magazines, the reading of American Typewriter face slows the reader approximately 5 per cent.[1] When stencil-duplicated, or mimeographed, American Typewriter face retards reading speed by as much as 6 per cent, depending upon the clarity of the impression.[2] Typewriter face is also known to affect the width of the reader's recognition, or fixation span. The average number of characters seen at one fixation in standard type is 8.5. Reading typewritten material shortens this to a fixation span of about five characters.[3] This would suggest that the reading of typewritten material reduces the fixation span by approximately 40 per cent, thereby reducing the fatigue factor considerably.

An easy-to-read page has an airiness about it. Psychologically, this reacts favorably on the reader. Space between words and lines and marginal space is highly important in heavy-duty reading. Much typewritten material is single-spaced, poorly duplicated, and cramped upon the page. As such it is decidedly suboptimal for easy reading.

While the reader can do nothing about the matter of visual presentation, the facts relating to it should be as enlightening to him as a knowledge of road conditions is to the motorist. The wise reader will simply face the fact that here are typewritten byroads over which he will probably not be able to travel with the same fleetness that he does along the fair lanes of print. It is the surface of the road itself which hinders him. He is wise who knows it and takes it into account in his reading.

[1] Donald G. Paterson and Miles A. Tinker, *How to Make Type Readable*, p. 27, Harper & Brothers, New York, 1940.

[2] Matthew Luckiesh and Frank K. Moss, *Reading as a Visual Task*, p. 253, D. Van Nostrand Company, Inc., New York, 1942.

[3] "Analysis of the Readability of Typewriter Type," a report issued by Remington Rand, Inc., New York.

But type is type and we must take the page as we find it. There is, however, a more manageable aspect of the complement of reading that comes across the desk. For reading is thinking; and the reader is a thinking, resourceful human being who still calls the plays regardless of his handicaps: the greater the handicap, the greater the need for skillfulness in reading. For that reason it is imperative that the businessman, the editor, anyone for that matter, who must deal with less-than-optimal typography, should have mastered every step to better reading which has been presented in the foregoing chapters. He should have already practiced his way to efficiency. There is no substitute for the mastering of the basic skills. He who plays a fiddle well has practiced many an hour. He who reads a page well has also practiced—the application of the basic skills—hour after hour.

We have discovered some ways in which printed materials are different. But there are still other differences. The very fact, for instance, that the material is to be printed invests it with a new dignity. It is more carefully prepared. The author himself is more careful to revise and polish his own writing. He will give attention to such matters as structure, syntax, and style.

After the author comes the editor. He goes to work on the author's words, revising, correcting, suggesting. His blue pencilings have only one excuse for being: to present the author's words in fresher, more attractive, more readable form. In this way, many of the kinks in the expression of the thought are straightened out. Exact and appropriate words are substituted, and the fundamental principles of unity, coherence, and emphasis are built into the whole piece. The final result is a presentation of thought that has undergone a substantial and rather rigid supervision with one aim only: to help the reader.

Contrast this with the preparation of the flood of words that pour daily through the channels of business. They, too, have been loosed with only one end in view: to communicate something to somebody else, whether it be the fellow at the next desk or to someone at the other end of the world. But these words have had a different origin from those of the writer. To get them on their way they have been droned down the tube of a dictating machine or into the ear of a secretary. And the man who dictates them is usually busy with other things. No wonder they are occasionally hackneyed and stereotyped. If edited at all, these words must be edited impromptu. This will account somewhat for "business style" being what it is.

Practical hints for reading business communications

What are some practical procedures, then, for reading this style of writing? Here are a few hints.

1. *Sweep Down Over the Communication with One Glance.* Have some questions in your mind as you look. The moment you pick up an item from your desk, your mind should bristle with questions. If it is a letter, glance at the letterhead. If it is a memorandum, look at the origin and content information at the top. How long is the communication? Can you see at a glance what it deals with? In the case of a letter, who wrote it? Do you know him?

Most letters are usually very simple. The writer is saying one, two, or three things. What are they? Are they worth the investment of time you are giving to them, or can you see at a glance what the writer wants? Letters, however, that *must* be read carefully, *should* be read carefully. Memorandums may be somewhat more lengthy than letters, but the once-over-lightly technique is still an excellent first step for any type of material.

2. *Get to the Heart of the Matter—Fast!* With letters particularly, use the first paragraph as a diver uses a springboard: to plunge into the depth of the matter at once. The first and the last paragraphs are usually unrewarding. They begin: "We have your letter . . . ," "Thank you for . . . ," "We note that . . . ," "Again, thanking you . . ." Those phrases betray the fact that there is nothing of importance there. If there is no thought content there, you can't put any there, even though you *do* read every word.

Run your eye down the left-hand margin. Note the signposts of non-communication: "As we have said . . . ," "I agree . . . ," "We appreciate . . . ," "We shall look forward . . ."

These phrases have their place. They are indications of good manners and the gentle amenities of social good taste, but from a reading standpoint they are merely sound and fury signifying nothing.

3. *Concentrate Your Attention at the Mid-page.* This is where you are likely to find the heart of the letter. In general this is the area of your slowest and most careful reading. Here you may have to be more alert, more careful in your reading. This is the critical zone. Here are statements on which you will have to base your decisions with regard to this particular letter. Perhaps when you get to this point in the letter,

you will discover that there is not much here that takes too much thought. The letter may not be really important after all. If such is the case, step on the gas. You can usually speed out of a letter the way you speed out of a little hamlet, once you have passed the crossroads at the center of town. The last paragraph and complementary close are merely the straggling outskirts. Negotiate them quickly.

4. *You May Expect Fairly Simple Sentence Structure in the Average Letter.* The average businessman makes no pretense at a literary style. His writing is, on the whole, confined to simple word order. The vocabulary is simple, and for the most part, entirely within the reading range of the average adult.

5. *Read Key Words.* The substance of every letter *could* be telegraphed, if necessary. Consider the letter as a telegram. Read only the key words. We have discussed this technique in Chapter Seven. Drive your eyes along the line; keep alert for the words that *really* count. Take, for instance, this letter:

Dear Sir:

Thank you for your letter of January 25, and your order for 6 dozen Buzz Bug Bombs.

We regret to inform you that your order cannot be filled immediately because of our depleted inventory at the moment.

We are, however, awaiting another shipment of Buzz Bug Bombs, which the manufacturer assures us will arrive within ten days to two weeks.

We will fill your order as soon as these arrive.

We are indeed sorry that we must cause you this inconvenience.

Very truly yours,

Buzz Bomb Distributors, Inc.

Now, read only the key words of that letter necessary to convey the thought:

REGRET ORDER CANNOT BE

FILLED IMMEDIATELY

DEPLETED INVENTORY

WILL FILL SOON

We have eliminated over 86 per cent of the verbiage.

Most letters can be reduced far more drastically than passages of comparable length in printed material. This is because the editor's blue pencil and the author's revisions have made printed material much less wordy. Hacking away all of the superfluous verbiage could reduce the average letter to ten or twenty words. But what man would write only a ten-word letter and sign his name to it? What *impression* would such a letter give? Therefore, we have to make it *look* like a letter, with ample proportion, whether the excess wordage says anything or not.

6. *Don't Be Fooled by the "Paragraph."* In business writing generally the paragraph is a rather amorphous thing. What look like paragraphs may be nothing more than fragments. Many businessmen are not paragraph-conscious. They begin a new paragraph whenever they feel that they have said enough following one indentation to warrant another one. In reports, on the other hand, the paragraph may drone on interminably. In a letter a paragraph usually means one or two sentences. Nothing comparable to conventional paragraph development will generally be found.

7. *Crumble the Cliché; Translate the Jargon.* Clichés are trite, threadworn phrases; jargon is verbal absurdity. Somewhere, somebody conceived the silly idea that business letters should be very formal. In consequence, a gibberish of the business letter grew up which is a kind of commercial gobbledygook. It is unnatural, squirrel-cage language that spins round and round without saying much. And although it is on its way out, you will find the wraiths of his ghastly phraseology still stalking abroad. Keep an eye out for them.

Their writers are always "regretting most sincerely" instead of just simply "being sorry," they are "not in a position to ascertain" when they merely "cannot," and they "will see that an investigation is made to determine" when they are going to do nothing more than "find out." From a reading standpoint, crumble this verbal nonsense and see it for what it's worth. One or two words will usually say what the whole rumbling phrase is trying to express. You simply cannot justify noise. Most of the time it expresses exactly nothing.

For example, what can be worse than this: "Your letter of the 25th has been received and contents carefully noted." The very fact that you have received a reply is ample evidence that your letter was received and its "contents noted." "We are hereby advising you that . . ." Of course they are; why not go ahead and do it? Why do they need to tell you? Such phrases are not only silly, they are verbal blockades that should be bypassed as soon as your eyes fall upon them. Get around them, and get on in pursuit of the thought.

8. *When Reading Reports, Try Reading Them Backward.* Many reports are clearly set up. They follow a prescribed form. Spacing, underlining, and enumerating are common devices employed to make the report more readable. In a great many reports the author summarizes what he has said in a concluding paragraph. When you pick up a report, look at the last page. See if it is summarized. The summary will tell you whether what is in the report is worth your time or whether this is something that another man, behind another desk, might better read. If the report is for you, the first thing that you will want to do is to read the summary carefully. Then read the rest of the report with the summary clearly in mind. You'll make time by doing so.

9. *Look in the Mirror Occasionally.* Remember that practically everything that comes across your desk has come from other people just like you. Most of the time they have done their best. But the man who wrote the memo or the letter or the report may never have been the top man in his class when it came to getting his thoughts down on paper. He is trying to reach you, but he needs your help. Give him a hand. Bring all your reading skill to play upon his page. To do so will probably help him. It will certainly help you. Remember, the material that comes across the desk probably does not represent an optimal reading situation. Even so, as a master reader, you can use your reading skill to get the thought which the man who wrote it is trying to convey —and if you use your skill, all of it, adeptly, you can get that thought efficiently and get it—quickly!

Learn to Read Rhythmically, Rapidly, and with Increased Eye Span

Read the following selection rhythmically, swinging down the page in two fixations to the line. Let your eyes swing, pendulum-like from midphrase to midphrase down the page. Refer back to p. 92 for further instructions in reading this type of exercise.

GRAPHIC PRESENTATION [4]

Graphic presentation is   a functional form of art
as much as modern painting   or architectural design.

[4] Mary Eleanor Spear, *Charting Statistics*, p. 3, McGraw-Hill Book Company, Inc., New York, 1952.

The painter studies his subject   to determine what colors
and style and design   will best express his ideas.
The same kind of imagination   is exercised by the graphic artist
and analyst.
   The chart has long been recognized   as the clearest
and most effective method   of interpreting and presenting
a subject visually.   Of equal or even greater importance
is the fact that such a chart   can also clarify
a complex problem.   It can reveal hidden facts
that were not obvious   from the original data.
   A graph is also an important means   of detecting mistakes
in statistical compilations   and reckonings.
It is a common experience   for statistical analysts
and researchers in scientific fields   to find that when
data are charted,   errors and omissions
that had previously been overlooked   are discovered.
   In the present day   when visual education
in all its aspects   has become not only an aid to,
but also a vital basis   of learning,
our attention is called   more than ever before
to the almost limitless   possibilities in this field.
The eye absorbs written statistics   but only slowly
does the brain receive   the message hidden behind
the written words and numbers.   The correct graph, however,
reveals that message   briefly and simply.

Seconds

   Each time that you repeat this exercise record your time.   1. _____
Swing your eyes faster and faster down the page. Try to show   2. _____
a definite record of improvement. Be sure that you *see* the   3. _____
whole of each fixation; be sure that you get the thought as   4. _____
you read.   5. _____
                                                                6. _____
                                                                7. _____
                                                                8. _____
                                                                9. _____
                                                               10. _____
                                                    Average time: _____

Reading for Speed of Comprehension

Everyone in today's world should know what jargon is. There is so much of it around. It lies thick, ofttimes, along the channels of business communication. In the selection which you are about to read a celebrated scholar discusses jargon in a most charming manner. Read it to get the meaning.

Time: MINUTES _____

SECONDS _____

ON JARGON [5]
by Sir Arthur Quiller-Couch

I ask leave to interpose some words upon a kind of writing which, from a superficial likeness, commonly passes for prose in these days, and by lazy folk is commonly written for prose, yet actually is not prose at all. It is with that infirmity of speech—that flux, that determination of words to the mouth, or to the pen,—which, though it be familiar to you in parliamentary debates, in newspapers, and as the staple language of Blue Books, Committees, Official Reports, I take leave to introduce to you as prose which is not prose and under its real name of Jargon.

Has a Minister to say "No" in the House of Commons? Some men are constitutionally incapable of saying no; but the Minister conveys it thus: "The answer to the question is in the negative." That means "no." Can you discover it to mean anything less, or anything more except that the speaker is a pompous person?—which was no part of the information demanded.

That is Jargon, and it happens to be accurate. But as a rule Jargon is by no means accurate, its method being to walk circumspectly around its target; and its faith, that having done so it has either hit the bull's eye or at least achieved something equivalent, and safer.

Thus the clerk of a Board of Guardians will minute that—

In the case of John Jenkins deceased the coffin provided was of the usual character.

Now this is not accurate. "In the case of John Jenkins deceased," for whom a coffin was supplied, it is wholly superfluous to tell us that

[5] Sir Arthur Quiller-Couch, *On the Art of Writing*, pp. 120–126, G P. Putnam's Sons, New York, 1916.

he is deceased. But actually John Jenkins never had more than one case, and that was the coffin. The clerk says he had two—a coffin in a case; but I suspect the clerk to be mistaken, and I am sure he errs in telling us that the coffin was of the usual character; for coffins have no character, usual or unusual.

Have you begun to detect the two main vices of Jargon? The first is that it uses circumlocution rather than short straight speech. It says: "In the case of John Jenkins deceased, the coffin" when it means "John Jenkins' coffin"; and its yea is not yea, neither is its nay nay; but its answer is in the affirmative or in the negative, as the foolish and superfluous "case" may be. The second vice is that it habitually chooses vague wholly abstract nouns rather than concrete ones.

The first rule of writing is: Whenever in your reading you come across one of these words, case, instance, character, nature, conditions, persuasion, degree—whenever in writing your pen betrays you to one or another of them—pull yourself up and take thought. If it be "case" (I choose it as Jargon's dearest child) turn to the dictionary, if you will, and seek out what meaning can be derived from *casus*, its Latin ancestor; then try how, with a little trouble, you can extricate yourself from that case. The odds are, you will feel like a butterfly that had discarded his chrysalis.

Here are some specimens to try your hand on:

(1) All those tears which inundated Lord Hugh Cecil's head were dry in the case of Mr. Harold Cox.

Poor Mr. Cox! left gasping in his aquarium!

(2) (From a cigar-merchant) In any case, let us send you a case on approval.

(3) It is contended that Consols have fallen in consequence: but such is by no means the case.

"*Such*," by the way, is another spoilt child of Jargon, especially in Committee's Rules.

Character—Nature. There can be no doubt that the accident was caused through the dangerous nature of the spot, the hidden character of the byroad, and the utter absence of any warning or danger signal.

Mark the foggy wording of it all! And yet the man hit something and broke his neck! Contrast that explanation with the verdict of a coroner's jury in the west of England on a drowned postman: "We find that deceased met his death by an act of God, caused by sudden overflowing of the river Walkham and helped out by the scandalous neglect of the way-wardens."

Condition. He was conveyed to his place of residence in an intoxicated condition.

"He was carried home drunk."

Now what I ask you to consider about these quotations is that in each the writer was using Jargon to shirk prose, palming off periphrases upon us when with a little trouble he could have gone straight to the point. "The accident was caused through the dangerous nature of the spot," "but such is by no means the case." We may not be capable of much; but we can all write better than that, if we take a little trouble.

Next, having trained yourself to keep a lookout for these worst offenders (and you will be surprised to find how quickly you get into the way of it), proceed to push your suspicions out among the whole cloudy host of abstract terms. "How excellent a thing is sleep," sighed Sancho Panza; "it wraps a man round like a cloak"—an excellent example, by the way, of how to say a thing concretely; a Jargoner would have said that "among the beneficent qualities of sleep its capacity for withdrawing the human consciousness from the contemplation of immediate circumstances may perhaps be accounted not the least remarkable." How vile a thing—shall we say?—is the abstract noun! It wraps a man's thoughts round like cotton-wool.

For another rule—just as rough and ready, but just as useful: Train your suspicions to bristle up whenever you come upon "as regards," "with regards to," "in respect of," "in connection with," "according as to whether," and the like. They are all dodges of Jargon, circumlocutions for evading this or that simple statement; and I say that it is not enough to avoid them nine times out of ten, or nine-and-ninety times out of a hundred. You should never use them. That is positive enough, I hope?

From a popular novelist:

I was entirely indifferent *as to* the results of the game, caring nothing at all *as to* whether *I had losses or gains*—

Cut out the first "as" in "as to," and the second "as to" altogether, and the sentence begins to be prose—"I was indifferent to the results of the game, caring nothing whether I had losses or gains."

But why, like Dogberry have "had losses"? Why not simply "lose."

Let us try again. "I was entirely indifferent to the results of the game, caring nothing at all whether I won or lost."

Still the sentence remains absurd; for the second clause but repeats the first without adding one jot. For if you care not at all whether you win or lose, you must be entirely indifferent to the results of the game. So why not say, "I was careless if I won or lost," and have done with it?

But let us illustrate Jargon by the converse method of taking a famous piece of English (say Hamlet's soliloquy) and remolding a few lines of it in this fashion:

To be, or the contrary? Whether the former or the latter be preferable would seem to admit of some difference of opinion; the answer in the present case being of an affirmative or of a negative character according as to whether one elects on the one hand to suffer mentally the disfavor of fortune, albeit in an extreme degree, or on the other to envisage boldly adverse conditions in the prospect of eventually bringing them to a conclusion. The condition of sleep is similar to, if not indistinguishable from that of death; and with the addition of finality the former might be considered identical with the latter: so that in this connection it might be argued with regard to sleep that, could the addition be effected, a termination would be put to the endurance of a multiplicity of inconveniences, not to mention a number of downright evils incidental to our fallen humanity, and thus a consummation achieved of a most gratifying nature.

That is Jargon: and to write Jargon is to be perpetually shuffling around in the fog and cotton-wool of abstract terms, to beat the air because it is easier than to flesh your sword in the thing. The first virtue, the touchstone of masculine style, is its use of the active verb and the concrete noun. When you write in the active voice, "They gave him a silver teapot," you write as a man. When you write "He was made the recipient of a silver teapot," you write Jargon. But at the beginning set even higher store on the concrete noun. I ask you to note how carefully the Parables—those exquisite short stories—speak only of "things which you can touch and see"—"A sower went forth to sow." "The Kingdom of Heaven is like unto leaven, which a woman took"—and not the Parables only, but the Sermon on the Mount and almost every verse of the Gospel. The Gospel does not, like my young essayist, fear to repeat a word, if the word be good. The Gospel says, "Render unto Caesar the things that are Caesar's"—not "Render unto Caesar the things that appertain to that potentate." The Gospel does not say "Consider the growth of lilies," or even "Consider how the lilies grow." It says, "Consider the lilies, how they grow."

Or take Shakespeare. I wager you that no writer of English so constantly chooses the concrete word, in phrase after phrase forcing you to touch and see. No writer so insistently teaches the general through the particular.

When Shakespeare has to describe a horse, mark how definite he is:

Round-hoof'd, short jointed, fetlocks shag and long,
Broad breast, full eye, small head, and nostrils wide,
High crest, short ears, straight legs, and passing strong,
Thin mane, thick tail, broad buttock, tender hide.

You may easily assure yourselves that men who have written learnedly on the art agree in treating our maxim—to prefer the concrete term to the abstract, the particular to the general, the definite to the vague—as a canon of rhetoric. "This particularizing style," comments Mr. Payne (in his prefaces to Burke) "is the essence of poetry; and in prose it is impossible not to be struck with the energy it produces."

A lesson about writing your language may go deeper than language; for language is your reason, your *logos*. So long as you prefer abstract words, which express other men's summarized concepts of things, to concrete ones which lie as near as can be reached to things themselves and are the first-hand material for your thoughts, you will remain, at the best, writers at second-hand. If your language be Jargon, your intellect, if not your whole character, will almost certainly correspond. Where your mind should go straight, it will dodge: the difficulties it should approach with a fair front and grip with a firm hand it will be seeking to evade or circumvent. For the style is the man, and where a man's treasure is there his heart, and his brain, and his writing, will be also.

What time is it now? MINUTES _____

SECONDS _____

What is your reading time for this selection? MINUTES _____

SECONDS _____

Now, test your level of comprehension by answering the following questions. Do not refer back to the article.

Comprehension quiz

Complete the following sentences with the proper word:

1. _____ is Jargon's dearest child.

2. Jargon employs _____ rather than straightforward expression.

3. Jargon habitually elects to use _____ nouns.

4. _____ is another spoilt child of Jargon.

5. As a rule, Jargon is by no means _____.

6. The author says that Jargon is not _____.

7. When you write in the active voice you write as a _____.

8. _____ is the master of the concrete style.

9. If your language be Jargon, your _____ will correspond.

10. The _____ is the man.

Check your answers with those in the Answer Key. Each correct answer is worth 10 per cent.

What is your level of comprehension? _____%

What is your speed of comprehension? _____wpm

What is your reading index $(R \times C/100)$? _____

Reading Habit Index

	Never	Rarely	Sometimes	Usually	Always
1. When I pick up a piece of writing, my first impulse is to look for those specific items which will give me a quick grasp of the piece as a whole.					
2. I know that in most writing the thought is logical and that it is usually well structured and organized. Hence, as I read, I look for the structural organization of the thought.					

Never Rarely Sometimes Usually Always

3. I spot jargon as soon as I come across it.

4. I am alert for "statistical jokers" and spot them immediately.

5. I am aware of "directional words" that change the flow of thought, noticing them as I read.

Reading habit index score: _____

(See directions for scoring, p. 75)

Date: _____

Chapter Seventeen

Reading
the technical report

THE TECHNICAL, or research report is writing which belongs to a distinctive category. The main purpose of the technical paper is to report on work in progress, to detail the particulars of some specialized operation or method, or to describe newer and more modern approaches to problems of the profession. In short, the technical report is a factual paper aimed to keep those who read it abreast of latest developments in their specialized field.

Frequently, professional journals are little more than a collection of technical papers, research reports, with the addition in some instances of items of a personal nature concerning the doings of certain members of the profession. The "journals" of the various departments of knowledge, with the exception of the book reviews which they may contain, are almost entirely devoted to reports on technical research.

The efficient reader knows how to handle the research or technical journal from a reading standpoint. Although it is not feasible to discuss each type of such journal, yet some general observations can be made about this class of writing which may help the reader to handle more quickly this type of material when he encounters it.

Suggestions for reading technical reports

1. *Do Not Be Fooled by Formidable Appearance.* Most technical articles have a very lofty, professional look. They are printed in formal columns, which frequently bristle with footnote indexes, and following the article is a bibliography usually consisting of an array of "selected references." In format alone the technical article is austere and formal, and it frequently has little appeal except to those who are really interested in its subject matter. On the whole, these articles appear to be very heavy and scholarly. Some of them are. Others are flimsy and unrewarding, but they masquerade under the severe garb of scholarship.

Look at a technical article in the same way that you would look at any other piece of writing which is becoming a part of your reading fare for the first time. There are certain basic assumptions which you are justified in making:

1. The person who wrote this must have had some organization in his own thinking;
2. That organization must be manifest somewhere within the article. Sometimes the organization is very apparent. The author gives you a 1, 2, 3 arrangement. This may be blatantly heralded with an arabic numeral at the beginning of each paragraph, or a group of paragraphs; or the author may be less obvious, and use "first," "second," "third." Or he may just let his thought pass from one phase to another, and let you find where the transition takes place.
3. Most professional journals require a prescribed format for the article. Such articles usually have a summary. Occasionally this comes first, preceding the body of the article; more often it appears in the concluding paragraphs or in a section at the end of the report. But it is good to know that one usually lurks somewhere—and it is tremendously helpful if you find it early in your reading.

2. *Try Skimming the Article.* See what you can do with a new technical article by applying the skimming techniques to it. You protest, "But the things that I read, I must get every word!" All right! What you are forgetting is that the skimming technique is only *one* step in the final reduction of the product. Chemists do not make gasoline with only one operation—there are dozens of processes between piped crude and super octane. In the laboratory there is a method of reduction called

fractional distillation. Reading is frequently done by the fractional distillation method also. Try skimming first. Skimming the article may help you to extract the essence of what the author is saying. You may be able to distill, by skimming, the sum and substance of the whole report.

Look the article over thoroughly. Apply the "look suggestions" which were made in Chapter Nine. If you have forgotten these, go back and review them. Then, after you have taken a minute or so to *look*, begin to read. Observe the way in which the author structures his writing. See where he states his main thought in the paragraph. Technical writers are usually fairly consistent stylists in writing. Wherever the author places the main idea in the first several paragraphs, it is fairly certain that in that position you may expect to find it in the remainder of the paragraphs.

The authors of technical papers are, as a general rule, not primarily interested in writing. They are more concerned with setting forth the results of their research. Occasionally the paragraph structure is somewhat irregular. In such instances the reader should be alert to the main ideas and their supporting facts. When the reader finds *two* main ideas in *one* paragraph—and he occasionally will—or when he finds only one main idea occupying two paragraphs, he should recognize such a situation and make his own paragraph divisions accordingly. When he looks at a paragraph he should analyze it immediately. His mental reaction in the case of a paragraph without a topic sentence might be something like this: "These are only facts and details—what this paragraph is really trying to say is . . ." and here follows his own clear statement of the main thought.

If the author has not clearly structured his thinking, then as a reader you must do it for him. Some writers, in this respect, place more of a burden upon their readers than others do, but in any event the prime interest of the reader should be to see the author's thought and its organization and to see it clearly and unmistakably.

For the most part, you will find the technical article fairly well organized, but it may tend to be less interesting stylistically than other reading because of its high factual content. It may also be heavy with documentation. From a research standpoint, documentation is important largely in terms of further research and to give authority for statements made, or for the material presented. Unless you are going into an exhaustive study of the subject, it is well, in reading to get the thought, largely to ignore the documentation.

3. *After You Have Surveyed the Report, Decide What You Will Do with It.* Because of their specialized nature, technical reports may have varying degrees of appeal for you. Reading specialists, for instance, do not read *every* article that comes out in the field of reading. Even at the adult level, the specialist may be more interested in certain investigations than in others. In true Baconian fashion some articles are to be tasted, others to be swallowed, and some few to be chewed and digested.

Stop to define *exactly* what you do when your trade, professional, or business journal comes to your hands. Do you turn to the table of contents to check on the most likely articles that you will want to read first? Do you practice priority in reading? Every efficient reader does. Pick out two or three of the most apparently appealing articles. Give these a quick skimming to see whether these really are what their title implies. That may be sufficient. You may not need to go any further. Maybe there is not as much in them as you thought there would be. Consequently, you saw all there was to see with a once-over glance. At a glance you may recognize that another of the articles is most worth while. This, like gold, is worthy of further refinement. It calls for the application of other techniques of reading, and it demands more time and care for the process.

4. *Select the Technique to Meet Your Need.* After you have settled upon your purpose, then you will want to select the reading technique that fits your purpose best. If you are reading the technical article to remember details, then you will want to recall the material contained in Chapter Eleven. Is this an article in which essentially you need to follow directions? Then keep in mind that material presented in Chapter Ten. The material in other chapters will also help you. Be conscious, however, that you are using a specific technique in reading with only one aim in view: to read a given type of material more efficiently.

5. *After You Have Finished the Report, Cover the Ground Again—Quickly.* Make it a habit, after you have finished reading a highly factual article, such as the technical report, to look back over it. No matter how well you think you comprehend the material, take one parting glance at the *entire* article before you put it aside. You should have a brief leave-taking with what you read as you have farewells with your friends. Don't just walk out on your article. Glance back to see what

there is in this article that you want to remember especially. The factual landscape is familiar now, but a final backward glance may help you to remember its salient features. This is the one act that may cement this article in your memory long after others who merely read and leave it may have forgotten it entirely.

The research report is a type of article with distinctive features. You can learn to read it rapidly and efficiently. Try the techniques suggested in this chapter in reading your next professional journal, and see whether much that is within its covers does not crumble before your eyes.

Measure Your Rapid-perception Span

Get out the card that you used last in Chapter Thirteen. You used it also in Chapter Six and Chapter Ten. We are going to do some more rapid-perception reading. Last time you had a 2¼-inch space between the arrows. Widen the bar for this practice to 2½ inches. Practice with this. Try to see in one split second all the words within this 2½-inch span. Below are blanks to record your achievement.

Phrase seen	Type units	Phrase seen	Type units
1. _____ ____		1. _____ ____	
2. _____ ____		2. _____ ____	
3. _____ ____		3. _____ ____	
4. _____ ____		4. _____ ____	
5. _____ ____		5. _____ ____	
6. _____ ____		6. _____ ____	
7. _____ ____		7. _____ ____	
8. _____ ____		8. _____ ____	
9. _____ ____		9. _____ ____	
10. _____ ____		10. _____ ____	

No. correct _____   No. correct _____

Av. type units _____   Av. type units _____

	Type			Type
Phrase seen	*units*		*Phrase seen*	*units*

1. _____ ____   1. _____ ____

2. _____ ____   2. _____ ____

3. _____ ____   3. _____ ____

4. _____ ____   4. _____ ____

5. _____ ____   5. _____ ____

6. _____ ____   6. _____ ____

7. _____ ____   7. _____ ____

8. _____ ____   8. _____ ____

9. _____ ____   9. _____ ____

10. _____ ____   10. _____ ____

No. correct _____   No. correct _____

Av. type units _____   Av. type units _____

Compare your achievement on this perception exercise with your achievements previously. Refer to your former records in earlier chapters.

Reading for Speed of Comprehension

Becoming tired is an experience that is common to all of us. We also know that on the job we sometimes feel a surge of energy, and at other times we are at low ebb. The matter of changes in fatigue during the eight-hour day is the subject of the technical report which you are about to read. Attack it as has been suggested earlier in this chapter. This is a report of easy to medium difficulty. Read it to get all the facts.

Time: MINUTES _____

SECONDS _____

CHANGES IN SUBJECTIVE FATIGUE AND READINESS FOR WORK DURING THE EIGHT-HOUR SHIFT [1]

by John W. Griffith, Willard A. Kerr,* Thomas B. Mayo, Jr.,
Illinois Institute of Technology
and John R. Topal, Belden Manufacturing Company

Although remarkable progress has been made in industrial psychology in recent decades, it is an interesting fact that remarkably little research has been reported on the changes which probably occur in the subjective fatigue and readiness for work of personnel from one part of a standard work shift to another. As Ryan (5) has pointed out, most "fatigue" research has reflected an academic preoccupation either with trying to measure objective fatigue or attempting to define fatigue with precision, the latter task being one which Muscio (3) decided as early as 1921 to be practically hopeless. Because of the relative absence of literature on the subjective feeling changes with work, the problem is largely unmentioned in existing textbooks on personnel and industrial psychology.

Production curves for the work day in various factory operations sometimes are presented for their possible relevance (1, 4) to fatigue, but it is admitted generally that many factors other than fatigue, however defined, determine the production curve. Feelings of tiredness do not necessarily change in expected directions with changes in rate of output. However, to date, the scheduling of work and locating of rest pauses in industry have been done largely according to guesswork or with reference to incidental practical considerations independent of worker readiness.

If considerable consistency is found in worker feelings of tiredness and readiness to work in various types of work, it is possible that such feeling curves will be useful in the more intelligent scheduling of work and rest pauses in business and industry.

The Present Research

The present research entertains the hypothesis that employees in representative types of work possess definite attitudes as to when during the work shift they are most ready to work and when they are most

[1] *Journal of Applied Psychology*, vol. 34 (1950), pp. 163–166.
* Senior author is W. A. Kerr.

tired. Employing the "tear ballot" technique (2) a measuring device was constructed which obtains from the worker his estimate of when in each half of the eight-hour shift he feels most rested and most tired. All replies of 379 employees were anonymous except that eleven ballots were temporarily coded for a crude test-retest reliability check in addition to other internal consistency evidence. Included in the sample were 232 male manual workers (handlers and sorters of light-to-100-pounds materials), 75 foremen in a rawhide factory, and 72 office workers (48 male, 24 female). Foremen were measured at a regular meeting of the Chicago Rawhide Management Club and the other personnel were measured while at work in a distributing organization (manual workers) and in an electronics plant (office workers). The supervisory and office personnel were regular day shift employees but the 232 manual workers began their various shifts in the three-hour period from 3:30 to 6:30 P.M.

Results

Obtained subjective reports of tiredness and readiness for work at various hours of work were analyzed with respect to age, sex, and type of work performed. Repeat-test reliability coefficients for small groups ranged from .69 to .92.

Age. Office and manual workers were studied separately as to possible age differences in work feelings. Each group was divided into younger (20–35) and older (36–65) personnel and per cent of each age group feeling tired (and rested) at each of the eight hours of the shift was calculated. Considering each half of the work shift separately, normal chance expectancy, assuming no change in work feelings with successive hours of work, would yield 25 per cent response at each hour of each half of the work shift. Actually, conspicuous changes in both tiredness and readiness for work are reported by both older and younger workers in successive hours of work. Older workers, both office and manual, report greater average feeling deviations from chance expectancy than do younger workers. This tendency, shown clearly in Table 1, seems to indicate that older workers are introspectively more conscious of feelings of tiredness and readiness for work at specific hours of the work shift than are younger workers. It is possible, of course, that "objective" fatigue is equally present in the younger workers but that the younger workers are less affected in their subjective feelings by their continually changing organic conditions than are older workers. Another explanatory hypothesis is that younger workers simply have less insight into their feeling changes with successive hours of work. Whatever the most tenable explanation, older workers in this study report significantly greater extremes of work feelings than do their younger associates.

Sex. Since all the manual workers are male, the sex comparison is limited to office personnel—48 males and 24 females—groups too small for any except suggestive comparisons. A suggestive tendency is present

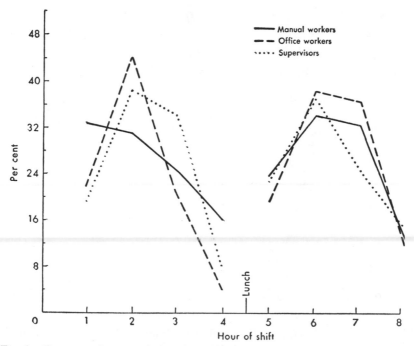

Fig. 1   Per cent of manual, office, and supervisory employees reporting maximal feelings of restedness at each hour of each half of the eight-hour work shift.

for female employees to report greater extremes of tiredness than do males.

Type of Work. Curves of work feeling throughout the work spell for manual work, office work, and supervising are displayed in Figures 1 and 2. It is significant that these three curves in each graph are all highly similar, despite the fact that they are derived from reports of employees doing dissimilar types of work and in different firms and industries. Introspectively, apparently, workers of widely differing types experience substantially the same feelings of tiredness and readiness for work at specific periods in the work spell. The similarity of these curves is all the more striking when it is considered that the manual workers are "swing" shift rather than regular day shift personnel. Extent of subjective tiredness feelings appears from Figure 2 to be in part a func tion of degree of manual effort involved in jobs performed. Supervisors

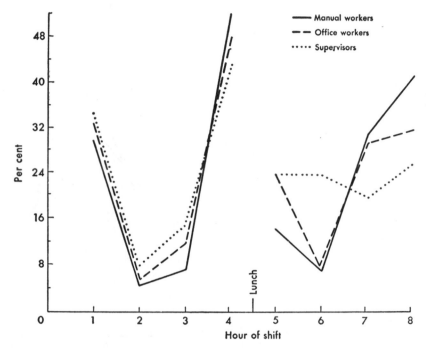

Fig. 2   Per cent of manual, office, and supervisory employees reporting maximal feelings of tiredness at each hour of each half of the eight-hour work shift.

show minimal variation about the line (25 per cent) of chance expectancy while manual workers show maximal variation for the three groups studied. Period of maximal tiredness seems to be the hour preceding the lunch period, while another peak of tiredness is during the last hour of the work shift. Readiness for work in terms of per cent of personnel reporting themselves as "most rested" is maximum in the second hour after the beginning of each work spell and it is minimal in the last hour of each work spell.

TABLE 1

Per Cent of Each Age Group Among Manual and Office Workers Reporting Feelings of "Most Tired" and "Most Rested" at Each Hour of the Work Shift and the Mean Deviations of Such Reports from Normal Expectancy

| | Per Cent "Most Tired" | | | | Per Cent "Most Rested" | | | | |
| | Manual | | Office | | Manual | | Office | | Chance |
Hour of Work Shift	Age 20–35	Age 36–65	Age 20–35	Age 36–65	Age 20–35	Age 36–65	Age 20–35	Age 36–65	Expectancy
1	32	20	27	41	27	38	31	6	25
2	5	7	3	18	36	29	51	53	25
3	16	18	18	0	20	15	15	35	25
4	47	55	52	41	17	18	3	6	25
	100	100	100	100	100	100	100	100	100
5	23	16	33	12	28	33	25	24	25
6	15	2	9	12	35	41	42	52	25
7	25	37	29	35	24	14	24	12	25
8	37	45	29	41	13	12	9	12	25
	100	100	100	100	100	100	100	100	100
MD	10.3	15.5	11.2	14.5	6.5	10.3	12.3	16.3	0
N	84	148	55	17	84	148	55	17	

Summary

Manual, office, and supervisory employees totalling 379 from three different establishments were measured with a Kerr "tear ballot" for subjective feelings of tiredness and restfulness in the various hours of the eight-hour work shift.

1. Manual, office, and supervisory personnel report significantly differential feelings of tiredness or restfulness for various periods in the work shift.

2. Older workers report significantly greater variation of such feelings than do employees under age 36.

3. Curves of tiredness feeling and restfulness feeling throughout the work shift are remarkably similar for the manual, office, and supervisory employees in this study. The similarities are more impressive than the dissimilarities.

4. Maximal subjective fatigue is reported in the fourth and eighth hours of the eight-hour shift.

5. Maximal restfulness feeling is reported in the second and sixth hours of the shift, the second hour of each four-hour work spell.

6. In possible future evaluation of the psychological and efficiency

advisability of the six-hour day, it is recommended that such data as these reported here be obtained on employees now engaged in six-hour shifts. Such new data should be examined particularly for: (a) less variability of tiredness feeling response; and (b) relative absence of high tiredness peaks just before the middle and end of the work shift.

Received September 16, 1949.

REFERENCES

1. Goldmark, M. D., Hopkins, P. S. F., and Lee, F. S. Studies in industrial physiology: fatigue in relation to working capacity: comparison of an eight-hour plant and a ten-hour plant. U. S. *Public Health Service, Public Health Bulletin No. 106, 1920.*
2. Kerr, W. A. Where they like to work; work place preference of 228 electrical workers in terms of music. *J. appl. Psychol.*, 1943, **27**, 438–442.
3. Muscio, B. Is a fatigue test possible? *British J. of Psychol.*, 1921, **12**, 31–46.
4. Rothe, H. F. Output rates among butter wrappers: I. Work curves and their stability. *J. appl. Psychol.*, 1946, **30**, 199–211.
5. Ryan, T. A. *Work and effort.* New York: Ronald Press Co., 1947.

What time is it now? MINUTES _____

SECONDS _____

What is your reading time for this selection? MINUTES _____

SECONDS _____

Now test your level of comprehension by answering the following questions:

Comprehension quiz   *Part One*

One of your skills in reading the technical article is to look for the way in which the author has organized and structured his thinking. After the introductory remarks the body of the report which you have just read assumes the form of the following outline. Fill in the blanks (for scoring purposes each blank is worth 7 per cent):

I. _____

II. _____

   A. _____

   B. _____

   C. _____

III. _____

IV. _____

Part Two

The following are either true or false. If the statement is true, place a T in the blank before the statement; if it is false, place an F in the blank. (For purposes of scoring, each correct answer is worth 2½ per cent.)

1 _____ The present study attempts to measure objective fatigue.

2 _____ The "tear ballot" technique was employed.

3 _____ A total of 232 subjects were sampled in this study.

4 _____ The study related the factors of fatigue to the day's production curve.

5 _____ Office and manual workers were studied separately.

6 _____ Each respective group was studied separately as to possible age differences in work feelings.

7 _____ Some of the personnel studied were measured while they attended a club meeting.

8 _____ In the office personnel there were twice as many women as men.

9 _____ Females on the whole report less variation in extremes of fatigue than do males.

10 _____ The tabulation of data makes no differentiation on the basis of sex differences.

11 _____ The older workers show a greater mean deviation in fatigue than do the younger group.

12 _____ The manual workers were engaged entirely in night work.

13 _____ According to the graph, office workers' efficiency drops more rapidly in the first four hours of work than that of either of the other groups.

14 _____ According to the graph, manual workers feel less rested than supervisors, but more than office workers.

15 _____ According to the graph, all groups have to get "warmed up" the first hour of work until they feel at their best.

16 _____ According to the graph, supervisors tire less easily the first four hours, more so the last four hours.

17 _____ According to the graph, manual workers feel more rested than either of the other groups after lunch.

18 _____ According to the graph, manual workers are more tired than either of the other groups upon beginning work.

19 _____ According to the graph, office workers are not so tired at the end of the day as they are before lunch.

20 _____ Maximal subjective fatigue is reported at the third and eighth hours of the eight-hour shift.

Check your answers against those given in the Answer Key. Allow credit for each answer as indicated above. The maximum total score for this comprehension quiz is 99 per cent.

What is your level of comprehension?   _____%

What is your speed of comprehension?   _____wpm

What is your reading index $(R \times C/100)$? _____

Reading Habit Index

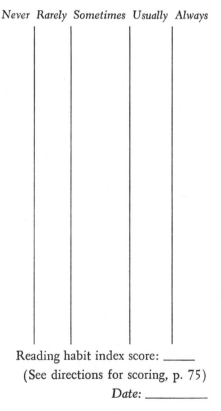

Never Rarely Sometimes Usually Always

1. I usually survey an article before reading it, in order to decide what is the best way to read it.
2. I notice jargon while reading.
3. When I read business letters, I look for the heart of the matter near the center of the letter, then I skim the rest of the letter.
4. I read key words and phrases, concentrating upon those particular words which are especially important in conveying the thought.
5. I notice the way a paragraph is structured and the way in which the author has developed his thought.

Reading habit index score: _____
(See directions for scoring, p. 75)
Date: _____

Chapter Eighteen

Reading for enjoyment

T HIS BOOK has been largely concerned with two things: the basic principles underlying all rapid, efficient reading, and the means of most efficiently attacking the load of reading which stems largely from occupational demands. But for those who have learned the first, and ceased from the second, there comes a time when they wish to read with entire abandon—for the sheer enjoyment of reading. And, as the library posters proclaim, "Reading *can* be fun!"

To get the most pleasure out of leisure reading, there is one rule to follow: Read what you like, when you like it. Don't be strait-jacketed. You are your own best critic and connoisseur of taste.

Most people who read for fun read fiction. And there is a way to read fiction. First, get acquainted with the people with whom you are going to associate in the book. They will be your companions for the length of the story. Get to know them. Observe them carefully at their first appearances. Consider them, not as characters but as human beings. These are people whom you might meet at a party. Read the first few chapters carefully. You will want to feel at home—with these people, and in their surroundings. You should read, therefore, with such scrutiny that you could draw the characters, and describe their various environments, just as if they were real people. Think about these characters

389

between readings. Picture them in your mind; see the backdrop against which they live and move. As you get on into the story read with greater and greater acceleration. At the sight of quotation marks you should *hear* your characters begin to speak. There will be no need to read such wooden comments of the author as "he said . . . ," "she assented . . . ," "they replied . . . ," "he scowled . . . ," "she laughed . . . ." All these moods and conditions you will sense. Strive to hear the characters *talk. See* the scenery as though you were riding through it.

You know how your friends will react to a given situation most of the time. When you read for the fun of it, try to guess what next the characters of the book will do. The elements of every denouement are told chapters ahead of the outcome. A hint here, a clue there, and then in due time the author ties them all together. Are you clever enough to synthesize all these and guess the denouement before it really happens? Once you do it, it's a thrill that you'll never forget. Reading *can* be fun.

Don't overlook the older great books, many of which you may never have read. Try a Greek play, the Book of Job, the Gospels, the *Divine Comedy, Don Quixote, Le Cid, Faust, Gulliver's Travels,* or *War and Peace.* All of these are magnificent. If you do not find them so, it means that you still have further to go until you are a really mature reader. Many a man who has read the *Odyssey,* the Bible, or Shakespeare for the first time for the sheer fun of reading has found them all exciting experiences. The great books are thrilling—every one of them. Of course, the trouble lies in convincing the average reader that this is so, and in getting him to taste and see.

He read many of the world's great books once; perhaps that was when he was young and in school. There he had neither experience nor appetite for such fare. Much of the time he read under compulsion and in the shadow of impending examinations. No wonder he failed to see the glory of the great books. They became for him lifeless academic exercises instead of magnificent epics of the soul of man. Could you but get him to go back to these springs to taste again, he would find out how excellent are these living waters that may irrigate the parched and shallow acres of his humdrum life.

To help you in selecting those books which generations of men and women have found thrilling and timeless, there is at the close of this chapter a selected list of those books and leisure-time reading aids which will help you to make your reading which is done for sheer enjoyment even more rewarding.

Excellent books are still appearing every day. Browse in the bookshops. You need not buy every time you go into a bookstore. The keepers of the shop will understand. They know the manner of the bibliophile and that he who likes books likes to be where new books are.

Read the reviews of the lastest books in your newspaper or in the book-review sections of magazines. Learn something about today's authors. They are a distinguished company, men and women whom you may someday come to know more intimately through the books which they have written. *The New York Times Book Review,* the *New York Herald Tribune Books,* *The Saturday Review,* and the book-review departments of the principal newspapers and magazines are all excellent sources for finding out which of the latest books other people like yourself are reading and enjoying.

Don't overlook the reprints, the pocket editions, the cheap paperbacked books. Remember that many of the great works of literature first appeared in shabbier garb than these. No man need want for the finest intellectual food in the world because he can't afford it. Nowadays it is within reach of all through the cheap reprint and the paperback edition.

Excellent titles are available in the nonfiction field. Modern man's exploration of the frontier of knowledge never stops. There is always something new, wonderful, and fascinating awaiting the reader. The pioneers of research are pushing further and further into the realms of the infinite. In this world and in the vast, mysterious regions of the unexplored universe, new and exciting things are happening, and a stream of amazingly intriguing books is pouring forth from the presses each day to tell you about them.

Visit your library. Get to know it thoroughly. Besides the general reading room and the stacks, you should be acquainted with the periodicals, the vertical file, the reference section, the special collections, such as phonograph records, including records for learning a new language, and the map and print division. Learn to use the card catalogue and the periodical indexes for looking up the information you desire. Look for special displays containing the new acquisitions and books on seasonally popular subjects such as boating, golf, camping, gardening, skiing, hunting and hobbies. Somewhere in every library there is a bulletin board which usually contains a wealth of information for readers: the ten best articles in current magazines, suggested reading lists by topic and interest, announcements of events of a cultural nature which are scheduled for the community, book-club meetings, and so forth. A library is in the best sense an educational center for the whole community and for all ages. Make the library habit one of your reading habits.

You can have a whale of a good time through reading if you let yourself go. In this hectic age read to follow the whims of your own free spirit. Go vagabonding in the realms of books. You *can* do this in reading, and such an approach to one area of your experience can help you to live a more balanced, sane, and healthy life. Every suggestion of this text was made for the purpose of making reading less of a chore and more of a pleasure. In reading for enjoyment the goal of pleasure should be your only aim. It should belong in the same category as an excursion, an adventure, or a picnic. You should look back upon it with deep satisfaction, and you should anticipate it with high expectancy.

This chapter would be incomplete without giving you further real help. You have certain interests, and in reading for pleasure you will probably want to follow those interests further and further. For that reason the following list of titles is given. These books will help you get acquainted in bookland. They are your guides, directing you into those areas where you will be happiest and where your reading for enjoyment can be most enjoyable. In the first list are books which will help you to select something to read; in the second list are those books which will help you to read whatever you select with greater understanding and more appreciation.

Books that will help you to select something to read

Ann M. Boyd and Rae E. Rips, *United States Government Publications*, The H. W. Wilson Company, New York, 1949, 3d ed.

> The United States government is one of the largest publishers of books and pamphlets in the world. This is a guide to United States government publications.

Everett F. Bleiler, *The Checklist of Fantastic Literature*, Shasta Publishers, Chicago, 1948.

A bibliography of fantastic literature, science fiction, mysteries, etc.

Marion Dargan, *Guide to American Biography 1607–1933*, The University of New Mexico Press, Albuquerque, 1949.

A comprehensive listing of American biographies with critical comments.

Asa D. Dickinson, *One Thousand Best Books*, The H. W. Wilson Company, New York, 1931.

A descriptive list and comparative rating of the choicest books of all time.

———, *The Best Books of Our Time 1901–1925*, Doubleday & Company, Inc., New York, 1928.

A work on the same plan as the author's *One Thousand Best Books.* This work also lists 1000 titles.

———, *The Best Books of the Decade 1936–1945*, The H. W. Wilson Company, New York, 1948.

An attempt to designate the best books produced for readers of English in a given period.

P. J. Fihe, V. Wallace, and M. Schulz, *Books for Adult Beginners*, American Library Association, Chicago, 1946.

Comprising a list of books for adults with simple text material.

Alice P. Hackett, *Fifty Years of Best Sellers: 1895–1945*, R. R. Bowker Company, New York, 1945.

There is also a supplement to this work, which carries the list from 1945 to 1951.

Helen E. Haines, *Living with Books: The Art of Book Selection*, Columbia University Press, New York, 1950, 2d ed.

A book to help you select your reading material.

Herbert S. Hirshberg, *Subject Guide to Reference Books*, American Library Association, Chicago, 1942.

An attempt to provide an alphabetical subject guide to the books most needed for answering reference questions frequently asked.

Hester R. Hoffman, ed., *Bessie Graham's Bookman's Manual: A Guide to Literature*, R. R. Bowker Company, New York, 1954, 7th ed.

The complete guide to modern and classical literature in print, with biographical and critical information.

Robert E. Kingery, *How-to-Do-It Books*, R. R. Bowker Company, New York, 1954, 2d ed.

A unique book which describes and lists by subject some 3500 books in 900 categories, such as home repair, hobbies, sports, etc.

W. Philip Leidy, A *Popular Guide to Government Publications*, Columbia University Press, New York, 1953.

> A list of 2500 free or inexpensive government publications having greatest appeal and widest practical value.

Elbert Lenrow, *Readers' Guide to Prose Fiction*, Appleton-Century-Crofts, Inc., New York, 1940.

> A list of 1500 novels topically classified.

Charlotte Matson and Lola Larson, *Books for Tired Eyes*, American Library Association, Chicago, 1951, 4th ed.

> Books in larger print for older readers.

Frank L. Mott, *Golden Multitudes: The Story of Best Sellers in the United States*, The Macmillan Company, New York, 1947.

> A survey of American best sellers, 1662 to 1945.

Reading Ladders for Human Relations, American Council on Education, Washington, 1947.

> Interesting, provocative list of titles to increase understanding in all areas of human relations. Titles suggest books for primary, intermediate, high school, and mature readers.

Ruth M. Strang, Christine B. Gilbert, and Margaret C. Scroggin, *Gateways to Readable Books*, The H. W. Wilson Company, New York, 1952.

> A list for adolescents who find reading difficult. Some of the more retarded adult readers may find this list helpful.

Atwood H. Townsend, Chairman, *Good Reading: A Guide to the World's Best Books*, 20th Anniversary Edition, Farrar, Straus and Cudahy, Inc., New York, 1952.

> A Mentor Books edition is also available, published by the New American Library. A "must" for the reader.

Books that will help you to read the books that you select

There are a few books which might well form the nucleus of a reference shelf in the library of anyone who expects to read widely, particularly in English and American literature.

James D. Hart, *The Oxford Companion to American Literature*, Oxford University Press, New York, 1948.

> A one-volume reference library for the general reader and the student of American literature.

Sir Paul Harvey, *The Oxford Companion to Classical Literature*. Oxford University Press, New York, 1937, 2d ed.

> An encyclopedic reference handbook of classical literature, and its background of history, society, politics, geography, and religion. Of great help to anyone interested in the ancient classics.

————, *The Oxford Companion to English Literature*, Oxford University Press, New York, 1938, 2d ed.

> A companion volume to the *Oxford Companion to American Literature*: an encyclopedic reference work which is an invaluable aid to anyone reading the classics of English Literature.

Hiram Haydn and Edmund Fuller, *Thesaurus of Book Digests*, Crown Publishers, Inc., New York, 1949.

> Digests of 2000 of the world's permanent writings from the ancient classics to current literature.

Mertice M. James and Dorothy Brown, eds., *The Book Review Digest* (issued annually) The H. W. Wilson Company, New York.

> Critical comments from recognized sources, excerpted from current reviews, of the principal titles published each year (may be found in most libraries).

Helen Rex Keller, *The Reader's Digest of Books*, The Macmillan Company, New York, 1949.

> A compilation of 2400 digests of novels, histories, books on science, essays, drama, and belles-lettres.

Donald MacCampbell, *Reading for Enjoyment*, Harper & Brothers, New York, 1941.

> An excellent book on the what and how of reading for enjoyment, with appended lists of 500 selected classics, 100 selected reference books, and 25 periodicals, classified and annotated.

Robert E. Spiller, Willard Thorp, T. H. Johnson, and H. S. Canby, eds., *Literary History of the United States* (3 vols.), The Macmillan Company, New York, 1948.

> The newest comprehensive history of American literature with sections written by 55 contributors and divided according to historical periods Volume 3 is a bibliography of American literature.

Alfred Stefferud, ed., *The Wonderful World of Books*, Houghton Mifflin Company, Boston, 1952.

> A Mentor Books edition is also available, published by the New American Library of World Literature, Inc. Sixty-seven experts in education and the world of books have contributed to this book. For its size and range there is nothing else like it.

Reading Habit Index

Never Rarely Sometimes Usually Always

1. There are certain authors, whose books I enjoy reading, and whom I might consider as "favorite authors."
2. I enjoy reading.
3. I read rather widely: many different types of reading than that required by my business or profession.
4. I make good use of my local library.
5. I like to browse among books.

Reading habit index score: _____

(See directions for scoring, p. 75)

Date: _____

Chapter Nineteen

How well
do you read—now?

W HEN YOU began to study this book, many pages ago, you took
three simple tests of your ability to read. You also marked an
inventory of your reading habits. In the intervening chapters you have
presumably been attempting to improve your reading skills: you have
been looking for main ideas and supporting details while you were
reading; you have been attempting to improve your vocabulary; you have
been striving to form newer and more beneficial habits.

Turn back to the table of contents and review it. A large part of the
domain of better reading has been explored. All along the way you
have been reading selections in each chapter designed to help you to
evaluate your own progress in the speed and level of comprehension.

Now we come to three other simple tests, very much like the first
ones. In fact, the reading material for the second and third tests is taken
from the same books as that for the corresponding tests which you took
earlier. The purpose for doing this was to keep the level of reading
difficulty as nearly the same as possible.

Take these tests as you did the earlier ones. You will want to plan to

397

take all three tests at one sitting, proceeding from one to the other without interruption. Select a quiet place in which to work, free from distractions. You will need, of course, a watch with a second hand, a pencil, an eraser, and a scratch pad. Observe the following simple directions:

1. *Read each selection only once.* Do not re-read or refer back to the selection after you have finished reading.
2. *Read as rapidly as you can.* Never sacrifice understanding for speed. Look for the thought—the main thoughts, the supporting details.
3. *These tests are similar to those you have already taken many times throughout the book.* There is nothing new, or special, about them. But try to do your best.

And now, here is the first test.

Test I [1]

Time now? MINUTES _____

　　　　　　SECONDS _____

Begin to read.

In each age there are outstanding minds. Each generation produces a few men who see more clearly than their fellows the pattern of reality and of man's eternal quest for answers to his problems. These are men of stature, men who, because they tower above their contemporaries, see with truer perspective and longer vision. They see man's universe whole and think in terms which go beyond the immediate and the trivial.

Men of such stature know that each man, everywhere and in every age, faces the same unchanging questions, questions concerning the nature of his basic relationships to his fellow man, his society, his universe, his God. The answers to these questions determine the way in which he will act, and, even more than that, what he will be.

Is justice simply a matter of "might makes right"? Is there a divine plan to the universe? Can man be happy? Are all men equal? These are the kinds of questions each man must answer for himself. It is man's

[1] From "The Great Books Program," by Charles F. Strubbe, Jr., in *The Wonderful World of Books,* edited by Alfred Stefferud, pp. 215–217, copyright, 1952, by Alfred Stefferud, published jointly by the New American Library of World Literature, Inc., and Houghton Mifflin Company.

The Great Books Foundation has five offices: 246 Fifth Ave., New York 1; care of Tacoma Public Library, Tacoma 3, Wash.; 59 E. Monroe St., Chicago 3; 421 Powell St., San Francisco 2; and 3305 Wilshire Blvd., Los Angeles 5.

nature always to be seeking answers, never to be satisfied, eternally seeking the nature of reality. And man cannot deny that nature. For, while truth may not be unattainable, it is elusive, and in this life we may expect the quest for truth never to cease.

The best answers men of each age formulate to questions such as these will survive to be examined and debated by the next generation, and the next. The best answers survive in books.

If it were not for books, for the written record of man's most profound thoughts, his loftiest achievements, each generation would have to rediscover for itself the truths of the past, with only the inadequate help of oral tradition, word-of-mouth handing down of human lore which would inevitably get distorted in the retelling. But books give us a permanent, accurate record of what others have thought about the very problems that face us now.

Those books which have made a lasting contribution to man's quest for truth, we call great books. A book is great if it has influenced profoundly the thinking of many people, over many years, about important things. And such books enrich every age, and give us the ability to see today, this week, this year in true perspective, against the background of other times, other peoples.

Because we prize the wisdom of the great books, we want to share them, to discuss them with others, to share the joy of discovering in them the most provocative answers man has ever evolved to the problems we face. And we want to have others share the great books with us for another reason: the great books are always beyond us, always over our heads, and so we seek the insight of our fellows to help us understand them. While a great book may be beyond the full comprehension and understanding of any one of us, it is not beyond the common wisdom, the pooled experience of the group.

So there exists in America today the program known as The Great Books Foundation discussion groups. It is the embodiment of two ideas: first, that books, the greatest books of each century, can help us understand the problems of our age; second, that groups of adults, meeting to talk about a great book they have read, can help each other acquire this insight. . . .

Today, in more than six hundred American communities, groups of fifteen to thirty persons meet for two hours each two weeks, under the guidance of two leaders to discuss a reading from a prescribed list. They gather in libraries, churches, schools, union halls, grange halls—any place large enough for them to meet informally around a square of tables. The leaders do not lecture. They ask questions designed to stimulate thinking. The reading list represents the pooled experience of thousands of groups and is constantly being changed to reflect that experience.

No conclusions are reached for the group, for these are important problems, questions that have perplexed men since time began. But each participant is encouraged to reach his own conclusions, if he can. The discussion period is not the end, but the beginning of the thinking process. Each participant goes forth from the discussion with clearer insight into the problems and possible solutions. No one does his thinking for him; he has to think for himself.

In a democracy, where each man has a voice in determining the future conduct of society, it is doubly important that he be able to think for himself. It is man's destiny to think, and to work with his fellow men toward common solutions to their common problems. But, above that, in a democracy, the ability to think clearly, to rise above passion and prejudice, must be as widespread as is the right to vote. Without it, we fall prey to every propagandist with his own ax to grind, to every philosophy or political system attractively presented. Only if every citizen can view the problems he faces with objectivity and with reason, can democracy survive.

The Great Books groups are democracy in action. Each man's opinion about the validity of the author's ideas is subjected to the searching scrutiny of his fellow participants. In this atmosphere, there is no room for bias or prejudice, but only for reason.

So it is that, through the medium of democratic group discussion, the wisdom of the ages is becoming the common property of Americans.

What time is it now? MINUTES _____

SECONDS _____

What is your reading time for this selection? MINUTES _____

SECONDS _____

Comprehension quiz

Test your comprehension of facts by completing the following sentences:

1. Today there are more than _____ American communities participating in the Great Books program.

2. Those books which have aided man to seek for _____, we call the great books.

3. Each Great Books discussion group meets _____ nours a month.

4. In the Great Books discussions prejudice is banned; there is room only for _____.

5. It is man's nature always to be seeking _____.

How Clearly Do You Recognize Main Ideas?

In the article which you have just read, the author has presented certain main ideas. These were amplified or supported by certain details or secondary data. Below are ten statements. Five of these are statements of main ideas. Five are statements of details, or statements of fact not mentioned at all in the article. Some of the statements are paraphrased, instead of being direct quotations from the article. Indicate the statements of main ideas by drawing a circle around the number of the sentence.

1. Without books we would have only oral tradition.
2. We like to share and discuss great books with others.
3. Great books are those we commonly regard as classics.
4. Each age has its outstanding minds.
5. The Great Books groups are democracy in action.
6. Man cannot deny his inquisitive nature.
7. The Great Books discussion group reaches no conclusions.
8. The leaders of the discussion groups do not lecture.
9. The great books are always beyond us.
10. It is especially important in a democracy for each person to learn to think for himself.

Now, go on to the next test. You will follow the same general procedure as you did with this test, although the *type* of comprehension questions may be different. After you have finished all of the tests, you will score them.

Are you ready to take Test II? You will want to time yourself on the reading portion of this test as you did on Test I.

Here is the second test:

Test II [2]

Time now? MINUTES _____

SECONDS _____

Begin to read.

It may be noted that there is a rough analogy between the increase in speed by using fewer fixations and the use of skimming. In each case, the reader foregoes the pleasure of dwelling even for an instant on what is not needed, looking only for the essentials. But in the first case, the rejected material is rejected only by the central vision; the peripheral vision is on the alert. In the second, the rejection is on a much larger scale, consisting of whole paragraphs or even pages when the reader has sufficient command of the material to warrant taking the chance of omission.

Other things which affect one's reading speed are of course the obvious matters of physical comfort, proper light, quiet, freedom from interruption. We all know about these, but it takes some of us a long time to learn that such conditions are not always to be had. People who fill their lives with books snatch the few minutes that come while riding a bus, or waiting for a meal to be served, or watching the coffee percolator. By all means, you should do everything you can to promote your comfort so that you may read faster and to greater advantage, but don't get the idea that all these matters are so essential that you just can't work otherwise.

Fatigue is also to be dealt with. A tired person takes more notes than one who is fresh, and it is usually true that he reads more slowly apart from whatever else he is doing. The most profitable way to rest is to change to another volume, or another part of the same volume. When you come to the time when you must really knock off, get a complete change. The longer you work, the shorter will be the periods of profitable application, and the longer should be the rest periods. And if you are actually to rest, don't just stop. Turn on a radio, take a shower, or otherwise completely alter your thoughts for a while.

[2] E. Wayne Marjarum, *How to Use a Book*, Chap. 2, pp. 38–42, Rutgers University Press, New Brunswick, N. J., 1947.

Personal differences must always be taken into account. Many people will tell you that they read and study most enjoyably and with complete efficiency in the presence of music. The psychologists who work on reading problems solemnly shake their heads, but the radio addict, despite the doubtful force of his defense, is seldom to be deterred. Some other persons are at their best (for the purposes of reading, that is), not during the early hours of the day but in the long hours of the evening and night. This may be true, but don't let a sense of being personally a little different from other men betray you into the romantic notion that you must read all night or under an apple tree because you're you. The writer once knew a sensitive young genius who could not work in a room where a clock was ticking until the Army showed him how. Your reading speed is also affected adversely by alcohol. Wine and poetry are alleged to be naturally concomitant; Longfellow enjoyed both in moderation, and Samuel Johnson, who read everything, was not a consistent teetotaller. But the laboratory shows conclusively that a few cocktails, despite their apparent stimulation, ultimately induce a post-alcoholic period of depression (this doesn't mean drunkenness) more marked and of longer duration than the initial "lift." If you have serious reading to do in a hurry, don't get the idea that you are Superman.

The worst handicap that confronts a vast number of readers is the lack of an adequate vocabulary. It presents a problem for which there is no very good solution. If you are to overcome the handicap, you must of course keep a good desk dictionary handy and look up what you don't know. But the time consumed is time gone from reading—there is no escape from that. Although this is not the place to deal with vocabulary building, it may not be amiss to point out that we learn words in several ways and with varying degrees of completeness. One way of learning is by inference, and where inference serves the purpose, it has much to recommend it. Before Hiroshima, few Americans had ever heard of "fissionable material." Now they use the word very readily, but few of them looked it up in a dictionary. They inferred the meaning. That is how words like *allergic, phobia, seismic,* or *totalitarian* receive much of their currency, and, it must be admitted, much of the loose usage and bad pronunciation that characterize them.

Let there be no mistake on this point: there is nothing so good as a good dictionary. Nothing else will take its place. The point made here is only this, that in the period between a learner's perplexities and his final command of an adequate vocabulary, much is going to be lost in time and in accuracy; whenever inference is warranted and opportunities for using a dictionary are limited, it must be allowed to serve as best it may.

One more caution by way of conclusion. You remember the tale of the sorcerer's apprentice who was told to carry in water during his master's absence, and how he conjured the broomstick into doing his task, but conjured so well that the broomstick broke into several pieces, each of which went to work despite the frantic efforts of the apprentice to end the spell he had cast. The principle is sometimes true of rapid reading. Don't let your broomstick get out of control. If you find your mind bewildered, or the quality of your results not quite useful, give the broomsticks a rest and take a few turns with the bucket yourself.

What time is it now? MINUTES _____

SECONDS _____

What is your reading time for this selection? MINUTES _____

SECONDS _____

Comprehension quiz

1. Physical comfort is
    a necessary for optimal reading.
    b desired for optimal reading.
    c immaterial to optimal reading.
    d not mentioned in the article.

2. The selection suggests that rest and fatigue are
    a in direct ratio.
    b in inverse ratio.
    c natural phenomena.
    d unrelated to reading.

3. According to psychologists who work with reading problems,
    a people read better who listen to the radio while reading.
    b people read best if they indulge their personal whims while reading.
    c people read better if they do not listen to the radio while reading.
    d it makes no difference what people do while reading, so long as it is educational.

4. Alcohol adversely affects
   a comprehension.
   b thinking.
   c speed.
   d concentration.

5. One of the major handicaps for a large group of readers is
   a music.
   b a clock ticking.
   c the fact that they were never taught to read.
   d inadequate vocabulary.

6. With serious reading one should
   a not be overconfident of his ability.
   b not underestimate his ability.
   c read slowly and critically.
   d not let sounds, like a clock ticking in the room, distract him.

7. In vocabulary building the author considers one of the best helps to be
   a learning words by inference.
   b reading widely.
   c a good dictionary.
   d careful correction of loose usage and poor pronunciation.

8. The reader with an inadequate vocabulary must expect to
   a pay for his deficiency by occasionally misunderstanding the meaning of what he reads.
   b pay for his deficiency in loss of time and accuracy for a while.
   c find reading sometimes a chore.
   d be bewildered and confused, like the sorcerer's apprentice.

9. The author refers to the story of the sorcerer's apprentice to say, in effect, *don't*
   a read faster than you can.
   b start something that you can't finish.
   c read faster than is reasonable.
   d read faster than you can comprehend.

10. Which of the following would be the best title for this selection?
    a Improving Your Vocabulary
    b Aids and Hindrances to Speed of Reading
    c Improving Comprehension
    d Words and Their Ways for the Rapid Reader

What Is Your Word Power?

The following ten words have been taken from the selection which you have read. Following each word are four choices. Check the choice which you feel is nearest the meaning of the key word. Do *not* refer back to the article.

1. allege: *a* assert   *b* divide   *c* distribute   *d* tempt
2. concomitant: *a* future   *b* present   *c* accompanying
        d past
3. conjure: *a* coincide   *b* join   *c* charge   *d* summon
4. fissionable: *a* radioactive   *b* splitting   *c* explosive
        d heavy
5. induce: *a* diminish   *b* extend   *c* persuade   *d* pamper
6. inference: *a* conclusion   *b* respect   *c* pull   *d* impress
7. obvious: *a* rectangular   *b* concealed   *c* impervious
        d evident
8. phobia: *a* attraction   *b* fear   *c* madness   *d* emotion
9. seismic: *a* pertaining to a volcano   *b* pertaining to the earth
        c pertaining to an earthquake   *d* pertaining to rock
10. warrant: *a* sanction   *b* sheriff   *c* adventure
        d rabbit-hutch

Do *not* score this test now. Go on to the final test. This test will be slightly more difficult. Do not sacrifice meaning for speed. Here is Test III.

Test III [3]

Time now? MINUTES _____

        SECONDS _____

Begin to read.

One phase of civilization does not replace another as a unit, in the way that a guard assigned to sentry duty takes over its post. For a while they mingle confusedly, until a moment comes when one realizes that the entire scene has changed and all the actors are different. So with the internal change that will produce the new person. After a transition period a critical point will come when it will be plain that the new personality has at last matured and that those who wear a different

[3] From *The Conduct of Life*, by Lewis Mumford, pp. 288–292, copyright, 1951, by Lewis Mumford. Reprinted by permission of Harcourt, Brace and Company, Inc.

mask look oddly antiquated and are "out of the picture." Though the object of this change is to make possible a new drama of culture, no one who understands the social process would pretend to write the lines or to describe, in any detail, the action and plot; for it is part of the very nature of the living drama that these things must be left to the actors. If here and there, I have ventured to anticipate the next moves, it is only because the first steps have already been taken.

How shall one describe the balanced man and woman, considered as an ideal type? Let me begin with a negative description. He no longer belongs exclusively to a single culture, identifies himself with a single area of the earth, or conceives himself as in possession, through his religion or his science, of an exclusive key to truth; nor does he pride himself on his race or his nationality, as if the accidents of birth were in some way specially laudable: that democratic parody of ancient feudal pride. His roots in his region, his family, his neighborhood will be deep, and that depth itself will be a tie with other men: but one part of his nature stays constantly in touch with the larger world through both his religion and his politics, and remains open to its influences and its demands.

The balanced man has the mobility of the migratory worker of the nineteenth century without his rootlessness: he has the friendliness toward people of other cultures that we see most admirably in the native Hawaiian; and with the habits so engendered goes a lessening of his conceit over what is exclusively indigenous. With respect to his own region, he observes two rules: first he cultivates every part of it to its utmost, not merely because it is near and dear, but because it can thus contribute its specialties and individualities to other places and peoples; and second, when he finds his own region deficient in what is essential for full human growth, he reaches out, to the ends of the earth if need be, to bring into it what is missing—seeking the best and making it his own, as Emerson and Thoreau, in little Concord, reached out for the Hindu and Persian classics.

Into the balance of the new man, accordingly, will go elements that are not native to his race, his culture, his region, even if the place he identifies himself with be as large and multifarious as Europe. The savor of his own idiosyncrasy and individuality will be brought out, rather than lessened, by this inclusiveness. So in him the old divisions between townsman and countryman, between Greek and barbarian, between Christian and pagan, between native and outlander, between Western civilization and Eastern civilization, will be softened and in time effaced. Instead of the harsh and coarse contrasts of the past, there will be rich fusions and blendings, with the strength and individuality that good hybrids so often show: this one-world intermixture will but carry further a process visible in the rise of most earlier civilizations.

The change that will produce the balanced man will perhaps occur first in the minds of the older generation: but it is the young who will have the audacity and courage to carry it through. In any event, the new person is, to begin with, one who has honestly confronted his own life, has digested its failures and been re-activated by his awareness of his sins, and has re-oriented his purposes. If need be, he has made public acknowledgment of such errors as involved any considerable part of his community. What has gone wrong outside himself he accepts as part and parcel of what has gone wrong within himself: but similarly, where in his own life he has had a fresh vision of the good or has given form to truth or beauty, he is eager to share it with his fellows.

The capital act of the new man is an assumption of responsibility: he does not transfer the blame for his personal misfortunes to his parents, his elders, his associates, his circumstances: he refuses to make his own burden lighter by treating himself as a victim of processes over which he could have no control, even when he has innocently suffered: for he knows that in the moral life future intentions are more significant than past causes. On the map that science and objective investigation supply him, he superimposes his own plan of life. So the balanced person treats his own situation, however formidable or threatening, as the raw material he must master and mold. But his humility, born of self-awareness, has another side to it: confidence in his own powers of creation.

Confidence in creation: a sense of the rich potentialities of life and of endless alternatives, beyond those that the immediate moment or the immediate culture offers. Confidence in creation, as opposed to the fixations, the rigidities, the narrow alternatives of the existing economic systems and cultural schemes: yes, here precisely is the deepest difference between the new person and the old, who gave to external conditions and external stimuli the initiative that living organisms and above all living persons must keep for themselves. Those who have this confidence are not afraid to break with the existing patterns, however compulsive and authoritative they may seem; and they are not afraid to make departures on radically different lines, merely because they may meet with rebuff or failure. Such confidence once existed in a high degree among the great industrialists who girdled the planet with railroad lines, steamships, ocean cables, and factories; and those whose task it is to build a new world on the ruins of our disintegrating civilization must have that faith in even fuller measure. The new person, because he has not feared to transform himself, is capable of facing the world in a similar mood of adventurous amelioration.

Only those who have confronted the present crisis in all its dimensions will have the strength to repent of their own sins and those of their community, to confront and overcome the evils that threaten us, and to re-affirm the goods of the past that will serve as foundation for the goods of the future that we have still to create. For those who have undergone these changes, life is good and the expansion and intensification of life is good. To live actively through every organ and still remain whole: to identify oneself loyally with the community and yet to emerge from it, with free choices and new goals: to live fully in the moment and to possess in that moment all that eternity might bring: to re-create in one's consciousness the whole in which man lives and moves and has his being—these are essential parts of the new affirmation of life. The rest lies with God.

Without fullness of experience, length of days is nothing. When fullness of life has been achieved, shortness of days is nothing. That is perhaps why the young, before they have been frustrated and lamed, have usually so little fear of death: they live by intensities that the elderly have forgotten.

This experience of fulfillment through wholeness is the true answer to the brevity of man's days. The awakened person seeks to live so that any day might be good enough to be his last. By the actuarial tables he knows, perhaps, that his expectation of life at birth is almost three score and ten; but he knows something more precious than this: that there are moments of such poignant intensity and fullness, moments when every part of the personality is mobilized into a single act or a single intuition, that they outweigh the contents of a whole tame lifetime. Those moments embrace eternity; and if they are fleeting, it is because men remain finite creatures whose days are measured.

When these awakened personalities begin to multiply, the load of anxiety that hangs over the men of our present-day culture will perhaps begin to lift. Instead of gnawing dread, there will be a healthy sense of expectancy, of hope without self-deception, based upon the ability to formulate new plans and purposes: purposes which, because they grow out of a personal reorientation and renewal, will in time lead to the general replenishment of life. Such goals will not lose value through the changes that time and chance and the wills of other men will work on them, in the course of their realization; nor will the prospect of many delays and disappointments keep those who are awakened from putting them into action at the earliest opportunity. Nothing is unthinkable, nothing impossible to the balanced person, provided it arises out of the needs of life and is dedicated to life's further development.

Even in his most rational procedures, the balanced person allows a place for the irrational and the unpredictable: he knows that catastrophe and miracle are both possible. Instead of feeling frustrated by these uncontrollable elements, he counts upon them to quicken the adventure of life by their very unforeseeableness: they are but part of the cosmic weather whose daily challenge enlivens every activity.

Life is itself forever precarious and unstable, and in no manner does it promise a tame idyll or a static utopia: the new person, no less than the old, will know bafflement, tragedy, sacrifice, and defeat, as well as fulfillment—but even in desperate situations he will be saved from despair by sharing Walt Whitman's consciousness that battles may be lost in the same spirit that they are won, and that a courageous effort consecrates an unhappy end. While the conditions he confronts are formidable, the initiative nevertheless remains with man, once he accepts his own responsibility as a guardian of life. With the knowledge man now possesses, he may control the knowledge that threatens to choke him: with the power he now commands he may control the power that would wipe him out: with the values he has created, he may replace a routine of life based upon a denial of values. Only treason to his own sense of the divine can rob the new person of his creativity.

Harsh days and bitter nights may still lie ahead for each of us in his own person, and for mankind as a whole, before we overcome the present forces of disintegration. But throughout the world, there is a faint glow of color on the topmost twigs, the glow of the swelling buds that announce, despite the frosts and storms to come, the approach of spring: signs of life, signs of integration, signs of a deeper faith for living and of an approaching general renewal of humanity. The day and the hour are at hand when our individual purposes and ideals, reenforced by our neighbors', will unite in a new drama of life that will serve other men as it serves ourselves.

The way we must follow is untried and heavy with difficulty; it will test to the utmost our faith and our powers. But it is the way toward life, and those who follow it will prevail.

What time is it now? MINUTES _____

SECONDS _____

What is your reading time for this selection? MINUTES _____

SECONDS _____

Now, answer the following questions. Do *not* refer back to the article.

Comprehension quiz

1. Changes in civilization take place
   a imperceptibly.
   b suddenly.
   c separately.
   d obviously.

2. The object of social change is to
   a cause changes in civilization.
   b produce a new social person.
   c force antiquated people and things "out of the picture."
   d make possible a new drama of culture.

3. The balanced individual is
   a exclusively indigenous.
   b in possession of an exclusive key to truth.
   c truly cosmopolitan.
   d incurably religious.

4. The characteristic individualism of the balanced man will be
   a resolved.
   b accentuated.
   c suppressed.
   d amalgamated.

5. The change that will produce the balanced man will perhaps occur first in the minds of
   a those men of vision of our own time.
   b the younger generation.
   c the older generation.
   d the mature thinkers of any civilization.

6. The deepest difference between the new person and the old is
    a an absence of prejudice.
    b an absence of provincialism.
    c a possession of confidence.
    d the ability to create.

7. The young have little fear of death because they live with
    a optimism.
    b hopefulness.
    c assurance.
    d intensity.

8. Which of the following quotations echoes a phase of Mumford's philosophy in this selection?
    a "They also serve who only stand and wait."
    b "Art is long, and time is fleeting."
    c "Whoso would be a man must be a nonconformist."
    d "The mills of God grind slowly, yet they grind exceedingly small."

9. Mumford's philosophy is basically a philosophy of
    a optimism.
    b pessimism.
    c theism.
    d materialism.

10. Select the best title for this selection:
    a The Main Trends in Today's World
    b Social Change
    c Man and Superman
    d Utopia Tomorrow

How Clearly Do You Recognize the Main Ideas?

The ability to recognize and to recall the main ideas of the author is one of the first steps in efficient reading. In Test I of this series you attempted to identify the main ideas from a selection which was easy to read. Now try again, on a selection which is somewhat more difficult.

As before, you will have a list of ten statements. Five of these are statements of main ideas, five are not main ideas. As in Test I, the thought may be paraphrased. Indicate your choice by encircling the number of the statement.

1. Nothing is impossible to the balanced person.

2. The balanced man will have deep roots in his own region, family and neighborhood.
3. The capital act of the new man is an assumption of responsibility.
4. The new person accepts what has gone wrong outside of himself as part and parcel of what has gone wrong within himself.
5. The way we must follow is heavy with difficulty.
6. Even in his most rational procedures the balanced person allows a place for the irrational and unpredictable.
7. The balanced man refuses to victimize himself.
8. The balanced man will exhibit certain fusions and blendings.
9. Life is forever precarious and unstable.
10. The great industrialists achieved because of their boundless ingenuity.

What Is Your GKQ (General-knowledge Quotient)?

In the test you have just read, there were a number of instances where you needed to call upon your general background knowledge for the text to be most meaningful. The following questions are a brief test of your GKQ on the selection which you have just read. Answer the following with a simple, straightforward, informative statement.

1. "Emerson and Thoreau, in little Concord, reached out for the Hindu and Persian classics." Explain.

----

2. "Instead of the harsh and coarse contrasts of the past, there will be rich fusions and blendings, with the strength and individuality that good hybrids so often show." What are hybrids?

----

3. ". . . his expectation of life at birth is almost three score [years] and ten." The words "three score [years] and ten" is a quoted phrase? What is its origin?

----

4. "Life . . . does not promise a static utopia." What is a utopia?

_____

_____

5. "By sharing Walt Whitman's consciousness that battles may be lost in the same spirit that they are won." Who was Walt Whitman?

_____

_____

What Is Your Word Power?

In the sentences given below, select a synonym for the italicized word from the choices which follow it. Although the sentences have been taken from the article which you read in connection with Test III, they have been edited for purposes of this test.

1. By the actuarial tables, he knows, perhaps . . .
   actuarial: *a* actual   *b* insurance   *c* census   *d* estimated

2. The new person is capable of facing the world in a mood of adventurous amelioration.
   amelioration: *a* merrymaking   *b* courage   *c* spirit
                       d improvement

3. The conditions he confronts are formidable.
   formidable: *a* friendly   *b* ceremonial   *c* dreadful
                     d harmful

4. There will be rich fusions.
   fusion: *a* blending   *b* design   *c* color   *d* metal

5. The savor of his own idiosyncrasy will be brought out.
   idiosyncrasy: *a* imbecility   *b* quality   *c* thought
                       d peculiarity

6. He has a lessened conceit over what is exclusively indigenous.
   indigenous: *a* foreign   *b* native   *c* unknown   *d* personal

7. He thinks that the accidents of birth are in someway especially laudable.
   laudable: *a* noteworthy   *b* outstanding   *c* praiseworthy
                   d important

8. He identifies himself with a place as large and multifarious as Europe.
   multifarious: *a* varied   *b* scattered   *c* populous
                       d growing

9. Those were moments of poignant intensity.

    poignant: *a* expectant   *b* fearful   *c* keen
    d unforgettable

10. He had a sense of the potentialities of life.

    potentialities: *a* responsibilities   *b* frustrations   *c* actualities
    d possibilities

Reading Habit Inventory

For each of the following statements, check under Never, Rarely, Sometimes, Usually, or Always. Do not omit any of the items. Be truthful and be utterly realistic. Represent your reading habits as they actually are.

	Never	Rarely	Sometimes	Usually	Always
1. When I pick up a page of print, I notice the paragraphs specifically.					
2. I read as I drive, with varying rates of speed, depending upon varying reading conditions.					
3. While reading, I find it easy to keep my mind on the material before me.					
4. After I have been reading for a while, I stop reading for a few moments and rest my eyes by looking at some distant object.					
5. I am alert to the role which punctuation plays in aiding me to get the meaning.					
6. When I pick up a piece of reading matter for the first time, I look for certain specific items which will aid me in reading the piece more efficiently.					
7. I read groups of words at one glance.					

	Never	Rarely	Sometimes	Usually	Always

8. I notice a distinctive style, or flavor, of the author.

9. I enjoy reading.

10. I can read for long periods of time without a feeling of eye-fatigue or tiredness.

11. After I read a paragraph, if required to do so, I could sum up the main idea clearly and briefly in my own words.

12. I make a practice of skimming articles frequently.

13. In reading a paragraph I usually try to see the organization of its thought content: I look for a main idea, and the details which support the main idea.

14. I do not lose my place, or skip words or lines, while reading.

15. I am mildly conscious of grammatical structure while reading.

16. I feel comfortable and perfectly at ease while reading.

17. In reading larger units of writing (articles, chapters, etc.) I try to see the outline and total structure of the author's thought.

18. I have little difficulty in remembering what I read.

19. When I read, especially for any length of time, I make sure that the page before me is adequately illuminated.

20. When I read, I am reading for some definite purpose, and I try to keep that purpose clearly in mind as I read.

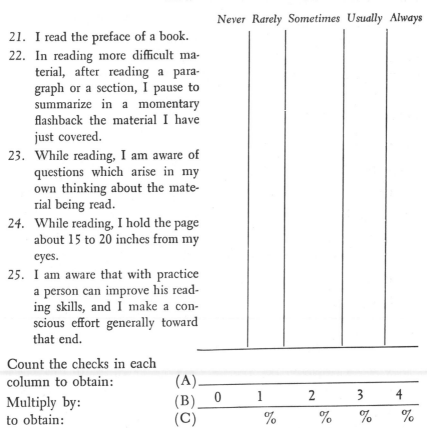

Never Rarely Sometimes Usually Always

21. I read the preface of a book.

22. In reading more difficult material, after reading a paragraph or a section, I pause to summarize in a momentary flashback the material I have just covered.

23. While reading, I am aware of questions which arise in my own thinking about the material being read.

24. While reading, I hold the page about 15 to 20 inches from my eyes.

25. I am aware that with practice a person can improve his reading skills, and I make a conscious effort generally toward that end.

Count the checks in each column to obtain: (A) _____

Multiply by: (B)   0   1   2   3   4

to obtain: (C)   %   %   %   %

Now add the figures in row C for your final score: _____%

How well do you read—now?

Turn back to the Answer Key and check your answers for each of the three tests against those given there. In the completion questions, if your answer is equivalent *in meaning*, but different in wording, allow full credit. If there is a difference in meaning between your answer and the one suggested in the Key, deny yourself credit. Mark the Summary Skill Sheet below.

Then, turn back to p. 46 and compare your scores for this set of tests with the ones there. The difference in the two sets of scores will indicate areas of improvement and areas where you still need to strive for further improvement in your reading skills. One thing you should remember: you have, perhaps, been reading inefficiently for many years. Some of your reading difficulty may reach back to the days of grade school. It takes time, and a great deal of persistent practice and effort to overcome the wrong habits that have been firmly fixed over the years. Study the two test summaries. Any improvement should be encouraging. Then compare your scores with your plottings on the improvement graphs.

Summary of Your Reading Skills

Your speed and level of comprehension:

Test I: Fairly Easy Reading

Rate _____wpm

Comprehension _____%

Reading Index _____

Test II: Standard, or Average Reading

Rate _____wpm

Comprehension _____%

Reading Index _____

Test III: Fairly Difficult to Difficult Reading

Rate _____wpm

Comprehension _____%

Reading Index _____

Your ability to comprehend main ideas:

Test I _____%

Test III _____%

Your Word Power:

Test II _____%

Test III _____%

Your General-knowledge Quotient:

Test III _____%

Your Habits of Reading:

Inventory of Reading Habits _____%

Date: _____

Chapter Twenty

Word power!

W ORDS ON the page are like red blood cells in the body. Both are carriers. As red corpuscles carry oxygen to the tissues, so words carry the thought of the writer to the mind of the reader.

Anemia can be fatal—whether it be in blood cells, or in word cells. He who reads words without knowing their meaning is suffering from reader's anemia.

Tests II and III may have revealed to you a need to acquire a broader, more useful vocabulary. If so, this chapter was designed for you.

Secure a good dictionary, and use it freely. In each chapter, either in the discussion or in the reading selections, certain words may be unfamiliar. In so far as you do not know these words, your reading will suffer. In this section those words which are likely to be troublesome are brought together under the heading of the chapter in which they appear.

When you look up a word in your dictionary, do a *thorough* job. Nearly everybody only half-uses a dictionary. A dictionary is a library of information in miniature, the eloquence of the orators piecemeal, the glory of English literature arranged alphabetically.

A dictionary is meant to be used exhaustively. Words that you do not know are the words which you should master completely. When you look up a word, read the *whole* definition. Read every word of the entry from the beginning to the end of it. And when you read a definition, look for certain matters specifically:

1. *Look at the word carefully:* note its spelling, configuration, its "look."
2. *Note the pronunciation of the word:* pronounce it to yourself, note the long and short vowels and the location of the accent mark.
3. *Scrutinize the parts of the word:* its prefix, root, and suffix.
4. *Study the etymology of the word:* every word has a history. It came into English from some other language—from Latin or Greek or Anglo-Saxon. Sometimes knowing what the word meant originally will help you remember its current meaning. This is the valuable information that you will find within brackets in the entry.
5. *Read the definitions carefully:* all of them. Remember that each number, 1, 2, 3, etc., means a new way in which the word is used. Sometimes a general meaning has submeanings indicated as *a, b, c,* under a numeral. Changes happen fast when you read definitions. Be alert.
6. *Pay attention to examples of usage:* the use of a word will frequently be illustrated in the definition. Note these examples carefully.
7. *Note the part of speech:* it will help you in using the word to express your own thoughts.
8. *Consider the synonyms:* every word has a distinctive quality, a shade of meaning which is peculiar to it alone. Sometimes the characteristic quality of a particular word can be best appreciated when that word is compared with its synonyms.
9. *Contrast the word with its antonyms:* you can appreciate the meaning of the word even more by making a direct contrast with the opposite meaning.

    On pp. 422–423 you will find specimen pages from a dictionary.[1] Notice how much information is condensed into a brief space.
10. *Apply what you have learned:* after you have studied a word with the dictionary, always do two additional things:

    a Be on the alert for this word in your reading. You are certain to come across it somewhere in the chapter. When you see it, note just how *the author* has used it.

    b Use it yourself as often as possible in your *thinking,* in your *writing,* in your *speaking.* Don't drag it in; just use it naturally. This will integrate the word into your usable vocabulary.

---

[1] By permission. From An Outline for Dictionary Study. Designed for Use with Webster's New Collegiate Dictionary, copyright, 1954, by G. & C. Merriam Co.

By processing each word that you do not know as suggested here, you will not only recognize that word the next time you see it, but you will also *know* it. It will be yours—all, totally, completely, and forever yours. You will be building power into your vocabulary.

How can you continue to improve your vocabulary?

While the words that may prove troublesome have been selected for you in this book, you will not want to stop your efforts with this list. Vocabulary improvement should become a lifelong habit. How are you to continue to add to your word hoard? Here are some suggestions:

1. *Keep on the Lookout for Words That You Do Not Know.* Many people with poor vocabularies are seldom alert to the new, the unfamiliar word. Unless it is a superobstacle, it makes no impression on them. Many people think that for a word to be difficult it must be a "big word," many-syllabled, capable of drawing attention to itself. This is not so. Many of the polysyllabic words are those that fall apart the most easily. A little knowledge of Latin and Greek prefixes, suffixes, and root elements, and the big words tumble fast. It's the litle fellows who make the trouble. Think of the simple words, the one-syllable words that are hazy in your thinking. Each day for a few minutes try to define those words that you feel you know, but whose meanings you cannot readily put into your own words. Because you have seen a word does not mean that you *know* it. You really know a word only when it comes freely, almost unconsciously to mind in expressing your thoughts.

2. *When You Meet Unfamiliar Words in Your Reading, Try to Get Their Meaning from the Context.* Maybe the word is not so difficult as you may think at first. Read on. Unless the whole thought goes to pieces, don't run for a dictionary at the sight of every new word. The rest of the sentence, or of the paragraph, may give you a hint as to the meaning of the new word. Let's take the word "quirt." Now, do you know the meaning of the word "quirt"? Probably not. But suppose you read this sentence: "He ran out of the house, jumped upon his horse, and, lashing the animal with his quirt, was gone in a cloud of dust." Still, you may not be *sure* what a quirt is, but the sentence has helped you a great deal. In fact, you might even *guess* that a quirt is a whip used by riders, which is precisely what it is: "a riding whip with a short handle, and a lash of braided rawhide." Thousands of words can be

Pronunciation

Centered Period for Syllabic Division

Subject Label

Principal Parts

Idiomatic Usage

Discriminated Synonyms

Verb Phrase

Usage Label

Foreign Word

Capitalization

Word Story

Plural Form

Antonym

pawn'er (pôn'ẽr), **pawn'or** (pôn'ẽr; pôn·ôr'), *n.* *Law.* One who pawns or pledges anything as security.

pawn'shop' (pôn'shŏp'), *n.* A pawnbroker's shop.

paw·paw' (*see* PAPAW), *n.* Var. of PAPAW.

pax (păks), *n.* [L.] **1.** Peace: — deified by the Romans. **2.** *R.C.Ch.* A tablet bearing a figure or symbol of Christ, the Virgin Mary, or a saint, which in medieval times was kissed by the priest and the people, before the Communion.

∥**pax vo·bis'cum** (vō·bĭs'kŭm). [L.] Peace (be) with you.

pax'wax' (păks'wăks'), *n.* [For *faxwax*, fr. AS. *feax* hair + a word akin to *weaxan* to grow.] In many mammals, the median ligament of the back of the neck, composed of yellow elastic tissue and used in supporting the head.

pay (pā), *v. t.*; PAYED (pād); PAY'ING. [OF. *peier*, *poier*, fr. L. *picare* to pitch, fr. *pix* pitch.] To smear or coat, as a vessel's bottom, a seam, etc., with a waterproof composition, as of tallow, resin, etc.

pay (pā), *v. t.*; PAID (pād) or. *Obs.* exc. in sense 6. PAYED; PAY'ING. [OF. *paier*, fr. L. *pacare* to pacify, appease, fr. *pax, pacis*, peace.] **1.** To satisfy (one) for service rendered, property delivered, etc.; remunerate. **2.** To give (something due) in return, satisfaction, or requital; also, to discharge indebtedness for; settle, as a bill. **3.** To make compensation or retaliation for. **4.** To give, offer, or make, freely or as fitting; as, to *pay* court or a visit. **5.** To be profitable to; also, bring in as a return. **6.** To pass out, as a rope; — now with *out* or *away*. — *v. i.* **1.** To give a recompense; make payment. **2.** To be profitable; to be worth the expense, effort, or the like.

Syn. Pay, compensate, remunerate, satisfy, reimburse, indemnify, repay, recompense, requite mean to give money or its equivalent in return for something. Pay implies the discharge of an obligation incurred; **compensate**, as here considered, a making up for services rendered or help given; remunerate, more clearly, a paying for services rendered; **satisfy**, paying a person that which is asked or required by law; reimburse, a return of money that has been expended; **indemnify**, a reimbursing for loss suffered through fire, accident, damage by war, or the like; repay, a paying back in kind or amount; recompense, often, a compensating for services rendered but, sometimes, for losses or injuries sustained; requite, a reciprocating or retaliation, often but not necessarily in kind.

pay off. **1.** To pay; specif., to pay in full and discharge. **2.** To requite. **3.** To allow to run off, as a thread or cord. **4.** *Colloq.* To yield full return, either to one's advantage or disadvantage; also, to attain full effectiveness. **5.** *Naut.* To turn (a vessel) to leeward. — *n.* Act of paying; payment. **2.** State or status of being paid,

pay'nim (pā'nĭm), *n.* [OF. *paienisme* heathendom, fr. LL. *paganismus* paganism.] *Archaic.* Pagans or pagan countries; also, a pagan; an infidel, esp. a Mohammedan.

pay'off' (pā'ôf'), *n.* *Chiefly Colloq.* **1.** Act or time of paying employees' wages. **2.** Repayment or accrual for settlement at the outcome of an enterprise; reward or retribution. **3.** Climax of an incident or enterprise; specif., the denouement of a narrative. **4.** Decisive fact or factor resolving a situation, bringing about a definitive conclusion; as, the opinion of the Tax Court on taxability is the *payoff*. — *adj.* *Colloq.* Yielding results in the final test; rewarding or decisive.

pay'roll' (pā'rōl'), *n.* A paymaster's list of persons entitled to pay, with the amounts due to each; also, the amount necessary, or the money, for distribution to those on such a list.

∥**pay'sage'** (pā'ē·zàzh'), *n.* [F.] A landscape or a landscape picture.

PC (pē'sē'). [patrol craft.] *U.S. Navy.* A fast patrol craft equipped with submarine-detection devices, 3-inch gun, machine guns, antiaircraft guns, and depth charges.

pea (pē), *n.*; *pl.* PEAS (pēz) or PEASE (pēz) (see *Note* below). [AS. *pise, pl. pisan*, fr. LL. *pisa*, fr. L. *pisum*, *pl. pisa*, fr. Gr. *pison*, *pl. pisos*. The vowel may have been influenced by OF. *peis*, fr. L. *pisum*. The final *s* was misunderstood in English as a plural ending.] **1.** Any plant of a family (Fabaceae, the pea family) of herbs, shrubs, and trees, the fruit of which is a true pod or legume. **2.** The round, smooth or wrinkled, edible seed borne severally in dehiscent pods by a vine (*Pisum sativum*) of this family; also, the similar angular seed of a related plant (*P. arvense*). **3.** Any of various leguminous plants or their seeds, resembling the common pea; as, the sweet *pea*, cow*pea*, etc. **4.** Something like a pea, as in size.

☞ The plural *peas* was formerly used to indicate a definite number, as contrasted with the collective plural *pease*; the tendency now is to use *peas* as plural in all senses.

peace (pēs), *n.* [OF. *pais, paiz* (F. *paix*), fr. L. *pax, pacis*.] **1.** A pact or agreement to end hostilities, between those who have been at war or in a state of hostility. **2.** A state of tranquillity or quiet; esp.: **a** Freedom from civil disturbance or war. **b** Public order or security, as provided by law; as, a breach of the *peace*. **3.** Harmony in personal relations; mutual concord. **4.** Freedom from fears, agitating passions, moral conflict, etc. **5.** One who or that which makes or maintains peace. — *v. i.* To become quiet; be silent; — *Obs.*, except in the imperative.

peace'a·ble (pēs'à·b'l), *adj.* Being in or at peace; not disposed to war, disorder, etc.; pacific. — **peace'a·ble·ness**, *n.* — **peace'a·bly**, *adv.*

peace'ful (-fŏŏl; -f'l), *adj.* **1.** *Now Rare.* Pacific; peaceable. **2.** Possessing, enjoying, or marked by, peace; tranquil; also, of or pert. to peace. — **Syn.** See CALM. — **Ant.** Turbulent. — **peace'ful·ly**, *adv.* — **peace'ful·ness**, *n.*

peace'mak'er (-māk'ẽr), *n.* One who makes peace or reconciles parties at variance. — **peace'mak'ing**, *n.* & *adj.*

peasant

peace offering. A propitiatory gift; esp., *Bib.*, a ceremonial propitiatory sacrifice.

Biblical Term

peace officer. A civil officer whose duty it is to preserve the public peace, as a sheriff, constable, or policeman.

peace pipe. The calumet.

peach (pēch), *v. t.* [ME. *apechen*, fr. AF.] *Obs.* To impeach; indict. — *v. i. Obs. exc. Slang.* To turn informer; to blab.

peach, *n.* [OF. *peche, pesche,* fr. LL. *persica,* fr. L. *Persicum* (sc. *malum*) Persian apple, peach.] **1.** Any of a family (Amygdalaceae the peach family) of trees and shrubs distinguished by the single pistil with united carpels, and the drupe, or stone fruit. **2.** The sweet, juicy fruit of a tree (*Amygdalus persica*), of this family, botanically a drupe, with a pulpy white or yellow mesocarp. **3.** The sessile pink flower (**peach blossom**) of this tree, borne on the naked twigs in early spring. It is the State flower of Delaware. **4.** One likened to a peach, as in beauty. **5.** A color, reddish red-yellow in hue, of low saturation and very high brilliance. See COLOR. — *adj.* Of the color peach.

peach′blow′ (pēch′blō′), *n.* [*peach* + *blow* a flower.] A glaze of a delicate purplish-pink color likened to that of peach blooms; — applied esp. to a Chinese porcelain.

pea′cock′ (pē′kŏk′), *n.* ⋯ PLURAL ʼote. 3. ⌈ ⌉ *vecok* ʼ ʼS. pēa

peacock blue. A color, bluish green-blue in hue, of medium saturation and low brilliance. See COLOR. — **pea′cock′-blue′,** *adj.*

Hyphened Word

pea′fowl′ (pē′foul′), *n.* The peacock or peahen.

peag (pēg), *n.* Also **peage** (pēg). Wampum.

pea green. A color, yellowish yellow-green in hue, of low saturation and medium brilliance. See COLOR. — **pea′-green′,** *adj.*

Noun Phrase in Alphabetic Place

pea′hen′ (pē′hĕn′), *n.* The female of the peacock.

pea jacket. [Prob. fr. D. *pij, pije,* coat of a coarse woolen stuff.] A sailor's thick loose woolen double-breasted coat.

peak (pēk), *v. i.* To grow thin and sickly.

peak, *n.* [Var. of 1st PIKE.] **1.** The sharp or pointed end of anything. **2.** [For earlier *pike,* fr. Sp. & Pg. *pico.*] Specif.: a *Now Local.* A headland or promontory. **b** The top of a hill or mountain ending in a point; one of the crests of a range; often, the whole mountain, esp. when isolated. **c** The projecting front part of a cap or the like. **3.** The topmost point; summit; also, the highest point, as in a graph; maximum. **4.** *Naut.* **a** The upper aftermost corner of a fore-and-aft sail. **b** The narrow part of a vessel's bow or stern, or the part of the hold in it. **5.** A point formed by the hair on the forehead; — chiefly in *widow's peak,* orig. such a point on a woman's forehead, now often a similar point on a man's forehead. — **Syn.** See SUMMIT. — *v. t.* To cause to come to a peak; specif., *Naut.,* to raise to a position perpendicular, or more nearly so, as a gaff.

Special Meaning

Subject Label

peaked (pēkt; pēk′ĕd; -ĭd), *adj.* **1.** Pointed; having a peak. **2.** (*pron. usually* pēk′ĕd; -ĭd) [From PEAK to grow thin.] *Chiefly Colloq.* Thin; emaciated.

peal (pēl), *n.* [Shortened fr. APPEAL.] **1.** *Bell Ringing.* **a** Loosely, a set of bells tuned to the tones of the major scale for change ringing. **b** A complete set of changes on a given number of bells; esp., the series on seven bells. **c** Any shorter performance than a full set of changes; as, a wedding *peal.* **2.** A loud sound, or a succession of loud sounds, as of bells or thunder. — *v. i.* To give out peals; resound. — *v. t.* **1.** *Obs.* To assail or din, as with noise or loud sounds. **2.** To sound forth in or as in a peal or peals; noise abroad.

pe′an (pē′ăn). Var. of PAEAN.

Variant Spelling

pea′nut′ (pē′nŭt′; -nŭt), *n.* A Brazilian herb (*Arachis hypogaea*) of the pea family, of erect habit, whose peduncles bend after fertilization and push the pods into the ground, where they ripen; also, the nutlike seed of this plant. **peanut oil** is expressed from these seeds; **peanut butter** is made from these seeds roasted, ground, and moistened.

pear (pâr), *n.* [AS. *pere, peru,* fr. LL. *pera, pira,* fr. L. *pirum,* pl. *pira.*] **a** The fleshy pome fruit of a tree (genus *Pyrus,* esp. *P. communis*) of the apple family. **b** The tree bearing this fruit.

pearl (pûrl), *n.* [OF. *perle,* fr. ML. *perla, perula.*] **1.** A dense concretion, lustrous and varying in color, formed as an abnormal growth within the shell of some mollusks, and used as a gem. **2.** Something resembling a pearl in shape, size, color, beauty, or value. **3. a** Mother-of-pearl; nacre. **b** In full **pearl blue.** The color of mother-of-pearl, a nearly neutral gray (slightly bluish) of high brilliance. See COLOR. **4.** *Print.* A size of type (5 point). See TYPE. — *v. t.* **1.** To adorn with pearls. **2.** To form into small round grains, as barley. **3.** To give to or suffuse with a pearly luster. — *v. i.* To fish or search for pearls. — *adj.* **1.** Of, like, or set with pearls. **2.** Formed into small round grains; as, pearl barley; pearl tapioca. — **pearl′er,** *n.*

pearl. Var. of PURL.

pearl′ash′ (pûrl′ăsh′), *n.* Purified potash. See POTASH, 1.

pearl gray. The color of a fine pearl, an early neutral gray of high brilliance. See COLOR. — **pearl′-gray′** (-grā′; 2), *adj.*

pearl′ite (pûrl′īt), *n.* [*pearl* + *-ite.*] **1.** *Metal.* The readily fusible alloy of carbon and iron, containing 0.85 per cent carbon. **2.** *Petrog.* = PERLITE. — **pearl-it′ic** (pûrl-ĭt′ĭk), *adj.*

pearl′y (pûr′lĭ), *adj.*; PEARL′I·ER (-lĭ-ĕr); -I·EST. Of or like pearl or mother-of-pearl; adorned with or abounding in pearls.

Cross Reference

pearly nautilus. See NAUTILUS, 1.

pear′main (pâr′mān), *n.* [OF. *permain, parmain.*] An apple of one of several different varieties.

peart (pērt), **peart′ly.** Dial. vars. of PERT, etc.

peas′ant (pĕz′ănt; -'nt), *n.* [OF. *paisant, paisent,* fr. *pais, pays,* land, country, fr. LL. *pagensis,* fr. L. *pagus* country district. See

Etymology

423

learned from their context. Guard against dashing for your dictionary every time you see an unfamiliar configuration of letters. Read on; you may not need your dictionary—at least, not at that moment. The reader's first job is always to read!

3. *Note Those Words That You Recognize as Strangers.* Even though you comprehend the meaning of new words from the context, reading with a pencil is a good habit when you are intent on enlarging your vocabulary. Always read as far as you can without the aid of a dictionary, but when you come across new words, put a check mark either immediately before the word or in the margin at the end of the line in which the word occurs. *After* you have finished reading, go back to clean up the debris.

4. *Keep a List of the New Words You Come Across in Your Reading.* Some people do this in a little memo book, like an address book, listing only the words. At odd moments, while waiting for a train, while riding on a bus, at those times when you cannot do much else—get out your memo book and test yourself to see how many of the words you know offhand. Other people put the word they do not know on one side of a 3- by 5-inch card, one word to a card. Only the word you are learning goes on one side of the card. On the other side you may put the data about the word: its pronunciation, meanings, etymology, and use in a sentence. You might even make a game of these cards—a kind of do-you-know-this-one contest, and play it either by yourself or with your friends. Learning words *can* be lots of fun, and nearly everyone, surprisingly enough, is interested in it.

5. *Carry a Pocket Dictionary with You.* Use it for down-the-column study, going straight through it, from beginning to end, use it to look up individual words that you do not know, or both. As you look up each unfamiliar word, put a little check mark in the margin before the word. These check marks are helpful in review. They will rebuke you gently if you look at the word later and do not immediately recall its meaning. They will say to you, in effect, "You have looked me up once; you should remember who I am."

6. *After You Have Looked Up New Words and Made a List of Them, Re-read the Material in Which These Words Occurred.* By so doing you will accomplish two things:

a. You will see those words again in the very same verbal environment in which you first met them. They will not look nearly so formidable or unusual to you the second time you read them.

b. You will see the way in which the author has used these words. In this way you will get the feeling for the word, the connotation, the "atmosphere" in which the word is at home.

7. *As You Read, Be Sensitive to the Fine Shades of Meaning of Some Words.* Sometimes one word will light up a whole sentence with new, added meaning. Such a word often has a deep, rich fullness which springs from the root of the word itself. Part of your vocabulary development is to have an appreciation for the delicate nuance as well as the power of the word.

8. *Play Word Games.* Crossword puzzles, Scrabble, charades, and similar games exercise your vocabulary. They place emphasis upon the importance of the exact word, a word of specified dimensions, of particular length. The more you work, or play, with words, the more interesting, familiar, and usable they become.

Words *can* be a great deal of fun, and the acquiring of a versatile and forceful vocabulary is an exciting game. What we need most is to start playing it!

Words that may be troublemakers in your reading

Chapter Four

adept	dominant	insomnia	subterranean
criteria	facet	medially	technique
denizen	frustration	mediocrity	truncate
denote	functional	peripheral	ultimate
deviate	harass	proclivity	unique

Chapter Five

accelerated	critical	imminent	pivot
aphetic	eddy	improvisation	rudiment
category	elude	ingenious	substantiality
cognizance	evanescent	ornate	vicissitude
copious	heft	pathos	vogue

Chapter Six

cardinal	ellipsis	metaphor	paradox
cumulus	exigencies	omniscience	postulate
deftly	indefeasibly	omnivorous	simile
demagogue	labyrinth	ordain	sublimation
diaphanous	lucidity	panorama	syntax

Chapter Seven

abracadabra	aurora	incredibly	nuance
abstruse	corona	ingest	redundant
adroit	corpuscles	metamorphosis	stereotype
alleviate	crucial	meticulous	tortuous
augment	demarcation	nacreous	unconscionable

Chapter Eight

affinity	ineptitude	molecule	savor
alchemy	infinitesimal	placid	synthetic
blandly	inordinate	pungent	tenacious
derogatory	intangible	ritual	umbrage
ferret	legion	role	unabridged

Chapter Nine

akin	contingent	integrate	potential
aperture	domain	naive	status quo
chronological	entity	nebulous	topographical
concomitant	expedite	optimum	trivia
conjecture	generic	orient (verb)	typographical

Chapter Ten

abstain	esthetic	monochromatic	spectral
audacity	flaunted	phenomenon	spectroscope
bombast	hypothetical	raze	stereoscope
colleague	irony	retaliation	succumb
corollary	languish	sequential	ultimate

Chapter Eleven

acrostic	dexterity	inherent	pertinent
authoritarianism	diametrically	ludicrous	scrupulous
avert	distorted	magnitude	theocracy
culminate	extrapolate	mnemonic	unwittingly
decadence	gregarious	parlance	variant

Chapter Twelve

bias	indiscretion	odyssey	stereotype
bizarre	innate	ornate	subtle
context	innocuous	pander	tabloid
fastidious	legacy	potent	ulterior
gullible	maxim	simultaneously	vicariously

Chapter Thirteen

antithesis	frugal	jargon	prodigious
avocation	germane	*laissez faire*	prognosis
batten	hatch	orthodox	purport
brigandage	idiomatic	postulate	spontaneously
cogent	infallible	probity	tentative

Chapter Fourteen

acuity	epicenter	meticulous	raucous
ancillary	garbled	milieu	scintillate
blatant	Gargantua	nomadic	telescope (verb)
cauldron	gossamer	peripheral	turbulence
ephemeral	itinerant	platen	verbiage

Chapter Fifteen

abscissa	coronary	hypothetical	percentile
bituminous	depict	median	schematic
caries	echelon	mitered	semantics
cessation	fluorine	nostrum	spatial
chicanery	homogeneous	odometer	spurious

Chapter Sixteen

amorphous	circumspect	flux	palm (verb)
ample	compliment	impromptu	periphrase
appertain	consummation	interpose	potentate
chrysalis	envisage	inundate	superfluous
circumlocution	extricate	negotiate	touchstone

Chapter Seventeen

array	fare (verb)	herald (verb)	priority
bristle	feasible	manual	salient
consistent	flimsy	octane	surge
documentation	format	personnel	transition
ebb	garb	prime	unrewarding

Chapter Eighteen

abandon (noun)	browse	tare (noun)	scrutiny
academic	chore	hectic	shabby
backdrop	connoisseur	impend	strait-jacket
bibliography	denouement	intrigue	synthesize
bibliophile	epic	parch	whim

Chapter Twenty

anemia	debris	hoard	rebuke
antonym	environment	lash (noun)	suffix
charade	etymology	piecemeal	synonym
configuration	exhaustively	polysyllable	versatile
corpuscle	formidable	prefix	vowel

Appendix

Reading Improvement and the Use of Instruments

In the professional reading schools the student has at his disposal a number of instruments by means of which he can aid himself in improving his rate of reading, his concentration, and his perceptual acuity and accuracy. These instrumental aids are the tachistoscope, or flashmeter; the reading pacer, or rate accelerator; and reading films. There have also been other devices used for measuring or observing eye movements.

All of these instruments have their place in the hands of the trained specialist. Basically they are motivating and disciplinary devices. They have been widely publicized to the point where nearly every article of a popular nature on reading improvement mentions them as an integral part of the improvement program. For this reason the average person feels that the use of some mechanical aid is almost a necessity if he is to make any real progress in improving his reading skills. This is readily understandable. We are for the most part a gadget-conscious nation. But sooner or later we come face to face with the brutal fact that nothing short of hard work and continuous, concentrated practice ever establishes new habits or improves our skills.

On the whole, the instruments used in reading improvement centers are quite expensive. Most of them are precision instruments, carefully engineered and produced for a limited market. Professional reading specialists who may wish to know where such equipment is available will find the list of principal manufacturers at the end of this section.

For the general reader, the same motivation and the same basic discipline can be had from a judicious use of some very common household items. You have already seen how an ordinary 3- by 5-inch filing card can be employed for improving visual span and simulating tachistoscopic training. There are many more ways of forcing you to improve. That is all the instruments do. Here is a list of suggestions of some simple things which you might try. Because they are simple, do not think that they are ineffective. They employ the same basic *principles* as an expensive piece of equipment. After all, improvement *does* depend upon you. The harder you work, the more you will progress. Here are several suggestions to help you increase your rate of reading.

Improving rate of reading

1. Read against the flowing sands of an ordinary egg timer. The sand takes three minutes to flow from the one compartment to the other. Turn the timer over, so that the sand begins to flow as you start a new paragraph. Put a check mark in the margin opposite the line where you started timing yourself. As you reach the end of each paragraph, glance at the sand in the glass to see if it is still flowing. When the sand stops flowing, check the sentence you have just finished reading.

Next, estimate your wordage. To do this:

a. Count *all* the words in ten consecutive lines.
b. Divide this number by 10. This is the average number of words per line.
c. Now, count the total number of lines read in three minutes.
d. Multiply the number of lines by the average number of words per line. This will give you the total words read.
e. Finally, divide this number by 3 to get your reading rate expressed in words per minute.

2. If you have a clock-type timer, set it for a given time. Usually five minutes is long enough. When it starts timing, you begin reading. At the signal compute your rate in the same way that you did above. This time, however, substitute 5 for 3. Another method of computing your words per minute is to *measure* the total length of the passage read. A ruler is always a handy tool for the reader. It, too, can be used in improving your rate of reading, which we will discuss later.

The reading rate accelerator is a mechanical device which helps you to read faster by means of a slowly descending shutter which slides down over the material being read, covering it at a given rate of speed. Many ways of getting the same result are available to the person who really wishes to improve.

3. Use an ordinary stiff piece of cardboard. Place your book on a firm support and at a slightly inclined angle. Hold the piece of cardboard, which should be wider than the opened book, with both hands. Begin slipping this cardboard screen down upon your reading area. Crowd yourself. Make yourself hurry to keep ahead of the shutter.

4. In place of cardboard use an ordinary ruler, or a 1-inch wooden dowel about a foot long. Grasp these at each end and pull the ruler or roll the dowel down over the page, evenly but steadily. Set a rate as before, which makes you hurry to keep ahead of these advancing objects. Each time you use these devices try to speed their descent just a little more.

5. Another very effective method of making yourself read faster is to take an ordinary sheet of heavy white typewriter paper. Cut into it about 2½ inches from the top a one-inch window, wide enough to reach a quarter of an inch beyond the side of the column of print on the page. With an ordinary book, such a window will frame five or six lines of print. Place the line at which you intend to start reading about the middle of the frame. Then begin to read. At the same time begin to pull the piece of paper toward you, moving the frame down over the page. The lines which you have read will disappear at the upper margin; new lines will appear at the lower one. Aim to keep reading in the mid-portion of the frame. By so doing, you will have some freedom of motion but not too much. Keep moving: while practicing this exercise, you should feel hurried.

Once you begin to draw any of these devices down over the page, do so with a steady, resistless advance. Do not give in to your inclination to slow down in some places and to hurry in others.

That you may find these devices a little distracting at first is only natural. Persevere, however, and in your effort to improve, you will soon forget about the distractions.

Observation of eye movements

Much emphasis has been laid in recent years on the importance of correct eye movements in reading. They are important, but they should not receive overemphasis. You read about eye movements in Chapter Two of this book.

In the laboratory the movements of the eyes in reading—or the saccadic movements, as they are known—are usually studied by means of a specially designed eye camera. There have been many types of these cameras designed by researchers for their own experimental use. Probably one of the best-known commercial instruments of this type is the ophthalmograph, an instrument designed by the American Optical Company and used widely in reading clinics for diagnostic purposes. With the ophthalmograph a beam of light is directed onto the cornea of the eye, from which it is reflected into the eye camera, tracing characteristic "stairways" on a moving 35mm film. Much can be told about the reading habits of the individual, as well as a diagnosis of some physiological factors, from a careful reading of the ophthalmographic record. But reading the ophthalmograph should be left to the specialist.

There are, however, much simpler ways to observe the eye movements of a person who is reading.

1. One simple method is the "pinhole-peep" method. Use this page for the experiment. With an ordinary pin, puncture the page at the center. Have the reader face toward a source of light which will illuminate his face, especially his eyes. Stand facing the reader. Hold the page with the pinhole in it at eye level. Sight through the pinhole. Ask the person to read the printed matter on the other side of the page. Watch carefully through the pinhole. You will see the reader's eyes move across the line with little jerks and stops. At the end of each line, you will see his eyes swing back to the beginning of the next line. Count each time the eyes stop in traversing the line. The efficient reader makes about three stops per line.

Divide the average number of fixations per line into the number of type units per line (a type unit is each letter *and* space in the line) to get the average fixation span in type units.

Note also the regressions which the person makes while reading. Regressions are those little backward movements of the eyes from right to left while you are reading across the line from left to right.

2. Another method of observing eye movements is to tilt a mirror placed beside the page so that the eyes of the reader may be clearly observed in the mirror. By watching closely the eye movements in the mirror, the observer may determine the fixations and regressions per line. This, however, may be somewhat distracting to the reader because your image will be reflected in the mirror for him in the same way that his image is reflected for you.

Improving perceptual skills

Many exercises and suggestions have already been given in this book for rapid-perception and visual-span development. This is a skill where opportunities for practice are practically everywhere you look.

1. Signs and lettering of all kinds provide excellent practice material. Improve your glance absorption. Look directly at the sign for only a split second; then drop your eyes, or look away. How much did you see? Take is as much as possible at a single glance.
2. As you wait for a bus, or walk along the street, try to read all the characters on the registration tags of the cars that speed by you.
3. When riding on trains or buses, try to read as many of the signs as you possibly can that flash past your field of vision.
4. Try to read *all* the names and the program information which appears on your television screen at the close of each show. This is an excellent exercise to indicate to yourself your ability in word attack. Many names will be challenging from a pronunciational standpoint. *Could* you pronounce them, if need be, after a single glance?
5. Flex the pages of an unfamiliar book. Let the pages slip in a continuous succession from under your thumb. Aim for a half-second exposure for each page. Try to see as much of the material on the page as possible, by glance absorption, in that brief time. When you have finished flexing the pages with your left hand, reverse the process. When you flex with your left hand, look at the right-hand pages only; when you flex with your right hand, look at the left-hand pages. Twice through the book in this way should give you a fairly accurate impression of the contents of the volume. When you have finished tell yourself as much as possible about the contents and the organization—or better yet, write it down.
6. Two people, both interested in the improvement of their perceptual skills, may help each other if each person prepares a set of flash cards with words, phrases, or sentences and flashes them at the other person. In preparing these cards, use a soft builder's pencil, with broad black lead for lettering them. Each person may keep score by seeing how many cards out of a given number he is able to read accurately.

None of these suggestions, however, are magic formulas. They are all simple, practical means of improving your skills. But they do require steady, persevering practice to prove their worth. Try them; every day in every way put them into practice in the odd moments when you would be doing nothing else. You will be surprised in a short while what they will do for you.

Principal professional instruments in the reading laboratory

Reading Accelerators

AVR Rateometer: Audio Visual Research, 531 S. Plymouth Court, Chicago 5, Ill.

Keystone Reading Pacer: Keystone View Co., Meadville, Pa.

Reading Rate Controller: Stereo Optical Company, 3539 N. Kenton Ave., Chicago 41, Ill.

Shadowscope: Lafayette Instrument Company, 26 N. 26th St., Lafayette, Ind.

SRA Accelerator: Science Research Associates, 57 W. Grand Ave., Chicago, Ill.

Tachistoscopes

Keystone Tachistoscope (group): Keystone View Co., Meadville, Pa.

Tachistoscope (individual): Lafayette Instrument Company, 26 N. 26th St., Lafayette, Ind.

Renshaw Tachistoscopic Trainer (individual): Stereo Optical Company, 3539 N. Kenton Ave., Chicago 41, Ill.

Visual Screening and Diagnostic Instruments

Keystone Visual-Survey Telebinocular: Keystone View Co., Meadville, Pa.

The Ortho-Rater (Bausch and Lomb Occupational Vision Test): Bausch & Lomb Optical Co., Rochester, N. Y.

The Ophthalmograph (for photographing eye movements while reading): American Optical Company, Southbridge, Mass.

Reading Tests

Reading tests may be secured by qualified persons from the following publishers (catalogues available on request):

California Test Bureau, 5916 Hollywod Blvd., Los Angeles 28, Calif.

Educational Testing Service, 20 Nassau St., Princeton, N. J.

The Psychological Corporation, 522 Fifth Ave., New York 36, N. Y.

Science Research Associates, 57 W. Grand Ave., Chicago 10, Ill.

World Book Company, Yonkers 5, N. Y.

Reading Films

Harvard Reading Films (college-adult level): Harvard University Press, Cambridge, Mass.

Iowa Reading Training Films (high-school level): Bureau of Audio-Visual Instruction, Extension Division, State University of Iowa, Iowa City, Iowa.

Table of Reading Rates

	Chapter Three			Chapter Nineteen		
Time	Test I	Test II	Test III	Test I	Test II	Test III
1:00	1190	1000	1130	910	960	1950
1:15	952	800	904	728	768	1560
1:30	793	667	753	607	640	1300
1:45	680	571	646	520	549	1114
2:00	595	500	566	455	480	975
2:15	529	444	502	405	427	867
2:30	476	400	452	364	384	780
2:45	433	364	411	331	349	713
3:00	397	333	377	303	320	650
3:15	368	308	348	280	295	600
3:30	340	286	323	260	275	557
3:45	317	267	302	243	256	520
4:00	298	250	283	228	240	488
4:15	280	235	266	214	226	459
4:30	265	222	251	202	213	433
4:45	251	211	238	192	202	412
5:00	238	200	226	182	192	390
5:15	227	190	215	173	183	371
5:30	216	182	205	165	174	355
5:45	207	174	197	158	167	339
6:00	198	167	188	152	160	325
6:15	190	160	181	146	154	312
6:30	183	154	174		148	300
6:45	176	148	168			289
7:00	170		161			279
7:15	164		156			269
7:30	159		151			260
7:45	154		146			252
8:00	149		141			244
8:15						236
8:30						229
8:45						223
9:00						217
9:15						211
9:30						205
9:45						200
10:00						195
10:15						190
10:30						186
10:45						182
11:00						177
11:15						173
11:30						169
11:45						166
12:00						163
12:15						159
12:30						156
12:45						153
13·00						150

TABLE OF READING RATES

Time	The Heritage of the Printed Word	What Is Work?	Homo Sapiens	What Do You Know about Locks?	On Finding Words	Our Amazing Network of Nerves
1:00	990	1330	1710	850	2910	1560
1:15	792	1064	1368	680	2328	1248
1:30	660	887	1140	566	1940	1040
1:45	566	760	977	486	1663	892
2:00	495	665	855	425	1455	780
2:15	440	591	760	378	1293	693
2:30	396	532	684	340	1164	624
2:45	360	484	622	309	1058	567
3:00	330	443	570	283	970	520
3:15	303	409	526	262	895	480
3:30	283	380	489	243	831	446
3:45	264	355	456	227	776	416
4:00	248	333	428	213	728	390
4:15	233	313	402	200	685	367
4:30	220	296	380	189	647	347
4:45	208	280	360	179	613	328
5:00	198	266	342	170	582	312
5:15	189	253	326	162	554	297
5:30	180	242	311	154	529	284
5:45	172	231	297	148	506	271
6:00	165	222	285		485	260
6:15	158	213	274		466	250
6:30	152	205	263		448	240
6:45	147	197	253		431	231
7:00		190	244		416	223
7:15		183	236		401	215
7:30		177	228		388	208
7:45		172	221		375	201
8:00		166	214		364	195
8:15		161	207		353	189
8:30		156	201		342	184
8:45		152	195		333	178
9:00		148	190		323	173
9:15			185		315	169
9:30			180		306	164
9:45			175		298	160
10:00			171		291	156
10:15			167		284	152
10:30			163		277	149
10:45			159		271	
11:00			155		265	
11:15			152		259	
11:30			149		253	
11:45					248	
12:00					243	
12:15					238	
12:30					233	

TABLE OF READING RATES (*continued*)

Time	The Heritage of the Printed Word	What Is Work?	Homo Sapiens	What Do You Know about Locks?	On Finding Words	Our Amazing Network of Nerves
12:45					228	
13:00					224	
13:15					220	
13:30					216	
13:45					212	
14:00					208	
14:15					204	
14:30					201	
14:45					197	
15:00					194	
15:15					191	
15:30					188	
15:45					185	
16:00					182	
16:15					179	
16:30					176	
16:45					174	
17:00					171	
17:15					169	
17:30					166	
17:45					164	
18:00					162	
18:15					159	
18:30					157	
18:45					155	
19:00					153	
19:15					151	

Time	This Most Excellent Canopy, the Air	The Businessman and His Reading	Architects of the Molecule	Taste That Word	How to Get an Idea Across *	The Sensations of Light and Colour
1:00	2090	1160	2170	710	2950	1760
1:15	1672	928	1736	568	2360	1408
1:30	1393	774	1447	473	1967	1173
1:45	1194	663	1240	406	1686	1006
2:00	1045	580	1085	355	1475	880
2:15	929	516	965	316	1311	782
2:30	836	464	868	284	1180	704
2:45	760	422	789	258	1073	640
3:00	697	387	723	237	983	587
3:15	643	357	668	218	908	542
3:30	597	332	620	203	843	503

TABLE OF READING RATES (*continued*)

Time	This Most Excellent Canopy, the Air	The Business-man and His Reading	Architects of the Molecule	Taste That Word	How to Get an Idea Across *	The Sensations of Light and Colour
3:45	557	309	579	189	787	469
4:00	523	290	543	178	738	440
4:15	492	273	511	167	694	414
4:30	465	258	483	158	656	391
4:45	440	244	457	149	621	371
5:00	418	232	434	142	590	352
5:15	398	221	413		562	335
5:30	380	211	395		537	320
5:45	363	202	378		513	306
6:00	348	193	362		492	294
6:15	334	186	347		472	282
6:30	322	178	334		454	271
6:45	310	172	322		437	261
7:00	299	166	310		421	251
7:15	288	160	299			243
7:30	279	155	289			235
7:45	270	150	280			227
8:00	261	145	271			220
8:15	253		263			214
8:30	246		255			207
8:45	239		248			201
9:00	232		241			196
9:15	226		234			190
9:30	220		228			185
9:45	214		223			181
10:00	209		217			176
10:15	204		212			172
10:30	199		207			168
10:45	194		202			164
11:00	190		197			160
11:15	186		193			157
11:30	182		189			153
11:45	178		185			150
12:00	174		181			147
12:15	171		177			
12:30	167		174			
12:45	164		170			
13:00	161		167			
13:15	158		164			
13:30	155		161			
13:45	152		158			
14:00	149		155			
14:15			152			
14:30			150			
14:45						

* Since this is a skimming exercise, the reader by applying the suggested techniques should have been able to have skimmed the article in seven minutes or less.

TABLE OF READING RATES (continued)

Time	Map-making	Can Memory Be Improved?	The Future of Democracy	The Reading of "Reading"	A Culture for Today	Finding Time to Read
1:00	1800	2190	1200	2020	1090	1280
1:15	1440	1752	960	1616	872	1024
1:30	1200	1460	800	1347	727	860
1:45	1029	1252	686	1154	623	732
2:00	900	1095	600	1010	545	640
2:15	800	973	533	898	485	569
2:30	720	876	480	808	436	512
2:45	654	796	436	735	396	465
3:00	600	730	400	673	363	427
3:15	554	674	369	622	335	394
3:30	514	626	343	577	312	368
3:45	480	584	320	539	291	343
4:00	450	548	300	505	273	320
4:15	420	515	282	475	257	301
4.30	400	487	267	449	242	285
4:45	380	461	253	425	229	270
5:00	360	438	240	404	218	256
5:15	343	418	229	385	208	244
5:30	327	398	218	367	198	233
5:45	313	381	209	351	190	223
6:00	300	365	200	337	182	213
6:15	284	350	192	323	174	205
6:30	277	337	185	311	168	197
6:45	267	324	178	299	161	190
7:00	257	313	171	289	156	183
7:15	248	302	166	279	150	177
7:30	240	292	160	269	145	171
7:45	232	283	155	261		165
8:00	225	274	150	253		160
8:15	218	265		245		155
8:30	212	258		238		150
8:45	206	250		231		
9:00	200	243		224		
9:15	195	237		218		
9:30	189	231		213		
9:45	185	225		207		
10:00	180	219		202		
10:15	176	214		197		
10:30	171	209		192		
10:45	168	204		188		
11:00	164	199		184		
11:15	160	195		180		
11:30	157	190		176		
11:45	153	186		172		
12:00	150	183		168		
12:15		179		165		
12:30		175		162		
12:45		172		158		

TABLE OF READING RATES (*continued*)

Time	Map-making	Can Memory Be Improved?	The Future of Democracy	The Reading of "Reading"	A Culture for Today	Finding Time to Read
13:00		168		155		
13:15		165		152		
13:30		162		150		
13:45		159				
14:00		156				
14:15		154				
14:30		151				
14:45		148				

Time	Religious Motives in Business	The News	How to Spot Statistical Jokers	On Jargon	Subjective Factors in Fatigue
1:00	2600	1640	1930	1880	1190
1:15	2080	1312	1544	1504	952
1:30	1735	1093	1286	1253	793
1:45	1486	937	1103	1074	680
2:00	1300	820	965	940	595
2:15	1156	729	858	836	529
2:30	1040	656	772	752	476
2:45	945	596	702	684	433
3:00	867	547	643	627	397
3:15	800	505	594	578	368
3:30	743	469	551	537	340
3:45	693	437	515	501	317
4:00	650	410	483	470	298
4:15	612	386	454	442	280
4:30	578	365	429	418	265
4:45	547	345	406	396	251
5:00	520	328	386	376	238
5:15	495	312	368	358	227
5:30	473	298	351	342	216
5:45	452	285	336	327	207
6:00	434	273	322	313	198
6:15	416	262	309	301	190
6:30	400	252	297	289	183
6:45	385	243	286	279	176
7:00	371	234	276	269	170
7:15	359	226	266	259	164
7:30	347	219	257	251	159
7:45	335	212	249	242	154
8:00	325	205	241	235	149
8:15	315	199	234	228	
8:30	306	193	227	221	

TABLE OF READING RATES (*continued*)

Time	Religious Motives in Business	The News	How to Spot Statistical Jokers	On Jargon	Subjective Factors in Fatigue
8:45	297	187	221	215	
9:00	289	182	214	209	
9:15	281	177	209	203	
9:30	274	173	203	198	
9:45	267	168	198	193	
10:00	260	164	193	188	
10:15	254	160	188	183	
10:30	248	156	184	179	
10:45	242	153	179	175	
11:00	236	149	175	171	
11:15	231		172	167	
11:30	226		168	163	
11:45	221		164	160	
12:00	217		161	157	
12:15	212		158	153	
12:30	208		154	150	
12:45	204		151		
13:00	200		148		
13:15	196				
13:30	193				
13:45	189				
14:00	186				
14:15	183				
14:30	179				
14:45	176				
15:00	173				
15:15	170				
15:30	168				
15:45	165				
16:00	163				
16:15	160				
16:30	158				
16:45	155				
17:00	153				
17:15	151				
17:30	149				

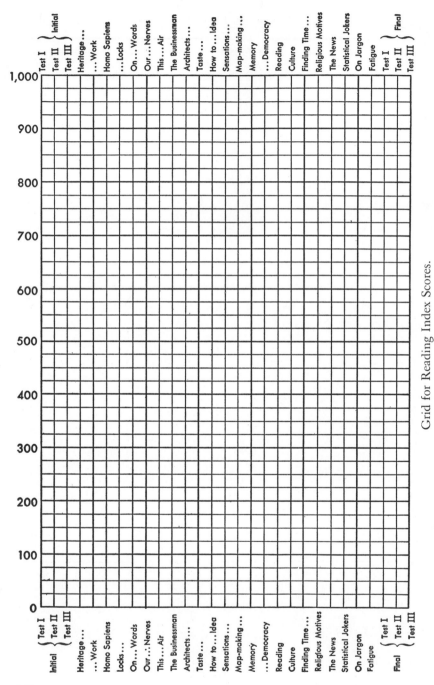

Grid for Reading Index Scores.

442

Selected Bibliography

Books

Adler, Mortimer, *How to Read a Book*, Simon and Schuster, Inc., New York, 1940.

Anderson, I. H., and W. F. Dearborn, *The Psychology of Teaching Reading*, The Ronald Press Company, New York, 1952.

Buswell, Guy T., *How Adults Read*, Supplementary Educational Monographs, No. 45, University of Chicago Press, Chicago, 1937.

Carmichael, Leonard, and Walter F. Dearborn, *Reading and Visual Fatigue*, Houghton Mifflin Company, Boston, 1947.

Causey, Oscar S., ed., *What the Colleges Are Doing in Planning and Improving College Reading Programs*, Texas Christian University Press, Fort Worth, 1955.

Center, Stella S., *The Art of Book Reading*, Charles Scribner's Sons, New York, 1952.

Howland, H. P., and others, *How to Read in Science and Technology*, The Norman W. Henley Publishing Company, New York, 1950.

Jackson, Holbrook, *The Reading of Books*, Charles Scribner's Sons, New York, 1947.

Lewis, Norman, *How to Read Better and Faster*, Thomas Y. Crowell Company, New York, 1951.

Shaw, Phillip B., *Effective Reading*, Thomas Y. Crowell Company, New York, 1955.

Strang, Ruth M., C. M. McCullough, and A. E. Traxler, *Problems in the Improvement of Reading*, McGraw-Hill Book Company, Inc., New York, 1955.

Articles and Research Papers

Averill, Laurence A., and A. D. Mueller, "Effect of Practice on Improvement of Silent Reading in Adults," *Journal of Educational Research*, vol. 17, pp. 125–129, February, 1928.

Bear, R. M., "Organization of a College Reading Program," *Education*, vol. 70, pp. 575–581, May, 1950.

Bellows, C. A., and C. H. Rush, Jr., "Reading Abilities of Business Executives," *Journal of Applied Psychology*, vol. 36, pp. 1–4, February, 1952.

Brickman, W. W., "Reading Process," *School and Society*, vol. 77, pp. 341–346, May 30, 1953.

Broxson, John A., "Teaching Adults to Read," *Peabody Journal of Education*, vol. 20, pp. 166–172, November, 1942.

Carlson, T. R., "Relationship between Speed and Accuracy of Comprehension," *Journal of Educational Research,* vol. 42, pp. 500–512, March, 1949.

Carrillo, L. W., and D. W. Sheldon, "Flexibility of Reading Rate," *Journal of Educational Psychology,* vol. 43, pp. 299–305, May, 1952.

Colby, A. N., and J. Tiffin, "Reading Ability of Industrial Supervisors," *Personnel,* vol. 9, pp. 156–159, 1950.

Connett, Theodore R., "How to Read Faster and Better," *Factory Management and Maintenance,* vol. 109, pp. 84–89, October, 1951.

Engle, L., "Improving Reading Skills of Executives," *Educational and Psychological Measurements,* vol. 14, no. 1, pp. 204–207, 1954.

Freeburne, C. M., "The Influence of Training in Perceptual Span and Perceptual Speed upon Reading Ability," *Journal of Educational Psychology,* vol. 40, pp. 321–352, October, 1949.

Fulker, E. N., and C. H. Lawshe, "Developmental Reading in Industry," *Journal of the American Society of Training Directors,* vol. 8, pp. 13–16, January–February, 1954.

Hunt, J. T., "The Relation among Vocabulary, Structural Analysis, and Reading," *Journal of Educational Psychology,* vol. 44, pp. 193–202, April, 1953.

Johnson, Granville B., "A Comparison of Two Techniques for the Improvement of Reading Skills at the College Level," *Journal of Educational Research,* vol. 46, pp. 193–205, November, 1952.

Lawshe, C. H., and R. E. Chandler, "How to Get Going with a Reading Improvement Program," *Personnel Journal,* vol. 34, pp. 15–18, May, 1955.

Lewis, Norman, "Investigation into Comparable Results Obtained from Two Methods of Increasing Reading Speed among Adults," *College English,* vol. 11, pp. 152–156, December, 1949.

McGinnis, D. J., "A Reading Laboratory at the College Level," *Journal of Higher Education,* vol. 22, pp. 98–101, February, 1951.

Manolakes, G., "The Effects of Tachistoscopic Training in an Adult Reading Program," *Journal of Applied Psychology,* vol. 36, pp. 410–412, December, 1952.

Massie, James S., "In-plant Training for Better Reading," *Factory Management and Maintenance,* March, 1953, pp. 110–112.

Mullins, C. J., and H. W. Mowry, "Does Reading Improvement Last?" *Personnel Journal,* vol. 32, pp. 416–417, April, 1954.

Potter, A. M., "Evaluation of the Reading Program of the United States Naval Academy during the Summer, 1951," *Educational and Psychological Measurements,* vol. 14, no. 1, pp. 193–203, 1954.

Preston, R. C., and M. Botel, "Reading Comprehension Tested under Timed and Untimed Conditions," *School and Society,* vol. 74, p. 71, August, 1951.

Sherrington, C. S., "Sherrington on the Eye" (excerpt from *Man and His Nature*), *Scientific American,* vol. 186, pp. 30–34, May, 1952.

Traxler, A. E., "Research in Reading in the United States," *Journal of Educational Research,* vol. 42, pp. 481–499, March, 1949.

——, "Value of Controlled Reading: Summary Opinion and Research," *Journal of Experimental Education,* vol. 7, pp. 280–292, 1953.

Answer Key

Pages 14–15
1. "Reading Is Thinking—Plus."
2. In the chapter thus far two subdivisions have been discussed. Preceding the first general subdivision were several introductory paragraphs. The titles of the subdivisions discussed thus far are: (1) "Why Do We Read As We Do?" and (2) "Reading Is Thinking—Plus."
3. If you are really reading, when you pick up a page of print, something happens.
4. Your answer should be: Yes.
5. "What Does It Mean to Read Well?"

Page 21
There are six *F's* in the sentence. The average reader finds only three of them. This is poor in terms of perceptual achievement. Seeing four is fair; five is good; six, excellent.

Test I

How Clearly Do You Recognize Main Ideas?

You should have encircled the following item numbers: 1, 4, 5, 8, 10. Each correct answer is worth 20 per cent. Score: _____%

How Well Did You Comprehend the Details?

1. horizons   2. map   3. printing   4. implied thought   5. read

Each correct answer in this section is worth 20 per cent. Score: _____%
To get Reading Comprehension Score for this test, add the above two scores and divide by 2. Reading comprehension score: _____%

Test II

Comprehension of Facts and Ideas

1. *a*   2. *c*   3. *d*   4. *a*   5. *b*

Each correct answer in this part is worth 20 per cent. Score: _____%

Word Power

1. *d*   2. *a*   3. *c*   4. *b*   5. *a*   6. *b*   7. *c*   8. *d*   9. *b*   10. *a*

Each correct answer in this part is worth 10 per cent. Score: _____%
Total test score: _____% (Add above two scores and divide by 2.)

Test III

Comprehending Facts and Ideas

    1. *b*   2. *c*   3. *a*   4. *d*   5. *b*

Each correct answer is worth 20 per cent. Score: _____%

Recognizing Main Ideas

The statements which you should have indicated as being those express-ing main ideas are 2, 3, 5, 7, 10. Each correct answer is worth 20 per cent. Score: _____%

To get Reading Comprehension Score for this test, add the above two scores and divide by 2. Reading comprehension score: _____%

General-knowledge Quotient

1. Man, the wise, the shrewd, the knowing one. (From the Latin, *homo*, man; and *sapiens*, from *sapere*, to taste, to know.)
2. Peking or Java Man, Heidelberg Man, Neanderthal Man, Cro-Magnon Man.
3. The Bible: St. John's Gospel, 1:1.
4. *The Tempest*, by William Shakespeare.
5. The most elementary charge of negative electricity. Electrons revolve about the proton in an atom. Their mass is approximately 1/1845 of that of a proton. They constitute the cathode rays and beta rays and are emitted by hot bodies.

Each question answered correctly is worth 20 per cent. GKQ score: _____%

Word Power

    1. *c* 2. *d* 3. *a* 4. *c* 5. *b* 6. *e* 7. *d* 8. *c* 9. *e* 10. *a*

Each correct answer is worth 10 per cent. Vocabulary score: _____%

The heritage of the printed word

Part One: 1. *d*   2. *b*   3. *d*   4. *c*   5. *c*

Part Two: The blanks should be numbered, reading down: 4, 2, 5, 1, 3.

What is work?

    1. *c*   2. *a*   3. *d*   4. *d*   5. *b*   6. *b*   7. *a*   8. *c*

Homo sapiens

    1. *b* 2. *d* 3. *c* 4. *c* 5. *a* 6. *a* 7. *d* 8. *b* 9. *d* 10. *c*

What do you know about that lock?

1. 4000
2. palace
3. Nineveh
4. wood
5. knots, rope (cord)
6. iron
7. British, English
8. eighteenth
9. nineteenth
10. pin-tumbler
11. last
12. Boston
13. case
14. plug
15. key
16. coil spring
17. ten
18. 100
19. thirty-six
20. master-keying

On finding words

1. *b*   2. *b*   3. *a*   4. *d*   5. *b*   6. *a*   7. *c*   8. *b*   9. *a*   10. *b*

Our amazing network of nerves

Part One: 1. *c*   2. *b*   3. *d*   4. *a*   5. *c*

Part Two: 1. twenty   2. normal, microscopic, and atomic.   3. two hundred, one-thousandth of an inch, two feet   4. molecules, universe   5. electrical

"This Most Excellent Canopy, the Air"

Part One

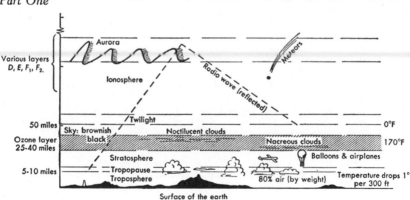

Part Two: 1. *b*   2. *c*   3. *c*   4. *d*   5. *a*   6. *c*   7. *d*   8. *a*   9. *a*   10. *d*

The businessman and his reading

Part One: You should have checked items 2, 5, 7, 8, 10.

Part Two: 1. redundant (or repetitious)   2. overconscientiousness, apprehension   3. reading, thinking   4. twenty   5. economics   6. subexecutive (or junior executive)   7. action   8. vision

Architects of the molecule

1. *c*   2. *d*   3. *d*   4. *c*   5. *d*   6. *b*   7. *a*   8. *c*   9. *b*   10. *b*

Taste that word

1. people   2. tongue   3. 1000   4. 12,000   5. understand, use   6. irritating (or offensive, or derogatory)   7. smile   8. decrease (or reduce)
9. judgment

How to get an idea across

Part One

1. The central idea, the "focal point" of the whole article as suggested in the title is *how* to get an idea across, i.e., the method, the manner, the way in which you get an idea across.
2. The author thinks in outline form and raises questions which he answers in the paragraphs following the question.
3. Yes, the outline of the "Four Step Method" presents the principal argument of the author.
4. Yes.
5. In the subheadings, and in the A, B, C arrangment of certain parts of the article.
6. By italics.
7. *a.*
8. The dash, the interrogation point, the exclamation point, quotation marks.
9. Supervisory personnel, specifically, but the article also has plenty of interest for the general reader.
10. To explain, principally to supervisory personnel, the most effective ways in which to communicate their ideas to those under their supervision.

Part Two: 1. *c*   2. *b*   3. *a*   4. *d*   5. *b*   6. *d*   7. *a*   8. *d*   9. *a*   10. *d*

Concentrate! *(pp. 213–214)*—The Woodchuck

The sensations of light and colour

This is a comprehension exercise as a part of the chapter entitled "Reading to Follow Directions." The directions for the marking of this exercise were plainly and explicitly given at the head of the statements. You were told to reverse the markings from the *conventional* way of marking a true-false test. You should, therefore, have the statements marked as follows:

1. T	5. 0	9. 0	13. T	17. T
2. T	6. F	10. F	14. F	18. F
3. F	7. T	11. F	15. F	19. T
4. T	8. F	12. F	16. T	20. 0

Map-making: from Ptolemy to photogrammetry

1. *d*   2. *b*   3. *b*   4. *c*   5. *b*   6. Greeks   7. sixteenth   8. *oblong* (or spherical)   9. hachuring   10. photogrammetry

Can memory be improved?

I. Rules for improving memory
   A.   Never toy with a memory image: verify it, if in doubt.

B. Get an accurate initial impression
C. Practice accurate recall (repetition)
II. Application of rules to specific situations
   A. Telephone numbers
   B. Names and faces
   C. Attention (alertness to details)
   D. Adult memory and learning
   E. Language and science

The future of democracy

1. *b* 2. *d* 3. *c* 4. *a* 5. *c* 6. *a* 7. *d* 8. *c* 9. *a* 10. *d*

The reading of reading

1. *c* 2. *d* 3. *d* 4. *b* 5. *a* 6. *c* 7. *d* 8. *a* 9. *c* 10. *c*

A culture for today

Part One: 1. *a* 2. *b* 3. *c* 4. *c* 5. *d*

Part Two: 1. tradition 2. choice 3. incidental (secondary) 4. bigotry
5. experience

Vocabulary test on one-syllable words

1. *a*	5. *c*	9. *a*	13. *d*	17. *b*
2. *a*	6. *a*	10. *d*	14. *b*	18. *a*
3. *d*	7. *d*	11. *c*	15. *b*	19. *c*
4. *b*	8. *b*	12. *a*	16. *d*	20. *a*

Test on the meanings of phrases

1. active duty: full-time duty in the active military service of the United States.
2. real action: a legal term designating an action at law in which things, such as land or chattels, are made the subject of the action, instead of persons.
3. bird blind: a tent, or place of concealment, from which birds may be observed or photographed.
4. black light: a popular name for near-ultraviolet energy in the 3200–4000-angstrom band. These invisible rays cause many materials to fluoresce.
5. wide gutters: a printer's term; the gutter is the margin of a book toward the binding edge. Wide gutters are, therefore, wide margins along the binding edge of a page.
6. shortstop bath: a photographic term indicating an acid solution, usually acetic acid, in which negatives or prints are immersed to stop the process of development, prior to fixing.
7. water glass: This term may be one of three things: (*a*) sodium silicate, used as a fireproofing and preserving agent; (*b*) a box with a glass bottom, used for observing objects and life below the surface of the water; (*c*) a water gauge for a steam boiler.
8. creep strength: The rate of continuous deformation of a metal under stress at a specified temperature. Creep strength is usually expressed

as pounds per square inch required to produce 1 per cent elongation in 10,000 hours at the temperature indicated.

9. flash point: The lowest temperature at which, under specified conditions, fuel oil gives off enough vapor to flash into momentary flame when ignited.

10. turtle deck: A nautical term, designating a convex deck at the bow or the stern of a vessel, so made that it will shed the seas quickly.

Finding time to read

Part One: 1. 300   2. 75,000   3. five   4. Sir Thomas Browne   5. twenty
6. bonus

Part Two: 1. *d*   2. *b*   3. *a*   4. *c*

Religious motives in business

1. *b*   2. *d*   3. *b*   4. *b*   5. *c*   6. *b*   7. *b*   8. *a*   9. *c*   10. *b*

The news

Part One: You should have checked statements numbered: 1, 4, 6, 7, 9.

Part Two: 1. *c*   2. *a*   3. *d*   4. *c*   5. *d*

How quickly and accurately can you see?

1. comprehend	5. reflection	9. think	13. concentrate
2. six	6. nonsense	10. tone	14. fake
3. signs	7. asset	11. winning	15. effective
4. axiom	8. photograph	12. neurons	

Statistical jokers

1. Six statistical jokers in this statement are

    a "The average American"—the unspecified average.

    b "owns one car"—owns? Does this mean he has paid for it, or is he still paying the monthly installments—in which case, he does not *own* it—yet.

    c "is a father"—apparently all average Americans are males!

    d "one car . . . two children"—this combination is not always invariable. Not every man with one car has two children, and vice versa.

    e "story-and-a-half house"—improbably precise.

    f "situated on 1.3 acres"—also very improbably precise.

2. Two statistical jokers in this statement are

    a "One out of every two smokers"—female as well as male? That means that approximately 25 per cent of El Ropo smokers are women. Unspecified average. Inadequate sample.

    b "prefer El Ropo"—to what? No alternative. Perhaps they prefer El Ropo to smoking corn silk.

3. Five statistical jokers are the following:

    a "the average traffic violator"—unspecified average.

    b "between twenty-one and twenty-five years old"—improbably precise.

    c "average intelligence"—unspecified average.

d "normal personality"—unspecified and ambiguous.

e "300 motorists . . . in Los Angeles"—inadequate sample. From this we cannot generalize about the "average traffic violator" in the nation generally.

4. Four statistical jokers in this advertisement are

  a unfounded statement. What makes the *Town Talk* a superior newspaper? The fact that it has more subscribers than any other paper.

  b "Read the *Town Talk* for best in news!" This statement does not logically follow either of the preceding statements.

  c a "gee-whiz" graph.

  d "10,000; 15,000; 20,000"—improbably precise figures.

5. Three statistical jokers in this table are

  a unspecified average.

  b improbably precise figures.

  c inadequate sample. We do not know how many seventeen-year-olds were measured, whether 4 or 400,000.

On jargon

1. case 2. circumlocution 3. abstract 4. such 5. accurate 6. prose 7. man 8. Shakespeare 9. character (or intellect) 10. style

Subjective fatigue

Part One: I. Present Research
  II. Results

   A. Age
   B. Sex
   C. Type of work

  III. Summary
  IV. References

Part Two:

1. F	5. T	9. F	13. T	17. T
2. T	6. T	10. T	14. F	18. F
3. F	7. T	11. T	15. F	19. T
4. F	8. F	12. T	16. T	20. F

Test I

Comprehension quiz

1. 600 2. truth 3. four 4. reason 5. answers (nature of reality)

  Each correct answer is worth 20 per cent. Score: _____%

How Clearly Do You Recognize Main Ideas?

  You should have marked the following: 2, 4, 5, 7, 10.
  Each correct answer is worth 20 per cent. Score: _____%
  To find reading comprehension score, add the two above scores and divide by 2. Score: _____%

Test II

Comprehension quiz

1. *b*   2. *a*   3. *c*   4. *c*   5. *d*   6. *a*   7. *c*   8. *b*   9. *d*   10. *b*

Each correct answer is worth 10 per cent. Score: _____%

Vocabulary

1. *a*   2. *c*   3. *d*   4. *b*   5. *c*   6. *a*   7. *d*   8. *b*   9. *c*   10. *a*

Each correct answer is worth 10 per cent. Score: _____%

To find reading comprehension score, add the above two scores and divide by 2. Score: _____%

Test III

Comprehension quiz

1. *a*   2. *d*   3. *c*   4. *b*   5. *c*   6. *c*   7. *d*   8. *c*   9. *a*   10. *c*

Each correct answer is worth 10 per cent. Score: _____%

How Clearly Do You Recognize the Main Ideas?

You should have marked 3, 5, 6, 8, 9. Each correct answer is worth 20 per cent. Score: _____%

To find reading comprehension score, add the above two scores and divide by 2. Score: _____%

What Is Your GKQ?

1. One phase of Transcendentalism was its preoccupation with Orientalism. Emerson, Thoreau, and Bronson Alcott, the father of Louisa May Alcott, author of *Little Women*, belonged to the Transcendental Club, where the Oriental classics were discussed. (See Arthur Christy, *The Orient in American Transcendentalism*. New York: 1932.)
2. A hybrid is an offspring which results from the crossing of two different species.
3. This quotation is from the Book of the Psalms: "The days of our years are three score years and ten . . ." (Psalm 90:10).
4. Utopia is an imaginary island, enjoying perfection in politics, law, etc. It is used generally to designate any place or idea of ideal perfection. Sir Thomas More described such an ideal commonwealth in his principal work, *Utopia* (1516). The word comes from the Greek, *ou*, not + *topos*, a place.
5. Walt Whitman (1819–1892) was an American poet whose most famous work is probably *Leaves of Grass*.
   Each item is worth 20 per cent. Score: _____%

What Is Your Word Power?

1. *b*   2. *d*   3. *c*   4. *a*   5. *d*   6. *b*   7. *c*   8. *a*   9. *c*   10. *d*

Each correct answer is worth 10 per cent. Score: _____%

Index